The People's Courts

THE PEOPLE'S COURTS

*Pursuing Judicial Independence
in America*

JED HANDELSMAN SHUGERMAN

Harvard University Press
Cambridge, Massachusetts, and London, England　2012

Library of Congress Cataloging-in-Publication Data

Shugerman, Jed Handelsman, 1974–
  The people's courts : pursuing judicial independence in America /
Jed Handelsman Shugerman.
      p.   cm.
  Includes bibliographical references and index.
  ISBN 978-0-674-05548-3
  1. Judges—United States—States—Election—History.
2. Judicial independence—United States—History.   I. Title.
  KF8776.S54 2012
    347.73'14—dc23   2011018540

For Danya

Contents

The People's Courts

Introduction:
America's Peculiar Institution

N 2002, a West Virginia jury hit Massey Energy, a West Virginia coal company, with a $50 million verdict for using illegal and fraudulent tactics to force a smaller company, Harman Mining, out of business. As Massey appealed this verdict in the court system, its CEO, Don Blankenship, recruited Brent Benjamin, a former state party treasurer with no judicial experience, to run against Justice Warren McGraw. Blankenship spent $3 million—the lion's share of the funding for Benjamin's campaign—to defeat Justice Warren McGraw. Most of Blankenship's money financed "And for the Sake of the Kids," an organization created just for this election which blitzed the state with television advertisements attacking McGraw for being soft on crime and dangerous to children. The most prominent ad alleged:

> Supreme Court Justice Warren McGraw voted to release child-rapist Tony Arbaugh from prison. Worse, McGraw agreed to let this convicted rapist work as a janitor in a West Virginia school. Letting a child rapist go free? To work in our schools? That's radical Supreme Court Justice Warren McGraw. [The word "radical" flashes onto the screen in red over McGraw's grainy picture.] Warren McGraw. Too soft on crime. Too dangerous for our kids.[1]

The McGraw campaign lacked the resources to overcome these attacks.[2] Benjamin beat McGraw 53 percent to 47 percent and became the deciding vote to overturn the jury verdict in 2007. Later, photos surfaced of a second justice, Spike Maynard, vacationing with CEO Blankenship in the French Riviera soon before he heard the case and also ruled in favor of

Massey Energy. Under pressure, Maynard recused himself from the 2008 rehearing, along with another justice who had called Blankenship a "clown" in the media and accused him of buying a Supreme Court seat. But again Benjamin refused to recuse himself, and again cast another deciding vote against the jury verdict.

In June 2009, the U.S. Supreme Court ruled for Caperton, Harman's president, against Blankenship's Massey Energy, deciding for the first time that an elected judge must recuse himself from a case involving a major campaign contributor.[3] In a five-to-four ruling, Justice Kennedy concluded, "There is a serious risk of actual bias . . . when a person with a personal stake in a particular case had a significant and disproportionate influence in placing the judge on the case by raising funds . . . when the case was pending or imminent."[4] Such political and financial influences on the court violate due process and "threaten to imperil public confidence in the fairness and integrity of the nation's elected judges."[5]

Caperton v. Massey was not an isolated case, and this decision has been the only time the Supreme Court has weighed in on the hardball politics of money and special interests in state judicial elections. In May 2003, the Illinois Supreme Court heard oral arguments in a class action against State Farm Insurance.[6] State Farm was challenging a $1 billion verdict, half of which was based on a questionable contractual damages claim. Instead of ruling, the judges decided to wait a year and a half for the election of a new judge in November 2004. With this case hanging in the balance, Republican Lloyd Karmeier and Democrat Gordon Maag ran for the open seat and together raised over $9 million. Most of that money came from the groups with something at stake in the State Farm case. State Farm employees and other insurance groups gave almost $1.5 million directly to Karmeier, and the U.S. Chamber of Commerce spent $2.3 million. Trial lawyers gave $2.8 million to Maag through the state Democratic Party.[7] Remarkably, the race was not even statewide, but just one of the rural districts in southern Illinois far from the expensive Chicago media market.

Political groups attacked both judges for being soft on crime. The Illinois Chamber of Commerce blamed Maag for voting to overturn the conviction of a man for sexually assaulting a six-year-old girl. Its ads did not mention the constitutional and evidentiary problems with the conviction.[8] On the other side, a group of trial lawyers and labor unions attacked Karmeier for giving "probation to kidnappers who tortured and nearly beat a 92-year-old grandmother to death."[9] Over ominous music and a blurry image of children at a playground, another anti-Karmeier ad warned, "He used candy to lure the children into the house. Once inside, the three children were sexually molested. A 4-year-old girl, raped. Despite prosecutors' objections, Judge Lloyd Karmeier gave him probation."[10] True,

Karmeier had sentenced Bryan Watters to probation, but only after the appeals court had directed him to.[11]

Karmeier survived these attacks (in part because of his financial advantage) and won the race. He commented that the fundraising was "obscene," but he did not recuse himself from the State Farm case. He cast the decisive vote overturning the verdict against State Farm for breach of contract. It is impossible to know if Karmeier voted solely on his view of the merits or if he was swayed on some level by politics. Whether State Farm had invested wisely in a true believer or a grateful candidate, either way the company received a return of $456 million on a savvy investment of about $1 million.[12] The U.S. Supreme Court declined to hear the appeal.[13] In more recent races, both left and right have attacked judges for aiding and abetting child molesters, sometimes by race-baiting and often by exaggerating the facts and misleading the public.[14] One recent race in Wisconsin left such raw animosity that it led to accusations of violence between the judges in closed chambers.[15]

Tennessee Supreme Court Justice Penny White generally upheld death sentences, but one sentence struck her as excessive in 1996. The court unanimously upheld the defendant's murder conviction, but also ordered a re-sentencing hearing because of procedural violations. Justice White joined a concurrence that more narrowly interpreted the "aggravating circumstances" that made a defendant eligible for a death sentence. She was the only one of the concurring judges up for reelection that year, and she was defeated by a coalition of conservative groups.[16] Afterward, Tennessee Governor Don Sundquist, who had fanned the flames over the death penalty controversy, remarked: "Should a judge look over his shoulder to the next election in determining how to rule on a case? I hope so. I hope so."[17]

One more example: In 2009, the Iowa Supreme Court ruled unanimously that the Iowa statute defining marriage as a union of a man and a woman violated the Iowa constitution's equal protection clause.[18] In the fall of 2010, three of those justices were up for their yes-or-no retention election. National organizations—the American Family Association, the National Organization for Marriage, and the Campaign for Working Families, which also fights for "pro-growth," "free enterprise" policies— spent over $800,000 against the three judges.[19] The judges decided not to campaign personally, and instead, other groups supported them independently, spending over $200,000 mostly on television ads.[20] In the end, all three justices lost their retention races.

Almost 90 percent of state judges face some kind of popular election.[21] Thirty-eight states put all of their judges up before the voters.[22] It has been a long-established practice for parties and lawyers to donate to the judges who will later hear their cases, but recently the size of such donations has increased dramatically.[23] Spending on judicial campaigns has doubled in the past decade, exceeding $200 million.[24] That figure does not include the millions spent on outside advertising. An Ohio Supreme Court justice confessed, "I never felt so much like a hooker down by the bus station . . . as I did in a judicial race. Everyone interested in contributing has very specific interests. They mean to be buying a vote."[25]

Today, judicial elections reduce state judges' willingness to apply the law or protect rights in the face of public opposition or special interests. Recent studies demonstrate that elected judges face more political pressure and reach legal results more in keeping with local public opinion than appointed judges do.[26] Other studies have found that elected judges disproportionately rule in favor of their campaign contributors.[27] Even though codes of judicial conduct bar personal solicitation of campaign contributions, there are many stories of judges directly asking for donations from the lawyers in their chambers in the middle of presiding over their cases.[28]

These stories and studies may be discomforting, but judicial elections certainly are not the only way for politics to influence the courts. Appointments are also political. We are reminded every few years in high-stakes battles over Supreme Court nominations that federal judges are appointed effectively for life, and the federal appointment process has grown increasingly partisan. The U.S. Constitution guarantees that "the Judges, both of the supreme and inferior Courts shall hold their offices during good behavior," which in effect gives them life tenure.[29] Even if lower federal judges have life tenure, they are tethered to public opinion and partisan politics if they hope to be promoted. And less well known is that some specialized federal judges are not covered by Article III of the Constitution and are appointed to shorter terms. In the dozen states that appoint judges, nine states appoint judges to relatively short terms. These federal and state judges are subject to the politics of reappointment that can be just as unseemly and corrupt as modern judicial elections. More troubling, those pressures are less visible.[30] One study found that the appointed judges in Virginia were the least likely to reverse death sentences among all the state courts, and South Carolina's were close behind.[31] An explanation is that these judges face reappointment by the state legislature, and state legislators have lots of incentive to make noise about judges who overturn death sentences. Penny White lost her Tennessee race 53 percent to 47 percent. If she had been facing reappointment by the governor and/or state legislators, her margin of defeat would have been much larger, and she almost certainly would not have been renominated at all. If West Virginia had judicial appointments, Massey's CEO would not have waited patiently on the sidelines. Likewise, State Farm and the Illinois trial lawyers would not have focused only on perfecting their legal briefs. They would have fought for the governorship and lobbied legislators—and made donations to them for the same purposes. These strategies would be less transparent than direct election spending—less obviously offensive to the casual observer, but more insidious. A nineteenth-century American lawyer-poet once quipped, "Laws, like sausages, cease to inspire respect in proportion as we know how they are made."[32] The same is true with judicial selection. With direct popular elections, we watch the sausage-making. With appointments, the sausage-making is out of sight, out of mind.

Many major democracies in Europe, Asia, South America, and Africa have turned over judicial selection to judges and judicial selection committees. France has one "marginal" specialized lower court with popular elections, but the rest of its system is a more insulated professional civil service. Law graduates interested in becoming judges must take a rigorous four-day exam, and only the top 5 percent are accepted to the École Nationale de Magistrature, an elite two-year judicial training program. They then enter the civil service, and they are evaluated by the Supreme Judicial Council, composed of judges, lawyers, and commissioners selected by the other branches of government. Many major democracies have adopted a similar system of civil service testing and bureaucratic internal promotion for the courts. This kind of appointment insulates the courts from popular politics, but it increases the influence of elite politics and judicial self-replication.[33]

One might think of judicial elections as America's truly unique institution. Many countries have copied American legal institutions, but almost no one else in the world has ever experimented with the popular election of judges.[34] Why have Americans adopted such a strange practice, when almost no one else has done so before or after?

Countless scholars describe judicial elections as a "threat to judicial independence."[35] In contrast, this book argues that the story of judicial elections is also the story of the ongoing American pursuit of judicial independence—and the changing understandings of what judicial independence means. Judicial independence has long been the rallying cry *in favor* of judicial elections in their various forms. "Judicial independence" and "judicial accountability" are not abstract concepts with fixed meanings over time. They depend on context, and they have evolved in the flow of events and crises. Interest group politics, economics, and specific events drive these stories of judicial design at each stage, yet at the same time, ideas mattered. The idea of judicial independence has been surprisingly resilient and popular throughout American history. At each stage, the goal of separating law from politics was a significant part of the campaign for each model of judicial elections. But the notion of what "politics" judges were supposed to be independent *from* changed over time, in part because the notions of what kinds of politics were necessary versus corrupting also changed over time.

It is too simplistic to link elections to judicial accountability and appointments to judicial independence. Alexis de Tocqueville predicted in 1835, when only three states held judicial elections of any sort, that "sooner or later these innovations will have dire results and that one day it will be seen that by diminishing the magistrates' independence, not judicial power only but the democratic republic itself has been attacked."[36] De Tocqueville presciently recognized the beginnings of a movement and the problems it would later create, but he missed the point about judicial power in his own time. In light of these stories of competitive and expensive judicial campaigns, one might imagine that Americans must have chosen this unique system because they opposed judicial independence. Scholars have suggested that states have turned to judicial elections in order to weaken the courts, "with little explanation of how an elective judiciary could protect constitutional rights."[37] To the contrary, advocates of judicial elections at each stage of American history have argued that elections bolster judicial independence and constitutional protections.[38] In the wave of judicial elections in the mid-nineteenth century, the agenda was more judicial power, not less. An economic crisis triggered a popular movement for fiscal restraint and limited government, and against partisan appointments and the weak courts they had produced. This movement had an economic ideology and a set of class interests, but its leaders also emphasized the abstract principles of judicial independence in their arguments for judicial elections. Reformers defined judicial independence as insulation from a certain kind of insider politics: the partisan patronage politics of appointments. Open partisan politics out-of-doors was their solution, not the problem. In that moment, reformers believed that direct elections gave "the people," mobilized by more participatory political parties, a check on insider politics. Intriguingly, they believed that partisan elections promised a *less* partisan and *less* politicized bench that would be emboldened to act as a stronger check and balance against the other branches. They were able to frame judicial elections as an improvement on the separation of powers and, even more remarkably, the separation of law and politics.

In the twentieth century, interest groups (chiefly business interests) drove the reform of judicial elections and the turn to merit selection, but they relied heavily on the rhetoric of judicial independence to legitimate their reform efforts. With time and experience, the definition of politics and corruption shifted: partisan elections were now perceived as having problems behind closed doors with party bosses, special interests, and crime, and now open campaigning was perceived as unbecoming of a judge's professional dignity. A new brand of insider politics was the solution: professional "merit" nominating commissions run by bar leaders and committee members. The indignity of open campaigning was supposed to be replaced by the dignity of uncompetitive retention elections without campaigning. This book traces the shifting perception of partisan politics, sometimes viewed as an engine of democracy and law, and sometimes as a threat to democracy and law.

Judicial independence has different meanings, but at its core, it refers to a judge's insulation from the political and personal consequences of his or her legal decisions. This historical account contrasts *relative* judicial independence (independence *from whom?*) with *general* judicial independence (*how much* independence from political pressure generally?). Some reforms foster "general" judicial independence: most importantly, length of tenure and job security, but also protection of jurisdiction, salary, and other resources. General independence does not mean absolute autonomy; a judge might still be influenced informally by public opinion, elite opinion, reputation, and ambitions for promotion. General independence simply means a judge is more insulated from direct political pressure from any source. By contrast, reforms in methods of judicial selection produce relative judicial independence. In the switch from one form of selection to another, judges become more independent from one set of powers but more accountable to another. The principal-agent problem is one key to understanding the history of judicial elections. Judicial appointments gave presidents, governors, and legislators (the agents) control over the courts instead of giving that power to the people (the principals). Many critics argued that short-term appointments made the judges agents of the agents, not agents of the people.

This book is a work of legal history and political history, and it is also a history of an idea. Political interests and economics shaped the evolving concepts of judicial independence, but those ideas were not only functions of those interests or simply mirroring society. The idea of judicial independence is so capacious and flexible that it has been manipulated to serve various political and economic interests over time. While reformers throughout American history have talked about separating law and politics, they often were seeking specific legal and political outcomes in particular kinds of cases, sometimes using "rule of law" rhetoric to thwart popular movements. These elites may have sincerely believed in judicial independence and the rule of law, they may have been cynically using this rhetoric only to persuade an audience, or somewhere in between, or they may have been trying to convince themselves of the moral correctness of their own positions. It is difficult to know from these sources. Nevertheless, advocates of judicial elections and their reform repeatedly emphasized judicial independence because that idea resonated with elites and the general public. Regardless of the sincerity of the leaders, the fact that they translated their specific reforms into general principles of fairness and justice indicates that they believed the public cared deeply enough about the concept of judicial independence. These stories illustrate that even if economic interests have been a driving force in legal change, they still needed to engage in a general discourse of ideas and public reason in order to legitimate those changes. Judicial independence became a principle that defined the terms of the debate, set boundaries on what amount of politicization was tolerable, and shaped the array of possible alternatives. Legal historians often use the phrase "constitutive" when describing how legal categories or legal ideas shape, define, and "constitute" social relationships.[39] In this book, broader ideas about justice, fairness, impartiality, and nonpartisanship roughly guided Americans' views, even when judicial independence sometimes might have created an obstacle to their political goals and might have been counter to their interests. This book suggests that a somewhat inchoate belief that law should be separate from politics influenced each change in judicial selection, even the adoption of partisan judicial elections, remarkably enough. Each chapter traces the role of interest groups or economics and the role of ideas about judicial independence, parties, and democratic politics in the evolution of judicial politics.

The development of judicial selection is also a story about the evolving concept of the separation of powers. Judicial independence and the separation of powers were political insurance, based on distrust and risk aversion.[40] Each generation feared concrete evils: imperious kings, incompetent legislators, corrupt political parties, corrupting special interests, demagoguery, and the masses. In various combinations, economic elites, political insiders, the dueling parties, and the general public distrusted each other more than they distrusted judges, so they were willing to entrust judges with more power and independence as a hedge against the other groups and the political branches of government. To insulate the judges from these evils, Americans in the late eighteenth century turned to life-tenure appointments. Nineteenth-century Americans switched to judicial elections, and then to elections to longer terms in office. In the twentieth century, the rise of the merit plan was a new separation of powers, separating courts from partisan politics (and, to an extent, from the masses). Nonpartisan "merit selection" commissions were a new mini-branch, separate from all of the other branches, but drawing their members from those branches and from civic leadership. At each stage, reformers focused on separating the courts from an immediate set of evils, but separating the judges from one set of interests often left them vulnerable to the next set of interests.

The concepts of general and relative independence can be traced over five stages in American history: the premodern unseparated judiciary, judicial aristocracy, judicial democracy, judicial meritocracy, and judicial plutocracy. Chapter 1 explains how colonial America's elected judges reflected the first stage, the premodern judiciary, with dependent judges and a mixed English system of powers. Because the premodern judiciary lacked separation of powers and judicial independence, elected officials played multiple roles, including judging. In England and America over the eighteenth century, judicial independence emerged in the rise of judicial aristocracy—not an aristocracy of birth, but in the minds of some of the Framers, a "natural" aristocracy of virtue insulated from political and partisan pressure. In the words of a leading historian on the Founding era, the U.S. Constitution was "in some sense an aristocratic document designed to curb the democratic excesses of the Revolution."[41] The Framers turned to tenure during "good behavior" in order to create a separate branch of government, a specialized judicial role with more job security. As the concept of separation of powers evolved, the elected colonial judges were vestiges of the less specialized premodern system. They were driven into extinction, replaced by a new species of independent appointed judges with life tenure and distinctly legal responsibilities.

Judicial democracy spread over the course of the nineteenth century. Judicial elections played only a minor role from 1800 through the 1830s. As Chapter 2 details, the democratic reformers in the Jeffersonian and Jacksonian eras were generally seeking to weaken courts, and there were more effective weapons for attacking judges, such as impeachment or getting rid of the judges' offices. The appointed judges of this era get credit for announcing the theory of judicial review to void unconstitutional legislation, but often they refused to put this theory into practice, and instead retreated from political conflict. A closer examination of the dramatic showdowns over the courts shows that these appointed judges were relatively weak and that judicial review was more paper than practice, more bark than bite. Appointments did not equal independence or power. Jeffersonians and other democratic opponents of judicial independence did not need judicial elections to expose the weaknesses of the early judiciary. Nevertheless, some judges still tested boundaries and risked their careers to lay a foundation for judicial review, and these efforts raised the profile of the courts, making judges a potential solution for democratic governance, not just an obstacle.

Chapter 3 shows that judicial elections arose in a few exceptional cases in these early years where there was more of a focus on the separation of powers and on insulating judges from corrupt governors and legislatures. These early experiments in Vermont, Georgia, Indiana, and Mississippi remained isolated cases even at the height of the Jacksonian era of the 1830s. The American "exceptionalism" of direct democracy had spread to most offices, but not the judiciary. Then came the Panics and the trigger of the wave of judicial democracy, discussed in Chapters 4 and 5. Economic and fiscal crises of the 1830s and 1840s triggered the American Revolutions of 1848, a wave of state constitutional conventions throughout the country. The fiscal crisis was blamed on legislative overspending on internal improvements (canals, roads, and railroads), so the conventions focused on limiting legislative powers and increased the separation of powers. Almost all of these conventions turned to judicial elections as a way to separate the courts from the other branches and to enforce the "people's" constitutional rights against government excess. The system of political appointment could have gone in various directions, but instead of making judicial appointments less political, these conventions decided to make them more directly political. Slavery, America's more infamous "peculiar institution,"[42] also influenced the design and practice of judicial elections in both the South and the North, but it was much less significant than the economic and fiscal crisis. The Panics occurred while the second "Two-Party System" (Democrats and Whigs) had flourished and mobilized astonishing numbers of voters—and just before that system collapsed in the mid-1850s over the new slavery crisis. At that moment, party politics and direct elections appeared to be a panacea. Ever since that turning point, popular elections have been a given part of state judicial politics, a path-dependent institution with a life of its own. The "exceptional" political culture of American direct democracy was one necessary condition for the switch to judicial elections, but the timing and the framing of the economic crisis were also necessary to trigger the constitutional conventions to make these changes nation-wide. It is not obvious that judicial democracy would have spread so broadly if judicial appointments had survived up to the Civil War.

Chapter 6 offers comprehensive evidence that these reformers' expectations were filled in at least one respect: the first generation of elected judges blocked far more legislation than any earlier era of judges. These elected judges also offered more general criticisms of public opinion and democracy in these cases than any earlier era of judges, a counterintuitive turn toward "countermajoritarianism." The elected judges of the 1840s and 1850s played a role in developing modern judicial power, modern constitutional law, and judicial resistance to progressive regulation over the next century. After the Civil War and Reconstruction, there were increasing concerns about the flaws of partisan elections. Judicial democracy emerged to promote judicial independence, but over time, party politics in those elections threatened judicial independence, too. In the late nineteenth century, reformers responded by lengthening judges' terms (discussed in Chapter 7), and early twentieth-century progressives turned to formally "nonpartisan" elections (a reform that failed, discussed in Chapter 8).

Then judicial meritocracy emerged during the Great Depression and spread in the 1950s through the 1970s, as told in Chapters 9 and 10. "Merit" commissions are a new twist on the separation of powers, a synthesis of appointment, election, and expertise that is not immune from politics but still is separated from the other branches and from the political parties. This campaign for judicial independence offers a strange puzzle of what, where, and when. *What*: In approving merit plans, voters were surrendering some of their voting rights—a very rare event generally in American history. *Where*: Merit plans emerged and then spread in relatively rural states in the Midwest, the Rockies, and the South, where one would imagine populism and antielite, antilawyer sentiment would block elite judicial selection. *When*: merit plans emerged in the 1930s and spread from the 1950s through the 1970s, in the very places that were most opposed to appointed judges and legal elites, first when the "Nine Old Men" blocked the New Deal and then during the most controversial decisions of the liberal Warren Court.

Chapters 9 and 10 do not solve this puzzle comprehensively, but they offer a number of clues based on a closer study of the early merit states. In both the early twentieth century and the late twentieth century, business interests drove the campaigns for merit plans, often behind the scenes, and often overcoming political resistance by using rhetoric to build broader coalitions. These puzzle pieces are a complicated balance of rural and urban dynamics; of business and labor, of plaintiffs' trial lawyers and the tort wars; reactions to World War II and the Cold War; the ideology of merit; and the politics of race, ethnicity, and crime. Ever since the 1980s, anticrime backlashes have threatened judicial independence, but oddly enough, crime waves in the 1930s and the late 1960s contributed to calls for *more* judicial independence from popular politics. Chapter 9 for the first time tells the story from the archives of a young prosecutor named Earl Warren leading the anticrime, pro-merit campaign on behalf of California businesses in 1934, launching his rise to power.

As Chapter 11 explains, modern America has shifted to an era of judicial plutocracy, not necessarily a judiciary of the wealthy, but a judiciary shaped by the massive campaign spending by lawyers, litigants, and interest groups. These advertising battles focus on crime and the death penalty (another peculiarly American institution), but are most often a front for the tort wars between trial lawyers and business interests.[43] Chapter 11 surveys the current practice of judicial elections and explores potential areas of reform.

The popular election of judges is an unusual and increasingly contentious practice. However, it must be understood in context, with a clear-eyed view of the alternatives. Judicial appointments are no panacea. Judicial elections were an understandable reaction to a crisis of appointments, corruption, and government excess. In judicial selection, there is no escape from politics, but only different forms of political influence. Today, judicial elections have reached their own crisis point of corruption and special interest excess. We can find some hope to face this challenge by recognizing that even if merit selection has its own politics and its own flaws, it better insulates the courts from money and partisan politics, and offers more job security than competitive elections. The key to judicial independence is not front-end selection, but rather, back-end retention and job security—that is, general judicial independence. It turns out that the American public often has embraced the idea of judicial independence, and even general independence. This tour of American legal and political history will explain why these leaders viewed judicial elections as the key to constitutional protections against the abuse of power, and why this system first succeeded and then failed. America is now at a crossroads between a flawed-but-promising judicial meritocracy and a flawed-and-worsening judicial plutocracy. One nineteenth-century leader warned that judicial elections would be a "route to hell" with no way back.[44] The lessons of this history may help us find a plausible path back to judicial independence.

Note on Historical Causation

Historical causation is complex, and it is difficult to pin down which factors were necessary or sufficient causes. I rely on a classic model of historical causation to sort out the factors: long-term *preconditions*, midterm *precipitants*, and short-term *triggers*.[45] In the wave of judicial elections in the mid-nineteenth century, a precondition was democratic ideology. Precipitants were the Panics, the states' fiscal crisis, and systematic abuses of the appointment process. The triggers were New York's 1846 convention and the wave of constitutional conventions thereafter. America's democratic culture was a necessary condition, but not clearly a sufficient condition to overcome a long-standing tradition of appointing judges. Without the precipitants and triggers, it is less likely that there would have been constitutional conventions proposing broad changes to state courts in the 1840s and early 1850s, and after the Civil War, it is unclear whether there would have been as much momentum for judicial elections. It is possible that judicial elections would have remained isolated to the American West, spreading only regionally and incrementally.

In the rise of merit selection in the mid-twentieth century, a precondition was a relatively rural society, but with increasing urbanization and industry. Another precondition was business interests seeking political control over the courts in labor and tort litigation. Precipitants varied from state to state. In some states, changes in voting rights and racial voting strength led to a backlash and a shift from popular participation to elite control by the bar. In other states, a precipitant was a crime wave, which created an opportunity to pitch merit selection as a way to produce a more effective bench in handling criminal prosecutions. World War II shaped Americans' views of judicial independence, and the Cold War led to renewed interest in "rule of law" ideology. Specific triggers also differed from state to state, such as Earl Warren's strategizing in California in 1934, corruption scandals in Missouri and Kansas, and Big Jim Folsom's cross-racial victory in Alabama. Often the preconditions and precipitants seem powerful enough to make a historical event appear almost inevitable. However, the triggers shape when and how these events took place, and sometimes whether they would take place at all. Sometimes it may appear that America's culture of popular democracy made judicial elections inevitable, but individual leadership, luck, and timing played a crucial role at each turning point.

CHAPTER ONE

Declaring Judicial Independence

N THE DECLARATION OF INDEPENDENCE, Thomas Jefferson included this in his list of American grievances against the Crown: "He [King George] has made Judges dependent on his Will alone, for the tenure of their offices, and the amount and payment of their salaries." Forty years later, Jefferson wrote a letter criticizing judicial appointments and life tenure. It began with a call for extending the founding principles by broadening suffrage and generally increasing the people's direct control of the government. Jefferson noted that the federal judges "are dependent on none but themselves." Life tenure had been progress for judicial independence from the king in an early age, "but in a government founded on the public will, this principle operates in an opposite direction, and against that will. . . . It has been thought that the people are not competent electors of judges *learned in the law*. But I do not know that this is true, and, if doubtful, we should follow principle. In this, as in many other elections, they would be guided by reputation, which would not err oftener, perhaps, than the present mode of appointment." Building on his faith in the people, he cited one example: "In one State of the Union, at least, it has long been tried, and with the most satisfactory success. The judges of Connecticut have been chosen by the people every six months, for nearly two centuries, and I believe there has hardly ever been an instance of change; so powerful is the curb of incessant responsibility."[1]

Jefferson embraced judicial independence in the Declaration of Independence, and then critiqued judicial independence in 1816, revealing the relativity of the concept. The Declaration of Independence had protested the colonial courts' dependence upon the Crown, and Jefferson sought a judiciary more responsive to the people. Similarly, his 1816 letter also endorsed a judiciary more responsive to the people. Jefferson was citing colonial history as precedent for judicial elections. This chapter digs into Jefferson's historical claim for the first time and shows that there was only some truth to Jefferson's example. Investigating Connecticut courts opens a window onto the development of judicial independence and, in particular, the rise of separation of powers in England and America. The many "elected judges" of colonial America reflected the premodern judiciary's lack of separation of powers, as elected officials often served a combination of executive, legislative, and judicial roles. Elected members of the legislative assemblies doubled as judges when the assemblies acted as appellate courts, and local elected officials wore the different hats of each branch of government. In the eighteenth century, these premodern elected judges disappeared as constitutions separated powers. The notion of a judge as a specialized appointed official, in contrast to an elected official, reflected a more modern division of labor and institutional checks and balances. The central legal device was the switch from appointments "at the pleasure of the king" to much more secure appointments "during good behaviour." These ideas and institutions—as well as economic interests— were the foundation for American judicial independence and the rise of a judicial aristocracy.

Judging in England and the Colonies

Until the modern era, England had no real separation of powers and no judicial independence. The king was sovereign, and Parliament and the courts were simply extensions of the Crown. In the medieval and early modern eras, Parliament considered itself the "High Court of Parliament," combining judicial and legislative authority.[2] It is not so much that it sometimes legislated and sometimes judged, but more that these powers were fused together and not distinguished. Parliament legislated very little in terms of general bills, but it passed many private laws as adjudications of private disputes. Meanwhile, common law courts made law. Members of the House of Lords served both as legislators and as the judges on the court of last resort in the common law system, but the House of Commons also served judicial functions through the seventeenth century. Even Sir Edward Coke, who sometimes is credited with developing judicial review of legislation, "recognized the supremacy of parliamentary authority precisely because it was transcendent in its judicial capacity."[3]

This English constitution—with legislators acting as judges—passed onto the colonies. Colonial assemblies not only exercised control over judges; they also served as judges, similar to the English House of Lords. Colonial assemblies adjudicated claims against the government and served a judicial function in trying individuals for crimes, including libel and sedition.[4] Eighteenth-century assemblies identified themselves "as a kind of medieval court making private judgments as well as public law."[5] They asserted equity and appellate jurisdiction over common law courts, often granting new trials. Even today, Massachusetts's legislature is officially called "the Massachusetts General Court," harkening back to its role as the court of last resort in the colonial and early republic eras. Because the members of colonial legislatures were elected popularly, most of colonial America's "supreme courts" were elected; they just happened to be elected assemblymen wearing multiple hats.

Other colonial officers also played multiple roles. The colonial councils in all of the colonies except Pennsylvania also served in executive, judicial, and legislative capacities. For example, in Virginia, the governor and the council sat together as the General Court, the state's chief trial court, throughout the colonial period.[6] The colonial courts also performed governmental functions, so that there was little distinction between administrative, legislative, and judicial roles.[7] Local courts in Massachusetts and Virginia performed a variety of day-to-day tasks of administration, such as assessing taxes, spending on local projects, licensing, and oversight.

In light of this mix of powers by both colonial legislative bodies and colonial courts, it is not surprising that colonial Connecticut's elected officers performed some judicial roles. Under Connecticut's first charter of 1636, the governor and magistrates were elected popularly to the general court, and sometimes acted like judges. At the same time, the colony established town courts, whose "principal men" or "selectmen" were elected popularly. In the 1660s, the colony created a court of assistants as the main judicial body, and it was made up of elected judges. In 1711, the superior court replaced the court of assistants, and its judges were partly appointed and partly elected.[8] The colonies (and then states) gradually separated their judiciaries from other elected bodies, but Connecticut hung onto its premodern mash-up of powers longer than the others. Well into the early nineteenth century, Connecticut continued to elect judges and give its elected legislators a judicial role. To the extent that Jefferson supported the separation of powers, his reliance on Connecticut as a model for electing judges was misplaced.

Meanwhile, in seventeenth-century England, one piece of evidence of the modern judiciary's evolution came from a source that also demonstrated its weakness. In 1610, Lord Coke established one of the early precedents for judicial independence and perhaps judicial review. In

Dr. Bonham's Case, a student alleged that the Board of Censors of the Royal College of Physicians had falsely imprisoned him, and the board itself had adjudicated the case. Lord Coke rejected the board's ruling because the board had a direct interest in the case, reflecting the principle that "no man shall judge his own case."[9] In 1616, King James I and the council called the justices of the King's Bench to demand that they stay a suit if the king so ordered. The other judges capitulated, but Lord Coke replied, "When that case should be, he would do that should be fit for a judge to do."[10] Even though Lord Coke was recognized as the greatest judge of his era, King James I removed him from his position as lord chief justice, just six years after *Dr. Bonham's Case.* For most of English history, judges held their offices *durante bene placito*—during the pleasure of the king—but increasingly, kings were displeased with their disagreeable judges. Over the next twenty-five years, a tumultuous period culminating in the English Civil War, James I and Charles I removed more judges who refused to submit. The remaining judges were viewed, fairly or unfairly, as tools of the Crown.[11]

The phrase "during good behavior" emerged out of this century of crisis, and it was the key to establishing judicial independence in England and America. The phrase literally means "so long as he should behave well," and it is the basis for tenure "during good behavior," which insulates judges from political removal and royal caprice. Starting in the fifteenth century, kings had opted to give some judges such charters. Under duress in 1642, at the beginning of the English Civil War, Charles I agreed to appoint judges "during good behavior." This practice continued throughout the civil war and the Interregnum, but the Stuarts returned to the throne in 1660 and returned to undermining the courts with "at pleasure" commissions in 1668. They ignored the sitting judges' "good behavior" guarantees, and over the next twenty years, they removed an increasing number of judges as a renewed political crisis brewed.[12]

These battles over the courts helped lead the way to the Glorious Revolution. In reaction to the Stuarts' abuses of power, English reformers first adopted the Bill of Rights in 1689, and then William III reinstated "good behaviour" appointments.[13] The Act of Settlement in 1701 set the royal "good behavior" protections into law, protected judicial salaries, and required "the Address of Both Houses of Parliament" for removal.[14] Seemingly, the job security of tenure during good behavior could be nullified by removal, which, on its face, could be with or without cause. However, the terms of removal fit with the late seventeenth century theory of judicial independence: undue political pressure could come from *either* the king *or* the people, as represented by Parliament, because the political conflict of the time was between the two. If the king and the people both agreed that a judge should be removed, then the presumption was that the judge's problems were more than political, and the judge surely was incompetent. [15]

After 1701, judges enjoyed a meaningful degree of independence from the Crown in law and in practice.[16] Initially, royal judges' commissions expired when the king or queen expired, but in 1760, an act announced that judges would continue in office during good behavior even after the monarch's death and the deaths of any of his or her successors. However, that same year, King George III declared that the Act of Settlement did not apply to the colonies, and colonial judges held their offices "at the pleasure of the Crown," without legal protection against removal. The king rarely exercised this power in the colonies, but the battles over the courts led to violent clashes in North Carolina, South Carolina, and Massachusetts in the 1760s and early 1770s. British threats against Massachusetts Bay Colony judges and closing their courts provoked revolutionary activity.[17] The colonial period is filled with instances of American colonists seeking to give their judges tenure "during good behavior" as protection from the Crown, and repeatedly the British pushed back.[18]

In the century between the Glorious Revolution and the American Revolution, political theorists were developing the idea of separation of powers. Historians credit John Locke, the theorist of the Glorious Revolution, with developing the first modern theory of "separation of powers."[19] However, Locke focused on separating the legislative from the executive, rather than separating the judicial from the executive.[20] Montesquieu extended the theory to judges as the defense of liberty: "Nor is there liberty if the power of judging is not separate from legislative power and from executive power. . . . If it were joined to executive power, the judge could have the force of an oppressor."[21] William Blackstone also defended the "distinct and separate existence of the judicial power . . . not removable at pleasure, by the crown." He concluded:

> Public liberty . . . cannot subsist long in any state, unless the administration of common justice be in some degree separated both from the legislative and also from the executive power. Were it joined with the legislature, the life, liberty, and property, of the subject would be in the hands of arbitrary judges, whose decisions would be then regulated only by their own opinions, and not by any fundamental principles of law; which, though legislators may depart from, yet judges are bound to observe.[22]

The English developed a separate judiciary by evolution; the Americans also solidified it by revolution. In 1776, John Adams continued Blackstone's themes: "The judicial power ought to be distinct from both the legislative and executive, and independent upon both, that so it may be a check upon both."[23] The state constitutional conventions followed Adams's lead.

The First Constitutions

As American colonists pursued independence from England, many demanded judicial independence as well. In particular, they called for judges to receive "good behaviour" commissions and more job security, not less—perhaps surprising given that their uprising focused on popular sovereignty and local democratic accountability. The fact that colonists found these positions consistent underscores how the rhetoric of judicial independence is often a response to whatever evil a political group is confronting in a particular moment.

In the 1750s, some colonial leaders declared that the common law mandated that judicial commissions were held during good behavior, and could be removed only for misbehavior in office.[24] Those favoring judicial independence argued that "good behaviour" was the "ancient and indubitable" common law, "by the usage and custom of ages; . . . by the rules of reason; . . . by covenant with the first founder of your government; . . . by the united consent of Kings, Lords, and Commons; . . . by birthright and as Englishmen."[25] In the years leading up to the Revolution, the independence of the judiciary from the Crown was a key issue in a majority of the colonies, and this debate focused on offices held during "good behaviour."[26] Benjamin Franklin took up the fight in the 1760s. In his "Causes of the American Discontents Before 1768," Franklin called for judicial commissions during good behavior, with secure, sufficient salaries.[27] The Crown's interference in the American colonial judiciary—real and perceived—was the basis of Jefferson's protest against "Judges dependent on his Will" in the Declaration of Independence. At this stage, judicial independence meant independence from a tyrannical central power, not independence from public opinion. Such independence arguably was consistent both with life tenure by appointment and with periodic popular elections.

Once the states won their independence, they wrote constitutions that separated the powers of government more clearly than ever before. Virginia's 1776 constitution explicitly declared the principle of the separation of powers, for the first time in the Anglo-American world since the 1650s: "The legislative, executive and judiciary departments shall be separate and distinct, so that neither exercise the powers properly belonging to the other: nor shall any person exercise the powers of more than one of them at the same time."[28]

But "separate" did not always mean the kind of separation we observe today. For example, most of the early state constitutions gave the legislature, not the voters, the power to choose the governor, and others used popular election only to create a slate of candidates from which the legislature could choose.[29] Not every new state constitution identified the judiciary as a separate branch, nor did every state give its judges life tenure or even long tenure.[30] Eight states adopted constitutions that guaranteed judicial commissions during good behavior, [31] and only three of those limited the removal of judges to a supermajority impeachment process. The other five exposed judges to the insecurity of a "removal by address" process by a bare legislative majority.[32] The remaining five states did not give judges life terms during good behavior. Pennsylvania and New Jersey provided their judges with seven-year terms, rather than life tenure.[33] Judges in Georgia and Rhode Island were elected by the legislature and served only at the pleasure of the assembly, that is, with no legal protection against removal.[34] Following its original colonial charter from 1662, Connecticut had a mix of one-year terms and tenure during the pleasure of the assembly.[35] Only six of the original state constitutions assured that judicial salaries would be "adequate," "fixed," or "permanent"; the other constitutions allowed legislatures to change salaries freely either explicitly or implicitly.[36]

These practices show that life tenure was not a dominant practice even in the Founding era. Even in the states granting life tenure, the legislatures controlled salaries, fees, and removal (often by the address of a simple legislative majority) in order to weaken judicial independence.[37] For example, early legislatures frequently vacated court decisions, suspended lawsuits, annulled judgments, granted new appeals and new trials, ruled on the merits of suits, and cancelled executions.[38]

The Federal Constitution

While the states were mixed on judicial job security, the federal Constitutional Convention marked a more decisive turn toward judicial independence. It is important to note that the judiciary was not a major subject of contention in the Convention. The Articles of Confederation, which the Convention had been called to revise, established no federal courts at all, and relied solely on the state courts and on Congress to resolve disputes between states. More or less, they were building from scratch, and they focused less on these details.

The Convention reached consensus that the federal judges should have the protection of tenure during good behavior and that the president should appoint the Supreme Court justices, subject to confirmation by the Senate.

The delegates divided over whether the rest of the judiciary should be appointed either by the president or by Congress. James Wilson of Pennsylvania argued that legislative appointment would lead to "intrigue, partiality, and concealment." John Rutledge of South Carolina countered that executive appointment was "leaning too much towards Monarchy," and that aside from a single federal Supreme Court, no other federal courts were necessary, because the state courts were sufficient.[39] At that point, Benjamin Franklin intervened to suggest other modes of appointment. As Madison recounted in his notes, Franklin "in a brief and entertaining manner" told a tale about Scotland. Scottish lawyers nominate the judges, according to Franklin, and they "always selected the ablest of the profession in order to get rid of him, and share his practice," to take his clients for themselves.[40] Perhaps Franklin was foreshadowing modern merit selection by bar leadership. Madison believed that the full Congress was too large and too untrained to choose judges, but he also had doubts about presidential appointments. He was inclined toward appointment by the Senate alone, because it was "numerous eno[ugh] to be confided in . . . and as being sufficiently stable and independent to follow their deliberate judgments." But he believed that they should leave this question for later, "to be hereafter filled on maturer reflection."[41]

In the end, they never did answer that question in the Constitution itself. The Constitution gave the president the power to appoint Supreme Court justices, with the advice and consent of the Senate, but the appointments clause does not mention other judges, and Article III on the judiciary simply left the question open for Congress.[42] Impeachment required a majority vote of the House and a two-thirds majority of the Senate to convict, and there was no provision for removal by address (a bare majority). Article III, Section 1 of the Constitution established the court system:

> The judicial Power of the United States, shall be vested in one supreme Court, and in such inferior Courts as the Congress may from time to time ordain and establish. The Judges, both of the supreme and inferior Courts, shall hold their Offices during good Behavior, and shall, at stated Times, receive for their Services a Compensation which shall not be diminished during their Continuance in Office.

This section set into constitutional stone several important features: a fixed Supreme Court; job security (tenure during good behavior, high threshold for removal); and salary security. But the Constitution did not clarify the structure of the "inferior courts," the number of Supreme Court justices, or other kinds of material resources—and no protection against the onerous "circuit-riding" around the country by horse and carriage, which would soon become a hot topic. Section 2 protected the Supreme Court's jurisdiction, but also limited it, and gave Congress an ambiguous power to make "Exceptions" and "Regulations" of its jurisdiction. Article VI's Supremacy Clause, making the Constitution "the supreme law of the land," was clearly meant to establish judicial review of state legislation (vertical review), but the Constitution did not specify a power of judicial review over federal legislation (horizontal review). The convention delegates themselves were divided or silent on this question; some believed the power was implicit, but they tolerated ambiguity.[43] The Constitution took very significant steps toward an independent judiciary, but there still were plenty of ways to change, challenge, or undermine the federal courts, too.

The convention delegates did not propose popular election of judges, and did not really challenge appointing judges with life tenure. Their only extended debate was whether to give the appointment power to the Senate or the president. A more complete separation of powers from other branches was not plausible for them, because their assumption was that judges had to be appointed by some combination of the other branches. Other models existed, such as New York's Council of Appointments, but this institution simply brought the governor together with four chosen senators, only a minor variation on the governor appointment/legislative confirmation model.

In *Federalist No. 78*, Alexander Hamilton defended Article III's guarantee of judicial offices during good behavior as "certainly one of the most valuable of the modern improvements in the practice of government. In a monarchy it is an excellent barrier to the despotism of the prince; in a republic it is a no less excellent barrier to the encroachments and oppressions of the representative body."[44] This explanation marks the transition of "good behaviour" from the colonial period to the early republic. Earlier, Americans had focused on life tenure as a protection against executive abuses. Hamilton shifted his focus to protect judges against legislative abuses. Hamilton argued generally for the "permanent tenure of judicial offices," so that the courts could fulfill their role as the "bulwarks of a limited Constitution against legislative encroachments."[45] He noted that the "good behavior" provision promoted the "impartial administration of the laws"[46] and that temporary appointments would "be fatal to their necessary independence."[47] He also contended that permanent tenure would attract those few individuals with the "integrity" and "sufficient skill in the laws to qualify them for the stations of judges."[48]

Historian Gordon Wood observed in the 1998 edition of his classic *Creation of the American Republic* that even though the historical interpretation of the Constitution's origin in the Framers' economic self-interest "in a narrow sense is undeniably dead, the general interpretation of the Progressive generation of historians—that the Constitution was in some sense an aristocratic document designed to curb the democratic excesses of the Revolution—still seems to me to be the most helpful framework for understanding the politics and ideology surrounding the Constitution."[49] Many Americans had concluded that "only the judiciary in America was impartial and free enough of private interests to . . . defend people's rights and property from the tyrannical wills of interested popular majorities."[50] For Hamilton and some of his fellow Federalists, judicial independence meant protecting commerce and credit from majoritarian meddling.[51] Hamilton had several concerns in mind, but high among them was the legislature's repudiation of public debts and its relief of private debts, against the individual rights of their creditors. For the next several decades, private and public debt led to fights over the courts and judicial independence, and ultimately to a wave of judicial elections.

Hamilton's *Federalist No. 78* reflected a shift in the understanding of judicial independence as independence from illegitimate *executive* power to independence from illegitimate *legislative* power. It articulated a more significant transition to our modern understanding of life tenure as independence from public opinion, party politics, and special interests. While Hamilton emphasized independence in order to protect the rights of the majority will against usurped public authority, he also discussed at length the protection of individual rights against majoritarian abuse, "those ill humors" that sometimes "disseminate among the people themselves" and "occasion dangerous innovations in the government, and *serious oppressions of the minor party in the community*" and of "*private rights of particular classes of citizens*, by unjust and partial laws." Hamilton concludes, "That inflexible and uniform adherence to the rights of the Constitution, and *of individuals,* which we perceive to be indispensable in the courts of justice, can certainly not be expected from judges who hold their offices by a temporary commission."[52]

Hamilton's explanation reflects the idea of judicial aristocracy—not in the pejorative sense of a privileged class of nobility, but in the sense of a separate and independent estate, enjoying the privileges of life tenure so that it can check the excesses of both monarchy and democracy. This usage was consistent with the Framers' "machine" metaphor as the mechanics of separation of powers to balance interests.[53] Most references to "aristocracy" in the convention were pejorative, often in critique of the Senate.[54] However, some Framers embraced the term, and often connected it to life tenure and the judiciary. Hamilton sought to create a federal institution to serve as a cosmopolitan elite, to represent "the rich and well born," and he believed the key was tenure for life or good behavior. "Nothing but a permanent body can check the imprudence of democracy. Their turbulent and uncontrouling disposition requires checks."[55] After he failed to persuade the convention that the senators should serve for life, he succeeded in establishing a judiciary with life tenure. Gouverneur Morris declared that "there never was, nor ever will be a civilized Society without an Aristocracy."[56] He endorsed life tenure because "Aristocracy should keep down Democracy."[57] Federalist James Kent, who would later become one of the most important judges in America, observed that Anti-Federalists called "men of talents & Property the natural aristocracy of the Country," and complained that the proposed constitution would put them in power. Kent replied that if that was the definition of aristocracy, he hoped he would "always be governed by an aristocracy."[58] Many Federalists embraced the concept of a "natural aristocracy," in contrast to the artificial and corrupt aristocracy by birth. Federalist James Wilson flagged even the most egalitarian state constitution, Pennsylvania's, for its provision that "representatives should consist of those most noted for wisdom and virtue," and Wilson hailed such men as a "natural aristocracy" that should govern.[59] Federalists meant to revive "aristocracy" in its original Greek sense: the rule of the virtuous and excellent. They wanted the courts to serve as "an aristocratic anchor," in the historian Louis Hartz's words, to check the democracy.[60]

One of the main Anti-Federalist critiques was that the proposed Constitution was "aristocratic" or "oligarchic." Around the time of the Revolution, some state judges already had generated fierce opposition by ruling in favor of Loyalists and their property claims. New York had passed the antiloyalist Trespass Act, and other states passed similar laws, taking property rights away from Loyalists. Risking public denunciation, Hamilton defended Loyalists and successfully challenged the constitutionality of New York's act. In a series of cases in the 1780s, courts in six states limited or overturned similar acts, and each time, they triggered a legislative backlash.[61] These decisions did not make American judges more popular as the Convention met and as the ratification debates began. Moreover, American courts imprisoned many debtors around this time, and opposition to prison for debtors was growing louder.[62] The general public had good reason to worry that the new federal courts with life-tenured judges would favor haves over have-nots, creditors over debtors, and federal power over state sovereignty. It also did not help that Federalist Judge Thomas McKean reportedly said at the Pennsylvania ratifying convention, "The wisdom, probity, and patriotism of the rulers will ever be the criterion for public prosperity; and hence it is, that despotism, if well administered, is the best form of government invented by human ingenuity."[63] In light of these unpopular cases, a political backlash, and the tone-deaf words of some Federalists, it is astonishing that Americans ratified the Constitution and accepted not only the creation of a federal court system, but also one that was designed to be so independent from political checks.

In contrast to McKean, Publius and other Federalists distrusted the wisdom of the rulers and were suspicious of mankind's "universal venality," so they constructed a system of separation of powers that relied on independent courts to check venality and despotism. Life tenure allowed judges to be insulated from popular opinion, and the Framers tended to equate disinterestedness and principle with virtue and natural aristocracy.[64] Hamilton had a more functional view of a judicial aristocracy as an institutional check on the other branches, rather than a faith in the inherent virtues of a ruling class. To construct this functional aristocracy, Hamilton focused on term length, which affects general independence, rather than method of selection, which affects relative independence. Judicial appointments by the executive and the legislature certainly do not guarantee judicial independence. After all, the federal Constitution could have given the president and Congress the power to appoint judges to short terms—just as some of the first state constitutions did. The federal Constitution also could have opted for electing judges to life terms, and those judges in theory would be just as independent. However, the Framers favored indirect democracy. Only the House of Representatives was directly elected. The electoral college chose the president, and the state legislatures appointed senators. By contrast, the advocates of judicial elections believed in direct democracy, and believed that life tenure obstructed the rule of the people. Thus, it is not surprising that the idea of appointment generally lined up with life tenure and that the idea of election lined up with short terms, but it is a mistake to think that this approach was universal or automatic.

The Anti-Federalists rejected the proposed federal judiciary because its appointed life-tenure judges would be too powerful and aristocratic. Some Anti-Federalists embraced the concept of a "natural" aristocracy, just like many Federalists, but they argued that the proposed constitution would create a more corrupt "oligarchy" instead.[65] Brutus, perhaps the most famous of the Anti-Federalist writers, titled one essay "The Supreme Court: They Will Mould the Government into Almost Any Shape They Please." The essay warned that the new government could tyrannize the people "through the medium of the judicial power," a power "unprecedented in a free country. . . . They are to be rendered totally independent, both of the people and the legislature, both with respect to their offices and salaries."[66] Obviously, tenure during good behavior came directly from English precedent, but Brutus foresaw a distinctly American invention of judicial supremacy in Article VI, which declares that the federal Constitution, statutes, and treaties are "the supreme law of the land."[67] Brutus recognized that the Supreme Court justices did not answer to anyone else. "No errors they may commit can be corrected by any power above them, if any such power there be, nor can they be removed from office for making ever so many erroneous adjudications," Brutus decried.[68]

A few months later, in an essay titled "The Supreme Court: No Power Above Them That Can Controul Their Decisions, or Correct Their Errors," Brutus carried forward this warning by distinguishing the proposed American constitution from the English constitution to explain why tenure during good behavior was acceptable in one but not the other. Even though English judges had tenure during good behavior, they did not have the power of judicial review and they were "under the controul of the legislature." By contrast, American judges under the proposed constitution "will controul the legislature. . . . [T]here is no power above them to set aside their judgment." The proposed combination of life tenure and judicial supremacy "transcends any power before given to a judicial by any free government under heaven," and threatened to kill America's democratic experiment. The English system of judicial independence meant only that judges had protected job security and fixed salaries. Brutus could accept these provisions if Congress could make those judges "properly responsible" to the people and could override their rulings. However, the proposed constitution has "made the judges independent in the fullest sense of the word. . . . In short, they are independent of the people, the legislature, and of every power under heaven. Men placed in this situation will generally soon feel themselves independent of heaven itself."[69]

The problem for Brutus and other Anti-Federalists was that the revolution had already changed the executive and legislative branches, and those changes altered the proper role of the courts.[70] In England, life tenure was crucial for republicanism, because it made the judges independent of the monarchy, but in America, the executive and legislature derived their power from the people, and thus these democratic branches had a more legitimate claim to control the judges.[71] Brutus addressed the threat of judicial tyranny with his own thinly veiled threat of rebellion:

> A constitution is a compact of a people with their rulers; if the rulers break the compact, the people have a right and ought to remove them and do themselves justice . . . but when this power [to determine the meaning of the compact] is lodged in the hands of men independent of the people, and of their representatives, and who are not, constitutionally, accountable for their

opinions, no way is left to controul them but *with a high hand and an out-stretched arm.*[72]

If Article III would not give the people a legal mechanism for removing judges, Brutus threatened to find extralegal means of fighting back. Brutus focused on the evils of judicial supremacy, and those evils were exacerbated by life tenure. Even though he seemed less than thrilled with either institution separately, he was open to life tenure without strong judicial review or strong judicial review without life tenure. But in a remarkable sign of the consensus against popular control of the courts, Brutus rejected judicial elections as "improper," because judging requires "a degree of law knowledge" (and the voters presumably were not capable of discerning law knowledge), and moreover, "it is fit that they should be placed, in a certain degree in an independent situation, that they may maintain firmness and steadiness in their decisions."[73] Brutus himself embraced general judicial independence, even while denouncing judicial supremacy.

Like Brutus, other Anti-Federalists did not use the occasion of their critiques of the proposed constitution to call for judicial elections.[74] One possible exception, implicitly, was "A Watchman," who wrote that Article III "deprives the inhabitants of each state of the power of choosing their superiour and inferiour judges."[75] But it is possible that this critic might have been satisfied by state legislatures appointing the federal judges in their states.

State Courts after Ratification

In the 1790s, the French Revolution went further and adopted popular election and short terms for judges.[76] The American states went the opposite direction, following Publius and the Federalists over Brutus and the Anti-Federalists in the 1790s. Pennsylvania switched to tenure during good behavior in 1790,[77] and Kentucky adopted it in 1792 when it entered the Union. Connecticut also conformed to this overall shift toward more independence and a clearer separation of powers. After the Revolution, Connecticut retained its colonial charter and its colonial court system, making it the first state to elect judges. However, it then moved entirely to appointment in a series of steps. In 1784, the general assembly passed a statute making all judges appointed by the general assembly, with tenure limited formally as year-to-year. At the same time, the assembly also created a Supreme Court of Errors, composed of elected officials (the governor and the council of the general assembly). Then the Supreme Court of Errors became a solely judicial body composed only of appointed superior court judges in 1806.[78] In 1818, Connecticut replaced its revised colonial charter with a new constitution that designated that all judges would be appointed by the general assembly.[79] The supreme and superior court judges would serve during good behavior, while lower court judges would be appointed annually. Thus, at the time Jefferson celebrated Connecticut's elected judges in his 1816 letter, Connecticut had not elected judges per se since 1784, and other elected officials ceased to hold judicial-type powers since 1806. Jefferson's letter, which was often cited by defenders of judicial elections, was technically right that Connecticut had once elected judges, but only because Connecticut had not separated judicial functions from other functions. In the rise of judicial aristocracy, judicial independence meant the end of these premodern, multipurpose, elected judges.

Connecticut was not the only state to hang onto the vestiges of a premodern judiciary without separation of powers. New York adopted a Court of Errors in both its 1777 constitution and its 1821 constitution as its court of last resort. The Court of Errors combined the state senators with the chancellor and supreme court justices, so that elected senators (with four-year terms) outnumbered appointed life-tenure judges by about eight to one.[80] The Massachusetts legislature continued to adjudicate cases, and Congress and most state legislatures continued to adjudicate "private bills" to address petitions for relief, very often functioning more like courts than legislatures.[81] Eventually, both New York and Connecticut would return to electing judges in the mid-nineteenth century—not in the premodern model without the separation of powers, but in the rise of judicial democracy to promote judicial independence and to strengthen the separation of powers.[82]

One could say that colonial America was full of elected judges, but it is more accurate to say that colonial America was full of elected officials who had some judicial responsibilities. As government modernized into separate and specialized branches, those mixed-role officials gradually were sifted out into more distinct categories of elected legislators, elected governors, and appointed judges. A major component of Founding era separation of powers was borrowing "good behavior" tenure from the English to create a judicial aristocracy. For the Federalists, the challenge was to protect a nascent democracy from itself, and their paradox was to protect democracy with a form of aristocracy. Judicial independence and life tenure were ways of protecting a constitutional democracy from democratic excess, and in the eyes of some Federalists, they were ways of protecting property and national economic development from democratic excess.[83] The most surprising part of this story is that, despite American judges issuing a series of unpopular decisions in the 1780s favoring pro-British loyalists, despite growing outrage at American judges imprisoning more debtors, despite general doubts about lawyers, and despite valid fears that life-tenured federal judges would run roughshod over state sovereignty, the state ratifying conventions still adopted the proposed Constitution and its powerful new federal judiciary. This remarkable event was the first of a pattern throughout American history: Even when lots of judges were making unpopular decisions, the public still accepted judicial independence.

The tension between popular democracy and judicial aristocracy increased in the next few decades. Brutus's descendants in the early republic and the Jeffersonian era continued to fight against judicial independence—sometimes using experiments in judicial elections, but more often using other tools.[84] Judicial aristocracy barely survived in the federal government, but most states overthrew it. Yet even in this transformation to judicial democracy, the values of judicial independence and separation of powers continued to thrive.

CHAPTER TWO

Judicial Challenges in the Early Republic

THOMAS JEFFERSON had called for judicial independence from England, but he intended that kind of independence to translate into judicial accountability to the public. Jefferson and his followers focused more on judicial accountability as they rose to power over the Federalists after the "Revolution of 1800." They took over the executive and the legislature on both the federal and state levels, and clashed with the Federalist holdovers in the judiciary. Their priority was to weaken the courts with their newfound powers in the other branches. An increased separation of powers or judicial independence would have undermined their strategy of using legislative power against the Federalist judges. Once the Jeffersonian Republicans seized power, opponents of the courts had many legislative weapons with which to attack the Federalist judges, while popular elections were viewed as unnecessary or unreliable in centralizing political control. Thus, judicial elections were not in the Jeffersonian repertoire, and they were uncommon in the early phase of judicial democracy from 1800 to the early 1830s.

This chapter focuses on the political vulnerability of early American judges *before* the era of judicial elections. This book argues that the 1840s and 1850s were a turning point in favor of judicial review and judicial power, driven by the first generation of elected judges. This argument invites a skeptical question: Weren't judicial review and judicial power firmly established in the Founding era and the early republic? Of course, the Marshall Court famously announced judicial review, and some scholars recently have produced outstanding research showing that early American courts exercised judicial review.[1] Colonial charters had given legislatures the power to pass their own laws, as long as they were not "repugnant to" English law, and these provisions were an early step toward written constitutions and judicial review.[2] Historians have demonstrated that judicial review was accepted as legitimate in the Founding era and in the convention and ratification debates themselves.[3] In the 1780s and 1790s, state judges endorsed the theory of judicial review, and sometimes they intervened and asserted their power in controversial disputes.[4] Unquestionably, these decisions were important early steps. But despite these announcements, judges were not yet putting this theory into practice regularly. They often avoided conflict with legislatures and political opposition. The Marshall Court famously announced and applied judicial review in *Marbury v. Madison,* but many scholars have pointed out how Chief Justice Marshall's decision in *Marbury* was a deft judicial sleight of hand avoiding political confrontation. After *Marbury,* the Marshall Court challenged federal legislation only in more subtle ways in low-profile cases.[5] In high-profile cases, it invalidated statutes in "vertical" judicial review of state law, rather than "horizontal" judicial review of the U.S. Congress.

While the Marshall Court solidified a moderate position on judicial review (occasionally challenging the states but not the federal government, generally speaking), the states' use of judicial review against state legislation was less frequent. This book offers a thorough study of state supreme court decisions from 1780 through the Civil War, depicted in Appendix D. The U.S. Supreme Court invalidated approximately one state statute every two years, but a thorough search of all state supreme court decisions through the Civil War shows that on average, each state supreme court invalidated only one or two state statutes per decade through the 1830s. Then state supreme courts sharply increased their exercise of judicial review in the 1840s and 1850s, almost quadrupling the rate between the 1830s and the 1850s. These decisions were predominantly the work of the first generation of elected judges.

Many of these decisions between 1800 and the 1830s came from a few sudden spikes: New York in the 1810s and 1820s, Kentucky and Vermont in the 1820s, and Tennessee in the 1830s. On the one hand, these bursts of judicial review show that some judges were testing boundaries and asserting their power. On the other hand, this chapter will show how partisan politicians punished these judges for their assertiveness by sweeping them off the bench or abolishing their jobs—even though the judges were supposedly protected on paper as life-tenure judges. In most states, the exercise of judicial review was either rare or nonexistent from the Founding through the 1830s, perhaps because of these political threats.

The announcement of judicial review on the pages of judicial decisions was a significant part of the judges contesting legislative power and building a foundation for judicial power. However, those announcements sometimes covered up political weakness that was apparent to contemporaries. As we dig deeper, the specific context of these cases illustrates how fragile these courts were, and how a court decision might trumpet formal legal power precisely because the court knew it lacked political power. This chapter focuses on one such state case as an example, the Maryland case *Whittington v. Polk*,[6] which has been identified by judges and historians for its announcement of judicial power one year before *Marbury* and for leading the way to *Marbury*.[7] The facts of *Whittington* are similar to those of *Marbury*. When the Republicans seized the Maryland legislature in 1801, they stripped Federalist justices of their offices, and an aggrieved Federalist justice, William Whittington, sued to reclaim his position. Only a few months before *Marbury*, the Maryland General Court proclaimed in *Whittington v. Polk:*

> It is the office and province of the court . . . to determine whether an act of the legislature, which assumes the appearance of a law, and is clothed with the garb of authority, is made pursuant to the power vested by the constitution in the legislature; for if it is not the result or emanation of authority derived from the constitution, it is not law, and cannot influence the judgment of the court in the decision of the question before them.[8]

The author was Judge Jeremiah Townley Chase, the cousin and close friend of Justice Samuel Chase on the U.S. Supreme Court. Samuel would soon thereafter join Chief Justice John Marshall's opinion in *Marbury*. Reading the texts of *Whittington* and *Marbury*, it appears these courts were establishing their power and their independence, but a closer look at context suggests that those appearances are deceiving. The Maryland Federalist ex-justices had been appointed to offices "during good behavior," and they had valid legal arguments for getting their offices back, but the Federalists on Maryland's General Court rejected their claims. *Whittington* is a particularly relevant case on two related levels: it simultaneously illustrates the vulnerability of the appointed judges of early America, and also reveals the weakness of early judicial review. Not only did the Maryland county justices lose their jobs, but the Republican legislature was on the verge of abolishing the Federalist-controlled General Court, too, even though on paper they were protected by "good behavior" life-tenure. And not only did the General Court try to hide its weakness with language about judicial review, their decision also underscores how the Marshall Court did the same thing.

This chapter also focuses attention on the case that was far more important than *Marbury* at the time: *Stuart v. Laird,* in which the U.S. Supreme rejected the claims of Federalists to their constitutional "good behavior" judgeships after the Republicans had repealed those offices. *Whittington* was a forerunner to the U.S. Supreme Court's capitulation in *Stuart v. Laird,* not a precedent for judicial review and judicial power. The Supreme Court justices were paying close attention to *Whittington,* and were drawing arguments from it as it was being litigated and as they were trying to decide whether to fight the Jeffersonians in defense of the Midnight Judges, or to capitulate. The Maryland judges' retreat in *Whittington* helped push the justices toward capitulation on the issue of the federal courts. Whether or not the law was on the side of the Federalist plaintiffs, this result reveals the judges' overall vulnerability: If the Federalist ex-justices had the stronger legal argument, then the Maryland General Court judges may have capitulated out of fear of political reprisal; if the Federalist ex-justices did not have a strong legal claim, then the Maryland General Court was confirming that the judges of this era had little formal protection from the other branches. Even after ruling in favor of the Republicans, the Maryland General Court itself was almost abolished by the Republican legislature, regardless of these judges' life tenure. Throughout the country in this period, other judges were political targets and similarly lost their seats because of the lack of independence from the political branches. Appointment "for life," even with constitutional protection, could not shield judges from the very real legislative weapons of impeachment, abolition of their courts ("ripper bills"), stripping the courts of jurisdiction, and other attacks.

This chapter title "judicial challenges in the early republic" has a triple meaning. First, the chapter investigates a few cases in which aggrieved Federalists, propertied interests, and others turned to the courts to challenge the constitutionality of legislation. Second, those judges faced enormous political challenges to their power, even though they were appointed with life tenure during good behavior. As a result, many Federalist judges backed down from these challenges, and those who did not back down were often removed from the bench. Third, even if the take-away message is that political pushback limited the appointed judges of this era, some of these judges were still pushing and willing to provoke some pushback. On the one hand, the Maryland General Court and the Marshall Court used the threat of judicial review as a fig leaf to conceal their nakedness against the opposition of the political branches. On the other hand, they did not offer a total surrender. In fact, both Federalist courts took risks in contesting the Jeffersonians by asserting the power of judicial review. They may not have given the Federalist plaintiffs their offices back, but they were still testing some institutional boundaries in significant ways. The Federalist judges in both courts opted to live to fight another day. It turns out that the early republic's courts often were struggling to survive political turmoil. The story of early American courts was not a steady march toward judicial supremacy or a story of constant retreat and defeat. American judges often were taking two steps forward, and one step back: gradual, slow growth, marked by occasional setbacks from Jefferson's presidency through Andrew Jackson's.

This chapter attempts to strike a balance between the stories of judicial triumphalism and judicial defeatism. Drawing on new archival records, it tells a story of how America was on the brink of a full-scale war over the courts and how the judges survived that conflict. This was an era of cautious contestation, of judges testing boundaries and planting the seeds of judicial review. In these years, judicial review was not as much bold practice; rather, it was more theory, dicta, sleight of hand, and grounds for removal from office. But because some of these judges were willing to take on the challenge, the seeds they planted would later blossom.

A High Hand against Judicial Independence

The Anti-Federalist Brutus had objected to federal judges' life tenure and judicial independence during the ratification debate in 1788, threatening judges with "a high hand and an outstretched arm."[9] This was a quotation from Deuteronomy, referring to God inflicting plagues on the Egyptians and freeing the Israelites.[10] The choice of the pseudonym Brutus sent another threatening message, a reference to Marcus Junius Brutus, one of Julius Caesar's assassins.[11] The assassins believed they were defending the republic from despotism. In the aftermath of the Revolution and the Shays Rebellion, a farmers' revolt against taxes and debt, Brutus was tapping into a culture of forceful popular constitutionalism—including mob violence—that would continue to shape the clashes between Federalists and Republicans in the 1790s.[12]

The election of 1800 was the turning point in the struggle between the two parties. Republican Thomas Jefferson and his running mate Aaron Burr each received seventy-three electoral votes, more than Federalist John Adams's sixty-five. Instead of that result automatically making Jefferson president and Burr vice president, a breakdown of constitutional foresight and political organization created a tie between Jefferson and Burr, leaving a divided House of Representatives to break the tie. In the ensuing deadlock, Washington buzzed with concern about the mobilization of Republican militias from Virginia and Pennsylvania, with the Federalist militia from Massachusetts joining in.[13] The Federalists in the House backed down from confrontation on the seventh day of voting, on the thirty-sixth ballot.

In his last days in office, President Adams pushed through a new set of federal judgeships and filled them with the Midnight Judges as a lame-duck blockade against Jefferson. Federalists in the state governments did the same thing. In response, Republicans overrode these Midnight Judges with impeachments and simple legislation, despite the fact that many of these federal and state judges were protected with life tenure. They removed one federal judge from office, impeached Supreme Court Justice Samuel Chase, and removed Federalist judges from the state bench.[14] This battle over the courts between Republicans and Federalists has been called "the Jeffersonian crisis."[15] The Republicans wanted to weaken their Federalist opponents on the courts, and many also wanted to weaken the courts generally.[16]

Whittington and *Marbury*: The Similarities

In the midst of the Federalist-orchestrated deadlock between Jefferson and Burr, the lame-duck Federalist Congress passed the Judiciary Act of 1801 on February 13, reorganizing the courts into six circuits and creating sixteen new life-term judicial appointments.[17] As their terms were about to expire, Adams and the Federalists appointed a series of judges known pejoratively as "the Midnight Judges." In addition, the Federalists appointed other officials at the last minute, including William Marbury as justice of the peace for Washington, D.C.

Once Jefferson was inaugurated in March, he and Secretary of State James Madison began carving away these appointments. William Marbury and other justices of the peace, confirmed for a five-year term to be held "in good behavior," never received their commissions from John Marshall while he was Adams's secretary of state. Given an easy opportunity to eliminate a handful of midnight appointments, Madison refused to grant Marbury and several other appointees their commissions, and these appointees sued. In December 1801, the Supreme Court required the new secretary of state, James Madison, to show cause for the failure to issue their commissions. In the meantime, the Republican Congress repealed the Judiciary Act of 1801 in March 1802, terminating the Midnight Judges' offices and the new circuit system, even though they held their judicial offices "during good behavior" under Article III of the U.S. Constitution. Congress then reinstated the Judiciary Act of 1789 (with some minor

revisions) one month later.[18] Fearing that the Supreme Court might intervene as soon as it had a chance, the Republicans rammed through Congress a bill on April 29, 1802 (the same month in which *Whittington* was
argued) that suspended the next two sessions of the Supreme Court, post-
poning the next session to February 1803.

The repeal went into effect without a chance for the Court to strike it
down, and the justices were expected to return to riding circuit in the fall,
despite the legal claims to the circuit courts by the Midnight Judges. In the
spring of 1802, Federalist leaders pressured the justices to take a stand,
and the justices considered boycotting the circuits and going on strike.
However, the justices reluctantly decided to ride their circuits in the fall.
The Midnight Judges unsuccessfully challenged the justices' jurisdiction in
the circuit courts in the fall of 1802. In Virginia, Federalist lawyers directly challenged Chief Justice Marshall's jurisdiction as a circuit judge for
the Fourth Circuit in *Laird v. Stuart,* arguing that the Adams appointees
were the rightful judges for the circuits. Marshall dismissed the argument
without issuing an opinion. Three similar challenges by Midnight Judges
in other circuits ended the same way. In February 1803, the Supreme
Court rejected Marbury's claim, striking down provisions of the Judiciary
Act of 1789 as unconstitutional for granting the Supreme Court jurisdiction beyond the scope of Article III of the U.S. Constitution.[19] A few days
later, in *Stuart v. Laird,*[20] the Court rejected the jurisdictional challenge
cursorily, asserting that the justices had acquiesced to riding circuit in the
past, and therefore they did not require specific commissions to ride circuit again. They avoided the question about whether the Midnight Judges
were entitled to those offices themselves as Article III appointments.

Whittington and *Marbury* are intertwined. The battle over the Maryland judiciary closely paralleled the battle over the federal judiciary in
chronology and in legal issues. The central characters in *Whittington* had
national political significance or were closely linked to the main characters in *Marbury*. Most significantly, *Whittington* received national attention in congressional debates, in the nation's newspapers, and in the letters of the Supreme Court justices, thus shaping the debate over the
federal controversy.

William Whittington was a "justice" of the county courts, an office
mentioned by the Maryland constitution in four different clauses.[21]
Maryland's Declaration of Rights, drafted together with the Constitution
in 1776, declared "that the independency and uprightness of Judges are
essential to the impartial administration of Justice, and a great security to
the rights and liberties of the people." To this end, the Declaration of
Rights guaranteed that "the Chancellor [and] all Judges shall hold their

commissions during good behavior."[22] However, even though "justices of the county court" were mentioned in the constitution, they were not considered constitutional "judges" for the purposes of "good behavior" tenure by the first Maryland legislatures from 1777 through 1790, because they were appointed annually and could be discharged by the governor.[23] Nevertheless, the justices of the county courts had extensive civil, criminal, and appellate jurisdiction since the eighteenth century.[24] In the Maryland judicial system, they were most analogous to trial court judges, even if they had other duties.

In the 1790s, the Federalists solidly controlled Maryland, and they retained power until 1800.[25] In 1796, the Federalists revised the state's judicial system by redistricting the county courts and then taking advantage politically by filling the new offices with Federalists.[26] The Act of 1796 designated that each justice "shall hold their commission during good behaviour, and may be removed for misbehaviour in the same manner as the chancellor and the judges may be removed agreeably to the constitution of this state, and not otherwise."[27] In February 1799, the Federalist governor appointed William Whittington chief justice of the state's fourth district.[28]

After Maryland's Republicans won the state's elections in 1800, the Federalists tried to shore up their control of the judiciary before their terms ran out, and appointed more loyal Federalists to the bench.[29] Noting the similarities with Adams's last days, Maryland Republicans also called these moves the midnight appointments[30] and vowed to overturn both the state and federal judges they regarded as illegitimate.[31] When the Republicans took over the Maryland government, they announced that they would send a message nationally against Adams's Judiciary Act of 1801.[32] They first repealed the Federalists' 1796 act, abolishing the offices by a statute, known as a "ripper bill," rather than impeaching the justices themselves.[33] In the U.S. Congress, the Republicans offered a rationale that the federal Judiciary Act of 1801 needed to be scrapped because it was unnecessary and expensive, and they followed through by scrapping it. In Maryland, there was little such pretense. The Maryland Republicans immediately reenacted exactly the same offices and filled them with Republicans for the same kind of "good behavior" life terms, proving that their motives were partisan.[34]

When the new bill took effect on January 26, 1802, Republican Governor Mercer appointed William Polk and two other Republicans to replace William Whittington and the other Federalist justices.[35] On March 24, 1802, Whittington sued, claiming that Polk had unlawfully "disseised" Whittington of his office.[36] The General Court had original jurisdiction over this suit, and its trial started on April 7, 1802.[37] Newspapers around the country reported on the case and emphasized its national importance.[38] Federalist writers denounced the Republicans' brazenness: "They do not even attempt to improve the system, but have repealed the law which established the system, and having thereby . . . turned out those judges which the Constitution declared independent, have *re-enacted the same law*! Such is the security afforded by written Constitutions, when Jacobins are to legislate under them!"[39]

According to these writers, Maryland's repeal was a dangerous legal precedent, and it served as a warning about the Jeffersonians' danger to the Constitution.[40] Congress scrutinized Maryland's actions during the debate over the repeal of the Federal Judiciary Act. Federalist Senator James Hillhouse of Connecticut condemned Maryland's revisions from the previous month: "What could be the object of this repeal? Surely none other than the turning the judges out of office. Could that be less a violation of their Constitution than the passing of a law directly removing from office the same judges?"[41] Republicans responded on the Senate floor at length to defend both the Maryland repeal and the federal repeal.[42]

The Federalists had more reason for confidence based on the composition of the three-judge General Court. The three judges of the General Court were Federalist Jeremiah Townley Chase, Federalist John Done, and Republican Gabriel Duvall. While they were judges on the General Court, Judge Chase and Judge Duvall had actively campaigned against one another for the electoral college in the 1800 presidential election for Adams and Jefferson, respectively.[43] Duvall won on behalf of Jefferson by a margin of three-to-one.[44] Jeremiah Chase was U.S. Supreme Court Justice Samuel Chase's cousin, and the two were very close.[45] When Jeremiah lost his father at age nine, Samuel's father Thomas took him in, and Samuel, then age sixteen, was like an older brother.[46] Samuel and Jeremiah married sisters Ann and Hester Baldwin, and the Chases remained close political allies, business partners, and loyal friends from the Revolution through their fight with the Jeffersonians.[47]

Duvall, the lone Republican, was also a relatively major figure, a former congressman, and a future U.S. Supreme Court justice. Marylanders hailed Duvall as a leader who has "done more in the cause of Republicanism than any man whatever."[48] The third General Court judge, John Done, was not as prominent, but he, too, established his commitment to the Federalists as an elector for John Adams in the 1796 presidential election,[49] and his continuing allegiance to the Federalists was publicly known.[50] Federalist writers took note of their solid two-to-one advantage on the Court, and predicted that the Maryland judges would "have firmness and independence" to stand up to the Republicans.[51]

The Supreme Court Justices

In March 1802, around the time that William Whittington filed his state lawsuit, the Republicans in Congress repealed the Judiciary Act of 1801, terminating the Midnight Judges' offices and the new circuit system, and then reinstated the old system, in which the justices rode the circuits themselves.[52] Congress had also suspended the next two Supreme Court terms, purposely to block the Supreme Court justices from hearing a challenge to the repeal until February 1803. In the interim, the justices faced a difficult decision: Should they set aside their legal principles, follow the new Republican Judicial Act, and ride circuit all around the country? Or should they disregard a law they regarded as invalid and boycott the circuits out of respect for their rightful office-holders, the Federalist Midnight Judges? They debated back and forth precisely when the Maryland trial in *Whittington v. Polk* was taking place. There were signals that the Supreme Court justices would dig in for a fight. As Federalist congressional leaders began organizing their resistance, they learned some exciting news in late March: Marshall would cooperate with their plans. One congressman visited Marshall in Richmond and reported "that the firmness of the Supreme Court may be depended on should the business be brought before 'em."[53] This report spread quickly among the Federalist leadership, and they were emboldened.[54] On April 6, Marshall wrote to Justice Paterson that he personally believed that the justices should boycott, and he wished that the Court would have an opportunity to hear a challenge to the repeal:

> I confess I have some strong constitutional scruples. I cannot well perceive how the performance of circuit duty by the Judges of the supreme court can be supported. If the question was new I should be unwilling to act in this character without a consultation of the Judges; but I consider it as decided & that whatever my own scruples may be I am bound by the decision. I cannot however but regret the loss of the next June term. I could have wished the Judges had convened before they proceeded to execute the new system.[55]

True to his leadership as chief justice, Marshall sought consensus, but his personal views favoring a boycott are very revealing.

These letters began a series of exchanges about the boycott plans. Justices Cushing, Paterson, and Washington preferred to ride circuit and avoid confrontation. Justice Samuel Chase argued strongly for the boycott. In his own letter to Justice Paterson on April 6, Chase argued that the justices should stand by their principles, regardless of the consequences.

He then explicitly mentioned *Whittington v. Polk,* which was to be argued the very next day:

> I expect we shall hear from our Chief Justice in about a fortnight. I hope we shall meet and consult. I believe a Day of severe trial is fast approaching for the friends of the Constitution, and we I fear must be principal actors, and may be sufferers therein. In this State [Maryland,] an assize of office is brought by Judge Whittington vs. Judge Polk to try the constitutionality of the act of our Legislature repealing our District Law. I would write to you fully my Sentiments, as far as I have formed an opinion, but I fear some accident. I will only say, if the office of the Circuit Judge is full, and it is so if not taken away by the repealing act, We are to be made the instruments to destroy the independence of the Judiciary.[56]

Chase regarded *Whittington* as an important test case that would influence the course of events. Chase seemed hopeful that the Maryland court would rule in favor of the Federalists, and if so, it would have been a strong precedent on his side in favor of a circuit boycott.

In an even more adamant letter to Chief Justice Marshall two weeks later, Chase again referred to the case and reiterated that "the Act is void" and that he would "restore the Judge to his Office."[57] At about the same time, Chief Justice Marshall informed the Federalist leadership that the justices had decided to ride circuit.[58] From this setback, the Federalist leaders in Congress and the Midnight Judges formulated a plan to contest the Supreme Court justices' jurisdiction in circuit courts that autumn.[59] The justices continued debating their decision, and even expressed some regrets about the situation.[60] As of June 8, Chase was still willing to fight.[61] On June 14, the Maryland General Court announced its decision. One might have imagined that the two ardent Federalist judges, Chase and Done, would vote to strike down the 1801 repeal, and the one Republican, Duvall, would dissent. Instead, the court unanimously rejected the Federalist challenges. Was this an act of impartiality and fair judging? Moderation? Calculated capitulation?

Whittington v. Polk: The Decision

Whittington was similar to the facts of *Marbury* and *Stuart v. Laird,* except for the fact that the Maryland Federalists had an even stronger legal and moral claim. Unlike *Marbury* and President Adams's other midnight appointments, William Whittington received a judicial appointment in 1799 in the midst of a Federalist mandate, and thus, his office was untainted by "lame duck" or "midnight" illegitimacy. Unlike *Marbury*'s five-year limited term as a justice of the peace, William Whittington's office was held during good behavior without any term limit. Thus, the office was "freehold" property under common law precedents. Moreover, even if the Maryland legislature had the power to repeal a legislatively created office, the Republican legislature re-created the same office, so Whittington had an even stronger legal claim to that office. Unlike the U.S. Supreme Court in *Marbury,* there was no doubt that the Maryland General Court had jurisdiction over the suit and had the power to return offices to their rightful owners.

Despite these advantages for the Federalists, the Maryland General Court rebuffed their arguments in June 1802, and cloaked its judicial surrender to the Republicans with mere dicta about judicial review. Judge Jeremiah Chase held, "1st. That an act of assembly repugnant to the constitution is void. 2d. That the court have [*sic*] a right to determine an act of assembly void, which is repugnant to the constitution."[62] Then for four pages, he touted the power of judicial review. He warned that if the legislature had the power to decide the constitutionality of its own acts, this power "would establish a despotism, and subvert that great principle of the constitution, which declares that the powers of making, judging, and executing the law, shall be separate and distinct from each other."[63] Judge Chase continued, "Whenever it does become necessary [to decide the constitutionality of legislation, the people] trust [that the judges] will not seek any evasion, or shrink from the determination of it, but act with caution and circumspection, and give it that consideration which the importance of it, and their duty, demand."[64] In fact, despite these strong pronouncements, the General Court did evade and shrink from their judicial duty. Judge Chase did take a chance by so visibly endorsing judicial power in theory, but that theory was much easier to tolerate when in practice, he was backing down from the fight.

After his endorsement of judicial review, Jeremiah Chase then turned to the case itself. Chase began by dodging the question of motives of the repeal: The motives "cannot be inquired into by the court in a question as to its constitutionality."[65] He then interpreted the Maryland Constitution's reference to "judges" (who hold their offices during good behavior) as not including "justices," and he concluded that the justice of the county court was a legislatively created office, not a constitutionally mandated office. He did not address the fact that the constitution refers to the justices of the county courts four separate times.[66] Chase granted that the general assembly had the power to "modify" the courts, but they could not create a life tenure office that endured beyond the life of the legislation. Though Whittington had "a right vested" in the office, that right lasted only "for the term of years limited for the continuance of the law." Still, Chase denounced the repeal as "an infraction of his right," as well as "incompatible with the principles of justice, and does not accord with sound legislation."[67] Nevertheless, the repeal was constitutional. Chase's implicit theory is that "good behaviour" meant one thing in a constitutional context: life tenure, with removal solely for misbehavior. It meant another thing in a legislative context: tenure for the duration of the legislation, with removal either for misbehavior or by repeal of the legislative act itself.

However, the Maryland General Court had plausible legal grounds for ruling the other way. Federalist leaders had been arguing that legislatures had the power to create such offices, citing several English precedents that undercut Chase's conclusions. In the *Washington Federalist,* "Lucius Junius Brutus" wrote a series opposing Congress's repeal in early 1802, just as the bill was being debated.[68] "Lucius Junius Brutus" has been identified as William Cranch, the judge of the D.C. Circuit (one of Adams's midnight appointments) and the very influential Supreme Court reporter beginning in 1801, using his own funds to publish the Court's opinions. In his defense of the Federalist judges, he cited Lord Coke's commentaries and a series of English decisions that explained that any grant during good behavior or "for any like incertain time" is "an estate for life,"[69] and is an "estate of freehold in the office."[70] The English Chief Justice Holt reaffirmed that "good behavior" offices are estates for life, and explained, "[Parliament's] design was, that men should have places not to hold precariously or determinable upon will and pleasure, but to have a certain, durable estate, that they might act in them without fear of losing them."[71] Cranch argued that Parliament ratified these cases in 1700, extending the property claim to the office holder's life, and not limiting it to the duration of the statute. He contended that the term "good behaviour" is not merely a restriction of power against executive power to replace at will, but that it is a conveyance of a right to the office holder against legislative alterations, too: *"The judge gains a title against all the world."*[72] A few years later, the Marshall Court further limited legislative alterations of contract and property rights in *Fletcher v. Peck*[73] and *Dartmouth College v. Woodward* (although those cases pertained to private property, not public offices).[74]

But even if Judges Chase and Done were unwilling to hold that a legislature could not repeal a freehold office, they did not address a strong claim in favor of Whittington: the Maryland legislature had immediately recreated the very same office. As long as the office existed, Whittington arguably had a vested freehold commission to that office. The other Federalists around the country would have preferred the Maryland General

Court to strike down the repeal itself as unconstitutional, a broader, bolder decision curbing legislative power. However, a more narrow holding (not ruling on the constitutionality of the repeal, but giving Whittington back his office on the reenacted court) would have signaled an important protection of Federalist judges, and a defense of property rights against legislative redistribution and meddling. Instead, the Maryland General Court was silent on this question.

Judge Jeremiah Chase briefly turned to the question of Whittington's choice of remedy, the writ of assize of novel disseisin. He concluded that the writ was not applicable, because Whittington's office was "only an interest for a term of years in the said office, determinable on the contingency of his being convicted of misbehaviour in a court of law; and that writ is not adapted to the recovery of any estate or interest . . . in an office less than a freehold."[75] As Judge Chase ruled, the legislature did not have the power to create such offices that would survive beyond the acts that created them. Even though the legislature might say that the office had no limit of years, the limit of years was implicitly the life of the statute— which could be repealed at any time. As a result, the office was not a freehold, and not subject to the assize. However, there was also legal support for the opposite conclusion. William Blackstone, in his classic *Commentaries* written almost four decades earlier, explained that a grant of property can be a freehold even if it does not state expressly that it is an "estate for life," but also "by a general grant, without defining or limiting any specific date."[76] Blackstone was focusing on real property, but he did not foreclose the assize's application to other kinds of property. Renowned English legal scholars have explained that government offices can be freehold rights, and observed that "the assize [of novel disseisin] which protects the possessor of land seems the natural defence for the possession of an office, at all events if that office has a local sphere."[77] English legislation in 1285 specified that the assize of novel disseisin applied to "offices in fee."[78] One might differentiate between royal offices in England and state offices in America, but that distinction was not dictated by law and not at all obvious.

Judge Duvall, the lone Republican, concurred in the result, but took exception to the passage in which Judge Chase decried the repeal as an "infraction" of the plaintiff's right and as "incompatible with the principles of justice."[79] Duvall flagged the inconsistency between recognizing such a right and then declining to remedy an infraction of that right. Duvall was implying that because there was no remedy, there could not have been a right. But the converse arguably was true: there was a legal right, and there should have been a remedy in the assize of novel disseisin.

If the Maryland legislature could repeal the circuit courts, then the *Whittington* decision was a legal precedent supporting the U.S. Congress's repeal of the Judiciary Act of 1801 and the Midnight Judges' lower federal courts. After all, the U.S. Constitution did not guarantee the existence of circuit courts or trial courts; it merely permitted Congress to create "inferior" courts. Similarly, the Maryland constitution mentioned the justices of the circuit courts, but did not explicitly require them. Even with its dicta advertising the power of judicial review, *Whittington v. Polk* was unhelpful for other Federalist litigation. Whittington could have appealed his case to the Maryland Court of Appeals, but that higher court was a very recent creation that actually had less prestige than the General Court, and its judges were less respected than the General Court's judges. Most significantly, the Republicans had just seized control of the Court of Appeals a year earlier. The Maryland Federalists had botched their appointments to the Court of Appeals while they still had control over the government. In 1801, Mercer, the Republican governor, took advantage of this opportunity, and made two appointments to the Court of Appeals. Then the legislature reduced the Court's membership from five to three that same year, leaving the Republicans a two-to-one majority.[80]

To sum up, there were two legal questions in the case: First, did Whittington have a right to the office of county justice? At the very least, the law did not foreclose a ruling in favor of Whittington. Second, was the assize of novel diseissin the appropriate remedy? Again, the Federalists had a plausible legal argument. The fact that Judge Jeremiah Chase so cursorily denied the validity of this writ is a signal of his desire to avoid confrontation, particularly because this writ could have been a relevant part of other litigation by Federalist ex-officeholders. Given that there were valid legal arguments in favor of the Federalist plaintiffs, and given that the majority on the General Court were partisan Federalists undoubtedly sympathetic to the Federalist plaintiffs, it was not difficult to perceive that the General Court was influenced by countervailing political pressure. The Federalist majority on the court had authored an opinion that was a defensible interpretation of English and American law, but it was not the only reasonable interpretation. Despite having access to legal sources that supported their Federalist ex-colleagues, Judge Chase and Judge Done had chosen retreat over conflict. They abandoned the legislatively established judgeships in the hopes of saving their own constitutionally established judgeships from the Republicans. After all, the Republican legislature had been dismantling the Maryland courts, and the next target in their sights was the General Court itself. Even though the Maryland General Court had ruled in favor of the Republicans, only a few months later the Republican legislature still voted to amend the state constitution to abolish the Maryland General Court.[81] The Maryland constitution's "good behavior" language was not enough to protect them.

The Reaction

The *Whittington* decision was a big deal. Many Federalists had been looking for a case to highlight these issues, make their arguments for the independence of the judiciary, and to win on the merits.[82] Instead, the Maryland decision was an enormous disappointment. National politicians on both sides recognized its political significance. The zealous Virginia congressman John Randolph gleefully mocked the Maryland Federalists' argument that their legislatively created "justices" were the same as the "judges" established by the state constitution. Randolph then remarked that it was fitting that these judges on the General Court had "disclaim[ed] all connection with Justice," and that they deserved impeachment for the "usurpation of sovereignty to pronounce on the constitutionality of law."[83] This extreme reaction foreshadowed Randolph's hard-line leadership in the impeachment and conviction of Judge John Pickering, and then in the impeachment of Justice Samuel Chase. On the other side of the aisle, Federalists grumbled about the *Whittington* opinion.[84]

The press immediately announced the opinion and its national significance, with prominent papers covering their front page with the entire text of the decision.[85] One paper's front page screamed, "Read! Assize of Novel Disseisin," with the full text below, and denounced the Federalist lawyers—as well as U.S. Supreme Court Justice Samuel Chase—for its hyperbolic warning that the nation "had arrived at the precipice of destruction."[86] Republican newspapers celebrated the victory, and emphasized that the decision was unanimous, including two partisan Federalists.[87] Several months later, in the midst of the circuit-by-circuit challenges by the unseated Federalist judges, the Republican press around the country continued to invoke *Whittington* as precedent,[88] reporting that it had deflated the Federalists' challenge to Congress's repeal, and the Federalists, "after all their brags and threats, do not seem inclined to hazard another defeat."[89]

Federalist papers scrambled to distinguish the Maryland defeat from the other pending lawsuits. One Federalist writer was too angry with the Maryland General Court to try to spin its decision or to distinguish it. Disheartened by the Judges Chase and Done, he found it "unaccountable" that the Maryland General Court would refer to the repeal as an "infraction," but would not reach the logical conclusion that the repeal was unconstitutional. "The spirit of the constitution was to bind the legislature as far as possible from doing injustice and violating [the public's] faith. The circumstance demonstrates the perpetual tendency of legislative powers to overstep its legitimate boundaries."[90]

A few months later, the U.S. Supreme Court decided *Marbury* with little reaction from either side. Republicans generally dismissed the decision as insignificant, and did not focus on the doctrine of judicial review. One writer described *Marbury* as a pained mutant and doomed animal, "its head in the rear, its tail in front, its legs mounted on high to support the burthen [burden], while its back was destined to tread the earth its bowels in the exterior, and its hide in the interior . . . As it was born in death so it died in life."[91] This assessment was more right than wrong in terms of *Marbury*'s impact over the next few decades: It would not be cited again by the U.S. Supreme Court until the end of the nineteenth century.[92]

Some historians have wondered why many observers failed to appreciate *Marbury* and its announcement of judicial review in its own time.[93] The major reason was that *Marbury*, a claim for a lowly local office, was not the main event. The main event was *Stuart v. Laird*, the Midnight Judges' challenge to keep their own higher-profile circuit judgeships.[94] When the Supreme Court issued its decision in *Marbury*, the political world was still waiting for *Stuart v. Laird*, issued six days later. The Supreme Court rejected the argument that the Midnight Judges should be riding circuit under the 1801 act, and not the justices under the preexisting system, based on an exceedingly narrow ruling that the Supreme Court justices did not need a specific commission to ride circuit. This case presented a more challenging question, beyond whether or not the Supreme Court justices could ever ride circuit. The real question was whether federal "inferior" judges could lose their seats by a mere statutory repeal. Whereas the Maryland General Court addressed this similar issue explicitly in *Whittington*, the U.S. Supreme Court dodged this issue entirely. But Federalists and Republicans alike had identified Whittington's relevance to the federal courts. The Maryland constitution specified the existence of a General Court and a Court of Appeals with the language "There be a Court of Appeals . . . ," but did not use such language for the county courts.[95] Instead, it mentioned the county courts in several places in terms of their jurisdiction. Article III of the U.S. Constitution specified a Supreme Court, but left the structure of the "inferior courts" to Congress as it "may from time to time ordain and establish."[96] In *Whittington*, the Court of Appeals and the General Court were treated as protected "constitutional" offices, and the "county courts" were treated as legislative offices vulnerable to repeal. The U.S. Supreme Court implicitly followed the same approach in *Laird:* The Supreme Court was protected, while all other Article III judicial offices were vulnerable to repeal. The *Stuart v. Laird* decision indicated more forcefully that the Supreme Court had capitulated to the Republicans on the judiciary, and Republican newspapers celebrated the *Stuart* decision.[97] After the Federalist-controlled lower courts refused to stand up to the Republicans, the Federalists hoped that the U.S. Supreme Court—appointed entirely by Federalists—might finally take a stand. Once the Supreme Court announced that it was passing the buck back to those same lower courts (like the Maryland General Court), the Federalists knew that the legal fight was probably over.

Historians have also wondered why Marbury and other Federalist plaintiffs did not pursue further litigation, considering that the Marshall Court had just announced that Marbury had a vested property right to his office, and simply needed to find another court with jurisdiction to provide a remedy for that right. One theory is that the Federalists were not actually trying to get their offices back, but were orchestrating a Supreme Court decision that they knew would invalidate part of the Judiciary Act of 1789 and would establish a precedent for judicial review.[98] Federalists may have found some solace in the consolation prize of judicial review, but this jurisdictional aspect of the Judiciary Act and the Constitution was so esoteric and such a questionable interpretation that it is hard to imagine that Marbury, his lawyers, or the Midnight Judges foresaw this result and were seeking only that result from the beginning.[99] Perhaps *Whittington* helps answer this question of why there was no further litigation. Observers on both sides understood that the Marshall Court had backed down in *Marbury* and *Stuart v. Laird.* There is some question as to whether state courts could provide a legal remedy for the Federalist plaintiffs, but even if they could, *Whittington* had sent an additional signal that lower courts were just as unwilling as the U.S. Supreme Court to stand up to the Republicans. *Whittington* sent a message to the Federalist litigants to lower their expectations from Federalist judges and to quit while they were ahead, even if being "ahead" was simply the weak threat of judicial review in *Marbury.* Rather than being mollified, the Maryland Republicans in the legislature proposed an even more radical attack on the state judiciary. In the fall of 1802, the legislature voted for a constitutional amendment to eliminate the General Court entirely, vesting all original jurisdiction in the new Republican county courts and all appellate jurisdiction in the Court of Appeals (which suddenly had a new Republican majority after Governor Mercer's two 1801 appointments).[100]

Under the Maryland constitution's rules for constitutional revision, the amendment had to be passed in two consecutive sessions, so the stakes were raised for the fall of 1803.[101] During this ongoing constitutional campaign, Justice Samuel Chase was speaking to a grand jury as he rode circuit when he flew into a tirade against these attacks on the judiciary. With a captive audience, Chase denounced the Republicans' repeal of the Judiciary Act of 1801 and the Maryland Republicans' attacks on the state courts. Chase warned that these revisions would:

> take away all security for property, and personal Liberty. The independence of the National Judiciary is already shaken to its foundation; and the virtue of the people alone can restore it. The independence of the Judges of this State will be entirely destroyed, if the Bill for the abolishing of the two Supreme Courts should be ratified by the next General Assembly.[102]

The Republican congressmen cited this tirade prominently as one of their four articles of impeachment of Justice Chase in 1804.[103]

Ultimately, moderate Republicans in Maryland broke away from the more radical wing, and they united with Federalists to defeat the final passage of the bill in the fall of 1803.[104] Maryland's moderate Republicans and moderate Federalists formed an open alliance that guided state politics in the following years.[105] Maryland again mirrored the national trend, as moderate Republican congressmen were satisfied that the Federalist judges had backed away from confrontation. They ceased their attacks on the judiciary, and a few refused to convict Samuel Chase in his impeachment trial.[106]

Because the Maryland General Court had backed down, the Federalist Party and its leaders were deflated instead of energized. In June 1802, when *Whittington* was decided, the justices were still debating whether or not to ride circuit.[107] The Maryland Federalists' retreat in *Whittington* provided additional support for the justices who opposed the boycott. If the Maryland General Court had held in favor of Whittington, riding circuit would have meant that Samuel Chase would have been abandoning his cousin Jeremiah. If Justice Samuel Chase, the Court's partisan hot-head, had boycotted on his own, or if any other justices had boycotted, many scenarios are possible. It is quite possible that the events might have turned out the same anyway, but one scenario is that the Republicans might have reacted by escalating the conflict. In 1804, when Samuel Chase was impeached by the House for his conduct on the bench, it was a stretch to label him guilty of "high crimes and misdemeanors." Even though he was acquitted by the Senate, the vote on the charge for his anti-Republican harangues before the Baltimore grand jury was nineteen for conviction, fifteen for acquittal (including six Republicans).[108] One reason why some Republicans did not vote to convict was that the Federalist judges generally had been backing down.[109] If Chase had boycotted the circuit assignment, such conduct would be more easily characterized as misbehavior and abdication of his legal duties. If four of the six acquitting Republicans had flipped to convict, Samuel Chase would have been removed from the bench, and such an event would have changed not only the Marshall Court's personnel but also its internal workings and its confidence.[110]

Of course, the Maryland General Court would have faced similar political pressure even if they were elected, rather than appointed. However, there were different political influences from the front end of selection and the back end of retention. In terms of the background of selection, as appointed judges, they did not have a direct mandate from the voters to exercise their power. Elected judges later in the nineteenth century were understood to have more confidence derived from a sense of democratic legitimacy to stand up to legislative power. In terms of retaining their jobs, Judge Chase and Judge Done faced a hostile Republican legislature threatening to abolish their court entirely, just as it had abolished the offices of the county court justices. Elected judges might have been more confident in taking their case to the voters that had already put them in office. Moreover, Judges Chase and Done had little reason to cater to the Federalist Party's interests, unlike in the system of partisan judicial elections in which retaining your party's nomination was necessary. Even in an elected system, the legislature could still threaten the judges, but elections channeled political opposition away from other political checks. The result in *Whittington* might have been the same in either system. The point here is to highlight the different political forces and perceptions in the two systems, and to highlight the vulnerability of the early republic's system of appointed judges, even with life tenure. A closer examination of these events illustrates that the early American courts were not as cohesive or independent as the received lore of the Marshall Court has portrayed.

Attacks on the Courts in the Jeffersonian and Jacksonian Eras

Around the country, the Jeffersonians were weakening other courts, too. Radical Jeffersonians increased their attacks on the judges, calling for more political control of the courts, as well as the abandonment of the common law ("lawyers' law") in favor of statutes and legislative codes ("the people's law"). The legal profession, one radical argued, was "evil" with "open enmity to the principles of free government, because free government is irreconcilable to the abuses on which they thrive [and] the tyranny which they display in the court. . . . [The] collusion which prevails among the members of the bench, the bar, and the officers of the court, demand the most serious interference of the legislature, and the jealousy of the people."[111] The dominant methods of checking the courts in this era were direct attacks on courts and judges: impeachment, repeal of courts (and their judges), and replacement with new courts. Some Jeffersonians called for judicial elections, but other than Jefferson himself, they were rarely major political actors. More often they were minor politicians who were ideologically committed to direct democracy. The Jeffersonian leadership found judicial appointments to be satisfactory, now that they had control of governorships and legislatures. The more common refrain was for increasing the jury's power, for converting the bar into a state-run service solely to assist the jury, and for leaving the judges only a minor role in the courtroom.[112] Once the Republicans had seized power, they had control of many reliable legislative tools for disciplining and punishing judges, whereas judicial elections were less reliable and not necessary. Moreover, it seems as if moderate Republicans had qualms about pushing popular control quite that far.

In addition to the battle over the Maryland judges, the federal Midnight Judges, William Marbury and the justices of the peace, and the impeachments of two federal judges (Judge John Pickering and Justice Samuel Chase), the Republicans also attacked Federalists on other state courts. In Kentucky, radicals had been seeking new circuit courts to take power away from the existing courts and to create seats for their allies. In 1801, the radicals succeeded in creating the circuit courts and weakened the existing court system.[113] Another step in the Jeffersonian assault on the courts was reducing judges' tenure. In its first constitution in 1803, Ohio rejected life tenure and adopted seven-year terms for all of its judges.[114] Then the Republican legislature shifted jurisdiction from the Federalist judges to the justices of the peace, a greater number of whom were Republicans. The Federalist justices on the Ohio Supreme Court struck down this legislation expressly because it violated the constitutional right to a jury trial, but under the surface, the court was fighting back in a partisan battle over the judiciary.[115] The Republican legislature then impeached the judges for "wilfully, wickedly, and maliciously" attempting "to introduce anarchy and confusion in the government of the state of Ohio."[116] The state senate voted fifteen to nine to convict, falling short of a two-thirds majority by one vote. Undaunted by the constitution's formal protections of the judges, the Republican majority in the legislature decided that these judges were only interim judges and not entitled by law to a full seven-year term. This interpretation had a shaky legal basis, and it was attacked as "arbitrary and revolutionary, as well as violent," but the Republicans forced the judges out anyway.[117]

When Pennsylvania Republicans defeated the Federalists in 1799, they turned to impeachment. The radicals in the Republican Party aimed to clean house. Judge Alexander Addison, the "Goliath of federalism," regularly used his charges to the grand jury to denounce the Republicans, and refused to allow his Republican colleagues to reply.[118] In 1802, the state assembly impeached Addison, without any traditional evidence of misbehavior. Then the senate convicted him by a vote of twenty to four, and barred him from holding judicial office again. Pennsylvania radicals did not stop there. They called for a series of impeachments of other Federalist judges, and campaigned on this issue in 1804 with success. With more power in the new legislature, the radicals impeached three more state supreme court justices on trumped-up charges of a "high misdemeanor." The house vote was a resounding fifty-seven to twenty-four. But moderates prevailed in the state senate, and the senate vote of thirteen to ten to convict fell short of the necessary two-thirds majority. Once it became clear that the Federalist judges in state and federal courts were not going to obstruct the Republicans, moderate Republicans split from the radicals and backed off of further attacks on the courts. The moderates formed a new coalition with the Federalists against these attacks, and this coalition won by the narrowest of margins.[119]

This alliance halted further impeachments, removals, and ripper bills during Jefferson's second term, but it was only a cease-fire, not a truce.[120] The Jeffersonians' political descendants continued to attack particular courts in the 1820s, too. The New York Supreme Court of Judicature started striking down statutes for the first time in the 1810s, and continued through 1821, often ruling against debtor relief statutes.[121] New York's Democratic-Republicans used their state constitutional convention in 1821 to wipe out the five more conservative justices on the Supreme Court, and to open up the court for their own appointments.[122] Between 1821 and 1823, the Missouri courts and the Kentucky Supreme Court, respectively, struck down statutes that protected debtors against their creditors.[123] The perception was that the courts had sided with city banks over the farmers and the people. Angry critics in Missouri suggested changes in judicial selection—but not judicial elections. Instead, they wanted to cut the governor out of the process, because they believed that the legislature by itself would be more reliably prodebtor. The only argument for judicial elections came from *supporters* of the courts who opposed the prodebtor populists and the legislature's meddling. Mocking the legislature, one procredit court supporter sarcastically suggested that "if the judges are to be made elective by irresponsible persons, then, I say, let the people themselves elect them, and not leave it to their servants."[124] In the end, Missouri populists chose an even more direct attack: They amended the constitution in 1822 to end the terms of the sitting judges and turn over their seats "as soon as their successors are, respectively, elected and qualified."[125] When the constitution had stood in their way, the opponents of the Missouri judges simply changed the constitution to clean house and install their own appointees. They did the same thing twelve years later.[126]

In Kentucky, the prodebtor opponents of the courts used similar tactics with more bizarre results. They did not have the two-thirds majority needed to impeach the procreditor judges, so they decided to abolish the existing supreme court and replaced it with a new one in 1823. They filled the new court with prodebtor judges and limited the court's power to strike down a statute to when the judges were unanimous. Disregarding the "new court," the "old court" judges ignored the legislature and kept hearing appeals. Thus, Kentucky had two supreme courts hearing appeals and issuing contradictory decisions for about two years. The old court's advocates won the next election and passed a bill to abolish the new court, but the governor vetoed it. After a third round of elections, procreditor forces won and finally abolished the new court, and Kentucky had one supreme court again.[127]

The Tennessee Supreme Court produced one of the most remarkable spikes in judicial review in the era of judicial appointments. Between 1830 and 1835, the Tennessee Supreme Court struck down statutes ten times, a unique burst that accounted for about one quarter of all invalidations of statutes in the 1830s. No other state reached double digits in any full decade before the era of judicial elections. Some of the most controversial cases also dealt with taxation, debt, and banks.[128] The Court also intervened on behalf of the Cherokee in three major cases.[129] Most intriguingly, the Court struck down a statute that permitted freed slaves to move to other states, because it held that there was a constitutional principle that freed slaves must be colonized to Africa, and not "inflicted" on fellow states to their peril. The author was Chief Judge John Catron, whom Andrew Jackson would appoint to the U.S. Supreme Court two years later, and who would vote with the majority in *Dred Scott* two decades later, holding that African descendants were not U.S. citizens and invalidating the Missouri Compromise, opening all of the western territories to slavery. One reason why John Catron was appointed to the U.S. Supreme Court was because he was no longer a Tennessee judge, and he was suddenly available. The state legislators were angry about the court's aggressive judicial review (mostly on the debt and Cherokee issues, not the ex-slave issue). After the state legislature tried for a few years to abolish his office, the state constitutional convention of 1835, which was called in part to reform the judiciary, swept the state supreme court clean, and dropped the guarantee of tenure during good behavior. Two incumbent judges retired, rather than fight to be reappointed by the legislature, and Judge Catron was rejected by a legislative vote of 71–27.[130] The Tennessee Supreme Court struck down a few statutes over the rest of the 1830s and 1840s, but not close to the same pace. After Tennessee adopted judicial elections in 1853, its supreme court went back to a binge of judicial review.[131]

These four states, New York, Kentucky, Missouri, and Tennessee, might represent some of the exceptions to the general pattern of the early Republic, the rarity of judicial review. But these spikes of judicial review actually underscore the weakness of judicial review, because of the vulnerability of the appointed judges who had attempted to stand up to the legislature. In these cases, the legislatures won their battles, as the judges found themselves off the bench and serving as cautionary tales against other judges testing these boundaries. These battles over the courts on the issue of debt and credit might seem like single-issue fights, but these battles were part of a broader war. Elements within the Jeffersonian Republican coalition opposed judicial independence as a matter of principle, and the debt-credit issue gave them the political opportunity to capitalize, so to speak. In the 1790s, the trend favored life tenure for judges; between 1800 and the 1830s, the trend moved sharply against life tenure in state courts. Beyond attacks on particular judges, Jeffersonian opponents of judicial power followed Ohio and continued to shorten judicial term lengths. By 1830, judges in six states had relatively short terms, ranging from no term ("at pleasure" tenure) to seven years.[132] In the 1830s, populists continued to focus on limiting judicial terms, rather than electing judges.[133]

Chief Justice John Marshall has received a lot of attention for building the power of the U.S. Supreme Court, and he deserves most of it. However, the *Marbury* mythology concealed how Marshall's construction project was slow, fragile, and dangerous during a broader trend of judicial weakness. Perhaps the most relevant language in *Whittington* was not its dicta about judicial supremacy, but its dicta about judicial caution. Judge Jeremiah Chase warned that the judiciary should not intervene every time a legislative act violated the Constitution, because such aggressive judicial review "subverts the government and reduces the people to a state of nature, and therefore cannot be the proper mode of redress to remedy the evils resulting from an act passed in violation of the constitution."[134] He suggested that the courts should weigh the interests on each side and then decide if their power is properly used case by case. The Marshall Court followed this thinking in practice by not recognizing a remedy for Marbury's right.

As it turns out, the Marshall Court's acquiescence in 1803 allowed it to survive and cultivate more judicial power. When it expanded its power in *Fletcher v. Peck,* it helped trigger a turn to judicial elections in Georgia in 1810 to 1812.[135] Its assertion of judicial power in the 1820s and 1830s sparked populist backlashes in the states.[136] Then in 1832, when the Marshall Court intervened for the Cherokee in *Worcester v. Georgia,* it helped Mississippi populists build the first successful case for electing all of the judges in a state (a case mixed with arguments for and against judicial independence).[137] President Jackson and other politicians simply ignored the Marshall Court's ruling in favor of the Cherokee, and they sent the Cherokee on the Trail of Tears—a crucial episode illustrating the weakness of early American courts.

Some scholars have identified "phases" of the Marshall Court: a "golden age" of unity and assertiveness (1812–1825), followed by fragmentation and more deference to Jacksonian democratic principles (1826–1835).[138] There is some debate about whether the Marshall Court was truly unified behind the scenes in the "golden age," or whether the justices hid their internal divisions when the Court's membership stayed the same (there were no new appointments between 1812 and 1823). In that era, the unanimous "opinion of the Court" was the norm. With new appointments, the justices wrote more concurrences and dissents.[139] The mix of new appointees and new internal and external factors made the Marshall Court less of a unified voice, and less of a bulwark against Jacksonian democracy in its later years.

The most famous of the Marshall Court's assertions of judicial authority, other than *Marbury,* were between 1810 and 1825.[140] For a decade after that, there were not the same kinds of groundbreaking cases, and in other cases, the U.S. Supreme Court scaled back its earlier pro-Federalist doctrines,[141] or it was ignored in high-profile cases (as in *Worcester v. Georgia* in 1830, when President Jackson proceeded with removing the Cherokee anyway). Between 1809 and 1824, the Supreme Court invalidated eleven state statutes (two every three years), but after that, it struck down only four more in the next sixteen years (once every four years). The late 1820s and the 1830s were more a period of leveling off of federal judicial power.

While the Marshall Court's vertical judicial review of states was quieting down, its horizontal review of Congress never raised much noise in the first place. The received wisdom had been that after *Marbury*, the Supreme Court did not strike down a federal statute again until *Dred Scott* overturned the Missouri Compromise and opened the western territories to slavery. Some recent careful research has shown that the Marshall Court did limit and even invalidate a handful of federal statutes. However, it seems that the Marshall Court may have been hiding some of these decisions themselves, because they were usually only one paragraph or even one cryptic sentence, they were low-profile cases, and most of these decisions did not draw much attention to the doctrine of judicial review or to a specific constitutional text.[142] The received wisdom was not correct in a technical sense, but its general point is still significant: the Supreme Court avoided confronting Congress and it kept a lid on horizontal judicial review.

The state courts remained more politically vulnerable in this era. The political trend was to weaken courts—*not by judicial elections*, but instead, by punishing judicial review, by impeachment, by "ripper bills," by constitutional amendment circumventions of formal protections, and by abolishing life tenure. In later confrontations in a more established legal system, reformers turned away from haphazard and potentially chaotic impeachments and ripper bills in favor of more stable institutions that would civilize or normalize judicial accountability. The idea of judicial independence was not obviously strong in these years, and thus the Republicans could successfully attack Federalist judges and disregard "good behavior" protections. However, some Republicans conceived of their "attacks" as defenses of judicial independence from the Federalists' partisan abuses and manipulations, particularly the midnight appointments that they believed broke the rules. And considering the intensity of the clash between Federalists and Republicans, the courts survived only because moderate Republicans either believed in a modicum of judicial independence or were constrained by public opinion favoring judicial independence, so that they pulled back from the brink and gave the Marshall Court and Federalists in the state courts enough breathing room to survive and rebuild. Though the early American courts suffered some defeats, they survived while also building a foundation for more power later. The Marshall Court extended judicial review vertically over state legislation, and state judges maintained just enough horizontal review of state legislatures to solidify their constitutional role and to attract the attention of later reformers.

One scholar has observed in this period a culture of "defiance" of the courts: "Independence is not the same as power . . . The resolution of the partisan conflicts of the early 1800s provided the judiciary with a certain degree of autonomy and security, yet the justices' authority remained profoundly open to question."[143] Elected officials regularly ignored the federal courts and openly attacked the state courts. Judicial review survived a series of political attacks on the courts, but it was not yet a robust practice. With opponents of judicial power willing to impeach, rip, or reduce terms in the first third of the century, it is no shock that judges in the early republic established judicial review gradually and cautiously.

Between the Revolution and the 1830s, a handful of states on the American periphery turned to judicial elections for one aspect of judicial power: the separation of the courts from the political branches and special interests. In the 1840s and the 1850s, reformers sought to increase another aspect of judicial power: judicial review. The judges of the Founding era and the early republic had incrementally increased the power of the courts. Even if their decisions often backed down from the bigger political showdowns, and even if they lost their offices over judicial review, some of these judges drew attention to the possibility that courts could be a threat to democracy, and also that they could be a potential weapon in democracy's arsenal. In the hands of appointed life-tenured judges, the weapon was likely to be used against majoritarianism, but down the road, when reformers experienced the failings of the other branches of government, they recognized that judicial review in the hands of popularly elected judges could be a democratic line of defense. Only once those reformers decided to bundle judicial review with judicial democracy, American judges would build the doctrine of judicial review into a more robust and regular power.

A lesson of the early republic is that formal legal protections in the wording of constitutions and statutes (such as provisions for "good behavior" tenure in office and restrictions against impeachments) were weak protections of judicial independence. These legal texts were often swept aside by the stronger force of party politics and democratic power. Some early-nineteenth century reformers who sought more judicial independence and more judicial power learned this lesson. Instead of relying just on writing new constitutional wording, they constructed a new institution—judicial elections—to bolster the courts' power and independence by harnessing the courts to the democratic engines of more direct popular control and party politics.

CHAPTER THREE

Judicial Elections as Separation of Powers

THOMAS JEFFERSON, in the same 1816 letter hailing Connecticut's history of electing judges, also endorsed weakening the courts by making it easier to impeach judges and remove judges from the bench. Then he concluded by criticizing legislative appointment: "To give it to the legislature, as we do, is a violation of the principle of the separation of powers."[1] Judicial elections had the potential to serve both of these goals: promoting judicial accountability to the people and judicial independence from the other branches.

In the early republic, critics of the courts had ample methods for limiting judicial independence: impeachment, repealing judicial offices, shortening terms, and creating new courts. When judicial accountability was the goal, judicial elections were not necessary. However, in a few places in the early republic, the separation of powers was an equally important goal, and these leaders turned to judicial elections to insulate judges from the political branches of government. In Vermont, Georgia, and Indiana, a combination of factors led to an increased focus on judicial independence from external forces and the abuses of other branches: localist backlashes against the state capital's abuses, legislative and executive excesses, and sometimes the political strategy of ambitious individuals. Where the separation of powers was a primary goal, judicial elections emerged. In Mississippi, the first state to adopt judicial elections for all of its judges in 1832, the economic elite in one region—the Natchez "Aristocrats"—had been manipulating the state's appointment process for years, and triggered a backlash by rural leaders—the "Whole Hogs"—in favor of local control. The simplest and most available mode of local control was direct local democracy and judicial elections.

At the same time, these four experiments were the exception, not the rule, from the early republic through the Jacksonian era. Many observers attribute the phenomenon of judicial elections to "Jacksonian democracy," but only one state—Mississippi—adopted judicial elections for its entire bench during Jackson's lifetime. Many other states strongly supported Andrew Jackson and switched many offices over to direct elections, but they still rejected judicial elections in the 1830s. Alabama, North Carolina, and Pennsylvania help illustrate the strong and enduring commitment to appointing judges in this era, and they help demonstrate that the revolution of judicial democracy required a game-changing series of events to shatter the tradition of judicial appointment. In terms of judicial elections, not much changed during the 1830s. But the turmoil in American politics and economic life during the 1830s set the stage for the revolution in judicial democracy.

The First Experiment: The Republic of Vermont

Judicial elections were not a major weapon in the Jeffersonian arsenal, but a few frontier states tried them in experiments that were not directly connected to the "Jeffersonian crisis." These lost stories of judicial elections reveal that opposition to judicial power was not the main impulse for judicial elections in the early republic. Instead, they were a shield to defend localities against the elite outsiders in more remote capitals, and they were a means of separating powers to increase the courts as a check against legislative power.

After Connecticut retained judicial elections from its colonial constitution, the next "state" to turn to judicial elections was the Republic of Vermont, which was not even a state yet. The independent Republic of Vermont wrote a constitution in 1777 in the hopes that Congress would recognize it as a free state. Vermont began as a territory known as "the New Hampshire Grants," and its settlers were in the middle of a land dispute with New York, which had been governing the territory and claimed the land as its own. After one unsuccessful attempt by a group of Vermont delegates to the Philadelphia Congress, they returned with a copy of the Pennsylvania constitution as a model for writing one of their own.[2]

While much of Vermont's first constitution tracks Pennsylvania's, it also contained some intriguing differences. Vermont's constitution began with a long preamble of almost 1,200 words listing grievances against New York, deliberately echoing the Declaration of Independence's grievances against England. It abolished slavery and gave all men the right to vote, regardless of property ownership or wealth.[3] The appellate judges were to be appointed by the governor with consent of the council, but it gave the voters the power to elect some of their judges: "the judges of inferior court of common pleas, sheriff, justices of the peace, and judges of probates."[4] Remarkably, these judges would be elected to commissions "during good behavior," and removable only for "mal-administration"— that is, life tenure. Vermont's elected judges marked a shift in relative independence, but more significantly, they enjoyed a major change in general independence. Their reaction to New York's abuse of power led only to a partial embrace of localism, because life tenure insulated the judges from local voters as well as outsiders. The Vermont constitution's list of grievances focused more on the misdeeds of New York's legislature and governors rather than its judges. Life tenure insulated these judges from political influences, and in the context of meddling legislators and governors, Vermonters were opting for a version of the separation of powers.[5]

Ethan Allen and his men had attracted other settlers to the Grants with the promise of self-government. They viewed New York's courts as corrupted by and for the wealthy and well-connected, and aimed to build a court system in the Grants to serve the less privileged.[6] These commitments became stronger when the powerful landowners of New York fought to invalidate the settlers' land titles in the Grants. New York judges were responsible for ejectment proceedings against the settlers, and they handed down severe fines without flexibility.[7] Just as Vermonters created the Green Mountain Boys militia to protect themselves when New Yorkers would not, they created a legal system to serve themselves when the New York courts would not. Focused on local matters of debt and land disputes, the settlers wanted local judges to be responsive to local settler opinion, and not outside interests. These judges and justices of the peace turned out to be more efficient (whereas New York judges delayed cases interminably) and more flexible on payment in-kind (whereas New York judges demanded currency), and on payment schedules (whereas New York judges demanded payment regardless of the harvest season).[8]

Like Connecticut's continuation of a colonial institution, Vermont's adoption of judicial elections under its 1777 constitution probably was a continuation of a colonial frontier practice. Elected lower court judges had been a practical part of frontier democracy in a rough colonial hinterland, while the established colonial capitals kept their appointed judges.[9] While the colonies rebelled against a distant and oppressive imperial/legal regime, Vermonters rebelled against New York's remote legal regime that they found similarly oppressive. The temporary means of ensuring local control of the law were local democracy and judicial elections. One could imagine a regime of judges appointed by local officials, but the established model of local government was direct democracy, especially on the frontier. When Vermont adopted a new constitution in 1786, it had been free of New York for a few years, and it was building its own central state institutions. In this changed context, it established appointments for all judicial posts with tenure for just one year.[10]

The voters of Connecticut and Vermont elected some of their judges in the early years of the republic as a continuation of colonial practices and as a practice of New England direct democracy. However, both states abandoned judicial elections in favor of appointments for short terms. In Vermont, this change to appointments decreased general judicial independence, and shifted relative independence, making judges more independent from voters and more dependent on the other branches. When Vermont was declaring its independence from New York, it adopted judicial elections partly because of localism, but life tenure limited localism, and underscored Vermont's commitment to judicial independence. To Vermonters in 1777, political insulation and a version of separation of powers were even more important than direct democracy and localism. Once they had solidly established their independence from New York by 1786, the impulses of localism, separation, and insulation were less significant, and they replaced life-tenure elections with short-term appointments.

The Second Experiment: Georgia in 1810–1812

Two more states, Georgia and Indiana, turned to judicial elections for lower court judges in the 1810s. These overlooked experiments foreshadowed the themes of the later wave of adoptions, when judicial independence, the separation of powers, and anti-corruption were the driving forces.

Georgia adopted judicial elections for its "inferior" courts in 1812, but not its appellate courts.[11] Georgia's 1798 constitution was already its third constitution since the revolution, and it created a few oddities: short terms for appellate judges, life terms for trial judges, and no statewide supreme court. Georgia's superior court judges were appointed by the general assembly to three-year terms, and its lower court judges were appointed by the general assembly for tenure during good behavior. Thus, the lower courts had more job security than the higher courts. There is a logic to this design: Appellate courts engage in a combined role of adjudication, lawmaking, and general interpretation, so it makes more sense under democratic theory for these judges to be more accountable to the public. By contrast, trial court judges engage more in case-by-case adjudication, where individualized fairness should trump public opinion.[12] Georgia had tried three different constitutions from the revolution, followed by two rounds of amendments revising the judiciary, and none created a supreme court. This void reflected the anticourt attitude of the era. Until 1845, Georgia's courts of last resort were the regional superior courts.

In 1810, the Georgia legislature began the amendment process to switch over to electing lower court judges, and to drop their term length from good behavior to four-year terms. At the same time, the legislature passed a debtor relief law, which was sure to face a constitutional challenge. The confluence of these two events suggests that the prodebtor statute was a specific trigger: The legislature wanted courts to be more responsive to prodebtor public opinion, and the combinations of elections and shorter terms would make judges less likely to block the legislation.

However, a second cause for judicial elections pushed in the opposite direction: to increase judicial independence and the separation of powers. The Yazoo Land Fraud led to a backlash against legislative corruption. From 1795 to 1803, a series of Georgia governors and legislatures sold off enormous tracts of land to their cronies for below market value. Many of these governors and legislators held stock in the land companies to whom they were selling the land. The Yazoo Land Fraud was the biggest of these scandals, and it provoked mob violence and murder.[13] The state government rescinded the sales, burned the bills, and offered refunds to subsequent purchasers of the land. The repeal of the land sales was popular with an outraged public, but it ran into a constitutional challenge. One Georgian, Robert Fletcher, bought Yazoo land from John Peck, after Peck had promised that the title to the land was not affected by Georgia's repeal. When Fletcher discovered otherwise, he sued. Peck argued that sale was valid, because the legislature's repeal of the sales was unconstitutional. The U.S. Supreme Court agreed in 1810.[14] Chief Justice Marshall ruled that the repeal was an unconstitutional "impairment of contract"—and *Fletcher v. Peck* marked the first time the Supreme Court struck down a state law.[15]

This decision reopened the wounds of the original scandal. On the one hand, Georgia's leaders might have turned to judicial elections in reaction to *Fletcher v. Peck* overturning a popular law. Impeaching Chief Justice Marshall was not really an option, but they could prevent little Marshall Courts from taking over the state trial courts. Georgia's courts had been dominated by Federalists for many years, and the Federalists had shouldered much of the blame for the Yazoo Fraud.[16] The Federalists lost the elections of 1796 in the wake of the scandal, but their judges remained on the courts with life tenure.[17]

Overhauling the state courts was one way to remove the remaining Federalist judges—but Republicans could have achieved that goal simply by abolishing the existing courts and creating a set of new courts with new Republican judicial appointments, much as the Jeffersonians had done often between 1802 and 1809 in other states. The change to judicial elections might have been a public rationalization—a good-government, bad-faith façade—for the dirty work of replacing the conservative Federalist judges with the new populist Jeffersonians, but if this was the purpose, then it is unclear why Georgia's Republicans waited from 1802 to 1812 to do so.

The reformers were also reacting to rampant legislative corruption. *Fletcher v. Peck* reopened the issue of the legislature's corruption throughout the past two decades. The Yazoo Land Fraud had been the worst scandal, but legislative corruption continued for years. Some criticized appointment power as the cause of corruption. "A Friend to Merit," writing soon after the scandal broke, charged that local land officials participated in the fraud because they had to pay kickbacks to the legislators who had appointed them. "I conceive that the legislature, having the appointment annually of county officers to be one main root of the evil of which we complain (*i.e.*, the low quality of the legislators).' "[18] Soon after the fraud came to light, the state had drawn up a new constitution in 1798 to limit the legislature's powers and to replace legislative appointment of the governor with popular election—a new separation of powers. The amendments to the 1798 constitution continued the same trend of shifting power from the legislature to other institutions, and according to a leading historian of Georgia's legal development, the amendment in 1812 for judicial elections was a post-Yazoo check on the legislature.[19]

Thus, there were two different forces for judicial elections in Georgia. One was a reaction to the unpopular judicial power exercised by the U.S. Supreme Court, and to the threat of Georgia courts blocking a prodebtor statute. Judicial elections in these contexts meant judicial weakness. The other reaction was against the state legislature's corruption. In the face of intractable legislative corruption, reformers produced a number of constitutional changes to check the legislature and to separate powers. The election of lower court judges was a way to shift power from the legislature to the people, to increase relative judicial independence, and to increase judicial power.

The Third Experiment: Indiana in 1816

The territory of Indiana became a state in 1816, and it also ventured into new legal territory by adopting judicial elections for its lower courts. This experiment was the result of a mix of frontier culture; a reaction to an overbearing federal administration over the territory; the fight over slavery in the Northwest Territory; and the political strategies of ambitious local leaders.

Indiana as a territory had chafed under federal rule, and by 1816, its residents were skeptical of outsider powers, including appointed judges, and sought more local autonomy. The Northwest Ordinance of 1787 called for the president to appoint a governor and three judges. This territorial government held broad legislative and judicial powers without any control by the residents of the territory. The first appointed officials in the territory were not frontiersmen, and were more identified with New England than the West—and they were unpopular.[20] They adopted a harsh penal code, perhaps appropriate for a frontier society with little law enforcement, but nonetheless, it cast these officials as punitive outsiders.[21] They were supposed to adhere to laws already in existence in other states, but they ignored these limitations and drew heavily on English precedents.[22] As the judges asserted more power based on the English common law, they clashed with the appointed governor. The governor questioned their integrity and alleged that they were involved with insider land deals.[23] The judges were vulnerable to these attacks, because they had an unusual amount of unpopular responsibilities in enforcing federal law on the frontier, and they were easy targets from above (the governor) and below (the settlers).[24]

The settlers increasingly chafed under the "arbitrary rule of the Governor and Judges" and pushed for more democratic power.[25] The territory's rapid growth also made the court docket grow unmanageable, and the judges gained a reputation for incompetence and bias.[26] In 1813, the territorial assembly passed "An Act Re-organizing the Courts of Justice" as an attempt to fix the court system and to bring it under the legislature's control.[27] Refusing to comply, the judges claimed that they were beyond the territorial legislature's authority, and that the assembly's act was "repugnant to the laws of the United States."[28] The judges won that battle, but the General Assembly continued pressing Congress for a more accountable judiciary.[29]

Around the same time as the fight over the courts, the Indiana settlers were also fighting over slavery. The future U.S. President William Henry Harrison was governor of the territory from its creation in 1800 until 1812. Harrison, who had been raised in a wealthy planter family in Tidewater Virginia, aligned himself with Indiana's proslavery conservatives and Virginia settlers. His vocal support for slavery and his aristocratic instincts alienated the majority of settlers who had migrated from Ohio and the Northeast.

The Northwest Ordinance of 1787 had prohibited slavery in the Northwest Territory and in the Indiana Territory. Governor Harrison called on Congress to repeal the slavery ban, but Congress ignored the request. In 1803, Governor Harrison and the Indiana territorial judges adopted Virginia's servant law to circumvent the ban on slavery.[30] Governor Harrison later proposed legislation to permit settlers to bring their own slaves into the state.[31] Meanwhile, the territory was becoming increasingly antislavery and anti-Harrison because of an influx of Quakers and Ohio settlers known as the "poor frontiersmen." They were ardent opponents of slavery and enthusiastic supporters of direct democracy, and they hated Harrison.[32] Their movement for popular local control gained more power in the territorial assembly, leading to more friction with Harrison.[33] When Harrison's second term was about to expire in 1806, the poor frontiersmen charged Harrison with bias and corruption in his appointments and interference in judicial proceedings.[34] Harrison was reappointed governor by President Jefferson, but the following year the assembly was even less friendly as antislavery forces grew stronger.[35]

Indiana residents called a constitutional convention in 1816 as soon as they reached the population benchmark for statehood. The convention split into two main camps: a strong, unified, antislavery majority of "poor frontiersmen" led by Jonathan Jennings, a lawyer from New Jersey who despised Harrison; and the "Virginia Aristocrats," a proslavery minority led by Harrison.[36] The "poor frontiersmen" (also called the Popular Party and the Frontier Majority) believed in vigilant popular mobilization to keep government officers in check.[37] The poor frontiersmen led a successful fight for judicial elections for lower courts and reducing judges' terms from good behavior to seven years.[38] Antislavery sentiment may have been correlated to a favorable view of judicial elections, rather than being causally related. The Aristocrats were wealthier Virginians, which may have been the root cause of both their proslavery views and their opposition to direct democracy. After all, they were called the "Aristocrats." And the "poor frontiersmen" were generally from Ohio, upstate New York, and New England, and their opposition to the southern "Aristocrats" led them to support direct democracy. The antislavery settlers had experienced the system of appointments as a tool for promoting slavery and thwarting the will of the majority. They also understood that antislavery had become a voting majority, and they had experienced direct democracy in the convention campaigns as a stronger protection for antislavery.

Moreover, personal ambitions of well-placed delegates also led to judicial elections. Judge Benjamin Parke chaired the judiciary committee at the convention. Parke was an odd combination: he was a Harrison supporter, but he was also strongly antislavery. Parke wanted to continue on the bench after statehood, but it was also apparent that Jennings, leader of the poor frontiersmen, would be the state's first governor. Parke and other Harrison supporters knew that they had a better chance of winning state office through local elections than by governor's appointment. Thus, some Aristocrats had strategic reasons for supporting local elections and for the separation of powers, to give the governor and the legislature less power over the courts.

The turn to electing lower court judges in Vermont, Georgia, and Indiana foreshadowed how the wave of judicial elections would play out several decades later. Local elections were a reaction to abuses of appointments by external executive powers. Slavery and antislavery influenced the Indiana convention, and they would play a role in the 1830s through the 1850s. The backlash against the Marshall Court would also arise again. Some of the supporters of judicial elections in Vermont, Georgia, and Indiana sought to weaken the courts, but this agenda was not a sufficient cause for their adoption of judicial elections. In each of these places, the separation of powers and judicial independence were an additional force in building a coalition for judicial elections. Declaring their independence from New York, Vermonters elected all of their lower court judges for life—a signal that judicial independence was a higher priority than localism. In Georgia, the Yazoo Land Fraud had framed the legislature as corrupt, and Georgians hoped that independent courts would be a stronger check against legislative abuse. Many of Indiana's delegates were motivated by a desire to separate the judges from past and future governors whom they did not trust. These places were certainly not the first to confront corrupt legislators and imperious executives. The change to elections required a combination of a culture of direct democracy, a reaction to abusive territorial appointees, and the maneuvers of particular leaders in the right place at the right time.

When populist reformers simply wanted to attack the courts, they tried many weapons—impeachment and "ripper bills," for example. But they did not use judicial elections because they were not as direct and effective for that purpose. They turned to judicial elections only when there was also a drive to separate the courts from the other branches and external political influences. In this context, the framing of judicial elections was judicial independence more than judicial accountability. Legislative corruption and the abuse of government power would also propel the later wave of judicial democracy in the 1840s and 1850s as a movement to strengthen judges.

The Fourth Experiment: Mississippi's Whole Hog Revolution, 1832

Mississippi's adoption of judicial elections in 1832 was the most significant exception that proves the rule of the early nineteenth century: judicial elections were rare, unless there was a unique political conflict that made the appointments process seem unfair or unrepresentative. Natchez, Mississippi's commercial center, had disproportionate control over the legislature, and its leaders abused the appointment process to monopolize the courts. The Natchez "Aristocrats," as they called themselves, triggered a rural backlash among the "Whole Hogs," who fought for local direct democracy, the separation of powers, and judicial independence from Natchez. Because of some lucky breaks, the Whole Hogs won by a very narrow margin, and they turned to judicial elections as one way to limit the Natchez Aristocrats.

In the middle of Mississippi's 1832 Convention, Stephen A. Duncan, a conservative delegate from the Natchez region, described to a friend the three factions at the convention on the hot topic of judicial reform. First were Duncan's "aristocrats," predominantly from the powerful commercial center around Natchez, who favored judicial appointments. Then there were the "Whole Hogs," who fought for the election of all judges. In between were the "Half Hogs," the moderates who supported a compromise: electing lower court judges, but appointing Supreme Court judges. Duncan had watched the Whole Hogs gain a narrow majority, and warned with regret, "You may . . . rest assured we will give you a constitution . . . much more democratic than any other in the U.S. Not *republican*—but downright and absolute *democracy.*"[39] For Duncan, this was bad news.

With the Whole Hogs winning the debate in the 1832 convention, Mississippi became the first state to elect all of its judges. Similar to many of the other turns to judicial elections, the reformers were motivated partly by democratic ideology, partly by a push for local control against the centralized control of Natchez (and Washington), and partly by political advantage. The aristocrats of Natchez had dominated the state through their disproportionate representation under the 1817 constitution, and like good aristocrats, they monopolized the judicial appointment process. The porcine populists—mainly from the backwoods—used judicial reform as a backhanded means of sweeping away sitting judges and replacing them with a more favorable set—what I term a "bench-clearing brawl."

Mississippi presents a challenging case for historical study, because the 1832 convention journal recorded only specific motions and roll call votes, and did not even provide summaries of the speeches' content. The few preserved newspapers also did not provide content from the convention debate, and few manuscripts or papers have survived. However, we can piece together from the sources a loose account of causation. One major factor was egalitarian democratic ideology on the frontier. Other factors were the original state constitution's disproportionate representation given to Natchez, which provoked an even stronger and more united movement for democratic reform in the backwoods; the state supreme court striking down a popular debtor statute (plus more minor rulings on slavery); and the manipulation of the appointment system by the Natchez elites to select their own allies for the backwoods judicial districts. The triggers were the 1832 convention itself, called to remedy the Natchez area's disproportionate power; the lucky timing of the elections for convention delegates favoring backbenchers; and the Marshall Court's decision in *Worcester v. Georgia* in favor of the Cherokee. The most significant forces were the Natchez-vs.-backcountry animosity, exacerbated by unpopular decisions by Natchez judges and the U.S. Supreme Court. The Whole Hogs had the same array of tools for checking the court that were available in the Jeffersonian era, but it was specifically the Natchez elites' abuse of the centralized judicial appointment process that turned the convention toward elections by a narrow margin.

Democratic ideology and frontier culture were significant in Mississippi's adoption of judicial elections, but they were not decisive. Other states that shared this background did not adopt judicial elections. The popular vote for Andrew Jackson in his three presidential elections can be used as a crude proxy for commitment to democratization. Mississippi gave Jackson 64 percent of the popular vote in 1824, 81 percent in 1828, and 100 percent in 1832. However, Georgia, Alabama, and Tennessee were even more consistently and more strongly for Jackson. North Carolina, Virginia, Missouri, and Pennsylvania (and probably South Carolina until 1832) had similar pro-Jackson voting records.[40] The strength of the Jacksonian Democrats did not yield more full-scale adoptions of judicial elections in the 1830s, even though most of these states and emerging frontier states had the same opportunities. Each of these states wrote new constitutions or amended their judiciary clauses in the 1830s and 1840s, but none followed Mississippi.[41]

In many parts of America, a raucous campaign culture favored populist candidates and treated elections as a public festival. Candidates generously provided free liquor to voters at the polls, and balloting often was by voice vote.[42] The more liquor the candidate provided, the louder his supporters became. This is apparently how one Whole Hog defeated a leading Mississippi aristocrat in 1832.[43] Yet elections in England and many parts of America (including Atlantic states) had been well lubricated with liquor

and mob revelry since at least the late eighteenth century.[44] Democratization and frontier culture may have been a necessary condition for
electing judges, but they were clearly not sufficient.

The story begins in Natchez, the heart of Mississippi's commerce and
cotton trade, and its seat of political power. The city's ruling class, known
as the "Natchez Junto," controlled the state's first constitutional convention in 1817.[45] Seventy percent of the convention delegates were from
the Natchez district, and they gave Natchez a grossly disproportionate
share of legislative representation.[46] They gave voting rights only to free
white males who paid taxes or served in the militia, and set a high property qualification for office holding—standards not very unusual in eastern states at the time, but out of step with the frontier states and soon to
be out of step with the East, too.[47] The constitution had no provision for
popular ratification. It simply took effect the day it was signed.[48]

The 1817 constitution gave the legislature the power to appoint judges,
and judges had tenure during good behavior.[49] The backwoods delegates
worried about Natchez consolidating its power, and they fell far short in
their push for judicial elections as a way of decentralizing the selection of
judges.[50] Their predictions were correct: the Natchez Junto dominated
Mississippi's courts, as well as most other offices, through the 1820s.[51]
The 1817 constitution established four judicial districts, and each district
had one representative on the four-member supreme court. One might
have guessed that this districting might have limited Natchez's influence,
but in fact, two districts and half of a third covered the Natchez area.[52]
Only one was completely rural. The 1817 convention coincided with the
peak of Natchez's political influence, but the power-consolidating devices
of the 1817 constitution could not hold off the inevitable tide of demographic change. Mississippi's white population grew rapidly over the
next two decades,[53] and most were settling the backwoods areas. Mississippians had been obtaining more and more land from the Choctaw and
Chickasaw tribes in the northern part of the state, and many Natchez
residents left to take over their land.[54]

In the 1820s, Natchez began to suffer a number of defeats, starting with
losing its status as the state capital to a new town named after a war hero:
Jackson. An English traveler quipped that Natchez was "the metropolis of
the state, . . . a center of communication, . . . and a natural and convenient" meeting place for the legislature, and thus "the Democratic Party
could not be expected to put up . . . with an arrangement of affairs so
reasonable and advantageous." The legislature decided to put a new capital in the state's geographic center, which turned out to be "in the middle
of a swamp," a proud tradition in American capital-building starting with

the creation of Washington, D.C. "This [swamp] was welcome news. . . . [A]ll might now be placed on a footing of equality, the spot being equally inaccessible and inconvenient for all."[55] The Natchez establishment had thought its concession on the state capital might calm the backwoods, but the rural population kept growing in numbers and in resentment, and a broad consensus emerged that the old constitution was obsolete.[56] Of the many pro-Jackson states, most lacked the kind of centralized elite power that Natchez held, and thus they developed their institutions and distributed power in a more egalitarian and steady way. The Virginia and South Carolina elites maintained their status while yielding power gradually. The Mississippi elites overreached and triggered a backlash. Nothing represented the power of the Natchez old guard and its overreach better than the courts.

The Natchez majority on the court then issued some decisions that undercut slavery's legal status. The court showed its lack of sympathy for slavery with some remarkable profreedom language in 1818:

> Slavery is condemned by reason and the laws of nature. It exists and can only exist, through municipal regulations, and in matters of doubt, . . . courts must lean in favorem vitae et libertatis [in favor of life and liberty]. . . . Slaves within the limits of the Northwest Territory became free men by virtue of the ordinance of 1787 [and the constitution of Indiana in 1816], and can assert their legal freedom in the courts of this state.[57]

Two years later, the court elevated the legal protections for slaves and rejected the notion that slavery was "natural." One of the Natchez judges reiterated that slavery "exists not by force of law of nature or of nations, but by virtue only of the positive law of the state," and the court also recognized the master's duty to feed and clothe slaves.[58] Major treatises on the law of slavery cited both cases, and one was later cited by an antislavery dissenter on the U.S. Supreme Court in *Dred Scott*.[59]

It turns out that such decisions respecting northern free soil legislation (sometimes called "comity") were not uncommon before the 1830s.[60] The comity in southern courts was partly the result of elite legal culture and its respect for common law principles and national unity. To lawyers and the commercial elite, these slavery decisions probably were not shocking, but slave owners—both in Natchez and in the backwoods— may have found the court out of touch, if they were paying attention. Fears of slave revolts were stirring, and slave emancipation was already making some Mississippians very nervous.[61] However, there seems to be no record of public reaction to these cases, and there is a gap of a dozen years between the slavery decisions and the 1832 convention, so the decisions played no more than a minor background role.

The debtor-versus-creditor struggles of the mid-1820s were more significant. In 1824, the Mississippi Supreme Court struck down a state statute protecting debtors from creditors in *Cochrane v. Kitchens*. The statute had created a one-year amnesty for any debtor after the creditor won a judgment for the repayment of debt, and it also limited the sheriffs' enforcement of procreditor judgments and forfeiture.[62] The state supreme court ruled that the statute violated both federal and state constitutional clauses on protecting the obligation of contracts. More stunning was the court's decision to fine a sheriff $100 for enforcing the statute.[63]

The legislators were incensed by the invalidation of the statute, and particularly by the court's punishment of the sheriffs for heeding the legislature's commands. The state legislature ordered the justices to appear before the legislature and "show cause, why they should not be removed from office."[64] The House of Representatives questioned whether the court had the power of judicial review at all.[65] It attempted to impeach and convict one Natchez justice for three consecutive sessions, partly because of his ruling in *Cochrane*.[66] About one year after the court decided *Cochrane*, the *Woodville Republican* called the Mississippi courts "a great and oppressive evil; and without any system or fixed rule of policy to guide us, are we not gradually approaching to a Kentucky anarchy?"[67] "Kentucky anarchy" referred to the Kentucky Supreme Court striking down a prodebtor statute in 1823, followed by the chaos of the Kentucky legislature creating a new one, and both courts hearing the same cases.

Meanwhile, the regional rivalry over the courts continued. In 1828, the backwoods appeared to win a round: the legislature added a fifth seat to the high court to represent the northern rural region. However, the legislature found a way, yet again, to appoint a Natchez lawyer for a rural judicial district.[68] In 1831, the Natchez Junto held four of the five supreme court seats.[69] One of those Natchez judges was an "active and violent political partisan[], entering personally into every canvass, and [was] often charged with political bias."[70] Natchez's power grab in 1831 helped trigger a vote for a convention that year. In August 1831, the voters approved the call for a convention by a vote of almost four to one. Even the Natchez leaders had to concede that the basic mechanics of the 1817 constitution were outdated, and they understood that the longer they waited, the more populist the next constitutional convention would become.[71] The land negotiations with Choctaw and Chickasaw tribes were heating up, and it was only a matter of time until new counties would be added to the state, and those counties would increase anti-Natchez representation in a future constitutional convention.[72] As long as a new convention was inevitable, Natchez understood that sooner was better than later.

After the vote to hold a convention, but before the convention itself, Indian removal became a lightning rod of judicial controversy. It already was one of the most important political issues in Mississippi in this era, and in 1832, Chief Justice John Marshall and the appointed justices on the U.S. Supreme Court made it more salient as an issue of judicial selection.[73] When Mississippi became a state in 1817, the Choctaw and Chickasaw controlled two thirds of the state's territory, but Mississippians aggressively settled that land and negotiated land treaties, often with threats of force.[74] Mississippians demanded forcible "Indian removal," and lionized Jackson for his lead role in Indian land negotiations in Mississippi in the 1810s and 1820s.[75] In 1832, Jackson was engaged in tough bargaining with the Chickasaw over an allotment treaty, which was signed later that year, and led to the relocation of the Chickasaw across the Mississippi in 1837. In 1832, Mississippians watched with great interest as a court battle continued between Georgia and the Cherokee, just as the Mississippi convention was about to meet.

The U.S. Supreme Court had been wrestling with Georgia and the Jackson administration over the treatment of the Cherokee. The Marshall Court first attempted to assert jurisdiction in a murder case against Corn Tassels in 1830, but instead of answering the court order, the State of Georgia executed Tassels. After Georgia passed a law asserting authority over Cherokee territory, the Marshall Court turned away the Cherokee claim of being a foreign nation in 1831, but left open other questions.[76] Just as Jackson's removal program and the Trail of Tears were getting underway, the Marshall Court ruled in favor of the Cherokee in *Worcester v. Georgia* on March 3, 1832.[77] The Marshall Court announced that Georgia's laws violated Cherokee sovereignty, and it rejected the "doctrine of discovery," which privileged Europeans as the "discoverers" of the Americas, as "extravagant and absurd": "It is difficult to comprehend that the discovery ... should give the discoverer rights in the country discovered, which annulled the pre-existing rights of its ancient possessors."[78] The Marshall Court had taken a stand that the Cherokee had sovereign rights, and that the United States government was legally bound to defend those rights against Georgia. Unfortunately, John Marshall did not have the tools to defend those rights. Hence the apocryphal quote attributed to Jackson: "Mr. Marshall has made his decision. Now let him enforce it!"

Most newspapers outside Natchez expressed outrage. They compared these events to the nullification crisis as threats to state sovereignty. In April, the *Mississippi Gazette* published the *Worcester* opinion and issued a tirade against the Marshall Court's attempt to become "all in all," "fulfill[ing]

the worst fears of the original republicans." Then the *Gazette* editorial
quoted at length Thomas Jefferson's critique of judicial supremacy and judicial independence. Jefferson concluded that judicial review is "dangerous," because the judges "are in office for life, and not responsible, as the
functionaries are, to the elective control. *The constitution has no single
tribunal. I know of no safe depository of the ultimate powers of society
but the people themselves.*" The *Gazette* immediately added, "Perhaps the
union will be wrecked by resisting [the U.S. Supreme Court's] rapacity for
power."[79] Thus, the advocates of Indian removal cranked up the volume in
calling for popular sovereignty. In an article entitled "The Voice of the
People!" the *Gazette* reported a resolution criticizing the Marshall Court
for "endangering the peace, prosperity, and safety" of the general public,
and calling for more of the "representative principle" throughout the government.[80] Then the *Gazette* approvingly reported on plans for impeachment: "*Whenever the Supreme Court is convicted of bending to party intrigue, let the articles of impeachment be in readiness; let the bolt fall on
whomsoever it may light!*"[81]

The *Vicksburg Mississippian* condemned "the fanatics of the North"
and "the recent decision of the Supreme Court, so flagrantly violative of
their sovereign rights." The letter included an implicit threat that "things
must come to their worst; and if in the last resort we need defenders, we
will find them everywhere among the honest men of the country to rally
to our Banner."[82] A week later a *Mississippian* editorial congratulated the
courts of Georgia for disregarding the Marshall Court's ruling. That
same spring, in the middle of the campaign for convention delegates, *The
Mississippian* published a series of editorials calling for judicial elections.
The Mississippian had already been a vocal advocate for judicial elections before the Marshall Court decision, but it had new fodder for its
argument. Even if the Cherokee cases may not have changed many minds
about judicial elections, the controversy helped focus attention on this
question and generate enough anger to move public opinion.

The Choctaw and Chickasaw removal also led to more tension between Natchez and the backwoods because of the fight over legal title to
the new lands. White settlers had been moving into these lands without
formal title, and the courts might consider them squatters and decide to
grant title over the land to the legislature. The Natchez-controlled legislature in turn could sell off the land, most likely to insider speculators in
Natchez. Judges elected in statewide or in truly rural districts would be
less likely to rule against the settlers in favor of speculators. If the reaction to the Marshall Court's Cherokee rulings was solely to increase political checks on the court, the convention could have achieved this goal

simply by limiting judicial terms and retaining the appointment process. Because the goal was also to strengthen the court to be able to stand up to the state legislature, the convention went further.

Soon after the Indian removal controversy exploded, the campaign for convention delegates began, building up to the vote in August 1832. Candidates focused on judicial elections more than any other topic.[83] They also criticized the commissioning of judges during good behavior, questioning why judges should be given "perfect independence."[84] They framed their argument for judicial elections in terms of relative judicial independence, in terms of separating the courts from the "unprincipled faction" of Natchez, but just as much, they also focused on judicial accountability to majority rule.[85] Meanwhile, the Aristocrats emphasized the importance of the courts' "independence and freedom from the excitement of electioneering contests, which they know to be essential to the firmness, and impartiality of judgment."[86] They focused on general judicial independence, to enable the courts to protect individual rights—specifically, property rights. Their rhetoric was lofty, but they also knew that their economic interests depended upon the protection of the judges from populist pressures.

The accident of timing was a factor beyond the coincidence of the Marshall Court's *Cherokee* decision. As it turns out, the convention did not include many of the state's preeminent leaders. Natchez City selected its most prominent "aristocrats," but convention delegates for the rest of the state were not a first-string team of state leaders, or even second-string. Only three of the 1832 delegates had served as delegates in the 1817 convention.[87] Over half of the delegates do not appear in any of the books on Mississippi's history, including the leading biographical guide to Mississippi for that era. Remarkably, over half of the 1832 convention made their only mark on history in those summer dog days, or rather, Whole Hog days.[88] The convention included a high number of backbenchers, partly because some party leaders lost, but even more because many prominent leaders—both in Natchez and in the rest of the state—chose not to run at all.[89] One explanation is the timing of the delegate election: The state conducted its elections for convention delegates at the same time as its elections for full-time offices. On the one hand, the goal may have been to increase turnout, and they achieved that goal.[90] On the other hand, the timing created a conflict for potential candidates. Candidates seem not to have run to be convention delegates while also running for full-time offices.[91] It is not clear whether there was a formal rule or an informal norm against campaigning for both or whether candidates, when choosing how to allocate their resources, made an understandable choice to focus on long-term offices with more prestige rather than to serve as a delegate for less time and less power. This conflict seems to have removed the established leaders who valued appointments and had benefited most from them. Lower-profile backbenchers and Whole Hog outsiders took their places. They were more likely to resent insider privilege, and they appreciated that local elections might give them more opportunity in the future. As it turns out, judicial elections passed by a very narrow margin. The timing of the convention election helped lead to judicial elections by skewing the convention from the party elites to the backbenchers, probably by accident.

When the convention met in the summer of 1832, the Whole Hogs had a slight upper hand. There is an unsurprising geographic pattern to the votes: the Natchez area delegates were unanimously opposed to judicial elections, and a large majority of the rural delegates were in favor. By reforming the courts, the Whole Hogs achieved their goals of reducing Natchez's potential influence of the courts: first by "clearing the bench," wiping away the otherwise entrenched judges; and second by creating three judicial districts. Two of the three were rural, and they would be directly controlled by rural voters, not the Natchez Junto. After several days of debate, the Whole Hogs won votes in favor of judicial elections for all judges by twenty-six to eighteen, twenty-five to nineteen, and on a final vote, twenty-six to eighteen. A switch in just four or five delegates would have blocked judicial elections. It is possible that if the voting for delegates simply had been on a different day than the general election, a few more elite leaders would have won seats instead of a few backbenchers, and that would have been enough to change these results.

The leading Aristocrat at the convention was John Quitman, one of Natchez's leading lawyers, the state's chancellor, and by all accounts a most deserving jurist for that position. One of Mississippi's most important antebellum leaders, Quitman was born in upstate New York and studied law in Pennsylvania, and then moved to Mississippi at the age of twenty-three to buy a plantation and practice law in Natchez. He embraced Southern Bourbon gentility and southern states' rights with the zeal of a true convert. Soon after his Aristocratic leadership in the 1832 convention, he would become Mississippi's first popularly elected chancellor and a founder of Mississippi's State Rights Party in the nullification fight against the federal tariff.[92] Quitman would later serve as Mississippi's governor, a brigadier general in the Mexican-American War, and one of the South's leading "Fire-Eater" secessionists in the U.S. Congress. Quitman's opposition to judicial elections was sincere, but he also may have had a personal stake. If he wanted to retain his office as chancellor, he had a much better chance of reappointment than of winning a statewide election. Quitman claimed to have lost twenty pounds at the convention from his draining fight against judicial elections.[93]

The convention gave the voters more power with one hand, but took it away with the other. At the end of the convention, a majority voted to make the constitution immediately effective by delegate vote, with no popular ratification or any other steps. Quitman denounced this as "one of the greatest outrages ever committed on a free people."[94] In a role reversal, the supporters of judicial elections opposed a popular ratification requirement (to avoid any threat to the constitution they favored), while the opponents of judicial elections supported a popular ratification requirement (to create another chance to defeat the constitution they opposed). Of the ten delegates who voted against the constitution, nine had opposed judicial elections.[95]

In a twist of fates, both Henry Foote, the leading proponent of judicial elections, and John Quitman, the leading opponent, reversed themselves later. Four decades later, Foote regretted that the change was "a great and most deplorable error," for it has "been impossible to keep politics out of judicial elections" and led to a "great and constantly increasing deterioration of the judicial department."[96] These sentiments were not likely sour grapes, because Foote was a successful political figure after 1832. Quitman, on the other hand, may have changed his mind because of sweet grapes, so to speak. Even if the prospect of elections had made him anxious at the convention, he won his race for chancellor in 1833. In 1845, after several years on the bench, he self-servingly noted that in Mississippi, judicial elections had proved to be "the best mode of selecting judicial officers," and said he had been wrong in 1832.[97] The first chief justice on the court had also opposed judicial elections in 1832, but then won three terms, despite being a "sta[u]nch Whig, while his constituency was as staunchly Democratic."[98] In fact, Mississippi voters, by casting ballots for the leading Aristocrats, partly dispelled the notion that voters would simply choose populist candidates with popular positions or local ties. For someone so opposed to elections in 1832, Quitman proved to be quite successful at elections throughout the rest of his career as a proslavery Fire-Eater, perhaps because he learned to play by the new democratic rules as a more democratic candidate.

The other Natchez judges did not fare as well. Only one of the four Natchez-linked incumbents won election to a supreme court seat in 1832. Under the new constitution, Natchez's political power dropped sharply, its bar declined, and it rarely elected anyone to the supreme court thereafter.[99] Demographic and economic shifts surely played a bigger role than structural judicial reforms, but the change in selection methods produced a very different court system after 1832.

Over time, Mississippi voters offered signs of hope to the defenders of judicial elections elsewhere. In general, Mississippians chose well-qualified, experienced judges. Mississippi voters did not allow Natchez to control the courts as it had before 1832, but they voted some prominent judges back into office, to the chagrin of some Whole Hogs.[100] Mississippi could have been a model for other states, but it was also perceived as an antimodel, a low-prestige state. In later constitutional conventions, delegates mocked Mississippi.[101] One delegate opposed judicial elections by denouncing Mississippi as "an instance of badly-administered laws, connected with popularly elected Judges."[102] Another observer claimed that judicial elections had destroyed law, order, and even civilization in Mississippi. Because of judicial elections, "life and property are less secure than in any other, and its public credit is lost beyond redemption. There *repudiation* [of debt] is openly avowed, and crime and murder stalk about in open day. And so far as we can gather from the public press, their system has *not* worked well. Shall we then discard the example and experience of all the other States, and follow the isolated course of Mississippi alone?"[103] By itself, Mississippi offered a laboratory with no prestige, and judicial elections remained rare for more than a decade after Mississippi's convention. By the time higher-status states adopted judicial elections, other convention delegates could set aside their distaste for Mississippi, and they took a second look at Mississippi's actual experience with relatively successful judicial elections. Some delegates in the 1840s and 1850s read from John Quitman's letters touting his conversion experience in favor of judicial elections and describing the wisdom of Mississippi's voters. A subtext was that if Mississippi voters could be trusted to vote for judges, certainly other states' voters could, too. At most, Mississippi had a mild influence, helping advocates make a case for judicial elections more than a decade later, but it was no catalyst or trigger for spreading judicial elections in the 1830s.

Mississippi's 1832 constitutional convention had another oddity that seemed unrelated to judicial elections but wound up putting judicial elections into focus before the U.S. Supreme Court. The 1832 constitution gave the legislature the power to ban the interstate importation of slaves because of financial and security concerns. The state legislature declined to enforce the ban.[104] As it turns out, this constitutional clause led to a debate about judicial elections before the U.S. Supreme Court in 1841.[105] Even though the legislature never enforced its power to prohibit slave importation, the state courts held that the constitutional provision was self-executing.[106] Henry Clay and Daniel Webster, the national leaders of the Whig Party, defended the legality of importing a slave into Mississippi, arguing that the state courts were wrong to hold that the provision was self-executing. Clay argued that because the Mississippi Supreme Court justices were elected, "The judges of Mississippi are sitting in their own cause; in the cause of those around them; of those who gave and take away their offices!"[107] In the end, the Taney Court agreed with Clay and Webster that the sale of the slave was valid, but it did not address the status of elected judges. Clay had elided the fact that most state judges circa 1841 also faced in-state political pressure, because they had short terms and faced the politics of reappointment. Whether elected or appointed, most state judges would find it in their self-interest to side with the in-state residents over out-of-state residents.

If, as Clay implied, the Mississippi convention was simply aiming to make judges politically accountable, then it might have stopped with the abolition of judicial life tenure. Of course, some delegates wanted to weaken the courts, whether they were motivated by debtor-creditor issues, slavery, or reaction to the Marshall Court. But in those cases, short terms plus reappointment would have constrained the courts. Instead, Mississippi went further, because more was at stake than general accountability. The backwoods delegates also focused on judicial independence, seeking to insulate the courts from Natchez's manipulation of the appointment process. They feared that appointed judges may have been beholden to wealthy Natchez speculators. Judicial elections with local districts would have produced a non-Natchez majority and a stronger court relative to those interests, powerful enough to recognize the settlers' "squatter" property rights against the challenges by wealthier interests. In the Mississippi debate over judicial selection, the framing was as much judicial independence as it was judicial accountability.

The Calm before the Storm

Looking backward, the simplest explanation for the rise of judicial elections has been "Jacksonian democracy." Jackson himself endorsed judicial elections and seven-year terms for federal judges, but neither he nor most other "Jacksonians" focused on this issue on either the state or federal level.[108] In Andrew Jackson's lifetime (from 1767 to 1845), only Mississippi adopted judicial elections for all of its courts, and only a small number of relatively isolated states tried it for any of their lower courts.[109] In the 1810s and 1820s, states were switching from appointing to electing many state officers, but not judges and justices of the peace.[110]

Justices of the peace were local officials who had a mix of minor judicial, prosecutorial, policing, and general administrative duties.[111] From the 1790s through the 1830s, eight states switched to electing justices of the peace along with other executive officials, such as attorneys general, sheriffs, constables, and clerks.[112] But most states still appointed justices of the peace until the wave of judicial elections in the 1840s–1850s.

States also had widely expanded suffrage in the early nineteenth century, so that by 1821, all but three of the twenty-four states had decoupled voting from property holding.[113] After the expansion of suffrage, it took a few years for popular participation to increase, but when it did, the increase was dramatic. Broader suffrage strengthened populism and led to new populist party organizations. They turned to General Jackson, the war hero from a modest background in the West, to be their figurehead. Thus, Andrew Jackson was as much a result of Jacksonian democracy as a cause of it.[114] In 1824, Jackson's first race in a crowded field, only 25 percent of adult white males voted for president. In the Jackson-Adams rematch of 1828, participation more than doubled, to 56.3 percent. This level of participation remained steady for the next two elections.[115]

The Democrats took the lead in populist ideology and rhetoric, and Whigs figured that if you couldn't beat populism, join it. In the 1830s, the Whigs, using log cabins, alcohol, coonskin hats, and populist imagery, sought to steal the Democrats' claim to being the party for the people.[116] Whig popular mobilization broke through in 1840 for Tippecanoe and Tyler, too, as voter participation shot up to a remarkable 78 percent.[117] With the Democrats and Whigs converging ideologically and competing to be the party of the people, the 1830s and early 1840s were ripe for democratizing the courts. Judicial elections could have been the low-hanging fruit for the next round of democratization, and yet they did not reach for that fruit. Instead, they pursued judicial accountability by shortening judges' terms from life to a set number of years.

The story of judicial elections in the 1830s was Mississippi and not much else. In fact, the story was more that judicial elections did not spread in the 1830s. By examining the two other states that revised their existing constitutions in the 1830s, plus another state that altered its judiciary by amendment, we can gain some insight into why more states did not turn to judicial elections earlier. Three other states that revised their court systems in the 1830s—Alabama, North Carolina, and Pennsylvania—illustrate that Jacksonian populism was an insufficient cause of judicial elections. Though given the opportunity, these states did not turn to judicial elections, because there was no similar crisis over appointments and the separation of powers.

Around the same time that Mississippi faced a legal fight over creditors and debtors, Alabama did, too. A self-proclaimed "Popular Party" represented debtor interests against procredit politicians, whom they labeled the "Royal" or "Aristocratic" party.[118] In 1827, the Alabama Supreme Court decided a controversial case in favor of creditors, sparking popular outrage and a "fierce and bitter" campaign.[119] The Popular Party won and began impeachment proceedings against the judges.[120] When impeachment fell short, they amended the constitution, reducing judicial tenure from good behavior to a term of six years.[121] But they did not focus on switching from appointment to popular election. The Popular Party had proposed more aggressive amendments, such as limiting judges to one term, but they provoked vocal defenses of "the independence of the judiciary." One newspaper editorial warned, "We should at all times be extremely cautious how we tamper with an instrument so sacred as the constitution of a state, which is not intended as a mere nose of wax, to be moulded and altered to suit the whims and caprices of the vicious and designing."[122] Around the same time as Mississippi's fight on the same issue, Alabama had enough support for judicial independence to protect an unpopular court from far-reaching changes.

Alabama also lacked the kind of regional divide that had plagued Mississippi. In the 1820s, Alabama's regional differences were replaced by stronger economic or class differences that cut across regional lines and created loose party-like alliances across the state.[123] Alabama's Popular Party would be able to control the court on debtor/creditor issues whether it used its majority through the appointment process or through direct elections. In Mississippi, the problem was particular to the way one region was able to dominate the appointment process, even though it was a minority of the state, and even after the state had switched regional districts. Mississippi's pro-Natchez governors and legislators could outmaneuver the design of districts by handpicking pro-Natchez judges nominally from the other districts. Local judicial elections in Mississippi were the most obvious way to guarantee that the residents of each district could actually choose a judge that represented their region. Local appointments, though imaginable, were simply not in their political vocabulary. Local elections were the familiar institution for local government. It is also worth noting the luck of timing: Alabama's judicial reform occurred before the Marshall Court's decision in *Worcester v. Georgia* in 1832.[124] Both Mississippi and Alabama had been negotiating for Indian removal in this era, and the Marshall Court's ruling was salient for both, but Alabama happened to debate judicial politics before the anti–Marshall Court backlash, and Mississippi was debating judicial politics in the midst of the backlash.

Another reason for the 1830s lull was that there were fewer constitutional conventions in the 1830s than in the decades before and after, partly because fewer states joined the Union in the 1830s. When a whole constitution was being drawn up from scratch, reformers could make more changes. In the 1830s, only two states joined the Union: Arkansas in 1836 and Michigan in 1837. Arkansas chose judicial appointments, and Michigan, with little fanfare, debate, or publicity, opted for an appointed supreme court and popularly elected lower courts. Generally, territories becoming new states avoided controversy—whether because Congress might raise objections in approving the new constitution for statehood, or whether the commercial interests in other states would have doubts about investing in a state with unusual institutions. Judicial elections swept through the country after 1846 in a wave of constitutional conventions, during a wider constitutional revolution. Judicial elections were a coherent piece of that revolution.

The 1830s may have been politically tumultuous, but Americans seemed content enough with their old state constitutions until the end of the decade. In earlier decades, most states had broadened suffrage, reapportioned state legislatures, or otherwise fixed the flaws of the founding constitutions.[125] North Carolina had not yet addressed its malapportioned legislature, so in 1835, it called a convention on this issue. The eastern part of the state, represented by elite planter Democrats, had dominated state offices and the appointment process since the Founding. The western populists demanding reapportionment mostly were Whigs. North Carolina regional politics were similar to Mississippi's Natchez-backcountry division, plus North Carolina had a more crystallized party system that should have exacerbated that tension. Then the Whigs gained the upper hand at the convention, which gave the western counties extra political clout. North Carolina's backcountry voters and rising Whig party should have been as ripe for judicial elections as Mississippi's had been.[126] It would have been a chance for the Whigs to sweep in a new court and for the backcountry to have more local control of the bench.

But North Carolina's Whig and western delegates still did not push for judicial elections. Instead, the convention retained judicial life tenure and adopted three provisions that *increased* the judges' independence: one securing judicial salaries, and two others making the removal of judges more difficult.[127] This result was quite the opposite of the events in Mississippi and Alabama. One possible explanation is that the judges of the North Carolina Supreme Court, and in particular Thomas Ruffin and William Gaston, were highly regarded and politically astute. Ruffin and Gaston had each joined the court only recently. Some credit them with saving the North Carolina Supreme Court from populist attacks at the 1835 convention.[128] Before they joined the court, North Carolina populists had been attacking the state judiciary since 1819, regularly proposing amendments to prohibit the increase of a judge's salary during his tenure and to make it easier for the legislature to remove judges.[129] The appointments of Ruffin and then Gaston helped to avert this fate. One newspaper observed that the "accession of Mr. Gaston to the Bench has made the Court stronger, if possible, than ever before. No open attack can now avail against it."[130] Another hailed the duo: "No State of the Union . . . not even the United States, ever had a superior Bench; few ever had its equal."[131] In a case much like *Marbury v. Madison,* their court struck down a popular statute. Ruffin and Gaston seized that opportunity to comment publicly on the importance of judicial independence and judicial review, arguing that the judiciary generally should be free from political pressure and legislative interference. As a measure of the public's respect for the supreme court, there was no backlash.[132] Ruffin and Gaston together helped defuse partisan tension over the courts. They united east and west, even crossing regional party lines: Gaston as an eastern Federalist-Whig sympathizer, Ruffin as a western Democrat. They reached across regional lines: Gaston supported internal improvements and other pro-western democratic reforms. Their reputations, politics, and backgrounds complemented each other and built trust in the court.[133]

However, there are problems with crediting Ruffin and Gaston for saving North Carolina's judicial independence so heroically. It is just as likely that such commanding figures on the court would have provoked more of a backlash, not less, particularly after the Ruffin-Gaston dynamic duo struck down a popular statute so soon after joining the court. And yet, just two years later, the constitutional convention not only dismissed attempts to check the courts, it actually added protection for judges. In the first third of the nineteenth century, the political impulse was to reduce state judicial power. But North Carolina demonstrates that there were limits to that trend, and perhaps even signs of a reversal in favor of judicial independence.

Pennsylvania was the next opportunity to change a state's judiciary through a constitutional convention. It also should have been fertile ground for judicial elections. Since the constitution's ratification in 1790, Jeffersonians and Democrats had been criticizing its judicial life tenure and had been calling for a new convention. They also repeatedly proposed switching to judicial elections. One of their main complaints was that the governors abused their appointment power as partisan patronage. By the time the Democrats succeeded in calling a convention in 1837, it happened to come at a time when the Whigs had formed a strong coalition with the populist Anti-Masons. The Whigs had been ideologically opposed to judicial elections, and the Anti-Masons had been ideologically in favor. It was easy for them to work out this philosophical difference, because self-interest trumped philosophy. By 1838, the Whig-Anti-Masons had gained control of the governorship and a one-seat majority at the constitutional convention. Now that they had the governorship, they had no interest in giving up the power to control appointments. Thus, the Anti-Masons toed the new party line hyperbolically, warning that judicial elections would lead to "Anarchy and Revolution . . . in their worst and most bloody forms" and would restore slavery to Pennsylvania. The opponents of judicial elections also feared being outliers, admonishing other delegates to take "great caution, and . . . not to make a change at all, unless on good and sufficient grounds." Inertia and risk aversion were powerful forces against judicial elections.[134]

The populist faction within the Democratic delegation realized that they did not have the votes in the convention for judicial elections. Instead, the Democrats united behind reducing judicial tenure from life to a term of years.[135] The convention voted to change the supreme court justices' terms from life to fifteen years—still a very long term tantamount to life—and the lower court judges' terms from life to five years. It was a matter of luck that the convention met in 1838—the only year of economic growth between 1837 and 1842. The economic crisis wound up changing the debate over judges.

Alabama's and Pennsylvania's focus on reducing term length rather than the method of judicial selection reflected the general trend of the 1830s. The states in the 1830s mostly continued the Jeffersonian era's approach of weakening the judiciary without using judicial elections. Before 1830, judges in twelve states held their positions during good behavior and judges in six states had much less job security.[136] Then, in the 1830s, Alabama and six more states switched to shorter terms for judges, generally ranging between six and eight years.[137] By the end of the decade, a majority of states limited judges' terms. These states were distributed fairly evenly through every region of the country. The overall effect was to increase the governors' and legislatures' appointment power, and thereby weaken judges' power.

Both Pennsylvania and Mississippi underscore the importance of luck, timing, and political self-interest. In Pennsylvania, it was a matter of luck that the Whigs had just taken hold of the governorship and then won a majority at the convention. It was a matter of self-interest that the Pennsylvania Whigs translated this timing into retaining appointments. In Mississippi, it was a matter of luck that the 1832 election timing shifted the convention from established politicians to backbenchers and Whole Hogs, and it was also a matter of luck that the convention races coincided with an unpopular Marshall Court decision on one of the most controversial issues in the state.

But the 1830s are not merely a story of contingency. As North Carolina illustrates, judicial independence was surprisingly robust in this era. The contrast of Alabama and Mississippi also reveals the role of judicial independence and the separation of powers in leading to judicial elections. When Alabama grappled with creditor-debtor relations, the Populist Party believed shortening judicial terms was a sufficient check on the courts. In Mississippi, the Whole Hogs faced that same issue, but went beyond that approach. They fought for judicial elections in order to separate the powers, insulating the courts from the other branches' manipulations of appointment. It was a classic move of relative independence: By making the judges more independent from the Natchez Junto, the Whole Hogs made the courts more accountable to local public opinion and the backwoods region. Even if Mississippi did not inspire many followers in the 1830s, the Whole Hogs' approach to relative judicial independence and to separating the courts from the other self-dealing political branches foreshadowed the wave of the near future. In Mississippi—as well as in Vermont, Georgia, and Indiana—interest groups framed judicial elections in terms of judicial independence.

CHAPTER FOUR

Panic and Trigger

TWO TURNING POINTS led to the wave of judicial elections in the 1840s–1850s: the economic crisis of the early 1840s and the New York Constitutional Convention of 1846. The Panics of 1837 and 1839 and the ensuing depression that followed transformed American politics. After New York moved heaven and earth to build the Erie Canal, state governments around the country overspent on new canals, roads, and railroads in the 1830s. They expected economic good times to pay off their massive debts, but the depression threatened many states with bankruptcy. State legislatures shouldered the blame for folly, fiscal irresponsibility, and corruption. A group of outsiders in the Democratic Party, known as the Radicals or "Barnburners," led a constitutional movement against public spending, public debt, and partisan patronage. They shocked the New York establishment by taking over the 1846 convention, and they sparked a nationwide revolution for stronger constitutional limits against legislative power. The Radicals understood that the courts had to be more independent from the other branches in order to check them, and judicial elections were the means to achieve this kind of relative independence. Although it may be hard to imagine from a modern perspective, New York's Radicals also believed that judicial elections would lead to general independence by giving judges more confidence and a stronger sense of democratic legitimacy. The leading Radical envisioned dramatic new powers by elected courts, that "if the judges should not find the rule fixed by society itself, that [the judges] must make the law" themselves, and that elected judges would have the insight to channel the "natural" law from "God himself."[1] The notion was not that elections would cabin judges within the limits of public opinions, but rather, that elections would liberate judges from the limits of machine politics to establish God's natural order and to enforce the people's Constitution.

For some Radical Barnburners, the natural order meant laissez-faire and opposition to special privileges doled out by the legislature and governors to party insiders. The Radical constitution aimed to separate judges from insider politics, and it also established a foundation for free market legal principles that would spread over the next several decades.

Panic

The Panics began in May 1837 as a banking crisis. For a short period, urban unemployment increased sharply, industry shut down, and credit collapsed, but this crisis was short-lived. The economy recovered in 1838, and the nation's nerves settled. The Pennsylvania constitutional convention coincided with the recovery, and thus it did not reflect economic or fiscal anxieties. However, the recovery was also short-lived. The Panic of 1839 caused severe deflation and economic stagnation into the mid-1840s. Bank notes in circulation dropped almost two-thirds, and European investors pulled out of the American economy almost entirely. Four states defaulted on their debts in 1841, and five more defaulted in 1842. Unemployment rates soared, food riots erupted in many cities, and a recession lasted until 1843.[2]

The crisis doomed Martin Van Buren's presidency, and many other political leaders took a fall after the Panics. The reputations of the legislatures around the country took an enormous and long-lasting hit after they had banked so heavily on new banks and expensive internal improvements. The push for internal improvements and state spending had, interestingly, been the overreaction to an earlier economic crisis, the Panic of 1819. Internal improvements were the craze and the fix-all for both Whigs (on the national and state levels) and Democrats (on the state level), building from the 1820s into the 1830s. New York's legislative energy began successfully with the Erie Canal. Initially, Governor DeWitt Clinton's plan for a 350-mile canal between Lake Erie and the Hudson River was mocked as "Clinton's Folly" or "Clinton's Ditch." However, it quickly drew enormous revenue and captured the public imagination for a transportation revolution.[3]

Drunk with the success of the Erie Canal, New Yorkers went on a binge of internal improvements. In 1825, the New York legislature authorized seventeen new canals, and many were completed at great expense. Other states around the country followed, all promising that the projects would bring great riches and that tolls would pay off the massive debts. State legislatures dramatically increased the number of special incorporations to accelerate economic growth and build infrastructure. In many states, the choice of where to build new canals and roads sparked bitter fights between regions and between towns within those regions. Designs failed and costs skyrocketed. The Panics of 1837 and 1839 further dashed those hopes. A severe depression stretched into the 1840s, with record lows in 1842. As other states defaulted or teetered on the edge of bankruptcy, New York literally tried to dig itself out of debt by building even more canals. Instead, its debts grew to more than fifty times the size of the annual state budget. Many states raised taxes sharply to pay down their debts.[4]

Debt in antebellum America was a moral problem, not just a fiscal problem. Personal debt had been considered a moral failing with religious dimensions, and catastrophic public debt was a sign of collective moral failure. "Paper aristocrats" was the English "Country Party" term for the political insiders who manipulated state debt for corporate profit. This English "Country" versus "Court" tradition carried on with many American revolutionaries, Anti-Federalists, Jeffersonians, and some Jacksonians. The Panics rekindled a deep hostility to debt and the "paper aristocracy."[5] Outraged citizens demanded a new constitution to prevent future fiscal crises by limiting debt and legislative power. The first state constitutions had established powerful legislatures as the voice of the public will and the engine of democracy. By the 1840s, the public viewed the legislatures as the broken engine that had gone off the rails of internal improvements. This constitutional movement had to wait a few years for the economic storm to pass, but it emerged with a bang in New York to the surprise of the political establishment.[6]

Trigger: New York's 1846 Convention

Judicial elections suddenly emerged from an isolated practice in the marginal frontier slave state of Mississippi to become a foregone conclusion in New York. New York then helped trigger their spread around the country immediately. Judicial elections were so widely accepted in New York's 1846 convention that no delegate even called for an up-or-down vote on elections versus appointments.[7] In the middle of the convention, Charles Kirkland, an opponent of judicial elections, said, "A majority of this Convention have doubtless decided that the judicial office shall be filled by election, and with that decision, so far as this body is concerned, I am not to quarrel."[8] At that point, the opposition acquiesced to judicial elections as a fait accompli. They simply moved on to fight over the details of elections. The story of this sudden reversal is in the fluid, treacherous mix of New York's partisan factions, particularly in the meteoric rise and fall of the Radical Barnburners.

"I don't pretend to comprehend [New York] politics. It is a labyrinth of wheels within wheels, and it is understood only by the managers," remarked one early republic observer.[9] In 1846, even the managers did not understand it so well, as a complicated web of factions jockeyed for power. New York's watershed adoption of judicial elections—triggering a wave over the next few years—was a combination of the economic crisis, ideological convergence on democracy, good factional management, bad political predictions, and luck.

Before stepping into the labyrinth, I offer the following scorecard of New York parties as they evolved from Hamilton's Federalists and Jefferson's Democratic-Republicans. The left column begins with the more populist Jeffersonian Democratic-Republican Party, and the right begins with the more conservative Federalists, but by the 1840s, both parties had populist factions (the Barnburners and the Anti-Renters) and conservative factions (the Hunkers and the regular Whigs). In the 1850s, the Barnburners and Whigs disappeared and re-emerged together in the Republican coalition.

1800s	Democratic-Republicans	Federalists
1810s	Democratic-Republicans	Federalists
1820s	Democratic-Republicans	Independent Republicans
1830s	Democrats (Loco Foco vs. Hunkers)	Whigs
1840s	**Radical Barnburners vs. Hunkers**	**Whigs / Anti-Renters**

Through most of these years, the Democratic-Republicans and then the Democrats held the upper hand in the state. The most important stage in the context of judicial elections was the split in the Democratic Party in the 1840s between the conservative, establishment Hunkers and the outsider Radical Barnburners. The name "Hunker" was derived from the notion that these insider Democrats "hunkered" for spoils or pursued a "hunk" of spoils from the appointment/patronage system. The term "hunk" comes from the Dutch "honk" (post, goal, or home), which eventually came to mean "office." Thus, it is not surprising that they opposed direct democracy. The Hunkers had formed a conservative coalition with the Whigs in the early 1830s to spend heavily on public works, and they continued to spend after the depression sent the state into heavy debt. They also supported the southern proslavery wing of the Democratic Party, and they supported the Southern-led Mexican-American War.[10]

The name "Barnburner" was an allusion to a legendary Dutch farmer who dealt with a rat problem by burning down his whole barn. The implication was that they were willing to destroy the canals, corporations, and banks in order to curb the debts, corruption, and abuses associated with them. One Radical leader commented, "They call us barnburners. Thunder and lightening are barnburners sometimes; but they greatly purify the whole atmosphere, and that, gentlemen, is what we propose to do."[11] The Barnburners were descended from the radical Loco-Focos of the 1830s, a mix of labor union leaders and anti–Tammany Hall, anti-corruption reformers. The Barnburners included some laborers, but they were more of a bourgeois coalition of rural smallholders, middle-class lawyers, and urban professionals from modest backgrounds, rising up against privilege and government corruption. The Barnburners were increasingly strong in New York City, and they also had strongholds throughout upstate New York—in regions that were the hotbed of the Second Great Awakening of populist religious revivalism.[12] They were truly a statewide insurgency against the statewide Hunker machine. They were liberal in the classical sense: Many of them focused on imposing stronger constitutional limits on state power, spending, and economic regulation. They perceived that the wealthy and the party insiders (both Whigs and Hunker Democrats) had captured state power and used the state for patronage, "class legislation," paper money, public debt, internal improvements, and redistributing property to play favorites and tighten their grip on power. One historian credits the Barnburners with the "birth of American liberalism," in the sense of laissez-faire.[13] The Barnburners also strongly opposed the extension of slavery.[14]

The Whigs also had been conservative on the judiciary and opposed populist reforms.[15] Between the conservative proappointment Hunkers and the Whigs' elite roots, it is odd that New York would be a populist pioneer for direct democracy. The first change was that the Whigs turned to populism and the separation of powers. The second change was that the Barnburner Democrats seized their moment in 1846, overtook the Hunkers, and embraced judicial elections.

First, the Whigs' partisan strategy trumped their traditionally conservative ideology, and then they changed their ideology to roll with the times. In the previous constitutional convention in 1821, the Whigs' antecedents, the Federalists, foreshadowed the Whig's prodemocracy strategy of 1846. By 1821, the New York Federalists had renamed themselves the "Independent Republicans." Casting aside their skepticism of direct democracy, they supported direct local elections for more offices, including some judges.[16] The Democrats had used the patronage system to appoint the state's 15,000 public officials and to build a "seemingly unbreakable political monopoly."[17] The ex-Federalists thought local elections were a necessary evil in breaking up that monopoly. Chancellor James Kent, the great conservative legal scholar and an Independent-Republican delegate, declared that universal suffrage would unleash "the power of the evil genius of democracy." At the same time, he warned that partisan appointments would impose "the disciplined force of fierce and vindictive majorities," that is, the Democratic patronage machine.[18] As a check against this abuse, Kent sought to harness the evil genius: He endorsed local voting for sheriffs and justices of the peace (who were part police, part local administrator, part judge), as something "like a quarantine laws into our constitution to prevent the introduction and rage of this great moral pestilence. . . . [U]nless we scatter [offices] in fragments among our counties, our future career will be exceedingly tempestuous and corrupt."[19] Drawing on the image of quarantining, Kent essentially was framing his argument for local elections in terms of the separation of powers. Other Independent-Republicans went further in proposing electing full-time judges, even as they admitted that they were "no clamorous advocate[s] of the people."[20] The Democrats took the opposite side, reflecting how partisanship drove the debate more than ideology. The Loco Foco leader Martin Van Buren replied that it was "wrong in principle to elect judicial officers."[21] But Van Buren, like Kent, was more worried about politics than principle, because he also understood that local judicial elections would reduce the power of the governor and the Democratic-Republicans' statewide patronage machine.[22] The Van Burenites went further, using the convention to wipe the Supreme Court clean, so that they could eliminate Chief Justice Ambrose Spencer and their other opponents on the court, and then appoint their own allies. The Independent-Republicans were a small faction at the 1821 convention, and they failed to save their Supreme Court justices or carve out local judicial havens safe from centralized Democratic control. However, in 1846, their Whig descendants would take advantage of another opportunity.

Their Whig descendants also moved ideologically and symbolically toward populism, particularly after the Panics. For much of the 1830s, the Whigs lacked coordination and a consistent message. They believed they could campaign as an antiparty, an informal coalition against the concept of parties. After their disorganized and doomed 1836 campaign, the Whigs learned they needed a party to beat a party. The Panics helped them organize a national structure with a national populist message. The Whigs blamed the economic crisis on "executive monarchy" and the Democrats' aristocratic appointments.[23] The Whigs won the elections of 1838 and 1840, and the key to their success was changing their image to more populist, rural, modest, and down-home. They turned nativist, portraying the new wave of European immigrants as a moral threat. They portrayed Democrats as drunks and as atheists. Horace Greeley, the New York Whig, alleged, "Wherever you find a bitter, blasphemous Atheist and an enemy of Marriage, Morality, and Social Order, there you may be certain of one vote for Van Buren."[24] But they played both sides on alcohol: William Henry Harrison, who had triggered the backlash for judicial elections in Indiana as the "Virginia Aristocrat" territorial governor, won the presidency with a frontier campaign theme of "Log Cabin and Hard Cider." Whigs also made the corruption of appointments a central message, attacking "the vain and insolent aristocracy of federal office holders."[25] The Whigs had adjusted to the new political climate, and by the mid-1840s, they were open to direct democracy, especially where it served their partisan interests.[26]

The Anti-Rent crisis, a tenant farmer uprising in upstate New York, was another powerful force pulling the Whigs toward populism and judicial elections. The Anti-Rent movement was the "most spectacular tenant rebellion in United States history," a popular mobilization of 10,000 tenant families and tens of thousands of their supporters in the Hudson Valley against an unfair property regime held over from the Dutch colonial aristocracy.[27] A few very wealthy Dutch families held their tenants to their land under extraordinary terms—binding generations to the land with bizarre requirements, such as requiring the tenants to deliver a specific number of chickens or other livestock on specific dates. The landowners turned to the court system to sue the farmers for failing to pay their debts. The farmers organized a massive rent strike that often turned violent. In 1845, the new Anti-Rent Party won seven state assembly seats, one state senate seat, and one seat in Congress.[28] The Whigs and the Anti-Renters made strange bedfellows, but they had just enough in common: The Whigs were more supportive of the Anti-Renters' legislative proposals, and both opposed the Hunker-dominated courts.[29] The Anti-Rent movement was at its zenith in 1845–1846, but it was not actually a cause of the convention.[30] Still, the Anti-Renters pulled the Whigs further toward populist reform, because some Anti-Renters had joined the Whigs formally, and because the tenant farmers offered an opportunity for Whigs to grow their base. By the time the convention met, the Whigs had many strategic, symbolic, and coalitional reasons to support judicial elections.

The next step toward judicial elections emerged in a factional struggle among the Democrats. In the middle of the depression, the Democratic Party was fracturing bitterly into two competing camps. The Hunkers, the conservative faction, had been more powerful than the radical factions, the Loco Focos and Barnburners, since the 1830s.[31] The first and only Democrat with Barnburner leanings to serve a full term as governor was elected in 1845, soon before the convention. In the midst of crisis over internal improvements and state debt, the Barnburners gained momentum, and the convention campaign played to all of their strengths and best issues. They campaigned so effectively that they overwhelmed the Hunkers and commanded a plurality at the convention of 1846.

The Panics and the depression of the 1840s led the way directly to New York's constitutional convention of 1846. In one prominent call for a convention, a New Yorker wrote in the *Democratic Review* (a Barnburner-affiliated magazine) that there were few calls for constitutional reform "until after the state had been threatened with bankruptcy," because of "the improvidence of the Legislature in contracting debts on behalf of the state."[32] The Barnburners took advantage of this call for change, running against the establishment free-spending Hunkers and Whigs. The *Democratic Review*'s motto was "The best government is that which governs least,"[33] reflecting the Barnburners' ideology of limited government.

Nevertheless, a convention was not inevitable. Most Democrats in the legislature did not want a convention.[34] Even the radical Barnburners took a more incrementalist approach, proposing a series of constitutional amendments rather than a full-blown convention. The first item on their agenda was a limit on the legislature's spending power. One antidebt solution was called "stop-and-tax,"[35] which required taxation to cover each spending measure, similar to modern "pay-as-you-go" proposals. In fact, the Barnburners even used "pay as it goes" to explain their fiscally conservative approach.[36] In addition, the proposal required public approval by referendum for large expenses.[37] Even though some Barnburners had supported judicial elections, they did not propose an amendment for such a change. Other amendments were a higher priority, so judicial elections were merely on the backburner for the Barnburners.[38]

Many Whigs supported the substance of the Barnburners' proposed amendments, but they did not vote for them. Instead, the Whigs gambled by voting against them, hoping to force the Barnburners to support a convention in order to adopt these changes.[39] As the minority party, the Whigs took a big risk, because the Democrats had a good chance of controlling the new convention and consolidating even more power. The Whigs were betting that they could play the Hunkers and the Barnburners against each other in a convention. The Whigs bet wisely: The Barnburners switched to supporting a convention as soon as they lost in the legislature, and they were eager to take on the Hunkers.

In November 1845, the voters approved the referendum calling for a convention by a sweeping vote of 213,257 to 33,860, almost a seven-to-one margin. Apparently, the Hunkers had been oblivious to public opinion by opposing a convention for so long. The special election for convention delegates was set for April 1846. In the planning for that election, the pro-Hunker New York Supreme Court intervened in the apportionment of delegates in favor of the Hunkers. The Hunkers had a longstanding monopoly on supreme court appointments, as they had in most appointed offices. In 1846, all three supreme court judges were Hunkers, and the three before them had been conservative Democrats, too. Judge Samuel Beardsley was an especially notorious Hunker on the court with a history of proslavery violence. As a Democratic congressman in 1835, he led a riot against the New York Anti-Slavery Society, destroying their press and their homes, and driving them out of Utica.[40] Despite this background—or perhaps because of it—Hunker Governor William Bouck appointed him to the New York Supreme Court in 1844.

The Barnburners already distrusted the Hunker Supreme Court, but this animosity increased right before the convention. This court unanimously apportioned the delegates based upon the 1836 legislative apportionment, rather than the 1846 legislative apportionment. The 1836 apportionment would have favored the Whigs first and the Hunkers second, and would have hurt the Barnburners, whereas the 1846 apportionment, taking into account the growth of New York City, would have favored the Barnburners the most. Even though the state had completed the apportionment for the legislature meeting in 1846, the Hunker judges ruled that because the legislature proposed the convention and the voters approved the proposal in 1845, the convention "shall be held in accordance with the provisions of the act of 1845," meaning that the 1836 apportionment was the relevant one.[41] The legal and logical basis for this decision was dubious. The factional basis for the decision was more apparent. At the last minute, the High Court of Errors, which included the full senate, overturned the supreme court's ruling, and the convention followed the more recent apportionment.[42] But Barnburner anger still smoldered. A Barnburner newspaper railed against the Hunker Supreme Court's "subversion of law" and called for the judges' ouster.[43]

However, impeachment was not necessary. Another way of getting rid of these judges was creating a new court, and a way of reducing the chance of Hunkers making it onto the new court was replacing the appointment system (which Hunkers had mastered) with elections (in which Barnburners had an advantage). The convention became the Barnburners' "bench-clearing brawl." In fact, the campaign literally became a brawl in Albany in March 1846. When the Albany Democrats met to nominate their delegates, violence broke out between the Hunkers and Barnburners. "Hard knock-down blows, and other violent demonstrations, were the order of the day," wrote the politically neutral *New York*

True Sun. The Hunkers were "routed and driven off the field," and the two factions met separately, plotting campaigns against each other.[44] The *True Sun* condemned this "spirit of demagoguism which has brought about this prostitution of public interests till it has ripened into open violence and riot."[45]

The newspapers did not report on individual delegates' races, but they did lay out the campaign themes and issues for each faction. The Barnburners explicitly called for judicial elections from the very beginning of the campaign, and they denounced the Hunkers for not embracing this proposal.[46] Barnburner newspapers mocked the Hunkers for being so similar to the Whig candidates, including their opposition to judicial elections.[47] If any Barnburners had doubts about judicial elections or their dislike for their fellow Democrats, the Hunker judges and brawlers surely removed those doubts.

Barnburning the Convention

The apportionment decision was not the last foray of the supreme court's Hunkers into the convention debate. Two of the three judges ran to be delegates. Chief Judge Greene Bronson and Judge Samuel Beardsley, the proslavery riot-leader, ran in Oneida County as part of the "Supreme Court" Party, as well as the "Old Hunker" or "Conservative" Party. In these races, Radical voters defected, splitting the Democratic vote. Both judges placed a distant second to the Whig candidates.[48] These races offer a hint at a general pattern that determined the overall composition of the convention: Barnburners voted strategically to defeat the Hunker Democrats, even if it meant more Whigs winning.

It turns out that the Barnburners did not simply sabotage the Hunkers. In a stunning upset, the Radicals were able to dominate the elections to the 1846 convention, winning fifty-two seats (41 percent), compared to the Hunkers' paltry seventeen seats (13 percent), and the Whigs' fifty seats (39 percent).[49] The convention immediately reflected a Radical agenda, and secondarily a Whig agenda. One of the most important law periodicals of the time reported:

> The four principal circumstances which led to the convocation of the body were the alleged abuses in the contraction of debt by the legislature; the accumulation of offices in the gift of the executive; the enormous growth of corporations together with the alleged irresponsibility of the banking companies; and the delays of right in the courts of justice. These were the principal sources of complaint. . . . [They] were beyond all doubt the real motives in the public mind.[50]

The Radicals opposed debt, state banks, and corporate monopoly power. The Radicals and Whigs together wanted to dismantle the Hunkers' executive patronage machine, and both supported streamlining the justice system. Judicial elections were not a high priority of either part of this alliance, but they were an important means for achieving their larger goals of separating powers and increasing judicial power.

The "People's Constitution," as the Barnburners named their work, reflected their goals of limiting government and regulation, with some Whig compromises mixed in. The Barnburners' chief accomplishment was constitutionalizing the stop-and-tax fiscal limits, which required popular referenda to approve new debts. For canal building, they entrenched (so to speak) strict budgeting rules and popular elections for canal commissioners and other formerly appointed officials. The Barnburners also constitutionalized the Free Bank Law of 1838 (which had been legislated after the Panic of 1837), sharply restricting special incorporation and charters, and adopting general incorporation statutes. Each statute would be limited to a single subject, making it more difficult for legislators to "logroll" and sneak less popular provisions into more popular bills, or otherwise bundle together compromise packages. Numerous other measures limited taxing, spending, and other specific legislative powers. The convention limited the traditional police powers that states had used to regulate daily life. Barnburners and Anti-Rent Whigs fought for measures that abolished the feudal forms of property that had caused the upstate Anti-Rent uprising, although these reforms offered little relief from preexisting leases, consistent with the doctrine of vested property rights.[51]

Most interesting was a new provision abolishing "all offices for the weighing, gauging, measuring, culling, or inspecting any merchandise, produce, manufacture, or commodity whatever."[52] This clause reflected three important goals of the 1846 convention: the dismantling of the Hunker patronage machine that multiplied state offices and filled them with partisans; limiting state expenses; and reducing state regulation that delegates believed had been corrupted by self-dealing, favoritism, and bribery. Together, these impulses drove an antiregulation, antilegislation ideology.[53] One delegate offered a defense of the free market:

> The acuteness of the great body of the people render them perfectly capable of taking care of themselves in all the transactions of life; and we have laws to enforce the fulfillment of contracts according to their plain, obvious and honest import. That is all the interference of government that is desired or wanted.[54]

New York's Barnburner constitution expanded individual property rights, limited state debt, and curtailed government powers generally. But that constitution was mere paper without judges willing to enforce it against the legislature. Thus, the convention devoted a lot of energy to the judiciary. The calls for a new convention often cited the inefficient and unresponsive court system, and particularly delays and exorbitant costs in the state's highest court, which was unironically called "the Court of Errors."[55] The court's full name was "the Court for the Trial of Impeachments and Correction of Errors," and it heard appeals from the Supreme Court of Judicature. It consisted of the lieutenant governor, the senators, the chancellor, and the supreme court justices. The Court of Errors was based partly on the colonial court of the royal governor and council, and partly on the English House of Lords, a body mostly of legislators who also served as the highest judges.[56] On the Court of Errors, elected officials (the senators) outnumbered appointed judges by a margin of five to one.[57] Thus, it is somewhat misleading to say that New York did not have elected judges until 1846, because most of the members of the state's highest court were elected. Advocates of judicial elections at the convention argued that the state had been voting for the senators on the Court of Errors for years, so electing judges would be no major change.[58] Given the amount of error by the Court of Errors, the convention delegates might have concluded that popular elections were part of the problem. Instead, they thought more elections would be part of the solution.

Together, the Whigs and Radical Democrats had an overwhelming majority in favor of judicial elections. The only debate was how to iron out a compromise between the Whigs' proposals for districted elections and Barnburners' preference for statewide elections.[59] Delegates from both parties argued that judicial elections would also strengthen the separation of powers and encourage the courts to check the legislature and strike down more statutes. The opposition to judicial elections in New York's 1846 convention offered the expected arguments in favor of judicial independence. Charles Kirkland, a conservative Whig lawyer on the judiciary committee, argued alliteratively that elections would lead judges "to yield to the popular caprices, or prejudices, or passions of a particular period."[60] Conservative Democrat Charles O'Conor, also a lawyer on the judiciary committee, continued the same argument against the populist bias created by judicial elections, referring to their effects as "evils."[61] Horatio Stow, a young Whig lawyer, focused on the "wide and decided distinction" between a judge's role and that of a governor or a legislator: "A majority elect the legislature and executive; and the reasons for this are very obvious. But a very different mode of selecting the Judges should be adopted. They are as the shield of the minority; to protect from the oppression (if tried) of the majority."[62]

Later, Stow added that an elective judiciary assumed "the right of the majority to be represented on the bench—whereas it was the law only that should be represented."[63] Stow believed that judges had counter-majoritarian duties to the rule of law and individual rights, and that judicial elections would allow public passions to undermine those principles.

A few delegates happily conceded that judicial elections were designed to limit judicial independence and the "aristocratic" courts in the name of the people.[64] However, more delegates argued that judicial elections promoted judicial independence and strengthened the constitution and the courts.[65] Both Barnburners and Whigs decried the Hunker patronage machine, which used appointments to promote its own interests and to keep judges in line.[66] They denounced the judicial appointment process for putting party insiders on the bench, rather than "the best men."[67] One delegate complained, "Who selects most of your judges now? The politicians of a party caucus."[68] A Radical leader added, "Judges were not only appointed on party grounds, but they were also removed to subserve party purposes. . . . This system . . . *must* be abolished."[69]

Radical Democrats generally opposed the power of elites, but many of these populists argued for giving more power to judges. Michael Hoffman, one of the top Radical leaders in the convention, argued that judicial elections were necessary to strengthen a judiciary that had been too permissive of legislative abuses in the past. Hoffman was a small-town lawyer before he linked up with Martin Van Buren's faction as it rose to power in the 1820s. He had written in 1842 that "under the pretence of public works equally useful to all and charging all with taxes[, insiders and corrupt legislators] have authorized such [projects] as are only beneficial to certain *districts* and *persons*."[70] As a result, he became an adherent of Adam Smith's *Wealth of Nations* and laissez-faire philosophy, and was the chief leader of the fiscally conservative "stop-and-tax" movement in the early 1840s. As the convention began, Hoffman wrote two articles laying out the Barnburner agenda, with twelve detailed pages on law reform. He complained that the judicial system had collapsed due to "an unfortunate use of the patronage of the courts." He also blamed the legislature's "unlimited power to create debts," often spent to purchase political support, for "failures, frauds, and crimes most appalling." His solution was to separate the powers by ending the senators' role in the Court for the Correction of Errors, to "stringently limit[]" the legislature, and to empower the courts to engage in "Judicial Legislation" in order to reverse "unjust" rules and laws. Hoffman, seeking more limited government, wanted a stronger court exercising judicial review more aggressively on behalf of "the people" and against special interests.[71]

In the convention itself, Hoffman was the leading voice for judicial elections. Hoffman conceded that he never would have supported judicial elections "if some strong and irrepressible evil did not require it," but maintained that the abuse of legislative power was such an evil. He recognized that, in an ideal world, legislatures should be trusted to legislate, and judges should merely interpret and apply the legislation. However, New Yorkers could no longer trust their legislators. The convention thus made the new legislature "less powerful . . . than it should be," and by "inevitable necessity, if the judges should not find the rule fixed by society itself, that [the judges] must make the law." Hoffman did not envision a passive judiciary that would defer to "the people," but rather, an activist judiciary making "judicial legislation" based on the judges' understanding of "natural right" as set by "God himself."[72] The theory was the judicial elections would install wiser and more virtuous judges onto the bench, and with more popular legitimacy, these judges would be inspired to act more boldly. "In reorganizing the legislative department, we have made it less powerful for general legislation. . . . [Thus] a large share of judicial legislation will be inevitable, and we must endeavor to supply it." Hoffman envisioned the elected judges acting as a superpopular superlegislature.[73]

Most fundamentally, elected judges would defend the written constitution against usurpations of power:

> There can be no Constitution in this country, unless the judges, or part of them, can be made to depend for their offices upon the people of the state. I looked in vain in any state, in our own state, or in the federal power, for a judiciary that had been able to stand by a Constitution, and to defend it against [legislative] usurpation. . . . [U]nless your judges are elected by the sovereign body, by the constituent, you will look in vain for judges [who] can stand by the constitution of the State against the encroachments of power.

Hoffman conceded that judicial appointments produced judges of "talent and integrity" and "intellect," but he concluded that these judges had not used their power to protect the people's rights.[74] Churchill Cambreleng, another leader of the Radical Democrats in the convention, denounced the "unrestricted and unlimited . . . legislative despotism" and argued that the new constitution would give the courts a popular foundation comparable to that of the other branches. The convention moved without much debate to switch from "good behavior" life commissions to eight-year terms, which diminished general judicial independence, but which also gave judges a similar popular foundation to legitimate their increased democratic power versus the legislature. The Barnburner theory of popular constitutionalism depended on elections and reelections to connect the judges to the people and to energize them.[75]

The Whig coalition included more legal conservatives, but they also vocally supported judicial elections. They resolved this apparent conflict by emphasizing that judicial elections protected judicial independence and the separation of powers. Whigs embraced the same message that judicial elections would lead to aggressive judicial review for the protection of individual rights.[76] Even the populist Anti-Rent delegates, who sought legislative solutions to the upstate tenant crisis, echoed the same goals of *increasing* judicial independence and power.[77] The Anti-Rent movement had been clashing with courts for years, whether in a futile search for a legal remedy for their subservient feudal relationships with landowners, or in the criminal convictions that resulted from their protests. Even though judicial review threatened their legislative proposals, the Anti-Rent delegates still embraced judicial power with the hope that they could win judicial elections and wield that power against the landlords.[78] One Whig Anti-Renter declared that judicial elections would liberate judges from partisan interests and "increase[] fidelity" to the people.[79] No doubt, the "people" for him meant the tenant farmers, but more generally, he imagined judges who would use their increased power for the public interest.

Even one of the most influential Hunkers in the convention, Charles Ruggles, called for more judicial resistance to legislation and for an end to the presumption that statutes were valid. His argument was that judges chosen by legislators would be too deferential to the legislature and fearful of its wrath.[80] And even the original conservative opponents, O'Conor and Kirkland, abandoned their criticism of the "evils" of judicial elections, and in the end voted in favor of them.

As the convention concluded, the delegates spoke for themselves. They included an official "Address of the Convention to the People" as they sent their draft to the people for ratification. The very first sentence of this address declared that the convention "wholly separated" the legislature from the judicial power, and then proclaimed that "after repeated failures in the legislature, [we] have provided a judicial system, adequate to the wants of a free people." The address then touted the new constitution's measures "to reduce and decentralize the patronage of the Executive," with judicial elections being part of that solution. It proceeded to emphasize all the ways that the new constitution limited legislative power and protected individual rights: "They have incorporated many useful provisions more effectually to secure the people in their rights of person and property against the abuses of delegated power."[81]

After the convention, the Barnburners promoted this reform by touting judicial elections as the separation of powers and the increasing of judicial power. One Democratic paper explained, without popular elections:

The vital principle of a republic—the separation and division of powers, has been sported with and set at nought. . . . [T]hat very branch of the government which is the most important of all others—which gives force and efficiency to the laws—which administers justice between man and man, and keeps the other departments from shooting madly from the spheres allotted to them, is the very one, which has been removed beyond the reach of all responsibility.[82]

In this context, responsibility to the other branches was the problem, and responsiveness to the people was the solution.

In the end, the voters ratified the "People's Constitution" by an overwhelming vote of 221,528 to 92,436.[83] The final result was a high court, called the "Court of Appeals," and a trial court system, oddly called the "Supreme Court," with eight geographic districts, each with four justices. On both levels, judges were elected to eight-year terms. The court of appeals had four permanent judges elected statewide, who were joined by four justices of the lower supreme court on a rotating basis annually. The combination of statewide elections and district elections was a compromise between Democrats and Whigs to balance their partisan interests, but the apparent big winners were the Barnburners. They had removed the despised Hunker judges from their life-tenured seats without having to impeach them, and Hunkers could no longer rely on their beloved appointment spoils system to get their jobs back. The voters had catapulted the Barnburners into power at the convention, and the Barnburners believed the voters would come through for them again in the next elections.

Things did not turn out as the Barnburners had imagined. During the first statewide party conventions to nominate judicial candidates, both parties were plagued by disunity and factional fighting. Some Whigs rejected the calls for party solidarity, and instead supported the Democratic ticket because it was more experienced and had better candidates. Other Whigs suggested that the Democrats join them in nominating a unity ticket "as may be satisfactory to the good men of all parties." This overture was partly tactical (considering the Whigs' electoral disadvantage), but the Whigs offered a valid criticism of the effects of partisan elections: "There is a great danger [when] a judge [is] nominated by a party only, and elected by that party and dependent upon that party for re-election, [and] may be more or less . . . prejudiced." The next day, a Whig editorial decried the partisanship that was dominating the election process, warning that judicial elections, "an anomaly in government that has never been tried," would "prostrate[] all those safeguards" of judicial independence.[84]

The Whigs may have had second thoughts about their partisan strategy supporting local judicial elections, because they realized that they were going to lose many of those elections, and because the Democratic factions were intent on playing hardball. The Democrats rejected the Whig proposal for a unity ticket as an elite-brokered subversion of competitive democracy. They contended that "any other mode of appointment other than by popular election would be an abrogation of that instrument as to the provision in question." The Democrats were not just rejecting unity with the Whigs—they were rejecting unity among themselves. The Hunkers and Barnburners organized separate conventions throughout the state. Dismissing the Whig overtures, the Democrats had embraced partisanship as a positive term, and likewise, both the Hunkers and Barnburners criticized each other's separate conventions as being "nonpartisan"— using the term pejoratively to signify a lack of partisan loyalty.[85]

The Hunkers pushed through the official nomination of four Hunkers for the four court of appeals spots, in part because the Hunker candidates had more judicial experience, and in part because Hunkers continued to control the established party machinery.[86] Frustrated, the Barnburners divided the party by running their own candidates for the general election in many races.[87] The Barnburners also returned to their strategy of supporting Whig candidates when it would hurt the Hunkers.[88] But the Barnburner strategy did not work out as well a year after the convention. Turnout for the July judicial elections was poor, and the Barnburners were routed.[89] Out of the blue, 1846 was a spectacular peak for the Barnburners, but 1847 was the beginning of their demise. The Hunkers won most of the 1847 races, and Barnburners never again saw nearly as much power as they had in the 1846 convention. By 1850, they effectively disappeared as a faction. A few years later, the Whigs also faded. After several years on the sidelines, ex-Barnburners and ex-Whigs returned to power in the Republican Party coalition.[90]

Coda: Codification and Trigger

The New York convention set the stage for another legal landmark: codification. In the early nineteenth century, codification was another tool for democratic control of the courts. Codes were comprehensive statutes that would replace areas of the judges' common law and its technicalities. Since the Founding era, the codification movement argued that law codes would elevate the people and their elected legislators over the unrepresentative judges. But the movement achieved little, even at the height of Jeffersonian and Jacksonian democratization. Then, in a rare victory for the codification movement, the 1846 constitution permitted the legislature to enact a legal code, and established a commission to draft that code. David Dudley Field, a New York Barnburner lawyer who tirelessly campaigned for codification, led the drafting of New York's Code of Civil Procedure—known as the Field Code. On the one hand, the code was a breakthrough for modernizing and simplifying the courts. Over the 1850s, it spread to a handful of midwestern and western states. On the other hand, the constitution limited the code to "the rules of practice, pleadings, forms and proceedings."[91] The constitutional convention had taken substance off the table, and at most, Field's committee could only squeeze in some substantive changes under the guise of procedure. The other states' codes were similarly restricted.[92]

The movement may have had a limited impact because judges and lawyers defused the codifiers' critiques by co-opting their ideas and incorporating some of their reforms.[93] Codification might also have buckled under the weight of the Field committee's unwieldy code, which was so long that it did not appear to simplify anything. The Panics offer another explanation for why populists in New York and around the country were so cautious about codes, not judicial elections. After the legislatures' disgrace in the 1840s, reformers had less faith in legislatures. They had more hope that judges, once they were elected, would respond to the people on issues of substance. Codification threatened to elevate the legislature over the courts and to reverse the separation of powers. The movement for judicial elections gained steam because it could go in the opposite direction: it could further separate the branches and it could increase the power of common-law judges to impose limits on legislators. Because the powerful force of this era was judicial independence, not judicial acquiescence, judicial elections overtook codification as the wave of reform.

After New York, constitutional conventions and judicial elections swept the country, demonstrating the power of bandwagons and the cascade effect. Some have questioned whether New York influenced other states, but the state convention debates frequently relied on other states' practices, especially New York's.[94] Many conventions studied and copied New York's new constitution. Wisconsin's delegates met just months later, and they focused closely on New York's work. Migrants from New York had settled much of Wisconsin, and they won a large number of seats in the Wisconsin convention. They even called themselves "Barnburners," "Loco Focos," and "Hunkers," and then they copied many of New York's constitutional provisions.[95] New Yorkers also settled other parts of the Midwest. Delegates in Illinois in 1847[96] and in Maryland in 1850[97] and commentators in Pennsylvania in 1847[98] sought support from New York's judicial elections, and in 1849, California's delegates drew heavily from New York's new constitution.[99] New York's adoption was pivotal in lending credibility to judicial elections and demonstrating that voters could be trusted to choose established, experienced, and qualified candidates.

Without a convention, New York's reformers would have been stuck with a more limited amendment process, and they would have invested energy on higher-profile fiscal issues. Without a convention, New York's populist factions in each party would not have gained enough control to reform the courts. And without New York's convention, judicial elections would have been perceived as a peculiar institution marginalized in pockets of the frontier. Reformers in other states probably would not have gained the political cover and inspiration to push for the same risky revolution in judicial politics. New York's Barnburners and Whig-Anti-Renters triggered more than a convention; they triggered a national revolution in judicial politics.

CHAPTER FIVE

The American Revolutions of 1848

I N THE REVOLUTIONS OF 1848, popular uprisings swept most of Europe. The urban poor, peasants, the working class, middle-class reformers, and socialists rose up in arms against their monarchies and nobility. The United States has been contrasted with Europe for its lack of violence in these years.[1] Nevertheless, Americans had their own overlooked revolutions midcentury. While Europe's poor and lower middle classes arose with the sword, their ethnonationalist leaders also arose with the pen, writing more than twenty new constitutions.[2] Many Americans also took up the same pen of constitution writing. The sheer volume of revisions between 1844 and 1853 was unprecedented. Soon after the depression ended, the states turned to constitutional conventions for long-term solutions. Twelve existing states adopted new constitutions with more widespread democratic power, and four states entered the Union with new constitutions.[3] In 1848, the Democratic Party platform hailed the European revolutions for following the principle of "the sovereignty of the people," just as American states were increasing popular sovereignty through new constitutions.[4] Democratic rhetoric reached an even higher pitch, with some skeptics complaining that the public was getting "carried away by the humbug of those omnipotent though often meaningless terms 'people's rights,' reform and democracy."[5] The people had become "a mystical entity of the popular consciousness," a "unified, morally infallible entity" that was "mainly myth."[6] But the myth was powerful.

These forgotten American revolutionaries were fiscally conservative and skeptical of government regulation. They reflected the classic Jacksonian opposition to "class legislation" and special interests, and some of them also adhered to a broader free market ideology. In the state constitutional conventions occurring between 1800 and 1830, the expansion of suffrage and legislative reapportionment were among the most important issues.[7] In the wave of conventions in the 1840s, however, the bipartisan focus was on limiting legislatures and restraining government.[8] In the wake of the economic crisis, "businessmen were heroes and politicians were villains, a balanced budget was a mark of state morality, and the menace of communism was . . . ground for constitutional argument. . . . [T]his philosophy comes closer to fitting the 'laissez-faire' label."[9] De Tocqueville had remarked in 1835 that "the legislature of each state is faced by no power capable of resisting it."[10] De Tocqueville had not seen the power of state conventions, which a decade later were capable of curtailing the legislatures. One Ohio delegate complained in 1850, "I wish to see the State Government brought back to its simple and appropriate functions, [leaving] railroad, canal, turnpike and other corporate associations, to get along on their own credit, without any connection or partnership with the State whatever."[11] An Indiana delegate in 1850 explained:

> The great vice of republics, of all popular governments, is excessive legislation. This is an evil which has afflicted our State, and all the States. It has cried aloud for correction. The new Constitutions have provided various means for the prevention of hasty, injudicious, fraudulent, or unconstitutional legislation. This has been one of the great objects of constitutional reform. A single bad law may, in mere money, cost the people of the State more than many sessions of the Legislature. Dearly has this State paid for improvident legislation.[12]

The conventions focused on limiting the legislatures and regulating their power to regulate. An example of "horizontal federalism," states learned from one another's mistakes in the 1830s and borrowed heavily from one another's constitutional innovations in the 1840s and early 1850s.[13] The conventions restricted state debt and eliminated "taxless finance." Similar to the "stop-and-tax" measure in New York's 1846 convention, the new state constitutions required states and localities to tax to cover all spending, and to hold referenda to authorize tax increases. The conventions restricted state debt and mandated equal taxation across the state. Most conventions prohibited "special incorporation," by which a set of investors had been given special privileges and sometimes monopolies. Special incorporation had been identified with cronyism and corruption, whereas the new general incorporation rules gave more open access to the public for entrepreneurship and investment. The conventions adopted broader procedural restraints on legislatures, including supermajority voting rules on particular issues and recorded votes legislator by legislator for taxing and spending measures. The constitutions shortened legislative sessions and permitted fewer amendments and fewer meetings (moving from annual sessions to biannual sessions), making it more difficult for legislatures to legislate. New constitutional provisions required more debate, more open deliberation, more readings of the bills, single subject per bill, and accurate titles and plain language for bills, as well as imposing other obstacles to legislation and measures for greater transparency. In the 1850s, therefore, it became much harder to regulate, to spend state money, and to make deals behind closed doors.[14]

Judicial elections were a part of this antilegislature agenda. The constitutional revolutionaries of the time believed elected judges were more likely to enforce limits against legislative excesses. From 1846 to 1851, twelve states adopted judicial elections for their entire court systems, and five states adopted partially elective systems. By 1860, out of thirty-one states in the Union, eighteen states elected all of their judges, and five more elected some of their judges. There were also proposals to subject federal judges to election, but the federal constitution was far more difficult to change.[15] (See Appendix A for a chronological list.)

The convention delegates heard the counterargument: If you can't trust the legislators whom the people elect, why trust the judges whom the people would elect? Another version of this argument in defense of appointments was that the people should simply elect better governors who would appoint better judges.[16] The delegates answered with a version of the principal/agent problem: The people are the principal, and the more removed the agents (i.e., the judges) are from the principal, the more they will stray from the principal's control. Judicial appointments add a layer of removal from the people and make the judges the agents of the governor and legislature more than of the people. Judicial elections would make the judges more direct agents of the people.[17] But they believed this relationship did more than simply foster accountability. They believed it would foster a more confident, pure, professional judiciary that would actually rise above politics and would be faithful to legal principle and "science" instead.[18]

More Judicial Review and More Judicial Power

The conventions offered powerful mandates for more judicial review: a mandate for creating new substantive and procedural limits on legislative power, and a mandate for creating a new institution (the elected judiciary) to make those paper limits a reality. This double mandate was a strong expressive signal to judges to assert themselves for the people, and that is exactly what the judges did. The delegates set forth a three-step theory for judicial elections to encourage more judicial review: elections would free judges from legislative control; elections would embolden judges by providing them with popular legitimacy; and voters would reward judges who defended popular constitutional rights and punish those who did not. Over the first half of the nineteenth century, the courts had been gaining a higher profile, from the Marshall Court's interventions to a gradually increasing number of state court decisions striking down statutes. Instead of extinguishing this fire, the Revolutionaries of 1848 wanted to fan those flames and blow them in a certain direction: at the legislatures.

In the Illinois convention of 1847, future U.S. Supreme Court Justice David Davis complained that appointed judges had "none of the confidence of the people," whereas elected judges "would always receive the support and protection of the people." He acknowledged that elected judges might abuse their power, but he said he "would rather see judges the weather-cocks of public sentiment, in preference to seeing them the instruments of power, to see them registering the mandates of the Legislature, and the edicts of the Governor." If the federal judges were elected, the people "would have chosen judges, instead of broken down politicians" nominated by the president.[19]

Soon after, an Illinois opponent of judicial elections mocked the supporters for "preach[ing] to us continually—distrust to the Legislature."[20] But "distrust to the Legislature" was the prevailing mood of this period:

> The object of the distribution of powers of the government was that the one department may check another. Suppose you give a few men the power to make laws and carry them into execution, it is simple and plain. Why not try that government? Because those few men may become corrupt. Gentlemen say, Let the Legislature and the Governor pass the laws, and before those laws can go into effect, the judiciary must give them an approval; therefore the judiciary has a control over the others.[21]

Delegates throughout these conventions argued for judicial elections to increase courts' independence and their power to check the legislature. In Indiana, supporters of judicial elections warned that, unless judges were removed from "the control of the other branches of the government," the state constitution's promises "to protect the rights of the people, and to preserve a proper equilibrium between the different departments" would be no more than "parchment barriers."[22] In Kentucky, Virginia, Ohio, and Maryland, delegates offered similar arguments for judicial independence and judicial power. Virginia's 1850 convention adopted judicial elections and explicitly introduced within its courts' appellate jurisdiction cases involving "the constitutionality of a law." Earlier Virginia constitutions had not mentioned such a power.[23]

The European Revolutions of 1848 had their various manifestos, including Karl Marx and Friedrich Engels's *The Communist Manifesto*. The American Revolutions of 1848 also had a manifesto, Samuel Medary's *The New Constitution*. In 1849, Medary edited and published a series of pamphlets calling for a constitutional convention in Ohio, which he distributed nationally.[24] As it turns out, Medary later became the proslavery governor of Kansas during its infamous "Bloody Kansas" battles in the late 1850s. *The New Constitution* reflects no proslavery agenda, but it does have some essays opposing black suffrage. *The New Constitution*'s issues frequently celebrated the European Revolutions as prodemocracy and antidespotism, in a manner consistent with the paper's antilegislature and antiregulation perspective.[25] *The New Constitution* reported on American "riot, confusion and violent contention" and "the cry of *revolution* which has come up from almost every part of the State" of Ohio. Instead, it called for a revolution "through the ballot box, what other nations and States are struggling to accomplish with the sword."[26] Writers often juxtaposed their peaceful movement for constitutional reform against European "anarchy and violence."[27] They reported on the details of New York's new constitution and celebrated its willingness to "dare[] the experiment" in electing judges.[28] *The New Constitution* regularly reported on the constitutional reforms in every region of the country and collected articles from other states making the same arguments against legislatures and for judicial power.[29]

Medary and his fellow writers were populist Democrats, but they still embraced stronger courts and judicial review. "Judicial independence" was a slogan throughout their essays, often in terms of general independence and increased job security. They called for judges' salaries to be constitutionally protected and increased, and for judges to serve longer terms with the goal of attracting better candidates and strengthening their hands.[30] More often, they focused on relative independence from the legislature. Again and again, *The New Constitution*'s essays railed against legislative excesses. Each issue was filled with statements like the following: "'The people are governed too much.' . . . We have too much law. . . . Give us but few laws and a simple government, and the people will be prosperous, happy and contented."[31] "Too much Legislation is the bane of all Republics."[32] "That Government is best which governs least."[33] In one issue, *The New Constitution* argued:

> The great evil of all free governments is a tendency to *over-legislation*. . . .
> [I]t is the people we would preserve from the tyranny of *legislators*. . . . Leg-
> islators also favored the tyranny of property in place of protecting the meri-
> torious and poor. . . . We want a Republican Constitution—laws few and
> simple—and above all, means devised to prevent the Legislature from heap-
> ing debts upon us. . . . We want a new Constitution, to give back to the
> people the power taken from them without their consent, to elect Judges. . . .
> As it now is, we see legislators spurning the good and wise [judicial candi-
> dates], and bribing men to become hypocrites, and to rob us, as has been
> done in our public works, where knaves have made fortunes in a few years
> out of the tax-ridden, oppressed people.[34]

The motto on its masthead in each issue was, "Power is always stealing
from the many to the few,"[35]and their chief villain was legislative power.

Some writers of *The New Constitution* favored debtors over creditors,
but even though judges in the past had blocked debtor relief, these writers still embraced judicial power. They called for judges' salaries to be
constitutionally protected and increased, and for judges to serve longer
terms with the goal of attracting better candidates and strengthening
their hands.[36] Writers claimed that the appointment process had filled the
bench with "broken down or defeated politicians," and argued that elections would "improve and heighten the character of our judiciary."[37]
They endorsed judicial review, even though in the past, they had bad experiences with courts striking down the prodebtor statutes that they had
supported. One writer, using the name "Madison," argued that judges—
even elected judges—were less politically biased than legislators, because
judges live up to the expectation of "honesty and integrity," and "a judge
should know and feel that the power conferred upon him is a *sacred*
trust." He emphasized the importance of the separation of powers and
the "duty of the Judicial branch to determine all questions of civil right."
Without judicial review, there would be "anarchy and many evils."[38] Another writer, "Veto," asked:

> Why have a constitution at all, if the legislature is unrestrained and may vio-
> late its plainest provisions with impunity? . . . Give [the judges] this power—
> make them elective by the people, and then indeed will we have an indepen-
> dent judiciary. But withhold it, and let the legislature continue to appoint
> them, and you make our judges mere tools in their hands—puppets who
> dance to any tune their masters play.[39]

The nom de plume "Veto" was appropriate because these writers adhered to a philosophy of negative liberty, championing more and more
hurdles against legislative action. The writers in *The New Constitution*
also called for expanding the governor's veto power, as a defense not

only for the "people's" rights, but also for "the rights of minorities."[40] Though most of the legal profession's periodicals opposed judicial elections, one major law journal endorsed judicial elections because they would increase judicial power and judicial review. It decried that appointments had "failed to secure either the independence of the Judiciary or the rights of the people."[41]

The convention delegates around the country shared *The New Constitution*'s view that the legislature was corrupt and incompetent. One Ohio delegate proposed:

> Whereas, There is a deep and just dissatisfaction amongst the people in regard to appointments to office—especially by the legislative department of government; converting that body, as they do to some extent, into a mere political arena, embittering the feelings of party spirit, and corrupting the pure fountain of legislation; Therefore—
> *Resolved*, That the new Constitution provide for the election of all State, County, and Township officers immediately by the people.[42]

Some Ohio delegates argued that a popularly elected court would better protect the rights of the people against the government. One declared that the courts should be "representatives of the people, [and] stand as sentinels to guard the constitutional rights of the people." The elected judges would be better able to protect "those great fundamental principles at the foundation of the State government, and preserve the landmarks of the Constitution."[43] Another Ohio delegate based stronger judicial review on a social contract argument:

> The people were the source of all power, and with the people should be left all power, except so far as it became necessary to take a part of it away in order to protect them in their rights and liberties under the form of a government. It became necessary that the people should delegate a part of the powers lodged with them, in order the more effectually to guard and protect them in that which they retained in their own hands.[44]

The new Ohio constitution limited legislative appointment powers, and restricted economic and special legislation.

A Massachusetts delegate contended that elected judges "will thus know that they are in the hands of the people, and knowing that, and feeling that their business is to administer the law to the people, they will be more likely to discharge their duties with fidelity" to the people.[45] In Pennsylvania, which adopted judicial elections by amendment, not in a recorded constitutional convention, the newspapers raised similar arguments to the public. When a Democrat was governor, Whig newspapers called for judicial elections so that judges would have more power and independence to check him.[46] Then, as soon as the Democratic governor died and was replaced by a Whig, Democratic newspapers adopted the same argument.[47] One Pennsylvania legislator argued, "Election always has and always will give us better men and better officers than appointment—more independent men, sir, for I hold a man elected to office by the will of the people, and having the confidence of the people, is freer to act than the autocrat of Russia."[48] A newspaper writer in Maryland argued that judicial elections fostered "human sympathy" on the bench, while appointments cultivated "selfishness, with all its little, bigoted, and concomitant auxiliaries."[49] Elections themselves shaped the judges' personalities and values. The *American Law Journal,* published in Philadelphia, embraced judicial elections because they would protect judicial power:

> When the Judges derive their authority immediately from the people, and can take an appeal to the same paramount power, the fear of removal . . . for resisting Legislative usurpations will no longer exist, and we shall probably hear less of the validity of retrospective acts destroying vested rights—of legislative reversals of Judgments without notice to the parties—and of other usurpations of Judicial power, under the new definition of *law,* that it is "a rule *postscribed*" instead of being "a rule *prescribed.*" It is a prevalent opinion that the present Judicial tenure has failed to secure either the independence of the Judiciary or the rights of the people.[50]

As the judicial election amendment was proceeding through its successive stages, an appointed justice on the Pennsylvania Supreme Court wrote:

> [Unconstitutional] retroactive legislation began and has been continued, because the judiciary has thought itself too weak to withstand; too weak, because it has neither the patronage nor the *prestige* necessary to sustain it against the antagonism of the legislature and the bar. Yet, had it taken its stand on the rampart of the constitution at the onset, there is some little reason to think it might have held its ground. Instead of that, it pursued a temporizing course till the mischief had become intolerable, and till it was compelled . . . to invalidate certain acts of legislation, or rather to reverse certain legislative decrees. . . . Yet the legislature attempted to divest it, by a general law it is true, but one impinging on particular rights.[51]

According to this appointed judge, the courts had lacked the confidence and "prestige" to confront the legislature over its constitutional encroachments until those abuses became intolerable.[52] Once a consensus emerged to curb the legislatures, judicial elections were one way of giving courts more confidence and democratic prestige. Prestige is often gained by eliteness, by rising above the people. But in mid-nineteenth-century America, it was "the people" who bestowed prestige with their ballots. Many delegates did not limit this authority to a narrow reading of the constitutional text. Some hoped that elected judges would use their new power to establish higher law. Michael Hoffman, the Radical who led the reform effort in New York, called for elected judges to engage in "judicial legislation" (that is, judicial lawmaking) and to enforce natural rights as "God himself" has established—a vision of transformative judicial power, not limitation.[53]

Separation of Law from Politics

Many scholars have contended that judicial elections were designed to reduce judicial independence and to make the courts more political. One has concluded that judicial elections were a Jacksonian reform to "rein in" the judges and "curtail[] the independent powers of judges themselves."[54] One piece of evidence for this interpretation is that in the courtroom, juries were increasing their power at the expense of judges. However, there are a few problems with this argument. The trend of weakening judges had preceded the Panics (such as the trend of switching "good behavior" tenure to shorter terms), and it largely was over by the time of the conventions of the 1840s–1850s.[55] Moreover, it is not clear that juries were gaining power relative to judges in the mid-nineteenth century. Juries gained power over fact-finding, but judges gained the exclusive power over "law-finding." Even in questions of fact, state judges increased their power with new procedures for jury instructions and for ruling on the sufficiency of the evidence. Moreover, the law of evidence emerged, giving judges more power to exclude evidence entirely from the jury fact-finder. Judges also gained dramatic new powers to direct verdicts (although a directed verdict was not at the time considered a binding final order) and to order new trials for verdicts "against law" or "against evidence."[56] By the 1830s, judges in many states routinely granted new trials for verdicts against the law, and the power was codified in New York's 1848 Field Code of Civil Procedure.[57] Judges also used interrogatories and special verdicts to guide and control juries.[58] The power to comment simply had shifted into new forms, as bold new judicial powers over juries. Judges were building their power over law, and judicial review was gradually increasing. If anything, the broader developments of nineteenth-century civil procedure confirmed that judges were gaining power over juries, as well as over other branches of government.

It might seem like common sense that the proelection delegates would have aimed to undermine the separation of law and politics. To the contrary, the convention delegates believed that appointments were a greater threat of politicizing the courts, and they believed—naïvely—that direct democracy would be better at insulating the courts. In these decades, the legal profession was building its own power and institutions, and it increasingly emphasized that law was different from politics.[59] Many convention delegates favored judicial elections not because they would merge law and politics, but because direct popular elections were better than insider appointments in protecting the unique judicial role from partisanship. In fact, the proelection delegates offered substantial arguments that appointments had been a greater threat to the rule of law. They emphasized that the "confidence of the people" would improve and strengthen the judiciary, and would make it less partisan than patronage appointments had.[60] Recall the Pennsylvania legislator who argued that the elected judge has "the confidence of the people" and thus "is freer to act than the autocrat of Russia."[61] Another advocate of judicial elections wrote that appointments had been "mercenary" and nepotistic, but voters go to the polls with no selfish bias whatever and would choose judges who "were the object of no personal or family partiality," and choose based upon "legal distinction," competence, and character. It would be "impossible" for such judges to display "unprincipled subserviency." This writer seemed to think judicial elections would lead to the best of both worlds. On the one hand, they would have attained "general popularity," but on the other hand, they would rise above politics and embrace the "professional, scientific, and extra-popular" expert role of the judge.[62] It may sound implausible that they believed popular elections would free judges from politics, but they had experienced the appointment process as so rotten that elections were purifying by comparison.

Vocal defenders of judicial elections in New York warned that, while the legislature preferred partisan judges, the voters would never tolerate partisan judges. "Nothing in this country would sooner seal the political doom of any judge, by all parties and every honest man, than the attempt to bend his decisions from the line of justice to make political capital. . . . He alone can be a popular judge who is honest, impartial, decided, and fearless."[63] They argued that "a faithful and independent judiciary" was vital to protecting constitutional rights of "the weak and defenceless" from political abuses.[64]

In short, they believed that the only kind of judge who is popular is an independent judge above politics, and elections, not appointments, would produce such a judge. The law periodicals of the time echoed the same view, arguing that the voters would pick "wiser and far better" judges than would legislators with their political "intrigue."[65] Such a judge would "be a bold man, utterly fearless in the discharge of duty, regardless of any thing but the right, and unmoved by fear, favor, or affection."[66] The supporters of judicial elections in other conventions echoed the views that judges had a unique and "strict" duty to rise above political pressure, and that voters would elect judges who performed these duties and toss out the ones who caved to politics.[67] These "countermajoritarian" defenses of judicial duties and judicial review—paradoxically used to defend direct judicial elections—would reemerge in the constitutional decisions of elected judges in the 1850s.

In hindsight, it is easy to question the faith among judicial election's supporters that directly elected judges would rise above partisanship. One might ask whether they were being disingenuous or simply naïve. It turns out they were sincere and sophisticated for their own time. It was the height of the second two-party system, and a much more fully participatory two-party system. These reformers believed that judicial elections with strong popular parties would lead to stronger courts and stronger constitutions. They embraced "partyism" as a means of protecting constitutional values. Some delegates surely believed that judicial elections would give their party a better chance of winning seats on the bench than appointments had, but this partisan strategy was probably a minor factor, because many proelection delegates belonged to the party already securely in power and expected to retain power. It is true that New York Radicals and Whigs opposed the Hunker monopoly of the courts, and that a major reason they favored judicial elections was to allow the Radicals and Whigs to gain seats on the bench. In addition, some have theorized that political leaders in power will prefer judicial independence when they foresee falling out of power and are risk averse.[68] It is likely that some delegates viewed judicial elections as insurance against the other party taking over the governorship. However, in several of the states adopting judicial elections, the Democrats had solid control of the governorship and the legislature, and would have foreseen maintaining control in the future.[69] Whigs had better chances with either statewide judicial races or in local judicial districts than with Democratic governors. Thus, the Democrats in these states took a greater risk in adopting judicial elections, so they had other reasons beyond partisan self-interest and risk aversion. Moreover, half a dozen states had a closer balance between the parties and had alternating control over the governorship and the legislature, but did not turn to judicial elections.[70] Thus, political insurance and partisan self-interest may have been additional precipitants in some states, but not a dominant factor overall.

At first glance, the convention delegates seem to have been critics of political parties. Opponents warned that, in popular elections, partisanship would take over the courts and would produce only "evil and evil continually."[71] Supporters argued that popular elections were simply the lesser evil: direct elections at least would be less partisan than appointments.[72] Whereas governors and legislators had exploited appointments for their own partisan benefit, the voters would be a check on party intrigue, cronyism, and abuse of power, even if parties played a major role in both systems.[73] The problems with party politics increased as direct popular control decreased. But with more direct control over partisan judicial elections, direct democracy through popular parties was perceived as a powerful mechanism for organizing the people against other monster institutions and against special interests. Some scholars have raised questions with impressive research about how deep and how widespread popular engagement actually was in this era.[74] Even if the reality was not the romanticized "golden age" of deeply meaningful popular participation, the leaders in these conventions reflect the belief that direct democracy through mobilized popular parties was still far more meaningful than the backroom insider politics of appointments, monster banks, and the interests.

This faith in party-run judicial elections reflects a long-term shift from the view that mass party politics threatened democracy to the view that mass party politics protected democracy.[75] In eighteenth-century England and America, the consensus was that organized political parties undermined authority, elevated faction above country, and subverted popular sovereignty. The Framers designed a "Constitution against Parties."[76] In the 1830s, a constitution *through* parties emerged.[77] Jacksonians (or more precisely, Van Burenites) feared that democratic government could not, by itself, withstand the overwhelmingly corrupting forces of the increasing concentration of wealth and corporate power and the seductiveness of banks, public projects, and self-dealing.[78] The only way to save democracy from a corrupt aristocracy was to counterbalance those forces with organized popular power: mass political parties. Parties could simultaneously concentrate political power for the people and also localize that power to mobilize the "country" against capture of the government by insider "court" parties and juntos. The only way to fight monster banks and monster corporations was with monster democracy: the political party.[79] By 1840, Illinois had a permanent two-party political system built on this ideology of parties as protectors of democracy and constitutional limits on power. Van Burenite Democrats mobilized their party to fight a powerful "Paper Aristocracy" (bank and corporate power and special privileges). Whigs mobilized their party to fight the "Spoils Aristocracy" (the Democrats' party machines that exploited appointments for patronage).[80] This development maps directly onto the perceived role of parties in appointing or electing judges. In appointments, Whigs and Democrats came to agree that parties had been a problem in concentrating power and increasing aristocratic self-dealing. But in elections, many believed parties could be a solution by organizing opposition to government abuses. The key to that solution was returning the parties and offices to direct popular control, and moving them away from appointments and special privileges. One writer argued that appointments made judges beholden to the governor and party insiders, and they then owed "individual favors," but elected judges more properly represent their whole party, "whose principles they have publicly espoused, and are supposed, in common honor and honesty, faithfully to maintain."[81] According to this interpretation, direct elections work precisely because they more directly connect the judge to the party, and they encourage judges to adhere to their party's principles. Not everyone was as sanguine about parties. Some delegates argued not that political parties were intrinsically good, but rather that they were a necessary evil. Antebellum America has been described as "a state of courts and parties."[82] Judicial elections combined the power of both courts and parties in the fight against corrupt and concentrated power.

The Legal Profession's Selfish Agenda?

An alternate theory is that the convention delegates were not sincerely concerned with the public interest, but were actually pursuing their own professional interests. Historian Kermit Hall's interpretation of the rise of judicial elections was that it was not so much a popular movement, but rather part of a hidden professional agenda of established lawyers to increase the popularity and status of the bench and bar in a democratic era. This theory relies on the fact that a large number of delegates were lawyers.[83] However, this argument oversimplifies the politics of these lawyer-delegates. New York's convention, the catalyst for this movement, is a good example. True, many of the strongest supporters of judicial elections were lawyers, but most of these lawyers were not "professional" representatives of the established bar. The most vocal supporter, Hoffman, was also the leading Radical Barnburner in the convention. He had been a small-town lawyer-politician, not an elite bar leader. The Radical Barnburners had to overcome the more "professional" Hunker lawyers' opposition. Many of the Whigs leading the fight for judicial elections were also leading the Anti-Rent uprising, which was at times an antilawyer uprising.[84] Lawyers made up about one third of the convention, and many of those lawyers opposed judicial elections.[85] The lawyers who were leading the fight for judicial elections were mostly "radicals" or populists, not leaders of the profession. The same dynamic was present in Wisconsin and Illinois, the next two states to adopt judicial elections after New York. Moreover, the votes in the conventions, legislatures, and public ratification generally were overwhelmingly in favor of judicial elections. In order to reach such broad consensus, majorities of the nonlawyers had voted for judicial elections.[86]

Furthermore, the conventions did not enact other items that would have been important to a lawyer's professional agenda.[87] Some delegates argued that judicial elections would improve the courts by opening them to lay judges, unless the constitution said otherwise. They thought lay judges would be more aggressive defenders of the people's rights and more able to clean up the bench and bar.[88] Only two conventions limited the courts to practicing lawyers and prohibited lay judges.[89]

Three conventions gave lay people more access to courts and opened up the legal profession to the broader public.[90] Such inclusiveness was not part of the bar's agenda. One delegate argued that opening the courts to nonlawyers would rid the profession of the corrupt and incompetent members of the bar.[91] Many conventions were filled with antilawyer rhetoric, even from lawyer-delegates themselves.[92] Some delegates argued for reforms that would reduce not only litigation and lawyers' fees, but also the number of lawyers themselves.[93]

Furthermore, almost all legal periodicals—the mouthpieces of the legal profession—opposed judicial elections throughout this period.[94] Only the *American Law Journal* supported them. It concluded that most of the legal profession opposed judicial elections because

> the education, habits of thought, and professional practice of lawyers, are calculated to make them ultra conservative; and it must be confessed that, unless the effects of the studies and practice of their profession be counteracted by other liberal studies, they are in no little danger of becoming bigoted and intolerant in regard to all changes in law and government.[95]

Either the lawyers in these conventions were very bad at pursuing their professional interests or, more likely, their professional interests were not their major concern. The agenda of these delegates—lawyers and nonlawyers—was roughly the public's agenda in the aftermath of a financial crisis. In the 1840s and 1850s, judicial elections commanded support from across the political spectrum and across classes because delegates believed that they would promote judicial power and constitutional constraints.

The Role of Slavery in the Adoption of Judicial Elections

It has been suggested that the fugitive slave crisis may have triggered the adoption of judicial elections. This theory posits that northern abolitionists surely had observed that appointed judges were too deferential to congressional rules on returning fugitive slaves and had ignored local public opinion. Elected judges would be more likely to ignore the national proslavery deal on fugitive slaves and would instead rule based on their own conscience and their local constituency.[96] It turns out that there is not much evidence to support this theory as a major factor.

New York's 1846 convention followed soon after the Supreme Court decided *Prigg v. Pennsylvania,* which had invalidated state laws that interfered with the return of fugitive slaves.[97] Justice Joseph Story, who was personally opposed to slavery, wrote the decision that recognized the constitutionality of the 1793 Fugitive Slave Law, and struck down Pennsylvania's "personal liberty law" of 1826 that had erected extra procedural hurdles for returning fugitive slaves. Justice Story ruled that masters had a right to recapture the slaves themselves without the approval of a judge or magistrate. However, state officials were not required by federal law to assist the masters, and states could enact statutes barring their officials from assisting.[98] Some northern states took advantage of this opening.

Right after *Prigg,* Massachusetts quickly passed its Personal Liberty Law of 1843, barring state employees from assisting in the return of fugitive slaves.[99] In New York, the legislature was divided: conservative "Hunker" Democrats called for the repeal of the state's 1828 personal liberty law. The repeal passed the state house, but not the state senate. Instead of fugitive slaves, New Yorkers focused more attention on the Mexican-American War and its implications for the expansion of slavery. The 1846 convention had no significant discussion of fugitive slaves. Through the 1840s, New Yorkers neither repealed the old statute nor enacted a new one, and few got very worked up over the fugitive issue.

Though New York's convention debates ignored fugitive slaves, a small number of delegates in other conventions made this argument. When Ohio delegates debated judicial elections, one argued that judicial elections "would strengthen the ability of judges to resist the demand of slave catchers and former slave owners without enhancing the rights of disenfranchised free blacks."[100] A Massachusetts delegate made a similar argument: Elected judges would be emboldened to stand up for local opinion against legal formalism in defending fugitive slaves.[101] Massachusetts had direct experience with its judges capitulating to slaveowners, so this issue was not merely theoretical. Still, Massachusetts did not adopt judicial elections.

Pennsylvania was the front line in the fight over fugitive slaves and personal liberty laws, and the timing of its adoption of judicial elections (starting the amendment process in 1848) coincides roughly with its adoption of a new personal liberty law in 1847. A few years after *Prigg,* Whigs and Democrats, conservatives and radicals, united on the measure in 1846, and it was signed into law in early 1847. The *Pennsylvania Freeman,* an abolitionist press, noted, "Anti-slavery public sentiment will make anti-slavery laws."[102] The act had four major provisions, operating in the space that *Prigg* arguably left open: punishment for purchasing or removing a free black to slavery; prohibiting state officials from assisting the return of fugitive slaves; penalties for "violent, tumultuous and unreasonable" means of capture and return; and the grant of broad powers to state judges to issue writs of habeas corpus and to investigate the legality of any detention.[103]

Because Pennsylvania adopted judicial elections between 1848 and 1850 by an amendment process and not by constitutional convention, there was no official record of debate. Abolitionists might have argued that the personal liberty law was a good start, but it needed sympathetic judges—elected judges attuned to public opinion—to enforce Pennsylvania law against the immoral slavery laws of southern states and a corrupt national compromise. However, the mainstream newspapers and the abolitionist press do not indicate a direct connection between fugitive slavery and judicial elections.[104] Instead, they focused on the post-Panic fiscal crisis, party corruption, and the most direct trigger, an ego-driven gridlock over judicial appointments. Between 1846 and 1847, the Democratic governor, Francis Shunk, and the Whig Senate fought to a stalemate over judicial appointments. Judge White, a respected jurist and an immensely popular Whig in a Whig area, finished his term and sought a reappointment. Governor Shunk refused to appoint Judge White, and the Whig Senate dug in and refused to confirm any of Shunk's eight Democratic nominees. The seat remained vacant for over a year, until Shunk won reelection in 1847 and the Whig Senate capitulated, but the Whigs blocked three other judicial appointments. The public generally blamed Governor Shunk for the partisan fight, and even after his death in 1847, the public called for a solution.[105] The interbranch obstructionism became another argument against appointments and in favor of the relatively smoother path of direct election. Over the three-year period required to amend the constitution, the state newspapers hailed the reform as an end to partisanship, depoliticizing the selection process. The votes in favor of judicial elections were more than two-to-one in both the state house and state senate, and the public's ratification vote was overwhelmingly in favor, too.[106] Thus, the issue of fugitive slaves could not have been a significant factor for Pennsylvania's adoption of judicial elections, just as it was not a major factor in other northern states.

Slavery actually shaped southern states' adoptions of judicial elections more than it did in the North. In Kentucky, proslavery forces were rebelling against a Whig urban elite that was often ambivalent about slavery. Judicial elections were a way to take the courts away from the Whigs' centralized control over appointments based in the state capital, and to shift control to the proslavery rural areas. Whigs had been in control in Kentucky for years, based on their urban commercial strongholds, and they had monopolized the courts through the power of appointment. The Whig elites of Kentucky's cities, led by Henry Clay, had grown more critical of slavery in the 1830s and 1840s. In the mid-1840s, Whig judges increasingly challenged slavery and crafted barriers against slave owners.[107]

At the same time, Kentucky Whigs became more and more visible as hostile to slavery. The Liberty Party presidential candidate in the 1840s, James G. Birney, was born in Kentucky, began his political career working for Henry Clay, and then organized "The Kentucky Society for the Gradual Relief of the State from Slavery" in the 1830s.[108] Kentucky abolitionists led a coalition in passing a slavery nonimportation bill, which imposed a $600 fine for bringing a slave into Kentucky, unless by inheritance.[109] The passage of this statute emboldened the abolitionists, and they fought off repeated attempts to repeal it. Cassius Marcellus Clay, Henry's cousin and the son of one of the wealthiest slave owners in Kentucky, campaigned against slavery in the state unequivocally: "I believe slavery to be an evil—an evil morally, economically, physically, intellectually, socially, religiously, politically . . . an unmixed evil."[110] Cassius Clay attracted more and more established Whig politicians in the cities, particularly in the capital Frankfort and in Louisville, especially among the growing German population.[111] Whig abolitionists believed the state's politics were ripe for gradual emancipation, and in 1847 they began a campaign for a new constitutional convention for that purpose. Proslavery Democrats read the political winds differently, and they gambled that a new convention would allow them to decrease the urban Whigs' power and increase direct local democracy. The legislature then scheduled the election for convention delegates in August 1849. The elections revealed that the abolitionists had badly misread the political climate. Perhaps their urban enclaves in Louisville and Frankfort were echo chambers. Perhaps they saw their supreme court judges ruling in favor of slaves and against slave owners, and gained confidence. But these city Whigs had no clue that the country Whigs and the Democrats were increasingly proslavery. As Clay's supporters grew, so did the zeal and violence of his proslavery opposition.[112] The Democratic Party was emerging from years of backwoods status into a more competitive, more ardently proslavery party.[113]

In February 1849, the legislature repealed the nonimportation act.[114] Meanwhile, Henry Clay endorsed gradual emancipation and colonization in a public letter, and the State Emancipation Convention met in April 1849, calling for a reinstatement of nonimportation and gradual emancipation. Over the summer, the campaign boiled over, with different candidates dueling and killing each other. Cassius Clay fatally wounded Cyrus Turner, the son of Henry Clay's main opponent, Squire Turner.[115] In the election on August 8, the proslavery candidates swept into the convention. Fewer than a dozen antislavery candidates won. Democrats won a narrow majority in the convention, in part because proslavery Whigs had been dragged down by their link to antislavery Whigs.[116]

The two biggest issues at the convention were first, slavery, and second, judicial reform and judicial elections.[117] The broad consensus at the convention favored judicial elections, but the details were more complicated. Proslavery Democrats pushed for elections by local judicial districts, not statewide elections. When Whigs warned that judicial elections would give parties too much power and would cede the courts to "cabals and caucuses," a leading Democratic newspaper answered that Frankfort's "cabals and cliques" had controlled appointments, and the Whigs' "unrighteous monopoly of judicial power" had ruled the state for decades.[118] Democrats worried that statewide control would maintain the elite Whigs' centralized power in Frankfort, while districts would connect judges to local public opinion throughout the state. Proslavery delegates were the most vocal on this point.[119] One delegate offered evidence that if a litigant lived farther from Frankfort, his chance of winning in court decreased.[120] Just as Mississippi reformers sought districts to reduce the control of the Natchez elite, and New York reformers sought districts to reduce the control of the Albany Regency, Kentucky reformers believed districts would limit the Whig elites in Frankfort and their abolitionist sympathies. The proslavery delegates got the results they wanted: Once the elected judges convened, their decisions turned in favor of slave owners.[121]

In the adoption of judicial elections from 1846 to 1851, slavery and antislavery played only a limited role, if at all. However, in the 1850s, slavery entered judicial politics more directly.[122] In Maryland, the appointed bench had been proslavery and aloof. When the state adopted judicial elections, one incumbent announced, "I expect to be excused from the indelicacy of 'taking the stump.'"[123] He and other veteran colleagues on the ballot lost to a slate of younger candidates who were more attuned to public opinion and to antislavery sentiment. In Missouri, the Democratic Party split into proslavery and antislavery factions, leading them each to support judicial elections and campaign against each other.[124] In Minnesota's constitutional convention of 1857, an opponent of judicial elections wrote, "We see it in Wisconsin, and in Iowa, and in all those states where popular excitement in reference to negro-worship and disunion has had its effect upon an elective Judiciary."[125] In Wisconsin, judicial elections turned on the question of fugitive slaves. These campaigns and court decisions lend support to the belief that elected judges would follow local sentiment over the formalism of federal law and comity.[126] As the politics of the 1850s increasingly turned on slavery and antislavery, these battle lines spilled over to judicial elections, as well. The Civil War battles also spilled into judicial elections in Maryland and Pennsylvania, where secessionist or Confederate-sympathizing judges lost to pro-Union candidates in the 1860s.[127]

Slavery and antislavery had a mixed role in promoting and reducing judicial power. In Kentucky, the advocates for judicial elections (and districts) tended to be the most ardently proslavery delegates who wanted the courts to defer to public opinion but also be willing to strike down any legislative encroachments on slave importation or gradual emancipation. Similarly, some northern supporters of judicial elections would drive judges to protect fugitive slaves and apply the state personal liberty laws—deferring to public opinion, but standing up to fight federal law. This was a mix of judicial strength (against the state legislature or Congress) and accountability (to the people).

The movement for judicial elections required a constellation of forces to line up, but once they did, the speed at which judicial elections swept the land between 1846 and 1851 is a historical marvel. The depression was the most significant factor of all in leading to the conventions and then to the adoption of judicial elections. But economic depressions do not ordinarily lead to more support for judicial review and judicial power. The key was how state leaders translated the depression into a movement against legislative power, and by extension, a movement for judicial power. Some opponents of judicial elections argued that a better solution for judicial accountability was more impeachments.[128] But the supporters of judicial elections were not seeking only judicial accountability. These reformers also believed that elections would produce judges who were less corrupt, more professional, and more committed to putting law above politics, even if that sounds incongruous to the modern reader. The revolutionaries of 1848 believed elections would transform and empower the courts more deeply. Like modern popular constitutionalists, they believed constitutional law was not the sole domain of the courts.[129] They trusted the people themselves to engage directly with the judges and to use the ballot to enforce their constitutional rights. They intended elected judges to stand up to the legislatures, and it turns out they were right.

CHAPTER SIX

The Boom in Judicial Review

N THE STATE CONVENTIONS of the 1840s and 1850s, supporters of judicial elections hoped for a more aggressive judiciary on behalf of "the people." They were at least half right. The first generation of elected judges certainly was aggressive: With an explosion of decisions striking down state statutes, they established a more widespread practice of judicial review in America. Many of these decisions dealt with the most controversial issues of the era, including slavery, liquor prohibition, takings of private property, taxation, school funding, private and public debt, corporate power, marriage and women's property rights, freedom of contract, and criminal procedure.[1] This boom in judicial review goes against the modern assumption that judicial elections should reduce judicial review, because elections would discourage judges from striking down popular legislation, and because elected judges would be more likely to line up politically with other elected officials. Another surprise is that they often denied that they were exercising this power on behalf of the people. In fact, they were the first generation of judges to offer countermajoritarian justifications for judicial review.[2]

The appointed judges of the early republic had relied mainly on majoritarian theory: the defense of popular majorities and their constitutional rights against the excesses of the ruling elites. Their justification was based on a version of the principal-agent problem, and these judges put themselves in the role of defending the principal (the people) against their agents (their untrustworthy and unrepresentative representatives). The delegates in the post-Panic constitutional conventions had emphasized this same vision in proposing judicial elections. But once judges actually became elected, they wrote as skeptics of democracy and increasingly turned to countermajoritarian theories, defending individual rights against majoritarian abuses. This reversal presents a paradox: Unelected judges defended democracy, and then elected judges criticized democracy. This reversal set the stage for the expansion of judicial review, as well as two other significant developments in American constitutional law: the rise of laissez-faire constitutionalism and the rise of countermajoritarian understandings of judicial review.[3]

The explosion of judicial review and the content of these decisions recounted here are based on a thorough study of state decisions from the Founding era up to the Civil War. This study is based on a search of electronic databases for the twenty-four states that joined the Union by 1820, plus California.[4] From the 1780s through the 1840s, each state averaged between one and two decisions striking down a statute per decade. But by the 1840s, there were signs already that elected judges were responsible for more judicial review. New York's elected judges struck down statutes thirteen times in that decade. The 1850s were even more decisive. States with appointed judiciaries averaged 2.5 decisions in that decade, not much more than earlier decades. States with elected judiciaries averaged ten decisions in the same period of time. The same pattern continued in the 1860s, and elected judges only increased their exercise of judicial review in the late nineteenth and early twentieth centuries. New England and the coastal South had the fewest elected judges and also the least judicial review. Meanwhile, one could find more judicial review in the elected courts elsewhere in the North, the South, and the West. Details of the results of this study are presented in the Appendixes.

Judicial elections influenced the spread of judicial review, but they were neither necessary (meaning that judicial review could spread in states without judicial elections) nor sufficient (meaning that judicial elections were not enough by themselves to increase judicial review). Before the switch to judicial elections, New York's and Pennsylvania's appointed judges in the 1840s started striking down statutes at an increased rate. Maine and North Carolina still appointed judges in the 1850s, and their appointed judges also started striking down more statutes. The timing and substance of these cases raise a question as to whether the 1840s depression or judicial elections were more responsible for the spread of judicial review. Historical causation is complex, and factors weave together. The economic crisis produced a deep skepticism of legislative power, which in turn produced a modest increase in judicial review by some appointed judges in the 1840s; new constitutional limits on legislatures in the late 1840s and early 1850s; judicial elections to foster a more independent, more vigilant judiciary to enforce those new limits through judicial review; and a sharp increase in judicial review by elected judges in the 1850s. The Panics influenced some appointed judges to become more suspicious of legislatures in New York and Pennsylvania in the 1840s. New York's appointed judges of the 1840s intervened against legislation principally related to the Panics and internal improvements.[5] At the same time, the Panics also triggered the conventions, the push for increased separation of powers, and the turn to judicial elections.

If the conventional wisdom today is that judicial elections deter courts from exercising judicial review, the 1850s challenge that assumption quite powerfully. But judicial elections did not merely coexist with judicial review. Convention delegates supported judicial elections in order to accomplish the very thing that happened: blocking more legislation. The fact that they intended elections to foster a more aggressive judiciary favors the hypothesis that judicial elections themselves contributed to the increase in judicial review. But it does not prove the point conclusively. It is also possible that the sentiments that produced judicial elections also produced judicial review, and it is possible that those underlying sentiments were more potent. But these possibilities are not mutually exclusive. These antilegislature sentiments and judicial elections were mutually reinforcing. Judicial elections harnessed those sentiments and made them more influential to judges. Moreover, observers in the 1850s saw the causal link between elections and judicial review.

The economic crisis and the rise of judicial elections in the 1840s and 1850s are part of a much larger story of American law: the broad expansion of judicial review and then the emergence of laissez-faire constitutionalism in the late nineteenth century. It has been noted that New York courts shifted from instrumentalism to formalism and laissez-faire in the wake of the Panic of 1837.[6] According to one interpretation, this change occurred because the ruling class feared the depression would spark a legislative redistribution of wealth, and the judges changed their tune to block this agenda. The fear of redistribution could have led some judges to set limits on legislatures, but it turns out that there is not much evidence that the general public was calling for economic regulation or prodebtor laws. Other depressions in American history (for example, those of the 1820s and the 1930s) followed that course. By contrast, political leaders framed the depression of the 1840s not in class terms, but as a crisis in governance requiring new limits on governmental power.[7] The constitutions of the late 1840s and 1850s, as well as the elected judges of the 1850s, demonstrate that the Panics and the economic crisis of the 1840s had a broader impact on public opinion, building a broader foundation for constitutional limits on government action. Other historians have suggested that the Jacksonian era was the democratization of free market capitalism.[8] The American Revolutions of 1848 and their elected judges were both an effect and a cause of the emerging liberal free market democracy and doctrine.

There are other potential explanations for the increasing number of cases striking down statutes, but either the evidence does not support them or, at most, they have some partial effect. These numbers do not seem skewed by the uneven reporting of cases. Almost all of the states in this era were reporting hundreds of cases per decade.[9] Nor do the increases in judicial review appear to be skewed by the changing amount of legislation in the 1840s and 1850s. It is true that legislatures generally passed more statutes over the course of the nineteenth century, so there were more and more targets to strike down over time, but the increasing rate of legislation was only gradual and did not line up with the rise of judicial review.[10]

One might wonder if legislatures were enacting new kinds of legislation in the 1840s and 1850s, and if that underlying cause was driving the increase in judicial review. In fact, three relatively new types of legislation were appearing: married women's property acts, liquor prohibition, and statutes permitting more referenda. However, only 10 percent of the total number of 1850s judicial review cases related to these new types of statutes. Still, some of these cases were the most fascinating and significant in these years. One Indiana case combined two of these innovations: a prohibition statute that had been passed as a popular referendum. Referenda, according to these Indiana judges who had been recently elected by the people, violated the republican principle of indirect democracy[11]— apparently judicial elections also increased judicial chutzpah. The New York Court of Appeals also struck down liquor prohibition laws, and in doing so, established one of the major precedents (*Wynehamer v. People*) for substantive due process for property rights, one of the pillars of laissez-faire constitutionalism for almost a century thereafter.[12]

Democracy and Counterdemocracy: A Puzzle

Americans in the Founding era and the early republic accepted the power of judicial review as a protection of majority rule. According to the theory of popular constitutionalism, judges were supposed to intervene on behalf of the people and their constitutions to slow down an overreaching legislature and to give the people a chance to deliberate and then confirm or reject the legislative program in the next election.[13] If the people voted for the same leaders to reinstate the same legislation, then the judges should step aside. The Constitution reflected the will of the people, whereas statutes could be the product of legislative error or corruption. Accordingly, judicial review could be consistent with majoritarian democracy. The appointed judges from the Founding through the 1830s often relied on such majoritarian theories to support their exercise of judicial review.[14]

One might expect that popularly elected judges would only emphasize these majoritarian and populist theories even more than appointed judges had. If anything, one might imagine that such recent constitutional conventions, which were called and then ratified by a majority of voters, would strengthen the majoritarian faith that these new constitutions reflected the people's will more than legislation did—especially older legislation. Instead, elected judges articulated antipopulist, countermajoritarian theories more often than ever before—a surprising reversal.[15] In the late eighteenth century, a few of the Framers had offered countermajoritarian perspectives. In the Constitutional Convention, James Madison warned, "In all cases where a majority are united by a common interest or passion, the rights of the minority are in danger. What motives are to restrain them?"[16] In his defense of the Constitution in the *Federalist Papers*, Alexander Hamilton argued for the "independence of judges" and the power of judicial review in order to protect "the rights of individuals" from the "ill humors which are the arts of designing men, or the influences of particular conjectures [that] sometimes disseminate among the people themselves."[17] However, few judges offered this defense of judicial review from the Founding through the 1830s. In the early nineteenth century, judges generally blamed government officials rather than the people as the threat to the people's higher law.

But then, in the 1840s and 1850s, state judges began to identify the people as a threat to higher law. Almost all of these state judges were elected by popular majorities, which made this a counterintuitive turn to countermajoritarianism. Of course, these nineteenth-century judges did not use the terms "majoritarian" or "countermajoritarian," but these labels are a helpful shorthand for two formulations: the courts defending the people (and their constitutions) against their agents' abuse of power and the courts defending individuals and minority communities against the majority's abuse of power.

The New York courts of the late 1840s and 1850s relied on antimajoritarian arguments more overtly than other courts, just as they were striking down more statutes than other courts. The 1846 New York convention helped lay the foundation for the laissez-faire constitutionalism that ascended after the Civil War. New York's courts dramatically increased their use of judicial review first in the 1840s, when elected judges struck down statutes thirteen times. By contrast, in that same decade, the twenty-two appointed state courts totaled only twenty-six cases. The New York Court of Appeals then accelerated this pace over the rest of the century, striking down statutes thirty-two times in the 1850s, thirty-four times in the 1860s, forty-four times in the 1870s, forty-two times in the 1880s, an astounding eighty-two times in the 1890s, and even more astoundingly, seventy times between 1900 and 1905.[18]

One engine driving judicial review was the expanding doctrine of vested property rights. The state can alter ordinary property rights and take ordinary property for a public purpose as long as it pays due compensation. But "vested" property rights are so complete that the state may not impair them or "divest" them without the owner's consent. This doctrine was well established in American law, but elected judges enforced it more frequently and broadly than ever before. A newer doctrine was "substantive due process." Ordinarily, a "due process" clause means that a state can take property or liberty if it has adhered to procedural requirements. But "substantive" due process is broader, restricting the state from infringing a property or liberty interest entirely. This doctrine would later be the basis of *Dred Scott* for slave owners' rights to take their slaves into the western territories, of *Lochner* and freedom of contract against maximum hours regulations, and even later, of *Roe v. Wade* and abortion rights. New York's elected judges used these doctrines to limit the Married Women's Property Act of 1848, the Anti-Liquor Act of 1855, and roughly twenty other statutes.[19]

At first, the elected judges added a minority-protection emphasis on top of their majority-protection theory of judicial review. In 1848, one defended judicial review because "excessive legislation is the great legal curse of the age . . . drawing every thing within its grasp."[20] The court justified judicial review as vindicating not only the will of the people but also "individual right[s]"[21] and "natural right and justice."[22] Over time, New York's elected judges became more critical of democracy itself. Striking down a statute for authorizing referenda, another New York judge rejected direct democracy, stating that it was wrong to think that "no harm can result from allowing the people to exercise, directly, the law-making power."[23] Skeptical of the voting public, the court observed that the people often followed "hasty and ill-advised zeal" and "unthinking clamor or partisan importunity,"[24] and that the courts' responsibility was to enforce the constitution's protection of "minorities against the caprices, recklessness, or prejudices of majorities."[25] In a similar case two years later, a different judge wrote that judicial review was necessary to protect "that great idea" of the Founding[26]—"liberty regulated by law"[27]—against "the evils . . . of a consolidated democracy."[28] Without a sense of irony, these elected judges—elected directly by voters— found that referenda were too much direct democracy.

The "vested rights" doctrine—the protection of certain interests "of which one cannot be deprived by the mere force of legislative enactment," but only in judicial proceedings—came up repeatedly in these 1840s– 1850s cases.[29] Many historians have identified this doctrine as a forerun- ner of the powerful substantive due process doctrine that blocked so much economic and labor regulation in the early twentieth century.[30] But sub- stantive due process itself—as a protection of liberty along with property— appeared in these cases, too. In *Wynehamer v. People* in 1856, the New York Court of Appeals struck down a liquor prohibition act on the inno- vative grounds of substantive due process.[31] The *Wynehamer* Court was divided five votes to three. Judge George Franklin Comstock, a conserva- tive Whig (and later an anti-Lincoln Democrat) wrote the lead opinion. The established doctrine of vested rights usually protected real estate and physical property. Comstock and Judge Alexander Johnson, in his concur- rence, used *Wynehamer* to declare a broader definition of property rights and the protections of due process. They clarified that property ownership meant more than physical ownership. Comstock wrote that any definition of property had to include "the power of disposition and sale, as well as the right of private use and enjoyment."[32] Johnson agreed that the due pro- cess right to property included "the right of any person to possess, use, enjoy, and dispose of a thing."[33] In many earlier "vested rights" decisions, the government action in question was the transfer of real property from one individual to another. In *Wynehamer,* the government action was a broader regulation of economic and commercial activity (prohibition of alcohol), and the court of appeals intervened to block this regulation and protect a general liberty interest. *Wynehamer* thus marks a step in the de- velopment from an earlier "vested property rights" doctrine toward the "substantive due process" doctrine, and later to the freedom of contract and the invalidation of economic regulation in the *Lochner* era.[34]

In addition, the *Wynehamer* decision also contained a robust argument for judicial review as a check against majoritarianism. Comstock justified judicial review on the grounds that legislation is sometimes the result of mistaken "theories of public good or public necessity [that] command popular majorities," and that the judiciary must protect the "vital princi- ples" of "free republican governments" against popular abuses.[35]

Many other states in the 1850s shifted to countermajoritarian argu- ments. Most, like New York, had adopted judicial elections recently. Chief Justice John Bannister Gibson of Pennsylvania had been a prominent critic of judicial review. Then in 1850, as he was running in the state's first judicial elections to retain his seat, he embraced judicial review.[36] In a civil case where the legislature had set aside a jury verdict and ordered a new trial, he ruled that this intervention overstepped the legislature's bounds.[37] Moreover, he offered a general critique of democratic elections: legislatures would sometimes pander to majorities, resulting in "the sacrifice of individual right[s]" because rights were "too remotely connected with the objects and contests of the masses to attract their attention."[38] Even if the people cared about individual rights in the abstract, Chief Justice Gibson doubted whether they would notice the actual breach of those rights or do anything in response.

One year later, the first elected Pennsylvania Supreme Court (including Gibson) further developed this countermajoritarian theory of judicial review. In a vested property case, the court observed that if statutes "are enacted, which bear . . . on the whole community . . . [and] are unjust and against the spirit of the constitution, [the community will] procure their repeal. . . . And that is the great security for just and fair legislation."[39] The people can control the legislature, but the same is not true for individuals targeted by the majority:

> But when individuals are selected from the mass, and laws are enacted affecting their property, without summons or notice, at the instigation of an interested party, who is to stand up for them, thus isolated from the mass, in injury and injustice, or where are they to seek relief from such acts of despotic power? They have no refuge but in the courts, the only secure place for determining conflicting rights by due course of law.[40]

The court's answer was that "the people" could protect themselves and did not need the courts to step in. Instead, they reserved the power of judicial review for individuals, because they would not be protected by the majority. In 1848, the Pennsylvania Supreme Court had admitted it had been "too weak" to stand up to the legislature,[41] but in the 1850s, it was making up for lost time and asserting its strength. Elected judges with limited terms would have been risking their careers if they aggressively defended individuals against popular majorities. Nevertheless, these judges apparently were feeling much stronger once they were elected. In 1855, two years after Justice Gibson's death, his friend and biographer attributed the sudden rise in judicial review to the rise of judicial elections:

> The tendency of the legislative branch (I had almost said *rod*,) is to swallow up both the others. Against its aggressions, the judiciary is our main reliance. Before it became elective, a case occasionally occurred of its succumb-

ing to those who were supposed to represent more nearly the wishes of the people, but that danger is now past, for the Courts are quite as near the people as the legislators themselves.[42]

According to Justice Gibson's friend, then, appointed judges were cowed by the democratic legitimacy of legislators, but elections gave judges more courage to assert their power on behalf of "the people."

One Ohio decision in 1855 demonstrated this shift in striking down a tax statute that gave special privileges and deductions to particular individuals and corporations.[43] The opinion started with the familiar principle that the three branches are each "servants of the people," but then emphasized that judicial review was more important in protecting individuals from the people as a whole:

> I do not admit that, in this respect, a whole community should be more favored than the most helpless individual member. . . . It is a trite saying, that eternal vigilance is the price of liberty; and so it is of a good government, and of freedom from oppression. A single individual, however vigilant, may sometimes suffer unjustly at the hands of a community. But communities rarely, if ever, suffer any injustice at the hands of those vested with authority, which cannot be traced to their own want of vigilance. . . . A community thus suffering under oppression, cannot apply to any Hercules for help, for it is with the people alone, under our system of government, that any such Herculean power resides. It is with them to make or unmake constitutions, laws, and officers.[44]

The people have the power to fight against government abuse, and if they suffer such abuse, it is their own fault for being complacent. Their remedy is the next election, not litigation. By contrast, individuals are powerless against the tyranny of the majority, and have only litigation as a remedy. Thus, courts have a countermajoritarian duty—and perhaps *no majoritarian duty*. This change would have been remarkable in any era, but it was particularly so in the context of the recent democratization of these courts.

An Indiana judge, concurring in striking down a liquor prohibition statute in 1855, worried that popular "interest or passion, or perhaps other dubious influences, often mould legislation," and that some laws were the result simply of "the fluctuating fever of the hour."[45] As it turns out, that judge had recently served in the Indiana legislature, so he had firsthand experience with the interests, passions, and dubious influences there. A Michigan Supreme Court justice voted in dissent to strike down a liquor prohibition statute, warning against allowing individuals to become "abject slaves to the majority."[46] An Ohio Supreme Court justice condemned local referenda as abuses of state power to take property and as "internal improvement piracy." He worried that "if the rights of *mi-norities* are not observed, it will not be long before the *majorities* will be in bondage. I look upon this thing of taking private property, or subjecting it to unusual burdens without the consent of the owner, as a great stride toward despotic power."[47] These new critics of democracy came from both parties: The judges were a relatively even mix of Democrats, Whigs, and Republicans, and of supporters and opponents of slavery.

Strikingly, there are almost no examples of countermajoritarian justifications from appointed judges, and few examples from before 1850.[48] One exception was a Delaware court in 1847 explaining the separation of powers in these terms: "These co-ordinate branches are intended to operate as balances, checks and restraints, not only upon each other, but upon the people themselves; to guard them against their own rashness, precipitancy, and misguided zeal; and to protect the minority against the injustice of the majority."[49] This court was confronting two legal issues that triggered some of the countermajoritarian arguments in the 1850s in elective states: local referenda and liquor prohibition.

Just as there were more instances of judicial review by courts in the mid-Atlantic and Midwestern states, there were also more countermajoritarian theories offered from those regions than from New England or the South. Some southern courts were relatively active in the 1840s and 1850s, but overall, southern courts asserted judicial review less often, and when they did offer a theory for judicial review, they adhered to the established majoritarian justification of defending the people and their constitution against legislative usurpers.[50] Southern judges seem not to have explicitly critiqued democracy and defended individual rights against majority rule in the 1850s.

One explanation for the rise of judicial review and countermajoritarian theory may be related to abolitionism. Abolitionism led some jurists to question majority rule and to turn to natural rights and fundamental principles.[51] Even though this style of judicial reasoning did not become more widespread until after the Civil War, it is possible that antislavery's ideology emerged in a few pre–Civil War cases as countermajoritarian critiques. It is also possible that judicial elections may have increased the influence of abolitionist politics.

The notion that abolitionism played a role in increasing judicial review and countermajoritarian theory is bolstered by geography, but it is also undermined by geography. On the one hand, southern courts were mixed on judicial review, and they did not generate critiques of democracy. On the other hand, New England, the bastion of antislavery thought, accounted for little of the judicial review in the antebellum era. It is perhaps no coincidence that New England's judges were appointed and also struck down few statutes. One might expect New England abolitionists to have advanced countermajoritiarian defenses of judicial review, but none can be found in court decisions. When their courts did strike down statutes, they offered the standard majoritarian theory as a justification, just as southern judges did.[52] The absence of judicial review and countermajoritarian theory in New England is surprising, considering that the Whigs (and their forerunners, the Federalists) had been the proponents of judicial review, stronger courts, and property rights, as well as skeptics of democracy. Thus, antislavery seems to have played only a minor role in the expansion of judicial review and countermajoritarianism.

Notably, state judges around the country generally used their new power not as much for the most important purpose of "the American revolutions of 1848" (fiscal restraint on legislative spending). The most frequent use of judicial review was for their own institutional self-interest: the protection and expansion of judicial power against legislative encroachment. While this result is consistent with some of the original purposes of the state conventions, the judges emphasized judicial departmental power more than any other general category of cases.[53] The elected judges struck down legislatures' attempts to override judicial decisions, to grant litigants new trials, to limit courts' jurisdiction, and to adjudicate cases in place of the courts. They policed the separation of powers vigilantly—but most often as the protection of their own judicial power, and not the protection of legislative or executive powers from encroachment. If anything, elected judges used their new separation of powers to encroach on legislative and executive powers, by limiting legislative procedures, taxing and spending, and appointment and removal powers. Taken together, these cases helped develop the principle that judicial decisions were final and not reviewable by the other branches. Popular constitutionalists may have created judicial elections, but the elected judges themselves often did not adhere to popular constitutionalism. Instead, they developed antipopular constitutionalism and judicial independence.

Judicial Elections, Theory and Practice

The theory behind judicial elections was consistent with the majoritarian theory of constitutional law. However, the actual practice of judicial elections themselves in the 1850s may have contributed to the rise of countermajoritarian theory. Party and faction were powerful forces that were not always consistent with majoritarianism. Judicial candidates fought harder for party nominations, with more competition among factions within the party. But then the candidates did not compete directly in the general election campaigns. This campaign dynamic was even more polarizing in the political climate of the 1850s, pushing judges from the center out to the edges of the political spectrum. Judicial elections emphasized local districts and factions rather than statewide public opinion and the "median voter." From the remaining records, it is even difficult to figure out many judges' party affiliations. Nevertheless, from some fragments we can reconstruct a grainy picture of party politics in judicial elections in the mid-nineteenth century.

The appointment process, for better and for worse, had been a centralizing force rewarding party cohesion. The party in power reinforced its strength and identity by building a machine through patronage. Of course, the elected officials also used appointments to reach out to smaller communities and constituencies, but convention delegates complained of cronyism in judicial appointments more than of special interests. Likewise, commentators argued that judicial appointments had been based on service to the party or other partisan interests.[54] But democratic reformers undermined patronage by making more and more offices popularly elected. Michael Holt observes: "The power to select officials had often provided glue to majority parties in state legislatures, helping to neutralize any tendencies toward factionalism on substantive issues. With patronage powers gone, such restraints on internal fragmentation disappeared." Holt quotes an unnamed observer blaming the disarray of the Ohio Democrats in 1852 on the recent constitutional reforms, which "ha[d] broken up their principle of cohesion to any central organization."[55]

This fragmentation of offices is emblematic of the larger political fragmentation in the 1850s. The founders of the second party system had sought to keep slavery out of American politics as long as possible, but by the early 1850s, it was no longer possible. Even though some had thought the Compromise of 1850 had saved the Union, this optimism was quickly squelched. The 1850s saw a decade-long "disintegration" of the national political order and of most state political orders, leading to "apathy, abstention, and alienation."[56] Americans of all regions and affiliations were disillusioned with their leaders, the party system, and their government. They felt betrayed and became pessimistic about the republic's survival.[57] Countermajoritarian theory, minority rights, and the rule of law all become more attractive when those in the majority confront the likelihood of falling out of power, become risk-averse, and seek legal protections from new coalitions rising into power.

The practice of judicial campaigns was like a centrifuge in this environment, producing even less cohesion. In an appointed system with competi-

tive parties, judges had to consider whether they would be reappointed by
a governor of the same party or possibly a governor of the other party, or
perhaps a legislature of their party or the opposing party. Uncertainty under these conditions pulled judges toward the center. Judicial elections,
however, tended to pull away from the center. Even though the parties
were less stable, they were still the vehicle for getting elected. The problem
was that the factions and interests within the parties were increasingly
powerful. The newspaper accounts of judicial elections in the 1850s and
later in the nineteenth century reveal a consistent pattern of judicial candidates competing actively for party nominations, relying on the support of
a faction, a region, a smaller constituency, or a special interest within the
party. After winning the party nod, judicial candidates did little to compete
for votes in the general election except for praying that their party machine was better at turning out its coalition of voters than was the other
side's machine. This political dynamic helps explain the increase of judicial review and the rise of countermajoritarian theory to justify factional
politics.

In New York's first judicial elections in 1847, the Democrats split bitterly into separate factional county conventions: one conservative Hunker convention and one radical Barnburner convention. The Hunkers
denounced the Barnburners' attempts to "produce alienation and division in the democratic ranks."[58] The factional infighting spread throughout the state, and their separate newspapers attacked each other daily.[59]
After being out of power in the constitutional convention, the Hunkers
returned to their strength as party insiders in the state Democratic nominating convention, converting their power over appointments into power
over party nominations. To the consternation of the Barnburners, the
Hunkers pushed through the nominations of four Hunkers for the four
court of appeals positions, in part because the Hunker candidates had
more judicial experience, and in part because Hunkers continued to control the party machinery. After the convention, the frustrated Barnburners divided the party by running their own candidates for the general
election in many races. Voter turnout for the judicial elections was relatively low, and the Hunkers swept the four statewide seats, taking advantage of the most consistent and reliable party machine.[60]

The New York newspapers of the 1850s similarly offered stories about
the factions' bargaining over judges in the state conventions, with judges
who represented different interests and regions jockeying for the party
nominations.[61] In the general election, however, the newspapers would
only print the party ticket, with no news about the judges campaigning
publicly, no editorials, and no open letters to the public. The Pennsylvania newspapers in the 1850s and the late nineteenth century displayed

the same pattern, including some intense factional fighting for party nominations, but no campaigning by judges in the general elections.[62] The veteran of the Pennsylvania Supreme Court, John Bannister Gibson, won his nomination in 1851 by only two votes in the party convention, despite being one of the most well-respected judges in the nation. He had not been a party insider and had no political base in a faction of the party, and therefore he faced a difficult challenge in the new era of judicial elections. He reported afterward that he did nothing to campaign for the general election. He simply rode the party machine to victory.[63] Judge Joseph R. Swan was not as lucky. He was a well-respected judge on the Ohio Supreme Court who expected an easy reelection in 1859. However, because he had enforced the Fugitive Slave Law, the Ohio Republican Party refused to renominate him.[64] The reelection campaigns of these two similarly established judges demonstrate the volatile nature of party support in the judicial elections of the mid-1800s.

Judges in the mid-Atlantic, the Midwest, and some border states drove the boom of judicial review in the 1850s. Many of these states had become more ethnically and religiously diverse, and their parties also became more diverse—the Democratic Party in particular.[65] Some judges' renominations and reelections may have depended upon defending the rights of a powerful minority community or interest group. An example is Judge Albert Cardozo, Benjamin Cardozo's father. In 1866, Albert Cardozo sat on the Court of Common Pleas and ruled that a "blue law" limiting the sale of liquor was unconstitutional.[66] In a personal letter defending his decision, Albert Cardozo wrote: "I have announced the law, as I believe it to be and while I do not doubt that any other conclusion would have been my political death, I know my own firmness sufficiently to assert that if I had had different convictions of the law, I should have boldly declared them."[67] He added, "The liquor law and the judges who had upheld it, will assuredly ultimately meet the condemnation which they deserve at the hands of the people, to who[m] I shall also make an appeal in due time."[68] Albert Cardozo's constituency of German and Irish voters in his urban judicial district were strongly opposed to the statute.[69] The episode illustrates that when judges in lower courts run for election in smaller districts, a majority-minority population (such as the Irish and German constituents in Albert Cardozo's district) can influence a judge in consideration of his "convictions" and lead him to adopt the legal theory that a judge should defend a local community against a statewide majority. On a related note about judicial elections, Albert Cardozo resigned in 1872 after being implicated in a corruption scandal connected to Tammany Hall and New York machine politics.[70]

The "countermajoritarian" judges of the 1850s also reflect some of this period's politics of fragmentation. George Comstock, one of the judges to warn against "popular majorities" in striking down a New York prohibition law, questioned the reliability of American democracy on several grounds.[71] He was a conservative Whig who was skeptical about another democratic institution, the jury,[72] and he embraced an earlier New York jurist who was a skeptic of democracy, Chancellor James Kent. The factionalizing of American politics contributed to Comstock's questioning of majoritarian democracy. By the time he ran for office in 1855, the Whigs were collapsing into factions, and the American Party (the anti-immigrant Know Nothings) had been rising to replace the Whigs. Comstock won the nominations of the "Silver Grays" (the faction of conservative Whigs) and the American Party, and he prevailed over a split multicandidate field.[73] As parties were splitting into battling factions, some judges unsurprisingly saw that the center could not hold. They were losing faith in the mechanics of democracy and the claims of popular majorities.

Other factors seemed to shape Comstock's doubts about popular majorities. Once the Whig Party and American Party folded and the Republican Party emerged, Comstock embraced the Democrats.[74] He was still an ardent Unionist and opposed southern secession, but he also strongly condemned abolitionists, the Republican Party, and Abraham Lincoln. He lost his reelection campaign during a Republican sweep of the state in 1861. During the war, he wrote:

> The Federal Government has no more right to invade one section of the Union for a purpose outside of the Constitution, no more right to propagate by force of arms in one State the theories, sentiments and opinions of other States, than it has to invade the Kingdom of Brazil to abolish slavery, or the Turkish Empire to abolish polygamy.[75]

Comstock adhered to states' rights and limited federal power: "Under the Constitution of the United States there is no shadow of right, in peace or war, by its laws or its military power, to spread or to propagate the opinions or sentiments of any class or section, upon social and moral questions."[76] Comstock had several reasons to voice his concerns about popular majorities in the 1850s, but among them was a growing commitment to states' rights in the political crisis of the 1850s.

Critics of democracy could be found in every party and faction in the 1850s. Democrats and Republicans joined Comstock and other Whigs in worrying about the dangers of popular majorities. William Yates Gholson, an Ohio judge, was born in Virginia and practiced law in Mississippi, and then left the South because of his antislavery views. After

138 THE PEOPLE'S COURTS

joining the Ohio Republican Party, he was elected to the superior court in 1854, and then to the state supreme court in 1859.[77] His son volunteered for the Union army and died in battle.[78] Judge Spalding, who had used images of slavery to criticize democratic excess, also joined the Republican Party early on.[79] From the opposite vantage point of Comstock's, Republicans in the mid-1850s had their own reasons to raise questions about popular majorities.

During these years, proslavery forces were pushing for popular sovereignty in western states and territories. In 1854, the Kansas-Nebraska Act marked a major step toward popular voting on slavery's status in the West, followed by a period known as Bloody Kansas. Meanwhile, proslavery forces were winning elections.[80] It is possible that northern judges observed these developments, began to distance themselves from "popular sovereignty" rhetoric, and became less enamored with public opinion and voters. It was also becoming clear that a national popular majority would be the strongest weapon for the Republicans against southern state majorities. Still, abolition would propel them to see a judge's role in protecting individual rights.

Local judicial districts further fragmented the bench. Before judicial elections, judges were appointed on a statewide basis, so they were more likely to line up with the composition of the legislature, and they had more incentive to stay in the good graces of the governor and statewide politicians in order to win reappointment. In the era of judicial elections, many judges ran for seats by district, shifting the base of support from statewide majoritarian opinion to local constituencies. In the wave of judicial elections, more than half of the states followed Mississippi and New York by basing all or some of their high court judges in geographic districts.[81]

Districts had little effect on the frequency of judicial review, because plenty of courts elected statewide struck down statutes more often than some of the district-based courts. But districts could have contributed to more countermajoritarian explanations for judicial review. Many of the judges who used their decisions to critique majority rule and defend smaller communities came from districted seats, not statewide seats.[82] Individual judges from districts would have focused more on their local constituencies than on statewide public opinion. A judge from a particular district might have conveyed that political focus in more abstract, theoretical terms of protecting minority groups against the whims of public opinion. It was simply local politics, translated into a more acceptable jurisprudence.

The convention delegates of the 1840s and 1850s had framed the turn to judicial elections as "democratizing" the courts, and they intended that democratization to empower the judges. But democratizing the courts also constrained judges due to the power of factions, special interests, and localism. It is important to remember that the supporters of judicial elections emphasized judicial independence: Elections would replace the appointments that gave legislators, governors, and cronyism power over the courts. Independent of these forces, the quality of judging was supposed to improve, and judges would be free to be judges. The opponents of judicial elections had the same goal; they simply disagreed about the means. For them, elections were a greater threat to judicial independence than appointments. The debates captured an ethos of the time that judges should be judges, just as lawyers were increasingly professionalizing and differentiating their role from mere politics. The fundamental question for many delegates was which selection method would allow judges to be more independent of politics and follow the rule of law. This development is often obscured when the debates are framed in simple "Jacksonian democracy" terms, as there is ample historical evidence that the legal profession was creating its own culture of expertise and aristocratic stewardship to save democracy from itself.[83]

The convention debates may have influenced judges' approaches to judicial review and individual rights. One might assume that the new constitutions had added more individual rights clauses, which would have offered a textual basis for more countermajoritarian theories. However, the changes in these constitutions were mainly structural and procedural, and their focus was not on establishing or reaffirming individual rights. Instead, it was the conventions' debates over popular elections that elicited individual rights arguments on both sides. Prodemocracy reformers used natural rights arguments, framed more as individual rights than as "the people's" rights, in favor of broader suffrage and more direct democracy. At the same time, some opponents of judicial elections feared that elected judges would not defend the rule of law and would not protect individual rights. Elected judges seem to have borrowed from both sides. They may have embraced the natural rights theory that justified self-determination, suffrage, and direct democracy,[84] but they also remained skeptical of voters and public opinion, as were the critics of judicial elections. Because opponents had raised doubts about elected judges' capacity to protect individuals, this first generation of elected judges might have tried harder to settle these doubts in action and in theory.

Another possibility is that these judges accepted the brave new democratized courts but also needed a way to distinguish themselves from legislators. If democracy is king, then why should a handful of infrequently elected judges have the final say over the work of the people's more frequently elected representatives? These judges offered the countermajoritarian arguments of liberty and rule of law to bolster their legitimacy: They could serve both the popular will and individual rights.

The rule of law was also a credential that distinguished the judges as a professional elite. When judges were appointed, they had to highlight their democratic bona fides to be more like everyone else. But once they were elected, they had to differentiate themselves from the other branches.

In an era of democratizing the courts, lawyers and judges were warding off efforts at broadening access to laymen who had been seeking to represent clients in court and pursuing seats on the bench. The legal profession was building its own identity and power in this era, and part of its ethos was the lawyer's responsibility in defending individual rights.[85] Asserting professional expertise in the rule of law was a way of fending off these challenges. The professionalization of bench and bar may have contributed both to more judicial review and to countermajoritarian arguments, as ways of defending judicial expertise.

The first generation of elected judges might have reacted against democracy once they experienced running in elections themselves. Some may have resented the inconveniences and discomforts of election campaigns, or those campaigns might have opened their eyes to the questionable world of electioneering and party machines. Like with sausage making, the judges found democracy less awe-inspiring once they got down and dirty in the electoral process.[86] The effect was an experiential basis for distrusting democracy.

It is important to note how judicial elections magnified the political crisis of the 1850s, but, of course, there is no denying the independent influence of the crises. The economic crisis of the 1840s and the political crisis of the 1850s were powerful enough to push judges toward more judicial review and more skepticism of democracy, even without judicial elections. Many Americans were disillusioned not only with politicians and parties after the 1840s economic crisis and the 1850s slavery crisis, but also with democracy itself.[87]

Going into the conventions that started in the mid-1840s, the leading interpretation of the crisis was that legislatures had been captured by special interests or their own interests. Delegates in state conventions argued that judicial elections would enlist the courts in restoring the will of the people against corrupt legislators. With or without elections, judges would have ridden that same wave of antilegislature sentiment. Judges also might have become skeptical of popular democracy in the wake of these events. An equally valid interpretation of the overspending and debt crises was that the public had helped generate the frenzy for new canals, turnpikes, and railroads, pushing the government into financial crisis. Neighboring towns and bordering regions had squabbled over the locations of the improvements, increasing pressure to pander and overbuild to keep the people happy. A reasonable reaction was skepticism of public opinion and the democratic process. However, if this interpretation of the crises had motivated judges to turn against democracy, then why did they not turn to antidemocratic arguments earlier, especially in the initial increase of judicial review in the 1840s? Instead, these arguments emerged mostly in the early and mid-1850s.

The new constitutions themselves offer another explanation. As suffrage and direct democracy expanded, and as voters controlled more and more of the government, courts might have become less concerned that legislators were out of touch with the popular will, and more concerned that they had become too responsive to the popular will. Or in the same vein, judges might have concluded that the reforms through the 1840s had made elected officials responsive enough to voters, and thus the judges shifted their attention from protecting "the people" (who no longer needed such help) to protecting individuals and minority communities. However, among the many reforms in the constitutions of the 1840s, the conventions had not made many changes to the mechanisms of popular control over the legislature or governor; those changes generally had come earlier in the century. In the 1840s and early 1850s, the constitutional changes focused on separation of powers and limits on legislative power. While some of the procedural changes for the passage of statutes were likely to slow down legislatures and keep them in line with public opinion, it is unlikely that the judges felt that changes in legislative process had dramatically increased popular sovereignty.

After the Civil War, state courts continued to strike down more and more statutes. In the 1840s and 1850s, state courts had delved into social and political controversies by striking down alcohol prohibitions, laws on slavery, laws on married women and property, and laws on internal improvements. After the Civil War, state courts took on new controversies over labor and progressive legislation, and they continued their exercise of judicial review at the same pace or even increased.[88] For example, New York courts struck down another 263 statutes from the end of the Civil War through 1905, over six per year.[89] The federal courts changed more dramatically. The U.S. Supreme Court increased its vertical review, overturning state legislation from a relatively consistent average of six decisions per decade between 1800 and 1860 to sixteen decisions in the 1860s, thirty-three in the 1870s, thirty-nine in the 1880s, and thirty in the 1890s—and often on the most controversial subjects of those times.[90] The Supreme Court had avoided confronting Congress before the Civil War, save for one titanic disaster in striking down the Missouri Compromise in

1857. Instead of shrinking from the embarrassment of *Dred Scott* and deferring more to Congress after the Civil War, the justices invalidated Congress in high-profile cases almost once per year for the next few decades: from the management of Reconstruction to black civil rights to commercial regulation, the income tax, and labor legislation.[91] Of course, federal judges were appointed, not elected, but many federal judges had come from practice in state courts or from the state bench itself, and had observed both judicial elections and judicial review, or had actually participated in them. For example, the author of the famous *Lochner* decision on the freedom of contract was Justice Rufus Peckham, who had been elected to the New York trial court and the court of appeals. He was joined by Justice David Brewer, a veteran of judicial elections from fourteen years on the Kansas Supreme Court; Justice Henry Brown, who had served as a state judge in Michigan and had actually lost a judicial election; Justice Joseph McKenna, who had practiced in California courts and had been elected twice a state district attorney; and Justice Fuller, who had been president of the Illinois Bar Association. Roughly one third of the Supreme Court justices appointed between the end of the Civil War and 1900 had served on elected state courts, and more had extensive experience in these courts, and still more had run in state elections for other offices. There are a number of different causes for the federal courts' aggressive turn in the late nineteenth century, but the bold institutional role asserted by elected state judges in the 1840s and 1850s appears to have set a precedent, influencing the federal courts directly in terms of personnel or more loosely by the transmission of ideas and practices.

At first glance, the boom of judicial review might seem to be a revolution in general judicial independence, as judges appear to be thumbing their noses at the legislature as well as at the voters. It is too simplistic to equate judicial review with "general" judicial independence, because even if a court obstructs a past legislative majority, the judges may be serving a powerful constituency or interest that is influential over the judges and their renomination and reelection. Judicial review indicates that a court is relatively independent from the other branches of government, but not necessarily independent from politics more broadly. The judges presented their power of judicial review and their antidemocratic rationales as standing up to politics, but they were also shaped by the politics of public opinion, the legal profession, business interests, and local constituencies. Even if that is true, the exercise of judicial review was still an exercise of judicial power at unprecedented levels.

Historians have discovered that local and state governments were active in economic and social regulation in the eighteenth and early nineteenth centuries, contrary to the mythology of America's free market origins.[92] Early American courts, legislatures, and other officials regulated the market place, commerce, public spaces, public health and safety, and morality.[93] State governments subsidized the transportation revolution directly and through corporate monopolies, and state courts subsidized growth through changes in the common law.[94] Even the federal government was creating more of a presence in administration and regulation of the economy and transportation.[95] But over time, the courts shifted against legislative power. One historian has identified a change in regimes from an active "well-regulated governance" to "the liberal state" of constitutional limits on regulation occurring in the late nineteenth century.[96] It turns out that in the 1840s and 1850s, the first generation of elected judges took significant steps in this regime change by boldly asserting constitutional limits on government power.

A common impression of the Age of Jackson is that Andrew Jackson clashed with John Marshall on the federal level and that a major platform of the Jacksonians was their opposition to judicial independence. But many Jacksonian Democrats believed in limited government and opposed the use of state power for the privileged, all the more so after the Panics of 1837 and 1839. The depression and the state fiscal crises of the 1840s underscored the problems of legislative folly and corruption and generated more support for laissez-faire constitutionalism in the American Revolutions of 1848. Reformers from both parties, from the North, South, and West, turned to judicial elections as part of a broader constitutional revolution against legislative power and in favor of limited government. In the years and then decades that followed, elected judges dramatically expanded judicial review and took steps toward the laissez-faire constitutional doctrine and substantive due process that would become the pillars of the *Lochner* era. The first elected judges also marked an important turning point in legal theory. Before judicial elections, courts relied on what scholars today call popular constitutionalism. Ever since then, countermajoritarian legal theory has captivated the minds of judges, lawyers, and scholars. Judicial power and judicial independence have thrived in America because they can be defended simultaneously as the guardians of democracy and the guardians against too much democracy.

CHAPTER SEVEN

Reconstructing Independence

OBSERVERS OF STATE COURTS have noticed a marked change in judicial elections. For most of the twentieth century, judicial elections were "sleepy" and "low key."[1] Then, in the last two decades, they have become more raucous, expensive, "noisy and nasty" affairs—in other words, more like normal elections.[2] Judicial elections were not always sleepy or under the radar. Late nineteenth-century judicial races were hotly competitive and intensely partisan in many states, with special interests taking an active role in party nominations. Still, only rarely do the records show judicial candidates announcing their positions on particular issues. By the 1870s, concerns about partisanship and corruption sparked a movement for more general judicial independence by extending judges' terms. Then the judges' response to a tragic episode—the Johnstown Flood in Pennsylvania—suggested that long terms could make elected judges *more* responsive, not less responsive, to disastrous events. In the wake of the flood, their turn toward strict liability for hazardous or unnatural industrial activity was a turn away from the elective judiciary's laissez-faire roots and toward populist regulation through tort law.

Competitive and Nasty

As judges ran in popular elections in the mid-nineteenth century, they did not campaign publicly or take positions on issues—at least not initially. Nevertheless, the partisan nomination process and the elections themselves were still competitive, and this competition was important for a few reasons: Close competition reinforced the populist aspects of elections, attracting more political personalities to the bench, instilling in judges a sense of duty to be responsive to public opinion, and bolstering public acceptance of the courts' legitimacy. Competitive judicial elections also seem to have made impeachments less common, because there was a new scheduled and apparently more appropriate channel for removing judges. Some opponents of judicial elections in the 1840s and 1850s had argued that a better solution for judicial accountability was more impeachments.[3] The age of judicial democracy showed that judicial elections replaced impeachments. Impeachments were rare after 1850, and were reserved for nonpolitical removals on grounds of incompetence or corruption.[4] Thus, judicial elections had some net benefits for judicial independence. On the other hand, close elections also increased the significance of party machines, and the significance of special interests and coalition politics. Elections were won or lost based on straight-ticket party voting and party mobilization.

According to one study of judicial elections in California, Ohio, Tennessee, and Texas from 1850 to 1920, judicial elections were remarkably close, even in states with one-party rule. In California and Ohio, the winning candidate garnered less than 55 percent of the vote (in two-party elections) in about three quarters of judicial elections in that period. Only 4 percent of California judicial elections were uncontested, and none of the Ohio races were uncontested. Tennessee and Texas were one-party states for most of this era, and yet the vast majority of races were contested, and the winners of judicial elections often commanded less than 55 percent, surprisingly low considering the dominance of the Democratic Party. Voter turnout was high compared to today.[5]

Pennsylvania records also show that races were highly competitive in this era. The election returns for Pennsylvania elections in the late nineteenth century no longer exist, but the state published a handbook recording the vote totals of nine state supreme court elections between 1877 and 1901.[6] The winning candidate prevailed with more than 52 percent of the state vote in only two elections (1893 and 1899).[7] In five of the other seven elections, the winning candidate garnered between 51 percent and 52.6 percent of the vote.[8] As for the other two elections, the winner in 1877 prevailed by about 1 percent (45.7 percent to 44.4 percent), and the winner in 1882 garnered a plurality of 48 percent to 43 percent.[9] In the late nineteenth century, judicial elections were no formality; they were close contests, which meant that judicial candidates had to stay close to the political parties that nominated them. The elections were partisan, with one Republican candidate, one Democratic candidate, and usually a few minor party candidates. The judges' margins of victory were almost always less than five percentage points—much closer than modern congressional and modern judicial elections, and often closer than the other statewide races in Pennsylvania. Pennsylvania judicial elections in the late nineteenth century were competitive.

Some competitive judicial elections gained national significance. In the late 1860s, farmers united to form a populist Granger movement that successfully pushed for legislation regulating railroad rates, warehouses, and corporations. In 1873, the Illinois Supreme Court ruled that the railroad statutes were unconstitutional. Then the Grangers led a successful campaign to oust Chief Justice C. B. Lawrence, a respected jurist who had ruled against them, in the next election. The election drew national media attention, with Charles Francis Adams outraged that a judge would be punished for ruling on "principles of law rather than in obedience to a popular demand." A major New York law periodical bemoaned that "a herd of dissatisfied farmers have put an ignorant demagogue in the seat of an able and upright judge."[10] *The Nation* advised, "All investors at home or abroad will do well to keep out of Illinois till the State chooses to set up an independent judiciary."[11] Thereafter, corporations tried harder to get their cases removed from elected state courts and into federal courts.[12]

An even more influential jurist met the same fate. Justice Thomas Cooley of Michigan, a Republican famous among lawyers for his learned treatises, had served for twenty distinguished years on the Michigan Supreme Court until the 1885 election, when he was targeted by a bitter and powerful loser of a case he had decided. In 1883, he upheld a jury verdict against the *Detroit Evening News* in a libel suit for $20,000. The *News* got its revenge by attacking him for favoring corporations and prohibition. The *Detroit Free Press* joined in the attacks, and Cooley was unequipped to fight back. In an election year that favored Michigan Democrats statewide, he lost by about 20,000 votes to a lawyer with no judicial experience. The *News* gloated that the votes were poetic justice: a 20,000-vote margin for $20,000 in damages. "The mills of the gods," its editorial celebrated, referring to the mills of the gods grinding slowly, but grinding exceedingly fine.[13]

In the general elections for the Pennsylvania Supreme Court, candidates mainly ran on party tickets, and usually they did not campaign actively for themselves on the stump or adopt particular stances on legal issues. Newspapers with partisan leanings simply published the party ticket, listing their candidates. However, the party nomination battles were often more contentious. In 1877, the conventions were competitive between judicial candidates, and particularly in a chaotic Democratic convention, where there was a "wild sense of confusion" as "personal altercations" erupted between the supporters of different candidates.[14] In the general election, party newspapers traded attacks on each other's judicial candidates and their integrity.

In 1882, Republican judicial candidates found themselves in the center of a factional civil war between populist and reformist "Independents" and machine-politics "Regulars." In the run-up to the convention, a Regular leader emphasized party loyalty (and loyalty to the machine): "We have scores of able, pure and learned lawyers who have always been staunch Republicans, and I think we should take one of them."[15] The Regulars pushed through their candidates with the support of Simon Cameron, the senator known among the reformers as the "party boss."[16] The Independent Republicans organized an opposition ticket and battled throughout the convention for their judicial candidates.[17] The Regulars represented industrial and mining interests in central and western Pennsylvania, while the Independents supported Philadelphia elites and commercial interests. Throughout the summer, these different factions and interests fought a nasty political battle in public, rather than their usual practice of fighting out nominations in conventions and backrooms.[18] The Independents declared that they were fighting "against the tyranny of bosses and the arrogance of placemen."[19] One official offered a strident speech:

> In early days the fathers of the republic declared the judiciary was the sheet-anchor of our liberty. In these later times, when education is general, this is a truism. The faction of a party which has undertaken to dictate your choice has invaded your liberties. . . . When the political manipulators extend their methods to the judiciary they should and must be put down.[20]

In the end, the Republican factions failed to mend their split, and the Democratic candidate prevailed by a 48 percent to 43 percent plurality.[21]

Sometimes hardball politics emerged in races for lower courts. In the 1889 elections for seven Pennsylvania lower court seats, five were contested by both parties, and of those, three were toss-ups. A Democratic candidate, L. W. Doty, accused his Republican opponent, A. D. McConnell, of infidelity. Doty warned that McConnell would bar liquor licenses, while Doty promised to grant liquor licenses "liberal[ly]." The Republican Pittsburgh newspaper angrily denounced his "bribes" and his "bitter" campaign.[22] Another Pennsylvania race also turned into a "bitter personal fight" with "a guerilla newspaper war waged in a way that has a tendency to lessen respect for the judiciary."[23]

An 1894 judicial election in New York was "fierce," with partisan thugs and "gangs of rowdies" beating each other senseless in a "free for all scuffle" at the ballot box.[24] One newspaper titled its article on the election "Disgraceful Scene."[25] The *New York Times,* a Republican-leaning newspaper at the time, criticized the Republican victor in the race, Judge William Werner, writing that "'the popular impression is that questionable methods were used in aiding Werner's canvass.' . . . [His] reputation as a politician [is] 'higher than his standing as a lawyer.'"[26] Parties tended to rely on political qualifications instead of more traditional legal qualifications for the bench. Thus, elections tended to attract judges who were, by temperament and training, more populist than appointed judges had been. In 1911, Werner wrote the decision for the New York Court of Appeals striking down the state's workers' compensation law on the grounds that employers had a due process right not to pay for their employees' injuries unless they were proven to have been at fault. He had his sights on the U.S. Supreme Court and imagined that this decision would draw the attention of national leaders. He had been a friend of Teddy Roosevelt's from their days as New York Republicans, and they continued to keep in touch. Instead, New Yorkers amended their constitution to override his decision in 1913, and they rejected him in his race for chief justice in the same election, ending his judicial career. In the middle of the race, newspapers reported that a regretful Werner had conceded to New York politicians that "if he had the *Ives* decision to go over again he would give a different decision."[27]

Judicial elections in the late nineteenth century were not always rough and tumble, but enough of them were controversial to focus attention on this issue and spark a debate about electioneering. The problem increasingly was identified not just with unseemly, raucous campaigning, but also biased and corrupt judging. In the wake of court corruption scandals after the Civil War, reformers rallied for changes. Some wanted an end to judicial elections—but judicial elections were too popular. Instead, the reformers turned their attention to lengthening judges' terms.

The Long Terms Solution

Partisan judicial elections might have many problems, but they had a commonsense logic in the beginning. The appointment process had allowed special interests and the other branches of government to capture and control the judiciary. Reformers believed that the emerging political parties were necessary for the people to organize and mobilize against the "monster banks," corporations, and the "interests." A generation later, in the 1860s and 1870s, many reformers recognized that "monster" parties themselves had become part of the problem. The early nineteenth-century faith in parties had turned among some to disgust. Critics believed that party insiders were able to seize control over elections through the control of small caucuses, central committees, and rigged conventions, which allowed them to stay several steps ahead of a less sophisticated and increasingly disenchanted general public.[28] Reformers had less confidence that elections would produce officials who represented the people, rather than the interests. In the wake of the assassination of President Garfield in 1883, Congress passed the Pendleton Act, which created a federal civil service as a protection against patronage and corruption. For judges, the state governments reached a different and even more paradoxical solution: lengthening the terms of judges to increase their independence from parties and to increase their responsiveness to the public.

The Civil War and Reconstruction in the South produced a flurry of new constitutions and tinkering with the courts, often for partisan self-interest. A few Confederate constitutions, such as the ones in Virginia, Florida, and Louisiana, returned from elections to appointment. At the end of the war, some defeated Confederate states also lengthened judicial terms, and their goal was a specific kind of political insulation: Old Confederate Democrats were lengthening terms to try to entrench themselves in the courts before the Reconstruction Republicans took over. Soon after, the Reconstruction Republicans took over the new state governments and overrode the entrenchment.[29] They rewrote most of the southern state constitutions, choosing appointment for six states and elections for four states.[30] Then, in 1868, the Republicans copied the Democrats' entrenchment strategy. They lengthened terms in Georgia, Arkansas, Florida, and Mississippi, using the courts as a hedge against Democratic "Redemption," the return of the Democrats to power.[31]

Union states also found the time to tinker with their judiciaries during the war, but they generally used longer terms for antipartisan purposes, rather than partisan entrenchment. James Bryce, the famous English observer of American politics in this era, wrote:

> Any one of the three phenomena I have described—popular elections, short terms, and small salaries—would be sufficient to lower the character of the judiciary. Popular elections throw the choice into the hands of political parties, that is to say, of knots of wirepullers inclined to use every office as a means of rewarding political services, and garrisoning with grateful partisans posts which may conceivably become of political importance. Short terms . . . oblige the judge to remember and keep on good terms with those who have made him what he is, and in whose hands his fortunes lie. They induce timidity, they discourage independence.[32]

Northern states focused on fixing one of Bryce's phenomena, short terms, to address the problem of political parties and their "wirepullers" in order to encourage more independence. In 1862, California extended judicial terms from six to ten years by amendment. In 1864, Maryland changed terms from ten to fifteen years by constitutional convention.[33] In 1869, New York voters ratified the state convention's Judicial Article extending judicial terms from eight to fourteen years, but rejected the rest of the convention's work.[34] In the 1870s, Missouri (by convention), Pennsylvania (by convention), Wisconsin (by amendment), and California (this time by convention) lengthened their supreme court judges' terms to double digits.[35] In most of these states, the goal was to insulate judges from party machines and corruption.

Maryland's 1864 convention was dominated by Unionists who focused primarily on abolishing slavery and disenfranchising anyone who would not take an oath of loyalty to the Union.[36] Yet it also found time to extend judicial terms from ten years to fifteen years.[37] The original judiciary committee report suggested a return to appointment by the governor and senate confirmation, with tenure during good behavior.[38] This proposal reopened the debate over elections versus appointments, but elections survived because the delegates still regarded appointments as more partisan, without popular elections serving as a check against backroom deals. As one supporter of judicial elections argued, it is better for the judge to "solicit [an appointment] at the hands of the people than at the hands of the executive."[39] Another reminded the convention that the *Dred Scott* Court "had acted as a partisan court. . . . [I]t is one of the evidences to show that the appointive system cannot change human nature." Ultimately, the amendment to continue judicial elections was accepted by a wide margin.[40]

The convention then debated whether to retain districts for judicial elections or to switch to statewide votes. The critics of statewide judicial elections feared that voters would know less about the candidates outside their district, and the voters' lack of familiarity would make the party machines more powerful. Some delegates worried that the parties would be able to foist unqualified candidates on the people in statewide elections, and they argued that short terms would be necessary for getting rid of them. But more delegates believed that this risk of partisan influence could be balanced out by lengthening judicial terms. If the parties gained power over judicial selection, longer terms would insulate judges from the parties once they were on the bench. Some delegates proposed life tenure, and in the end, they compromised on fifteen-year terms without possibility of reelection.[41]

New York followed a similar strategy after the war. In the mid-nineteenth century, many Americans regarded New York judges as the most corrupt in the country. Machine politicians controlled offices throughout the state with patronage—either by appointment or by rigging the party nomination process for elected offices, such as judgeships. In New York City, the Democratic nomination was a guarantee of election. A contemporary observer described the Democratic judicial nominating convention as a swarm of sycophants, and the nominations were compromises ironed out by ward bosses and their patronage demands. A notable example of partisan corruption of the courts was New York trial court judge Albert Cardozo, Justice Benjamin Cardozo's father. Albert Cardozo was caught in an enormous Tammany Hall scandal over Erie Railroad business deals during the late 1860s, engineered by financier Jay Gould and reaching almost every level of state government. Cardozo resigned in 1872, and many other judges in this period were swept up in similar scandals.[42]

Judicial reform was a top priority of New York's constitutional convention in 1867.[43] The elite bar had much more power in this convention than they had in the Radical Barnburner convention of 1846. Even though these elite lawyers did not appreciate the Barnburners or their constitution, they shared the Barnburners' priorities of anticorruption, judicial independence, and judicial power. They thought the courts had declined sharply, and nearly all blamed the Constitution of 1846 for having created judicial elections, for creating short judicial terms, or both.[44] Delegates complained that the New York bench's prestige had declined sharply since 1846 and that other states were no longer following New York precedents. Judge Charles Daly, a Democrat elected to the court of common pleas in New York City and a delegate at the 1867 convention, declared from experience: "The real evil at present is that, after [a judge] goes upon the bench, he depends for his continuance there upon . . . all the influences which affect political parties."[45] Daly suggested:

> [A judge] soon learns that his continuance in office does not depend upon his learning, his ability or his integrity. . . . He may have the learning of Mansfield and the integrity of Hale, but it will avail him little if his party is not in power, and if he is not an active, leading and influential member of it.[46]

As a result, judges remained deeply involved in party politics:

> Within the last six or seven years, the name of almost every judge in the city of New York has been heralded in the newspapers as president or vice-president of some political meeting, not from their own choice in all cases, but because the exigencies of party demanded it.[47]

Daly also blamed short terms and party politics for removing good judges from the bench.[48] Other convention delegates from both parties added names of good judges who were not reelected, with some blaming Boss Tweed and party corruption.[49] All implied that the New York bench's declining prestige was due to the replacement of these judges with less able judges. The New York convention reached a consensus to extend terms on the court of appeals (the state's highest court) from eight years to fourteen years, which many delegates compared to life tenure. They also scheduled a referendum on judicial elections versus judicial appointments for 1873, allowing several years for the public to observe the new constitution and its extended judicial terms in practice. In 1869, the voters separately ratified the convention's Judiciary Article, but rejected the other parts.[50]

In the referendum campaign of 1873, in the midst of new political and judicial scandals, reformers renewed their efforts to abolish judicial elections. One reformer, Dorman Eaton, produced extensive statistical and anecdotal evidence purporting to show the corrupting influence of elections: more appeals, more new trials, more reversals of civil cases, and a declining rate of conviction.[51] All of these changes were probably attributable to broader social factors, but he suggested that elections caused these failings. He also offered this statistic: "The unexampled number of five judges . . . awaiting trial for official corruption [in 1872]—a number greater than were arraigned in the whole period of appointed judges in this state from 1777 to 1846."[52] Despite the scandals of the early 1870s, the voters rejected the proposed amendment to reestablish appointments, illustrating how difficult it has been to switch back from judicial elections to appointments, or alternatively, illustrating how the public was hopeful that longer terms would change the integrity of the courts.

By the 1870s, Pennsylvania elites, much like New Yorkers, were increasingly exasperated by corruption and party machines. These leaders called for a new constitutional convention in 1873, in which the tenure of state supreme court justices was lengthened from fifteen to twenty-one years.[53] Reformers did not attack elections themselves, perhaps because the existing fifteen-year state supreme court terms had already created more judicial independence. However, across the spectrum, the debate over selection of judges was significantly focused on further insulating the judiciary from the corrupting partisanship that infected the political branches of Pennsylvania government.[54]

One of the main purposes of the 1873 convention was to address political patronage of the courts. In the 1870s, Pennsylvania's urban machine politics led to "the tyranny of local political bosses of the majority party."[55] The governor went so far as to suggest that partisanship in the legislature and in the courts "had almost destroyed the theory of representative government."[56] The convention delegates discussed proposed changes to the judiciary for fourteen consecutive days.[57] The Committee on the Judiciary recommended that justices of the supreme court be appointed by the governor with the concurrence of two thirds of the senate,[58] sparking a fiery debate among the delegates.

A small number of delegates who opposed electing judges argued that free and fair elections were essentially impossible. One delegate asserted that "if it was safe to elect judges in 1850, when our elections were free and pure, it is not safe to elect them now, when, by common consent, popular elections have ceased to be either free or pure." Another asked, "Do any of us who are familiar with the manner in which these elections are brought about, believe that the mass of the people have any voice in the nomination or election of a judge?"[59]

However, most delegates believed that judicial elections were relatively *less partisan* than appointments. One delegate asserted that "the people, in their votes, have been less governed by party ties than the Governor."[60] Another imagined a judge appointed "by a corrupt Governor, and confirmed by a Senate combining for a corrupt purpose."[61] As the debate wrapped up, the rhetoric increased: "One of the great evils in this country has been this matter of executive patronage, and out of that has grown the evil of having in office incompetent persons."[62] Some proponents of elections still were concerned that the corrupting influences affecting the appointment process could infect sitting elected judges as well, overcoming the insulation of the already lengthy fifteen-year terms for supreme court justices.[63] The convention ended in a rejection of the committee's recommendation to return to appointments, and instead extended the terms of supreme court judges to the quasi-life term of twenty-one years.[64] These delegates turned to longer terms not to insulate judges from the people, but rather, to insulate judges from corruption so that they could better serve the people that had elected them in the first place.

California voters had extended judicial terms to ten years by amendment in 1862, and the constitutional convention of 1878–1879 further extended the state supreme court terms from ten to twelve years.[65] In an extensive debate, the more dominant position favored longer terms, and the dominant rhetoric was pro–judicial independence.[66] One delegate argued:

> The only safety is in having a bench independent of all things; independent of money influence, independent of the influence of popular clamor, independent of political influence; and, without that, you cannot have a pure and independent judiciary. . . . Where you take a man in the prime of life,

and put him in the office of Judge of the Supreme Court, you should give him a term that he may expect for a great portion of the balance of his life. Put him there under these circumstances, and give him salary enough so that he does not have to look after his own private interest, and to pinch himself for money to pay his monthly bills, and you have an independent judiciary; and that is the only way.[67]

He added that these elections were swung by party machines and timing more than the candidates themselves. He and other delegates concluded that voters did not base their decisions on the quality of the judicial candidate, but more on party labels.[68] Reelection was luck, so it was more important to take whatever mediocre bench the parties and voters chose, and at least insulate that bench from the parties and the voters. The delegates had observed that the "Eastern States" had tried short terms and it only produced corruption. "Give us a long term, and by that means we obviate the necessity of men going into politics for judicial positions. They also learn what is the interest of the people of the State. This is what the people want."[69] The convention then voted to lengthen the judicial term to twelve years.[70]

In these four conventions, the rhetoric of judicial independence prevailed. Many states in this era sacrificed direct judicial accountability in favor of more general judicial independence. Delegates focused more on insulating judges from parties and corruption than on removing judges from popular control. Some delegates argued that long terms would allow judges to be more responsive to the public once they were protected from special interests. To the modern reader, these reformers' belief that longer terms would lead judges to make more publicly minded decisions might seem far-fetched. In fact, there is at least one piece of doctrinal evidence from the late nineteenth century that appears to confirm their view.

The Johnstown Flood and the Twist of Long Terms

Pittsburgh's titans of industry—including Andrew Carnegie, Andrew Mellon, and Henry Clay Frick—belonged to the South Fork Fishing and Hunting Club, also known as "The Bosses' Club."[71] The club owned one of the largest reservoirs in the world and used it for recreation. The club's owners and employees ignored many warnings of the reservoir dam's decay, and it collapsed in the middle of a violent night storm in 1889. Twenty million tons of water crashed into the valley below at one hundred miles an hour. The flood completely destroyed Johnstown, killing two thousand people, and even flooded Washington, D.C. It became the legendary "Johnstown Flood," one of the most deadly disasters in American history and "the biggest news story since the murder of Abraham Lincoln." Public opinion turned against the club's wealthy members and newspapers demanded justice. A county commission quickly investigated the dam, and on June 7 it announced that the owners were "culpable" and "responsible" for the deaths. Throughout the country, newspapers accused the club of being "negligent," criminally negligent, or even guilty of manslaughter. Mobs gathered and attacked the club.[72]

Two months after the Johnstown Flood, one of the most prestigious legal periodicals of the time, the *American Law Review,* published an article detailing the flood's carnage and calling for courts to change tort law by expanding strict liability for bursting reservoirs. The Johnstown Flood had transformed a vibrant town into "a great mass of earth, stones, trees, houses, railway locomotives, cars, human bodies, and what not . . . very deep and . . . very solid." The author then concludes that one particular English precedent, *Fletcher v. Rylands,* was "the best answer which has ever yet been given."[73]

Fletcher v. Rylands was a case of a reservoir crashing into abandoned coal mines and then destroying a neighbor's active coal mines. A lower court had ruled that the coal mine owner could not recover because the reservoir owner had not been proven negligent. But two appellate courts ruled in favor of the coal mine owner, holding that he did not have to prove negligence. The Exchequer Chamber ruled that a person who "for his own purposes brings on his lands and collects and keeps there anything likely to do mischief if it escapes, must keep it in at his peril," and pay for the damage if it escapes.[74] The House of Lords affirmed, focusing on "non-natural uses . . . likely to do mischief."[75] The facts of the case may have been unusual, but the court's language was very broad. Because *Rylands* imposed liability without regard to fault—that is, regardless of whether the owner had been careful in building and maintaining the reservoir—the ruling portended a far-reaching, plaintiff-friendly liability regime, especially if its "strict liability" approach applied to other activities.

However, English courts narrowly limited the rule thereafter, and American courts opposed it—at least initially.[76] The highest courts in New York,[77] New Hampshire,[78] and New Jersey[79] rejected *Rylands* in the 1870s in cases that many of today's tort casebooks continue to offer as representative of American tort law. The Pennsylvania Supreme Court then rejected *Rylands* in 1886.[80] After these prominent eastern state supreme courts rejected *Rylands,* America's treatise writers followed.[81] This initial reaction helped what would become the modern conventional wisdom about American tort law: in the nineteenth century, a general proindustry negligence rule replaced premodern strict liability rules,[82] and only in the mid-twentieth century did pockets of provictim strict liability return.[83] To this day, most modern tort casebooks include some note with this historical interpretation after *Rylands,* often including one or two of the American cases rejecting *Rylands* as representative of American law.[84]

In the post-flood article in the *American Law Review,* the author acknowledged that *Rylands* had been "adopted by several American courts, though denied by some."[85] He nonetheless defended it as necessary to provide justice for victims like Johnstown's.[86] Pennsylvania courts confirmed the *American Law Review*'s concerns, because suits by the victims of the Johnstown Flood failed against the club and its members. The most direct legal problem appeared to be the courts' refusal to pierce the "corporate veil" separating the judgment-proof club from its deep-pocket members (who were not legally liable for the club's actions). However, the media reported that the obstacle was the negligence requirement.[87] Newspapers offered lawyers' explanations that the club itself was not a good target for a suit because it had no assets, and that individual members of the club would be liable only if the plaintiffs could prove individual negligence.[88]

While the trial courts frustrated the flood's victims, the Pennsylvania Supreme Court was responding quickly on a broader doctrinal level. Three years before the flood, the Pennsylvania Supreme Court had gone out of its way to repudiate *Rylands* in *Pennsylvania Coal Co. v. Sanderson.*[89] Even though the court ruled that *Rylands* was inapplicable to the facts before it, it still took the opportunity to attack *Rylands,* declaring that the English precedent had been rejected in America and that its rule was "arbitrary."[90] The court also emphasized the "great public interest" of industry's unfettered development, dismissing the "mere personal" and "trifling inconveniences" that were caused by industrial damage and that must "give way to the necessities of a great community."[91]

The Johnstown Flood swept in a new attitude toward big industry and liability. In *Robb v. Carnegie Bros.,* an 1891 case involving Andrew Carnegie—the most prominent figure connected to the flood—the Pennsylvania Supreme Court applied strict liability to a basic and necessary function in the manufacturing of coal.[92] The plaintiff's counsel cited *Fletcher v. Rylands* and argued that the damage caused by the coal factory, unlike the damage caused by the mine water in *Sanderson,* was not caused by a "natural product," but rather by one that was "brought" to the defendants' property.[93] The appeal was first argued on October 10, 1889,[94] just five months after the Johnstown Flood.

The court adopted a rule of strict liability in a unanimous decision, with three of the *Sanderson* judges changing their pre-flood stance, including the author of *Sanderson*.[95] The *Robb* ruling limited "natural" activities to the natural "develop[ment of] the resources of his property," which sharply distinguished *Sanderson*.[96] The key distinction between *Sanderson* and *Robb* rested on the natural/unnatural dichotomy: coal mining itself was natural, but any further development or manufacturing of the coal was not natural.[97] Again, this dispute over naturalness and nonnaturalness was an implicit reference to *Rylands*.

Robb further eviscerated *Sanderson* by rejecting *Sanderson*'s reasoning about the greater public importance of industrial development. *Robb* first asserted that "it is a fundamental principle of our system of government that the interest of the public is higher than that of the individual."[98] The opinion then stated that industry is not public, like roads, rails, highways, and canals, but rather private. The industrialist "is serving himself in his own way, and has no right to claim exemption from the natural consequences of his own act."[99] The Pennsylvania Supreme Court expanded strict liability for unnatural activities in a series of cases in the 1890s.[100] After the Johnstown Flood, federal courts continued to ignore *Rylands,* but many state courts adopted it. By the turn of the twentieth century, eighteen states had adopted *Rylands* explicitly and seven more had adopted a general strict liability rule for unnatural activities, hazardous activities, or *Rylands*-like storage of large amounts of water.[101] Most of these states adopted *Rylands* in the 1890s. See Appendix F.

Broad social and economic conditions had set the table for the adoption of strict liability: increasingly heavy industries developing side-by-side with urban or residential areas; business cycles (bust in the 1870s, boom in the 1880s, and bust in the 1890s); and the rise of the Populists as critics of industry's excess in the 1890s. However, there was no geographic, industrial/agricultural, or business cycle pattern to the adoption of strict liability. It was also not a partisan issue: Republican-leaning and Democratic-leaning states both overwhelmingly adopted *Rylands* in the 1890s and the early 1900s. The trigger for this wave of adoptions was the Johnstown Flood, assisted by other flooding disasters in California and Texas. And the politics of judicial elections shaped the way that trigger influenced state courts.[102]

Conventional scholarly wisdom has held that the modern American tort doctrine of strict liability for hazardous activities emerged in the middle of the twentieth century around the time of the New Deal, but, in fact, it burst onto the scene in the wake of bursting reservoirs and flooding disasters in the late nineteenth century, and mostly through the rulings of elected judges. Federal judges (who are appointed, of course) and *appointed* state judges mostly ignored or rejected *Rylands* after the flood.

The Johnstown Flood added hydraulic pressure in favor of strict liability for activities that seemed "unnatural." There was no mass movement against the fault rule, no "Strict Liability" political party, no "The People for *Rylands*" street protests. Even though strict liability was never a campaign issue, elected judges translated a disaster into a narrow, focused (but somewhat esoteric) doctrinal change.[103] Even if the adoption of *Rylands* had no effect on a judge's popularity, elected judges were attuned to current events and outrage.

That elected judges might be more responsive to current events is not shocking. The real surprise is that longer terms did not make judges less responsive to events. Admittedly, this study is limited to one area of tort law over a decade or two. Nevertheless, the Johnstown Flood episode offers a hint that longer terms might make elected judges more responsive to recent events, rather than special interests. This counterintuitive effect is what the Reconstruction-era reformers had intended in lengthening judges' terms. Pennsylvania, New York, California, Maryland, and other states lengthened terms explicitly to give judges *more* freedom from special interests and from political corruption, so that judges could decide cases without being cabined by their party base. These reforms arguably paved the way for *Rylands*'s adoption to spread two decades later.

The Johnstown Flood and *Rylands*'s overlooked adoption are a story of tragedy and democracy shaping the law. It is important not to romanticize the responsiveness of elected state judges, because their responsiveness led to a confusing and unstable body of tort doctrine in the nineteenth century. Nevertheless, the Reconstruction era was another example of Americans' enduring commitment to "general" judicial independence in the form of long terms. The judges they elected to long terms then showed in the Johnstown-*Rylands* episode that they could balance this general judicial independence with responsiveness to events.

CHAPTER EIGHT

The Progressives' Failed Solutions

THE EARLY TWENTIETH CENTURY was a turning point in the perception of parties and of courts. The problems of party corruption and special interests had been apparent for a long time, but the progressives took on the issue more directly. The courts had their own crisis in a constitutional stand-off with progressive legislatures. In their efforts to reform both courts and parties, the progressives proposed several failed solutions, including nonpartisan elections and procedural checks on courts, as well as a solution that failed to catch on for a few decades: expert judicial selection by the professional bar.

The constitutional conflict is now known as the *Lochner* Era, named for the U.S. Supreme Court decision striking down a New York law that had limited bakers to a maximum of sixty hours a week.[1] *Lochner v. New York* was one of a series of decisions expanding the freedom of contract and limiting government regulation of the economy. From the 1890s through the 1920s, the U.S. Supreme Court famously struck down the progressive income tax, protective labor and unionization laws, child labor laws, and minimum wage laws, often by five-to-four votes.[2]

Many state courts also blocked progressive legislation. Ohio's legislature passed a series of progressive statutes around the turn of the century, and the state supreme court struck many of them down: the state inheritance tax, water sanitation regulations, teacher pensions, the eight-hour workday for public employees, and railroad liability for injuries. The court also ruled that the city charter was an unconstitutional type of local legislation, and upheld the state's *optional* workers' compensation plan by only a four-to-two vote. This narrow margin raised the workers' fears that the court would strike down any compulsory plan in the near future, as New York's high court had done in 1911.[3]

As Ohio goes, so goes the country. The state that picked all but two of the presidential winners of the twentieth century also was a microcosm of the early twentieth century's great constitutional crisis and a renewed struggle over partisanship. These challenges led to Ohio's constitutional convention in 1912 being a battleground for the nation's leading progressives over the courts, and it was part of a new wave of constitutional revision. The constitutional convention was a focal point of the progressive agenda in many states. Thirteen states held conventions between 1900 and 1920. Ohio's 1912 convention was perhaps the most remarkable spectacle of them, as it became a major event in one of the most dramatic presidential campaigns in American history. President William Taft, Teddy Roosevelt, and other presidential aspirants used Ohio as a platform to declare their stance on judicial independence and judicial accountability.

Ohio's convention led the next evolutionary stage of judicial politics, the switch from partisan to nonpartisan judicial elections. Eight other states made this move in the 1910s, and ten more followed soon after. At the turn of the twentieth century, twenty states still used nonpartisan competitive elections for most of their courts, making it the most common method of judicial selection. However, this reform was more a façade than a real solution. Progressives also proposed other checks on the judiciary, such as judicial recall, overriding court decisions by popular vote, and limiting the power of judicial review. Despite a number of conditions favoring the success of these progressive initiatives, all of them failed in this era. The year 1912 was pivotal. On the national stage, Teddy Roosevelt offered a more confrontational and creative agenda of judicial reform, but he lost to Woodrow Wilson and his more incremental, nonconfrontational campaign, and Roosevelt's ideas disappeared. Ohio's 1912 convention suggests that state-level efforts also failed because reformers were too incrementalist, too unimaginative, and too naïve about party politics. The public and even the courts' critics in the midst of this crisis still were committed to the idea of judicial independence, so they turned back from aggressive checks and opted for window dressing. But at the same time, progressive lawyers came up with a new idea for deeper structural independence from the political parties, a plan for nonpartisan expert selection that did not catch on during these years but would eventually would catch on as the "merit" plan, and it would be much more than window dressing.

Ohio's Star-Studded Convention

In Ohio, a progressive coalition of political reformers, professionals, labor unions, and prohibitionists—united by their opposition to laissez-faire capitalism and party machines—campaigned for a new constitutional convention partly to address these judicial decisions and generally to modernize the constitution. While there was no specific movement for nonpartisan judicial elections, the idea fit in with the progressives' broader agenda to counter a court they regarded as partisan and obstructionist. Ohio conservatives and businesses were pleased with the court decisions, but they had their own reason to support a convention: to restructure the tax system. The Ohio State Board of Commerce spearheaded the drive to repeal the constitution's uniform tax rule and to reduce taxes on businesses, so it formed an unlikely alliance with progressives favoring a convention. The public's vote for a convention was ten to one.[4]

Once the convention met, it scheduled a series of high-profile speakers. President William Taft (an Ohioan), presidential candidate Teddy Roosevelt, William Jennings Bryan, and California Governor Hiram Johnson, one of the nation's most important progressive leaders, spoke in the first few weeks of the long convention. Senator Robert LaFollette, a progressive Republican running for president, also spoke in the run-up to the convention. Teddy Roosevelt was the first to appear. He had earlier endorsed the recall of federal judges, in part because he was "so disappointed" in the judges he had appointed himself.[5] Roosevelt titled his address "A Charter of Democracy," and it was reprinted and distributed nationally as part of his Bull Moose Progressive candidacy. In the aggressive speech directed mainly against the judiciary, he recommended the introduction of both "judicial removal" by a simple majority of the legislature and "judicial recall," in which the voters remove a judge from office.[6]

Roosevelt's rhetoric suggested that adopting these measures was a matter of life or death: "The recall is not so much a recall of judges from office as it is a recall of the administration of justice back to life, so that it shall become, as it ought to be, the most efficient of all agencies for making this earth a better place to live in. Judges have set their rules above life. . . . Both law and life are to be considered in order that the law and the Constitution shall become, in John Marshall's words, 'a living instrument and not a dead letter.' Justice between man and man, between the State and its citizens, is a living thing, whereas legalistic justice is a dead thing." Recall would kill some judges' careers, but more importantly for Roosevelt, it would "recall" the judiciary "back to life" as a transformative force.[7]

California Governor Hiram Johnson, one of the most prominent progressives in the country, had led the fight in California to extend recall to judges, and he focused almost half of his address to the convention on this point. He also ratcheted up the rhetoric: "The recall . . . menaces just one kind of judge, and that is the corrupt judge, and he ought to be menaced by something. By pointing a pistol at a man you do not make him a coward; you only prove him one."[8] The perennial Democratic-Populist presidential candidate William Jennings Bryan also championed judicial recall in his Ohio convention speech,[9] and Senator LaFollette fought to add a judicial recall plank to the Republican platform that year.[10]

Recall was no lightning bolt out of the blue in 1912. Since at least the 1890s, other progressive and populist officials and journalists had been clamoring for judicial recall and the popular election of federal judges.[11] One of the most frequently proposed federal amendments in this era was the establishment of federal judicial elections.[12] Of course, these efforts failed, in large part because the hurdles for amending the federal constitution are so onerous: two thirds of both houses of Congress, and then three quarters of the states. Contrast these hurdles with the much simpler process of state constitutional amendments, which generally require only simple majority votes by the legislature and the public. This basic difference explains much of the disparity between the evolving elected state judiciary and the stable appointed federal judiciary.

Furthermore, while populists were enthusiastic about judicial elections, their usual allies, the progressives, were more ambivalent. Populists and progressives were united in their opposition to laissez-faire law and politics around the turn of the twentieth century, and usually worked together for political reform. The Populist Party, after some success in the late 1880s and 1890s, receded after 1900, and its followers joined progressive groups.[13] It is not easy to distinguish between populism and progressivism as historical movements. However, judicial elections reveal the more subtle differences between the two groups.

The populist wing tended to believe that more direct democracy was the solution to most social problems. The progressive wing, however, believed that in some contexts, less democracy and more expertise were necessary. The populists of the early twentieth century had a strong faith that voters could purify politics. The populists were more likely to support the popular election and recall of federal judges, but the progressives were not. Progressives preferred direct democracy to insider politics, of course, but they also preferred expertise to direct democracy in certain professional domains, including technical regulation and the law. Many progressives urged conservative judges to yield to public opinion,

THE PROGRESSIVES' FAILED SOLUTIONS   163

but also argued that the rule of law generally should be insulated from public opinion. Roosevelt's speech to the Ohio convention itself voiced these conflicting sentiments.[14]

The critical point here is that the idea of judicial independence retained its sway even among the progressives who were so frustrated by it. Populists and progressives retreated from these attacks out of a fear of backlash. Even William Jennings Bryan, who built his presidential candidacy based on attacking judicial decisions and spared no conservative force in America from his fiery oratory, exempted the U.S. Supreme Court. In his legendary "Cross of Gold" speech at the 1896 Democratic nominating convention, Bryan vigorously denied that he was criticizing the Court itself, and emphasized that the party platform made "no suggestion of an attempt to dispute the authority of the Supreme Court."[15] By that time, Bryan already privately supported proposals for the election of federal judges, but he feared that a public endorsement would trigger fears that he was too radical.[16] Perhaps his fear was justified, because McKinley, the Republican nominee, had already won political advantage by warning that Bryan would undermine the power of the courts.

Samuel Gompers, the head of the American Federation of Labor, the largest labor organization in America, also tempered his attacks on the federal judiciary during this era. Gompers certainly criticized the Court's antilabor decisions, and when speaking or writing to a labor audience, he often turned to strong rhetoric, such as calling antilabor injunctions the "judicial reenactment of slavery."[17] However, even in front of these sympathetic audiences, he also felt the need to balance his criticisms with conciliatory comments. In 1908, he softened his criticisms by conceding that the justices acted "honestly and conscientiously," adding, "We do not agree with those who charge the court with being influenced by sinister motives, or under the domination of corporate influence."[18] Gompers avoided any mention of reforming the judiciary's power, and instead urged union members to ask their congressmen to revise labor statutes. Gompers spent more time telling laborers to obey court orders than to disobey them. Instead of disobedience, Gompers urged labor to go to the polls to defeat antilabor legislators and state judges. Only after World War I did Gompers abandon his moderate path.[19] Gompers and other labor leaders feared that an attack on the judiciary would offend the public, just as Bryan had feared. They perceived that the American people had a deep attachment to the courts as a symbol of American law, even if they disagreed with the content of the courts' decisions. Some populists and labor leaders were conflicted about judicial power. Even though they had been frustrated by federal and state judges for decades, many still believed that the judiciary would someday become a vanguard for defending their own rights claims.[20]

In 1912, Roosevelt had an uphill battle as a third-party candidate, but he thought he could ride antijudicial anger back to the White House. Instead, his attacks triggered a backlash robbing him of momentum. Roosevelt's target and foil was William Howard Taft, a staunch defender of the courts. When the territory of Arizona included judicial recall in its proposed constitution in 1911, President Taft vetoed it because recall was "so pernicious in its effect, so destructive of independence in the judiciary . . . that I must disapprove a Constitution containing it."[21] He called judicial recall "legalized terrorism."[22] Arizona's drafters dropped the provision to win statehood, and then promptly reproposed it and adopted it after they no longer had to answer to Taft. In fact, far fewer Americans had to answer to Taft after he lost the dramatic 1912 election. Taft had something of a last laugh on the topic of judicial independence when he became a stridently independent chief justice in 1921.

On judicial politics circa 1912, Roosevelt was too hot, Taft was too cold, but perhaps Woodrow Wilson was just right. Wilson opposed the idea of recalling judges and took mild positions on the courts.[23] Both Wilson and the Democratic platform avoided advocating any structural reforms of the courts themselves. Instead, Wilson campaigned on specific policies and social legislation, an incrementalist vision of progressivism that avoided a direct confrontation with the Supreme Court. Roosevelt's campaign failed to persuade the Democratic and Republican parties and failed to win public support for his judicial proposals. Roosevelt's defeat, despite his outpolling Taft, spelled the demise of sweeping judicial reform, and his aggressive proposals disappeared from political debate.

There was yet another problem with national leaders proposing checks on Ohio's courts and most other state judiciaries: They fundamentally misdiagnosed the problem they sought to address. Judicial elections were not the solution to the progressives' frustrations with judicial review. Elected state judges were about as likely as appointed federal judges to strike down regulatory legislation in favor of business or individual rights.[24] Most states already had their own form of judicial recall: judicial elections to relatively short terms. Considering that most judges had terms of about six to eight years, and that most state supreme courts had five or seven members, the public probably had a shot every year or two at "recalling" a judge who had voted to strike down a popular statute or otherwise crossed the progressives' causes. New Yorkers voted Judge William Werner out of office soon after he had written the decision striking down the state's workers' compensation law. In the same election, New Yorkers also amended their state constitution to override the decision.[25] This is an example of another progressive solution: checks on the courts, instead of attacks on judges.

"Independent Judges, Dependent Judiciary"

Ohio's delegates offered some alternatives that limited judicial power, but did not limit judges' job security. These proposals fit what some leading scholars have called "independent judges, dependent judiciary."[26] Another way of thinking about these alternatives is that they curtailed judicial supremacy, but not judicial independence. They could overturn the judges' decisions without turning the judges out of office.

One example was Teddy Roosevelt's pet proposal: the recall of judicial decisions as opposed to the recall of the judges themselves. Roosevelt suggested that if a court were to strike down a statute, the voters should have a final say after a two-year period of deliberation. The voters could then reinstate the statute, overriding the court's decision. At the Ohio constitutional convention, Roosevelt explained, "When a judge decides a constitutional question, when he decides what the people as a whole can or cannot do, the people should have the right to recall that decision if they think it wrong. We should hold the judiciary in all respect; but it is both absurd and degrading to make a fetish of a judge or of any one else."[27] For the remainder of the presidential campaign, Roosevelt replaced his demand for the recall of judges with the recall of decisions,[28] but this idea did not get far either. The only state to implement it was Colorado in 1913, and the state supreme court struck down this provision eight years later.[29]

Rather than adopt a formal recall process, the Ohio convention turned to a much more traditional form of this strategy: the constitutional amendment. Progressives had already used the federal amendment process to "recall" or reverse a U.S. Supreme Court decision. The Supreme Court struck down the federal income tax in 1895 in *Pollock,* and for almost two decades progressives pursued a constitutional amendment to overcome the Court's opposition. The Sixteenth Amendment was ratified in 1913, the first in almost a half-century. Over the next three years, reformers prevailed in ratifying three more federal amendments. The Seventeenth Amendment, which established the direct election of senators, was ratified the same year. The Eighteenth Amendment—Prohibition— was ratified in 1919, and was a kind of "recall" of various state decisions that had limited state prohibition laws. One year later, the Nineteenth Amendment gave women the vote. The Ohio convention itself was an example of this strategy. Progressives organized the convention in part to override a series of conservative decisions invalidating statutes. The convention—and later the voters—adopted seven clauses to override court decisions against workers' compensation, the establishment of an eight-hour workday, and teachers' pension funds.[30]

Another example of the "independent judges, dependent judiciary" model of judicial reform was the supermajority voting rule: a state supreme court should need a supermajority, not just a bare majority, of its judges to strike down legislation. From the Marshall Court through the Taney Court and then Reconstruction, other critics of judicial power had proposed such rules, but they never succeeded on the state or federal level until Ohio in 1912.[31] Like the U.S. Supreme Court in these years, the Ohio Supreme Court invalidated several progressive statutes by narrow votes.[32] In his Ohio convention speech, William Jennings Bryan called for a unanimity rule among the state's supreme court judges to limit their power to invalidate statutes.[33] A superior court judge, Hiram Peck, proposed such an amendment as a convention delegate.[34] Frustrated with the judges as "stumbling blocks to progress," Peck conceded, "We cannot look into the breast of a judge to see whether a matter of political expediency has influenced him."[35] Because of this reluctance to impeach a judge's credibility or to impeach a judge formally, Judge Peck wanted to check judges together as an institution. The convention adopted a rule requiring the concurrence of all but one of the judges to void state legislation.[36] Fittingly, the delegates voted for this near-unanimity rule nearly unanimously: ninety-seven to five in one round, and ninety-three to six in the final round.[37] Two more states followed Ohio. In 1918, North Dakota amended its constitution with a rule requiring four of the five supreme court judges to concur in order to strike down a statute,[38] and in 1920, Nebraska changed its constitution to require the concurrence of five out of seven supreme court judges.[39] Ohio rescinded its amendment in 1968, but North Dakota's and Nebraska's supermajority rules are still in effect today.

The supermajority rule was appealing to many progressives, but it failed to capture the public's imagination. It was a technical procedural remedy, rather than a simple substantive proposal. And there were many ways for the judges to evade this rule. For example, the judges could say that they were not striking down the statute on constitutional grounds, but that they were ruling on other grounds, like statutory interpretation. Moreover, even if the public was sometimes frustrated by close votes among a small group of judges, much of the public also wanted the court to be able to protect constitutional limits, and feared that supermajority rules might turn out to be a way of crippling the courts' independent check on government excess. For a combination of reasons, the supermajority rule did not spread very far in an era disposed to embrace it, nor did it spread during similar backlashes in the 1930s and the 1960s– 1970s. Americans were attached not only to independence for judges but also to the independence of the court as an institution.

The Emergence of Nonpartisan Judicial Elections

Partisan judicial elections had a commonsense logic in the beginning. The appointment process had allowed special interests and the other branches of government to capture and control the judiciary. Reformers believed that public-minded individuals could not take on the insiders and the interests on their own. The emerging political parties were necessary for the people to organize and mobilize against "monster banks" and corporations. Parties could fight for the public interest against the "interests." A generation later, during Reconstruction, many reformers recognized that "monster" parties themselves and the corruption they bred had become part of the problem, and their answer was to lengthen the terms of judges to increase their independence from the parties.

A generation after that, when the parties were at the height of their power, progressives continued the struggle against partisanship, capture, and corruption. A new perspective on partisanship developed: Partisan elections created a judiciary that was more easily captured by ideology and special interests. Candidates had to rely heavily on party connections to be nominated and elected. Then elected judges were perceived as being beholden to their party, and their independence and integrity were questioned once they were on the bench. Some observers noted that the parties were run by lawyers, and those party leaders had some skill and interest in picking competent judges.[40] On the other hand, they also had the legal skills and special legal interests to pick judges who would be favorable to their side and their machine. One contemporary observed, "The use of the Republican or Democratic insignia in city elections served as a sort of 'smoke-screen,' behind which municipal spoilsmen and office-brokers could hide in safety."[41] Surveys of lawyers suggest that state bars were evenly split between favoring appointment and election, but the upper echelons of the bar, including the American Bar Association and its first president, supported a return to appointment for life.[42]

Another perception was that partisan elections pushed judges toward judicial review in favor of business interests and against the public interest.[43] In Ohio and around the country, judges from both parties voted to strike down progressive legislation, so the problem was not the product of one party or the other, but was the product of party interests structurally trumping majority preferences. In 1911, Nebraska Governor Chester Aldrich, a progressive, blamed this "trouble" on the fact that courts were "composed of lawyers who owe their position, not so much to legal attainment and profound learning, as they do to political services rendered."[44] Just as both parties had a progressive wing, both also had their own business interests and special interests that opposed the progressive agenda. Thus, progressives fought to free the political system from the party system. Progressives hoped to reduce the influence of party machines and special interests, and they believed that nonpartisan elections would be a way to do so.[45] In 1873, a group of judges in Cook County, Illinois, decided on their own to run on a nonpartisan ballot, and their tradition continued in later elections.[46] But this practice came from willing judges, not from any legal mandate. A few western states began to experiment with some nonpartisan elections for local offices. In 1911, Ohio applied that experiment to judges.

After Ohio voters approved the calling of a constitutional convention, the state legislature went to work on judicial reform even before the convention assembled. The Non-Partisan Judiciary Act of 1911 required the candidates' names "to be placed on a separate ballot without party designation."[47] The statute applied only to the ballots in general elections, and it did not affect the partisan nomination process. Judicial candidates still had to win party nominations to get on the ballot. Some progressives tried to use the convention to push for further reforms, but the delegates botched the effort because of their incrementalism and lack of imagination. Even though most progressives came to the convention as critics of partisanship, they were unable to commit to real nonpartisanship because they remained partisan themselves. This failure in Ohio has been a microcosm for the overall failure of nonpartisan judicial elections since the Progressive era.

After the Non-Partisan Judiciary Act had only tinkered with the general election ballot, progressives at the convention wanted to go deeper to the root of the problem. Delegates blamed the inefficiencies of the court system on partisan politics leading to incompetent crony judges. One endorsed a version of expert merit selection, but conceded that the convention and the public were not ready for such a major change. Instead, the delegates focused on a more acceptable target: the party convention. They argued that the party convention allowed the bosses to foist bad candidates on the voters and rob the public of real choices at the ballot box.[48]

A progressive delegate, the newspaper editor J. W. Tannehill, called the Non-Partisan Judiciary Act a "joke" of a solution.[49] "I would as soon have our people menaced with the cholera or black death as to run the gauntlet of another legislature such as the last. . . . [T]he people have been trifled with and betrayed by corrupt legislators until they will endure the perfidy and infamy no longer. They are going to demand their rights."[50] He and other progressive delegates regarded the Non-Partisan Judiciary Act not as a helpful first step, but rather as proof of the partisan capture of the legislature producing a façade of reform but preserving the bosses' control.[51] Tannehill proposed a constitutional measure that would abolish the party convention and replace it with the direct party primary. He condemned the "tyranny" by the party bosses and their insider conventions. "The chief cause of the frequent failure of representative government," he claimed, "lies in the corrupt, boss-controlled, drunken, debauched and often hysterical nominating convention. The convention must go."[52] So long as "the manner of their [judges and other elected officials] selection is such that party bosses . . . can name both the democrat and republican candidates for each office, there can be no hope of improvement in representative government."[53] Tannehill believed that direct primaries would wrest control from party bosses.

Other delegates wanted to go further. As long as the convention was considering direct primaries, it should make them open nonpartisan direct primaries. All of the candidates would run in one primary, and the top two finishers would face each other in a runoff general election. They argued that this system of nonpartisan direct democracy was more legitimate.[54] They also suggested nominations by petitions *only* and general elections with no party designations, or at least a path to get on the ballot by petition without a party nomination.[55] The goal was to find ways for judicial candidates to stay out of the partisan process, and give voters a choice of candidates with no connection to parties.[56] But these proposals were tabled, and Tannehill's direct party primary language was passed by a vote of seventy-eight to twenty-three and became part of the new Ohio constitution.[57] Instead of making more structural changes and entrenching them in the constitution, the convention merely gave the legislature more power to alter election methods.[58] The convention appeared to have momentum for separating judicial elections from partisan machinery and creating nonpartisan open primaries. Instead, the progressive delegates reverted to the party system. It is possible that some naïvely believed that direct democracy would fix the party nomination process, and that they believed they were giving the legislature more power over election law so that it would improve elections further. More likely, they were cynically voting for the appearance of reform, while making sure that they were not ceding their parties' control to a more open system.

In 1913, the Ohio legislature passed the Direct Primary Law, giving effect to the constitutional amendment and still leaving the parties in control of the primaries.[59] That same year, the legislature used its new authority over elections to make them more partisan. It required every candidate running for party nomination—including judicial candidates—to pledge their support for the principles of the party if elected.[60] This hackery validated Tannehill's fears about the partisans in the legislature undermining the convention's reform efforts, but considering Tannehill's cynicism about the legislature, it is all the more puzzling that he and other progressives did not build higher walls against partisan and legislative manipulations.

Other states adopted nonpartisan judicial elections at the same time, and most went further than Ohio by making the primaries formally nonpartisan, as some Ohio delegates had suggested in vain. North Dakota made its change in 1910, one year before Ohio's Non-Partisan Judiciary Act, and California under progressive Governor Hiram Johnson adopted nonpartisan elections the same year as Ohio. Washington State and Minnesota followed one year later, and then Nebraska, Wisconsin, Wyoming, and South Dakota in the rest of the 1910s. Ten more states joined the bandwagon over the next few decades, and by the end of the twentieth century, about twice as many states had nonpartisan judicial elections than had partisan elections.

These reforms failed to live up to the aspirations of the progressives, and they failed immediately. Ohio's superficial ballot changes failed to make the judiciary any less partisan, and it is possible that the direct primary only intensified partisanship. Contemporaries observed that the nonpartisan judges were less experienced than the ones who ascended to the bench under the partisan system, and were more focused on generating publicity than on developing skills.[61] Moreover, the absence of party identification on the general ballot was only cosmetic, and merely removed a piece of information from the voter in the voting booth. Although the delegates to the convention may have accomplished one goal in directly involving the electorate in the selection of judges, they did not really address judges' partisanship.

In the early twentieth century, it appears that progressive reforms dampened voter participation in judicial elections. Voter participation had peaked in the 1890s. Elections were formally partisan, and the two-party system was at its peak in terms of mobilization and straight-ticket voting. In a study of four states (Ohio, Tennessee, Texas, and California), participation in judicial elections equaled or even exceeded voting at the top of the ticket on governors' races and legislative races.[62] These races generated more interest because of the increasingly high stakes of labor-versus-management and the judicial review of populist legislation. Because many states lengthened the terms of judges in the 1860s and 1870s, the stakes of each election were greater. After the reforms of 1911 and 1912, Ohio voter turnout decreased by over 20 percent, and "roll-off" (where a voter casts a vote in major races at the top of the ticket, but not in more minor races further down the ballot) increased sharply. Progressives had experimented with moving judicial elections off-cycle, that is, not on the same day as major federal or state races, and they also adopted measures to eliminate automatic straight-ticket voting. The intent was to make these races less partisan, but the effect was to decrease participation even further.

Progressives had aimed to increase public control and participation in judicial elections, but their reforms seemed to have the opposite effect. At best, progressives could claim that even if the quantity of voters in judicial elections declined, the quality of their votes increased. The casual voters who simply pulled the straight-party ticket dropped out, while perhaps the better-informed voters stuck around. On the other hand, removing the party label took away at least a marginally helpful signal from voters, and thus more voters would choose based on the ethnic signal of the candidate's last name. In the next few years, some observers reported that because judicial candidates could not rely on party organization to raise money, make connections, and get out the vote, they turned to another kind of organization: organized crime. In 1914, a California organization of businessmen complained that because California law had recently prohibited candidates from "the assistance of any regular political organizations, [a judicial candidate] must in some way lift his personality out of the mass of citizens." One method was winning "the sympathy of the underworld by drinking, carousing, and dicing," as well as coddling corrupt police officers. Another method was turning a case into a media circus to gain publicity, at the expense of "some unhappy family" or misfortune.[63]

Former President Taft quickly called the nonpartisan system a failure. He contended that it increased pressure on judicial candidates to campaign more aggressively, and it did not lessen the influence of party machines.[64] Party conventions could select highly qualified candidates and put them on a party ticket, without requiring those candidates to campaign at all. But direct party primaries forced all judicial candidates to campaign twice: once for the party nomination, and again in the general election. Taft pointed out that judicial candidates also had to be more aggressive in nonpartisan general elections, because they could not rely on the party label on the ballot as a shorthand for less informed voters. He added that nonpartisan ballots made luck more important: The name appearing first on the list would have the arbitrary advantage in attracting more votes. Without party loyalty to rely on, the candidates had to pander even more loudly to gain name recognition, and had to resort to "disgraceful . . . demagogic methods."[65] Nonpartisan elections were backfiring, because they made the candidates even more factional and reliant on interest groups to compensate for the removal of explicit party support. Taft called these judicial candidates "supplicants before the people" and asserted that "nothing could more impair the quality of lawyers available as candidates or depreciate the standards of the judiciary."[66] Judge Harvey Keeler, an incumbent who lost his reelection campaign in Ohio in 1913, reported afterward that both political parties were just as active as before, campaigning openly "in utter defiance of the spirit and purpose of the statute."[67]

One should take these critiques with a grain of salt. They were written in 1913, at a time when the Non-Partisan Judiciary Act had been in place only for a short period of time. Taft had already formed his own views on judicial independence, but it is intriguing that as much as he opposed partisan elections, he publicly opposed nonpartisan elections even more. And Taft and Judge Keeler were not the only ones. By 1927, three states had tried nonpartisan judicial elections and abandoned the idea.[68] Even though the spread of nonpartisan changes had slowed down, this format overtook the partisan format.

The failure of nonpartisan elections in the early twentieth century continued to the end of the twentieth century. More recent studies show that the absence of party labels removes a signal for voters, and makes the order of names and the ethnic signal of the names more influential. Nonpartisan elections have been even more expensive than partisan elections, because the candidates needed to spend more to increase their name recognition and to overcome the absence of party labels to get their message out. Studies also suggest that candidates in nonpartisan races tend to campaign even more aggressively and negatively, and with more overt political stances, for the same reason. And yet these candidates still must rely on the political parties to get out the vote and to tell their members which candidate to support.[69]

The failure of the judicial recall and the supermajority rules was partly caused by a national attachment to judicial independence, but the failure of nonpartisan elections was influenced more by a deep ambivalence about judicial independence. Whereas partisan elections offended some sensibilities about the proper role of judges, the reform movement was unable or unwilling to embrace a more robust agenda for judicial independence. The reformers succeeded only in adopting half-measures and superficial changes that arguably made judicial elections more politicized, more partisan, and more expensive. Their compromises only compromised the state judiciary. Nonpartisan elections produced less judicial accountability to the people and less judicial independence from politics.

A New Approach

In 1906, the president of the American Bar Association (ABA) invited the thirty-five-year-old dean of the University of Nebraska College of Law to address the organization's annual meeting on the topic of legal reform. Roscoe Pound was at that point a relative unknown with a doctorate in botany but no law degree, who would soon become a Harvard Law School professor, a dean, and an early leader of the legal progressives and the American Legal Realists before publicly repudiating both groups. Pound was ultimately one of the most influential, combative, and mercurial figures in American law in the first half of the twentieth century.

Pound's address, "The Causes of Popular Dissatisfaction with the Administration of Justice," began with the title's premise: that the American people were increasingly disillusioned with the legal system. Pound focused on a long list of problems. One was that the court system was bogged down in outdated, expensive procedures that delayed justice and often denied justice. Another was the doctrine of judicial supremacy and its misuse in blocking progressive legislation that had been passed to solve modern problems. Toward the end of the speech, Pound lamented, "Putting courts into politics and compelling judges to become politicians, in many jurisdictions has almost destroyed the traditional respect for the Bench."[70]

The audience split dramatically. Many leaders of the ABA condemned Pound for his critique of civil procedure and judicial supremacy, but many of the younger lawyers and professors at the meeting were inspired, and they challenged the ABA's status quo. While the populist wing of the progressives tended to think more direct democracy was a solution to all problems, an opposing wing preferred professional expertise and bureaucratic management. Academics like John Parker Hall, the dean of the University of Chicago School of Law, went around the country criticizing all forms of judicial elections and touting appointments. However, Hall did not give a blanket endorsement of appointments. He reminded his audience that appointments were political, too, noting that in states with legislative appointments, the legislators often took turns appointing themselves to the courts.[71] The expert, academic branch of the progressives was looking for a new approach to judicial selection, an alternative to the regular politics of election and appointment. Its alternative was professionalization.

Inspired by Pound, a cadre of younger bar leaders and academics founded the American Judicature Society (AJS) in 1913. The AJS was supported by a handful of business leaders who supported reforms to create a more efficient, expert bench, partly because such reforms would help business interests.[72] One of the AJS's founders and directors, Professor Albert Kales, suggested a reform that went beyond a nonpartisan ballot. He proposed reviving appointments, but instead of the governor appointing judges, he proposed that an elected chief justice appoint the rest of the judges, with the help of a judicial council's recommendations. After serving on the bench, these appointed judges would run in unopposed retention elections.[73] Kales and other lawyers believed that these noncompetitive elections would increase judicial independence and job security and therefore attract better lawyers to the bench, while also retaining a concrete opportunity for public participation that would win public support for the plan.[74] Kales called this proposal "the nonpartisan court plan"[75]—a bland name that failed to distinguish it from the ineffectual turn to nonpartisan general elections. However, Kales's original idea for an elected chief justice to have the power of appointment was perhaps the worst of all worlds: a higher-stakes popular election of a single judge, who then has the power and the pressure to appoint the lawyers, partisans, and cronies who helped elect him or her. Instead of balancing judicial selection among more decision makers, this plan concentrated more power in a single decision maker. The associate judges selected by the chief judge would feel indebted to the chief judge, and would be more likely to share his philosophy and politics. A court would have much less diversity of perspectives.

Over the next few years, other reformers suggested variations on the appointment steps, each with some combination of judges and legal professionals who would draft lists of nominees or who would make the appointments themselves.[76] Bar leaders took note of the de facto role played by bar leadership in many states in advising governors on vacancy appointments, in advising parties for nominations, and in sponsoring and endorsing candidates.[77] As part of the Progressive Era's urban professional reform programs, the bar associations in Chicago, Cleveland, Denver, Detroit, Duluth, Pittsburgh, San Francisco, Los Angeles, and St. Louis created "bar primaries" (notably, San Francisco, Los Angeles, and St. Louis led the efforts for professionalized selection in the 1930s). In these bar primaries, the city's many bar members voted by secret ballot in two steps: to evaluate incumbent judges, and then to endorse candidates for the general election. These endorsements were questionably "nonpartisan," because the bar associations were often affiliated with one party or another, but they established a stronger formal model of bar evaluation and selection.[78] Reformers also built on the existing institution of advisory "judicial councils," which were often a mix of bar leaders and judges and had been growing in significance around the country. Bar leadership around the country suggested creating a more formal panel of bar members—selected randomly, elected by their peers, or appointed by other elected officials.[79] Some suggested that the bar nominating committees provide a list to the chief judge, who would then choose from this short list.[80] Eventually, the chief-judge-selection part of the plan disappeared over time, but the bar's role on a nominating commission survived. Soon this bar-based plan became known as the "AJS plan" and, after 1937, the "ABA plan"—acronyms that captured only the elite, the bureaucratic, and the arcane aspects of the plan. Around the same time, progressives were using the phrase "merit system" for civil service reform in various bureaucracies, addressing the problem of partisanship and patronage.[81] However, the phrase "merit" for the AJS plan and professional judicial selection emerged only in the late 1950s.

In the 1910s and 1920s, these ideas spread to various state bar associations, and in the 1920s, major urban bar associations and the ABA itself stepped up their focus on judicial selection and tenure with a series of studies and reform campaigns.[82] The ABA committee reports found that judicial elections were rife with problems, but they observed that judicial elections functioned better when the local bar association played formal or informal roles. In 1924, an ABA committee called upon local bar associations to redouble their efforts to clean up judicial elections and influence public opinion.[83] Despite this increased bar association activity, no state came close—yet—to returning to appointment, whether by governors or by professional commissions. Meanwhile, "the merit system" of civil service reform spread through administrative bureaucracies in local, state, and then federal government. Major cities were the focal point of merit civil service reforms. Merit reform had an easier time in bureaucratic offices because they had remained appointed systems. The switch from patronage appointment to merit or civil service was a smoother institutional change. It was impractical to suggest direct elections for the expanding number of administrative offices in this era, and there was no democratic inertia: the resistance to changing from a direct democratic form of selection to a less democratic form.

There has been an active historical debate about who the "progressives" were, and the debate's answer has been that there were many strands of progressivism from many sources.[84] The emergence of expert judicial selection was a kind of progressive reform that underscored first, the role of professionals from *both* the public and the private spheres, and second, the role of cities and urban leaders all around the country. A key to progressivism was skepticism of insider party politics, but the progressive movement also included skeptics of mass democracy generally—who were often businessmen who opposed labor, farmers, and populism.[85] Businessmen and corporate interests joined the progressive cause of professional judicial selection through the AJS, seeking a more expert, efficient bench for the benefit of industry. Even though expertise made important advances in this period, direct democracy still trumped expertise in state courts. It would always be an uphill battle to convince the public to sacrifice direct democracy in favor of elite control, and the leadership of the AJS and the bar associations barely tried to sell their nominating commission proposals to the general public. They took their message to the political elite, thinking they would find a sympathetic audience, but their plan fell on deaf ears.[86] Legislators had relied on party politics to get into power, and they had little interest in undermining their parties' power. Oddly, only during the Great Depression did the elite and professionalized "nonpartisan court plan" gain a foothold. The Progressive Era was littered with failed judicial reforms, but it planted an idea that grew through the rest of the century.

CHAPTER NINE

The Great Depression, Crime, and the Revival of Appointment

T HE MODEL of professional selection and retention elections suggested by progressive lawyers was mostly ignored in the Progressive Era, but it established its first beachhead in California during the Great Depression, propelled by the creative use of anticrime rhetoric. The appeal of this appointment model was its promise to separate judges from electioneering and partisan politics, a new separation of powers through expertise. However, the California business interests behind the scenes found a way to tweak the design back to party control in their favor.

In the wake of widespread corruption scandals and a crime wave, a young Oakland prosecutor called for sweeping reforms of the partisan California judiciary. In the Chamber of Commerce's *California Journal of Development*, this prosecutor—a political newcomer by the name of Earl Warren—wrote an article, "Organized Crime vs. Unorganized Law Enforcement," in support of anticrime measures. He recited the villains of a 1930s crime wave: the Dillingers, the Lindbergh baby kidnappers on the loose, and many others. Warren praised recent changes in criminal procedure to speed up trials and convict more criminals, but he concluded that procedural changes were irrelevant as long as incompetent judges were either passive "umpires" or ambitious publicity-seekers:

> It has been my observation over a period of years that when a judge assumes the role of a baseball umpire, merely calling balls and strikes, and lets it be understood that it makes no difference to him what action the jury takes, that justice is seldom done in important cases, but that on the other hand, where the judge assumes the responsibility placed upon him by the

law—where he conducts the trial in a dignified manner—where he refuses to turn his courtroom into a sideshow where he [gets] everyone in the courtroom to understand that they are there for the purpose of seeing to it that innocent people are acquitted and guilty people convicted, justice is usually accomplished.[1]

Warren's target was judicial elections. They produced the passive umpire who avoids both controversy and justice (a very different connotation than the contemporary umpire metaphor), or they spawned the self-promoting politician who turns the courtroom into a circus.[2] Warren then offered a third evil of partisan elections: judicial corruption.

> If the judges seek favor with the underworld by dismissing cases or suspending judgments or granting probation to confirmed criminals, or meting out inadequate sentences, then the whole structure falls. . . . [W]here we fall down is when the law comes into contact with organized criminals—then we meet money influence, brains, organization and armaments. The law attempts to meet this situation without organization and in many instances with corruption.[3]

One part of the problem was that judges chosen by party machines are more corrupt and more corruptible than ones screened for merit. Organized party patronage was one step away from organized crime for Warren. But Warren made another argument against judicial elections: They were part of "the old system of decentralization of our law enforcement agencies," an obsolete localism leaving every stage of law enforcement too disorganized to control crime or prevent corruption. Warren's answer to the 1930s crime wave was not more populism, but instead, a version of elitism: a revival of gubernatorial appointment and the first state bar nomination panel.

The next two chapters offer new research from the archives and newspaper records to help answer one of the strangest puzzles in the history of judicial reform. Merit reforms emerged during the Great Depression and then, after a long lull, they spread starting in the late 1950s. There are some particularly odd features of this wave, mostly overlooked by observers: what, where, and when. What: It is exceedingly rare for states to abandon direct democracy, and especially for voters themselves to go to the ballot box to surrender their power to vote. Where: Merit plans started in western and midwestern states, and spread first through rural, populist areas (the Great Plains, the Rockies, and the Deep South). It is surprising that these populist rural states would lead the way to elite merit selection. When: These rural states would do so during populist reactions to an appointed U.S. Supreme Court and the elite legal establishment: the Great Depression, the McCarthy era of the 1950s, and then the backlash against the Warren Court in the 1960s and early 1970s. It is most helpful to take a look at a timeline of merit plan adoptions to see this pattern (see Appendix G).

There is an obvious pattern: rural state after rural state, from Kansas, Iowa, and Nebraska through the Rockies. Some suggest that there is something about rural political culture that embraces merit selection.[4] But appearances can be misleading. The three most important factors in merit's spread were first, business interests driving the campaign for merit reforms; second, urban leaders supporting merit reform; and third, the ability for these interests and leaders to win voters and broaden their coalitions. Voters generally had been skeptical of a switch from direct democracy to elite control. However, in the 1930s and again in the 1970s, business leaders and urban leaders used fear of crime to persuade voters that expertise and professionalization were better than popular elections in producing judges who could manage a crime problem. Recently, anticrime rhetoric has been used to make the case for judicial accountability to popular control, not independence from popular control, so the reversal in the 1930s and the 1970s is remarkable.

Scholars have not yet provided an adequate explanation for merit's diffusion.[5] If business and urban support were the key to merit's success, then it is even more puzzling that the early merit states were rural. However, the key is the relative balance between emerging business strength versus emerging labor unions and urbanization. True, the merit states tended to be rural, but among rural states, they were urbanizing and industrializing.[6] Within those states, rural voters were divided about or opposed to merit plans. They may have liked the idea of nonpartisan elections, but they did not like the idea of giving up their vote in favor of bar elites on merit commissions. Merit selection was carried by a larger margin of urban support, and it was driven by urban leaders and urban interests, addressing urban issues. More than 60 percent of the legislative sponsors of these proposals represented urban areas in these rural states.[7] Merit reform often targeted urban courts and urban problems, and sometimes exempted rural courts.[8]

Why would merit plans succeed in rural-but-urbanizing states among urban voters, but not in more rural areas or in more urban states? The answer is in the timing of industrialization and urbanization, and in the balance of power between business, labor, and urban voting blocs. In most rural states, business interests were not strong enough to get merit campaigns off the ground and overcome rural voters' entrenched preferences for direct democracy. In more urban industrialized states, business interests were strong, but labor unions and ethnic voting blocs had grown strong enough to defeat their merit campaigns. In rural-but-urbanizing states, business was strong enough to mount a campaign with support from the bar and urban leaders, and there were enough signs of growing labor power or growing ethnic diversity to motivate business interests and urban elites to act fast. By seizing these moments in the 1930s and the 1950s–1970s, business and urban elites had good timing, because they had a temporary political advantage over the opposition. They also took advantage of the timing of crime waves to make an anti-crime campaign in favor of merit.

California and Missouri in the 1930s are examples of states where the climate was just right: business had grown powerful enough to support merit, but unions and urban ethnic blocs had not yet grown strong enough to resist. California's industrial union membership lagged in 1934, before New Deal legislation sparked more rapid growth only after California voters passed the judicial appointment plan.[9] In the 1930s, California and Missouri ranked tenth and fourteenth, respectively, in terms of union membership per capita, strong enough to indicate an increasing political threat, but not quite as strong as New York, Pennsylvania, or the industrial Great Lakes, where unions were already politically powerful enough to fight business interests and win.[10] As it turns out, union membership in California and Missouri skyrocketed over the next decade, just after business succeeded in replacing judicial elections. Business seized its window of opportunity, but only when it combined with other opportune events. California's story shows that anticrime anxiety was one such opportunity. Earl Warren was both opportunistic and sincere in successfully framing this campaign in terms of crime, a role that has been overlooked by his biographers and historians.[11]

Earl Warren, Crime, and the Return to Appointment

Since California's constitutional convention in 1849, the state had used popular elections to select its judges at all levels.[12] In 1911, the legislature switched to nonpartisan judicial elections, and in 1926, the voters ratified this change in a constitutional amendment. California shared the same experience with formal nonpartisan reforms as Ohio and other states that found they did not solve the real problems of partisanship and political corruption. Businesses had started a campaign to replace partisan elections with merit selection in 1912, a year before the founding of the American Judicature Society. Around the country, unions had poured more resources into judicial elections, and by the 1910s and especially

THE GREAT DEPRESSION, CRIME, AND APPOINTMENT   181

the 1930s, they were electing more prolabor judges.[13] They also were increasingly outraged by appointed judges and the legal establishment. Thus, the labor movement increasingly favored partisan judicial elections. And as the labor movement gained an advantage in partisan elections, businesses began thinking about changing the rules of the game.

The San Francisco–based Commonwealth Club met to discuss the problem of trial delays, and concluded that the problem was bad judges, not bad rules.[14] The Commonwealth Club was founded in 1903 as a bipartisan organization, but its membership was generally Republican, wealthy, and probusiness throughout this era. Its original members included major bankers, business executives, prominent Republicans (such as Herbert Hoover), and conservative Democrats.[15] When California had switched to nonpartisan judicial elections around the same time as Ohio in the early 1910s, the Commonwealth Club had presented an astute critique of the nonpartisan format that remains true today. Because of the new ban on party assistance, club members argued that a judicial candidate "must in some way lift his personality out of the mass of citizens," and some candidates switch from organized parties to organized crime in order to raise their profile and campaign cash.[16] Club members contended that judicial candidates would condemn police corruption on the stump, but behind the scenes at the policemen's fraternal meetings, they would glad-hand and fraternize with those same officers. A few years later, newspapers were reporting that in Chicago, the judges of the criminal courts were "placed in office by the underworld element." Because the parties were "too evenly divided," according to a Chicago probation officer, "an outside factor to give a balance of power and majority of votes to one man is needed. It is supplied by the underworld." Officers complained that the endorsement of major bar associations did not ensure nomination, let alone election.[17] Both partisan and nonpartisan elections were blamed for contributing to crime.

Citing the crime and corruption problem, and citing the need for more expert judges in increasingly technical cases, the Commonwealth Club began a campaign for judicial appointments.[18] The committee reported that the state judges who had been vacancy appointments were much more efficient and competent than the elected judges, and it recommended a return to appointment, without discussing the details.[19] In 1926, the Commonwealth Club focused on crime and juvenile delinquency from a number of perspectives in a special issue titled "The 'Crime Wave.' " The committee chairman on this topic blamed judicial elections for putting "untrained" judges on the bench and for giving a vote to criminals so that they can corrupt the courts legally. "So long as our municipalities hold on to the out[-]worn fetish of electing . . . judges by popular vote, just so long will criminals prey upon society with relative impunity."[20] The Commonwealth Club's devotion of an entire issue to crime from a variety of angles suggests that they were sincerely concerned about the issue, and some club members seemed to believe sincerely that judicial elections exacerbated the problem. Later in the reform campaign, "curb crime" became such a relentless slogan for judicial reform that business interests with their own motives apparently took an earnest policy argument and turned it into propaganda.

The state bench and bar were divided contentiously on the issue. Merit was perceived to benefit the most elite lawyers, and the less established or wealthy members of the bar thought their own chances for a judicial career were better served through direct elections. Sitting judges liked the partisan election system that got them on the bench, and understandably feared that a governor might have other interests and political supporters in mind.[21]

The state legislature debated the club's proposed constitutional amendment five times from the 1910s through the early 1930s,[22] but neither house passed it after several years of consideration. As long as organized labor and the incumbent judges opposed it, the legislature was sure to kill it. State legislators relied heavily on the state parties to stay in office, and the state parties had no interest in giving up their control of picking their own judicial candidates. Resistance by partisan professionalized legislators would be a recurring theme around the country. In the early 1930s, the club considered a new strategy: bypassing the legislature and taking the amendment directly to the people.

Around the same time, the bar associations got off the fence and committed themselves to merit selection. Like several other major urban bar associations around the country, the San Francisco and Los Angeles bar associations had been organizing "bar primaries" in which bar members first rated incumbent judges and then endorsed specific candidates in pamphlets distributed to voters.[23] The bar primaries laid a foundation for more direct control over nominations. The bar associations were then motivated by scandal to fix the courts. In 1932, three Los Angeles judges were caught giving out lucrative state receiverships to party officials in return for money and gifts ("pay to play" corruption), and they were recalled by the voters.[24] Another Los Angeles judge was discovered to be frequently intoxicated on the bench.[25] In the wake of these scandals, the Los Angeles County Bar Association began its own reform effort to rebuild confidence in the courts. It made more progress in the legislature with a proposed merit panel consisting of the chief justice, the presiding justice of the intermediate court, and the relevant state senator, followed by a retention election every four years. However, one San Francisco legislator amended the proposal so that it applied only to counties with more than 1,500,000 residents—and that meant only Los Angeles.[26] Thus limited, it passed both houses of the legislature. The next step would be voter ratification in the 1934 election as "Assembly Constitutional Amendment No. 98." The state bar backed this limited plan. California's population was growing more diverse ethnically and racially, especially its cities. The total nonwhite population quadrupled from 1920 to 1930, with especially sharp growth in Los Angeles.[27] Minorities were playing a more powerful role in urban machines and at the ballot box. Merit plans were a means of shifting control away from a more diverse urban voting population to a white legal elite.[28]

Meanwhile, a crime wave was spurring a separate reform movement. This was the "Public Enemies" era of legendary Great Depression bank robbers, following the Prohibition era's infamous gangsters. Al Capone went to prison in 1932, and Bonnie and Clyde's infamous exploits from Missouri to Texas were from late 1932 through May 1934. John Dillinger's and Baby Face Nelson's sprees of midwestern bank robberies and murders ran from the spring of 1933 through the summer of 1934. Ma Barker's gang was robbing midwestern banks at the same time. This crime wave led to J. Edgar Hoover's expansion of the FBI's powers and the use of the "Public Enemies" media campaign.[29] The fear of crime was national, but it was not a sufficient condition for judicial reform. Most states did not turn to merit then. However, California (and Missouri soon after) had a number of unique factors contributing to reform, including the creative political strategy of a few dynamic lawyers and businessmen.

It appears that there was no real increase in national crime rates in the Great Depression, and in fact, crime may have been decreasing around the country in the mid-1930s.[30] However, California had a more localized increase in crime in this period. Between the 1910s and the 1930s, California's population had tripled, its felony conviction had quadrupled, and its crime costs had quintupled.[31] The state experienced its own series of murders, brutal crimes, and notorious armed robberies of trains in 1933 and 1934 that made the crime issue even more salient. In two of these robberies in Northern California, the culprits could have been caught if there had been cooperation between two county police departments, but they failed to coordinate. Some felt that organized crime was moving west, and perceived that California was reverting back to the Old West lawlessness.[32] In 1934, a mob broke into a Santa Clara County jail and lynched two confessed killers.[33] These events inspired Earl Warren, then an Oakland district attorney, to take the lead in modernizing and centralizing state law enforcement. He was frustrated by the lack of resources for prosecutors and the weakness of the attorney general's office. At that time, the attorney general simply offered legal advice to the governor and represented the state in civil suits, while tending to his own private practice on the side. Earl Warren wanted the job, and he also wanted that job to be more powerful.[34] To achieve both goals, he joined a new effort to overhaul the state's courts.[35]

The Chamber of Commerce was not satisfied with the state bar's plan because it only covered Los Angeles. In the fall of 1933, the Chamber of Commerce teamed up with Earl Warren and brought together a variety of groups—police chiefs, business groups, bar leaders, and women's organizations—to plan a coordinated campaign. In January 1934, they formed the California Committee on the Better Administration of Law, with a stated mission to propose legislation that would "curb crime in California."[36] The twelve-member board included District Attorney Earl Warren, the chiefs of police of Los Angeles and San Francisco, and a representative of the Crime Problems Advisory Committee of California. The bar was not part of this committee, strangely enough, but it included leaders of the California Federation of Women's Clubs, the California League of Women Voters, the Crime Problems Advisory Committee of California, and the American Legion.[37]

The League of Women Voters and other women's groups had a few reasons for joining this coalition. Many women's groups emerged in the campaign for women's suffrage and the Nineteenth Amendment, and their coalition-building strategy had been to embrace nonpartisanship. If the suffrage groups appeared to lean toward one party, then the other party would have reason to oppose suffrage. If the groups reinforced the message that women would be a swing bloc of voters up for grabs, then the parties would have more reason to cater to women and support suffrage once it became obvious that suffrage was inevitable in the long run. After the passage of the Nineteenth Amendment, suffragists formed the League of Women Voters in 1920. Now that they had won the vote, these women's groups also understood that their vocal nonpartisanship would continue to entice both Democrats and Republicans to compete for their votes by being responsive to their concerns.

Anticorruption was another important link. In campaigning for suffrage, women's groups had cultivated an image that women voters would clean up government and promote virtue and the public interest. These groups were looking for new issues after winning suffrage, and anticorruption court reform was consistent with their message.[38] Some of these women's groups also believed that party patronage systematically discriminated against women as outsiders to the party system, and in the 1920s and 1930s, the League of Women Voters generally pressed for merit reforms in government to open up more jobs for women.[39] Furthermore, the leaders of these groups were white, middle class, urban, and professionally oriented. This background would lead them to be concerned about urban crime and the demographic changes in urban party machines and more sympathetic to professional expertise in place of partisan politics.

Warren and two of his deputies drafted a four-part "Curb Crime" package of constitutional amendments for the committee.[40] The minutes from these committee meetings have been lost from the archives, but fortunately, a graduate student in 1951 summarized them before Warren became chief justice of the Supreme Court, and noted that Earl Warren was the leader on the committee.[41] Warren had a vision of executive appointment and life tenure, and he wanted the governor and a commission of professionals to review not only future appointments but also the sitting judges. The current judges, Warren said, should not be "blanketed in" for life tenure, and should face professional scrutiny to be reappointed.[42] The existing California bench needed to be overhauled and reevaluated through a merit commission.

As the first proposed amendment in this Curb Crime campaign, Earl Warren's judicial selection plan had three steps, relatively consistent with the Judicature Society's merit nomination model:

1. A nominating board—the chief justice of the supreme court, the presiding judge of the district court of appeal, and the attorney general—offering two candidates to the governor.
2. The governor would appoint one of those two candidates.
3. In the next general election, the judge's name would appear on the ballot, with only a "yes" or "no" option for retention. Judges receiving a majority of "yes" votes would hold their seats for life. The committee purposely drafted the ballot question as "Should Judge —— be retained in office?" without mentioning the term "for life," because it feared the public would recoil when confronted explicitly with life tenure.[43] This proposal eventually became Proposition No. 3.

Warren's committee drafted three more amendments comprising the Curb Crime package: creating a state department of justice headed by the attorney general as the chief law enforcement officer of the state, with power to coordinate and even to take over for a deficient county (Proposition No. 4); allowing judges to comment on the evidence at trial, and—remarkably—allowing judges and prosecutors to comment on a criminal defendant's failure to testify (Proposition No. 5); and permitting a defendant to plead guilty when he is first taken before a magistrate, rather than a judge (Proposition No. 6).

Up to that point, the Commonwealth Club, the elite group of San Francisco businessmen, had stayed on the sidelines. They had been working on judicial reform for decades and had been burned out by legislative obstinacy. But once the state bar had advanced a Los Angeles–only reform, and once Earl Warren and the Chamber of Commerce had made progress for a statewide reform, the Commonwealth Club jumped back into the fray in late February 1934. These San Francisco businessmen persuaded the committee that a twelve-year term would be more likely to gain voter support than life tenure. The club also convinced Warren and the committee that they should convert their proposed nominating board into a reviewing board (a "Commission on Qualifications," with the same membership of the chief justice, the presiding justice on the court of appeals and the attorney general) that would confirm a governor's nominee.[44] This switch would later have a major impact on California and the future of judicial politics in the 1980s. When the process starts with the commission's nominations, as Warren had proposed, there is less control by the governor over the appointment and less predictability about the appointee's ideological leanings. The membership of the commission can change, and it is difficult to put pressure on the judges on the commission, who would be serving in the middle of long terms. Outside groups who dislike an incumbent judge will be cautious about opposing that judge, because those groups would be uncertain about the replacement. When the governor starts the process, the governor has strong control over the appointment, especially when the governor sends only one name to the commission, as the club proposed. Because the governor is a known quantity and is also influenced by political pressure, outside groups will know when it is worthwhile to pour their resources in defeating an incumbent that they dislike, because they would have a fairly good guess about the leanings of the replacement. It is possible that the Commonwealth Club had figured out this dynamic, and they wanted a little more predictability. This institutional redesign in 1934 paid dividends in 1986, when businesses fought to defeat Rose Bird, knowing that a conservative governor would name her replacement.

Earl Warren wrote other amendments for the 1934 election, including one that placed most state jobs under the civil service, making them independent from political considerations. This antipartisan reform was popular with the state Republican Party leaders, who feared losing to a New Deal Democratic wave at the polls—and subsequently political firings in the statehouse.[45] In the 1930s, the California Republicans fared better than other Republicans around the country, but they were still nervous about Franklin Roosevelt's growing popularity, the state's changing demographics, and losing the governorship for the first time since 1895.

The California Committee on Better Administration of Law's constitutional strategy was to cut out the implacably partisan legislature by using the initiative petition. The irony of using direct democracy in order to abandon direct democracy would be repeated throughout future merit reform efforts. The challenge for this strategy was that it required an enormous number of petition signatures. In the spring of 1934, this coalition went forward with an aggressive and well-organized campaign.[46] With its mix of lay leaders, police chiefs, and women's groups, the California Committee was a better public face for the campaign than the Chamber of Commerce, the wealthy Commonwealth Club, or the state bar association. The League of Women Voters and the California Federation of Women's Clubs took the lead in gathering 119,000 signatures, a daunting obstacle requiring a lot of foot soldiers.[47] The Curb Crime package became Propositions Nos. 3, 4, 5, and 6 on the November ballot, with the merit plan as No. 3. In fact, this reform of judicial selection was not called the "merit plan" or any specific name in this campaign. It simply became "No. 3" and it had no separate identity from the Curb Crime package—a packaging that shrewdly focused voters on crime, rather than on the more controversial notion of merit and diluting voter control.[48] The Commonwealth Club and the Chamber of Commerce financed the printing of 122,000 pamphlets and 100,000 voter reminder cards—as well as hundreds of billboard, radio, and newspaper advertisements.[49]

Figure 9.1 shows one example of a billboard in the campaign. In campaigning for his amendments, Warren focused on the most notorious criminals of the 1930s: "The manner in which the Dillingers, the Baby Face Nelsons, the Machine Gun Kellys, . . . and numerous other criminal gangs have been playing hide-and-seek with the public authorities has truly become a national disgrace. . . . [F]ault has largely been in the lack of organization of our law-enforcement agencies. [The law enforcement] business of California is a gigantic business costing the State thirty million dollars a year, and it is being run in a most unbusinesslike manner."[50] Warren's rhetoric is classic Republican progressivism: analogizing government to business, and seeking businesslike efficiency and management in the public interest. Merit selection for judges, as opposed to party politics, fit that progressive worldview. Over the course of the twentieth century, a more populist view of crime—"throw the book at 'em"—grew dominant, but the progressives had their own program for crime control: a mix of efficiency, expertise, and prevention. The entrepreneurial leaders

Figure 9.1. The billboard used during the campaign. Reprinted with permission from the California Chamber of Commerce (www.calchamber.com).

of the merit selection campaigns would draw on both populism and progressivism, but Warren led the way by emphasizing the progressive/efficiency/management message. Warren's plan aimed to curtail the local power of parties and voters, and recentralize and reorganize judicial selection with governors' appointments and a more statewide and professional Commission on Qualifications to vet those appointments. His answer to modern organized crime was a more modern and reorganized nonpartisan judiciary. As Warren wrote in "Organized Crime vs. Unorganized Law Enforcement," there would be no more party-patronage "umpire" judges who don't care about justice, and no more circus clown judges who only seek attention. Warren's Curb Crime plan would produce judges with the ability, the vision, and the integrity to clean up the state.

Warren's allies made similar links between judicial selection and crime. In an article titled "California Girds for War on Crime," Joseph Knowland, the president of the Chamber of Commerce, connected Proposition No. 3 to crime control by arguing that partisan elections produced a distracted and less competent bench. Politics took up a quarter of judges' working time, and these local elections were flooded with candidates and were too confusing to allow voters to make the best choice.[51] Knowland, the

THE GREAT DEPRESSION, CRIME, AND APPOINTMENT 189

Chamber of Commerce, and the Commonwealth Club may have believed that merit selection would help the courts manage crime more efficiently, but this cause was not their primary motivation, and their commitment to reducing crime was questionable. Warren, on the other hand, was passionate about cracking down on crime.

Newspapers emphasized the "curb crime" message of the legal reforms, reflected in a montage of headlines during the campaign (see Figure 9.2), assembled by the California Chamber of Commerce in their "Crime Can Be Curbed" pamphlet. Most of the major newspapers endorsed No. 3, particularly the conservative *San Francisco Chronicle* and *Los Angeles Times*. A survey of judges indicated that they spent about 25 to 40 percent of their time dealing with their own political matters.[52] Retention elections would produce more job security with less competition, less campaigning, and less partisanship. Party machinations dissuaded many worthy candidates from pursuing the bench.[53] The bar argued that merit selection would make judges more efficient, because it would spare them the draining distraction of raising money and campaigning.[54] They linked this issue to crime control: less party politicking meant more focus on the crime crisis.

The media suggested that the voters might have liked the concept of voting for judges, but in practice, voters did not really care. The *Los Angeles Times* noted, "60 percent of those who voted for governor in this county (Los Angeles) did not vote on judges at all."[55] And even the ones who voted did not know much about the candidates, if they knew

Figure 9.2. Typical newspaper headlines showing popular demand for crime legislation. Reprinted with permission from the California Chamber of Commerce (www.calchamber.com).

anything at all. One observer claimed that several judges had won simply because they had the same names as more famous judges.[56]

Organized labor and the American Legion were the chief opponents of Proposition No. 3. Labor had understandable reasons for opposing the merit plan. For years, labor unions had faced severe obstacles from appointed federal judges and from state judges elected by business interests. Just as labor was strong enough to win judicial elections and defeat the probusiness candidates, the Chamber of Commerce was changing the rules. The Chamber of Commerce's financial and organizational support for the ballot initiative only provoked stronger skepticism from union leaders of the merit plan's likely outcomes.[57] In a debate at the Commonwealth Club, Edward D. Vandeleur, president of the San Francisco Labor Council, mocked the idea that the governor was more nonpartisan and nonpolitical than direct democracy.[58] Vandeleur predicted that special interests would have more access in the appointment process, and judges would face even more pressure to rule in favor of powerful elites in a merit selection system. He concluded, "A reform more treacherous to public welfare was never devised."[59] Liberals also doubted whether appointments by a politician would really clean up a corrupt system.

Upton Sinclair, the prolabor socialist author of *The Jungle* and eighty-nine other books, was the Democratic candidate for governor, running on the "EPIC" platform (End Poverty in California). His coalition opposed the merit proposition as well,[60] but Sinclair himself did not campaign against it. Sinclair's campaign may have galvanized conservative opposition, and conservatives fearing a Sinclair win supported a more independent judiciary. One theory about the merit plan's adoption is that states were more likely to switch to merit plans if they had relative parity between the two parties, compared to states that did not adopt merit plans. The notion is that political parties with a weaker grip on power have been risk averse, and out of a fear of losing power, these party leaders prefer an independent judiciary that could protect them in the long term, even if it might frustrate them in the short term. [61] This theory does not appear to bear out in most states that adopted merit, because most of those states had one dominant party during their merit campaigns, but political risk aversion seems to have been one factor in California in 1934.[62] California Republicans had the upper hand from the mid-nineteenth century through the Great Depression, but Upton Sinclair's left coalition in 1934 worried Republicans more than ever before—not only of losing power, but also of living under a socialist regime. Risk-averse Republicans might have viewed a more nonpartisan and more independent judiciary as insurance against such a doomsday scenario. Indeed, the Republicans lost seats in the 1934 and 1936 elections, even losing the state house in 1936.[63] Warren's plan shifted power from the voters and parties to legal elites, a more reliable bulwark against socialism.

As it turns out, the combined resources and political strategy of the merit coalition (business, professionals, and Republicans) were more powerful than labor and Democrats, even in the midst of the Great Depression. Propositions 4, 5, and 6—the measures giving the attorney general more power and changing criminal procedure—passed by overwhelming majorities. Proposition No. 3 on merit selection passed by less than 5 percent.[64] Its support came from the urban counties of San Francisco, Los Angeles, San Diego, and especially Alameda (home of Earl Warren and Oakland), which voted in favor 92,000 to 49,000. Outside of those four urban areas, the rest of the state split evenly.

Meanwhile, the bar association offered something akin to a control group: a merit proposal "untreated" by anticrime medicine. The bar's Amendment No. 98 was a proposed merit plan only for Los Angeles County, and it was defeated 55 percent to 45 percent. It was not linked with the Curb Crime campaign either in the media or on the ballot. Some concluded that the Chamber of Commerce's financial support for the statewide plan was the difference between Proposition No. 3's passage and No. 98's failure,[65] and it is important to note that the ballot included an argument against No. 98 on the ballot but not against No. 3, meaning that opposition groups like labor decided not to contest the Curb Crime amendment.[66] Furthermore, the California Committee members had debated whether to include No. 98 but decided to put their support only behind the statewide plan. If No. 98 were offered as an alternative within the Curb Crime campaign, it carried the risk of dividing support for statewide merit. So they ignored No. 98, and they made No. 3 the leading proposal of the anticrime package.[67]

Basking in their victory, the California Committee published a thirty-page pamphlet two years later, titled "Crime Can Be Curbed."[68] It would be fair to say that the pamphlet had two layers of propaganda: It was intended to persuade like-minded political groups in other states to pursue merit reforms, and it was a playbook for how to win those campaigns with a clear anticrime message. The committee noted that the American Bar Association (ABA) and New York politicians had already taken notice of California's Curb Crime campaign, and the pamphlet was immediately cited by leaders of other state bars halfway across the country.[69] Diffusion of this plan would take a few more decades, but nevertheless, California was a creative political/rhetorical entrepreneur and an influential anticrime/merit plan beachhead.

Proposition No. 3 was the first switch back from election to any kind of appointment in any state since Reconstruction, and it was a major departure from the partisan appointment process by replacing legislative confirmation with the professionalized review by sitting judges and the attorney general. This system would not be the precise "merit" model for other states in the twentieth century, because the California governor was the first mover in the nomination process, not the professional panel. Still, it offered a more general model for replacing politicians with legal professionals, and other states also followed a similar political campaign, drawing on crime waves and urban problems to build popular support for more expert control.

The Rise of Earl Warren

The Curb Crime campaign catapulted Earl Warren into statewide prominence as a conservative figure. In the vitriolic 1934 governor's race between socialist Upton Sinclair and probusiness Republican Merriam, Earl Warren was the California Republican Party chairman. He had been elected just six weeks before the general election, so his role was limited.[70] However, with his nonpartisan reputation and his role as a crime-fighting prosecutor, Warren was active in wooing moderate Democrats. He did grow more partisan nearer the election, writing that Sinclair's "election would mean a threat to private industry . . . a menace to every investor. . . . It means chaos to California." He also said the election was no longer a political campaign, but "a crusade of Americans and Californians against Radicalism and Socialism."[71] In a radio address, Warren warned, "The battle is between two conflicting philosophies of government—one that is proud of our flag, our governmental institutions and our honored history, the other that glorifies the Red Flag of Russia and hopes to establish on American soil a despotism based on class hatred and tyranny."[72] This tone was consistent with the Merriam campaign, which had billboards that read, "Take California out of the red; the Red out of California."[73]

The success of the Curb Crime campaign helped Warren politically in many ways. Warren won strong and enduring support from the entire law enforcement establishment. He claimed of his state campaigns: "They (law enforcement officers) supported me actively in all parts of the state."[74] The amendment that Warren had drafted to expand the powers of the attorney general drove out the aging incumbent, because he was overwhelmed by the office's new responsibilities.[75] His retirement opened an opportunity for Warren. He campaigned for the job with the same anticrime, probusiness, anti-Communist message and coalition that had propelled the

Curb Crime campaign. The attorney general position's statewide powers gave Warren an even better stepping stone to the governor's mansion, which he won on the same platform four years later. In addition to anti-crime and anti-Communism, Warren campaigned on nativism.[76] As governor of California, he supervised California's role in the Japanese internment. Warren's anticrime, probusiness, anti-Communist, nativist politics of the 1930s and 1940s made him a credible Republican presidential candidate and a likely conservative vote on the Supreme Court, but they certainly did not presage his actual role on the Supreme Court.

In the first few years of the new judicial selection plan, the Republican governor Merriam appointed experienced conservatives, and then pro–New Deal Democratic Governor Culbert Olson appointed experienced liberals. In 1940, Olson nominated Berkeley law professor Max Radin, a Polish-born Jew who had arrived in America at the age of four and a legal historian specializing in Athens and Rome. Justice Felix Frankfurter and Thurman Arnold were among Radin's long list of endorsers, but Radin's opponents questioned his "Americanism."[77] The Commission on Qualifications rejected him two to one, with Attorney General Earl Warren voting no. Earlier, Radin had publicly criticized three murder convictions, and apparently Warren had been offended.[78] After Radin's rejection, Olson nominated forty-year-old Roger Traynor, Radin's Berkeley colleague. The commission confirmed Traynor after only half an hour of discussion. Radin was the only nominee to be rejected by the commission through 1950 (and perhaps longer).

Earl Warren defeated Olson for the governorship in 1942, and he inherited a Commission on Qualifications with two Olson appointees (the chief justice and the presiding appellate judge), a potential two-to-one disadvantage for Warren. Nevertheless, Warren reaffirmed his support for the commission: "I am of the opinion that no man should aspire to the bench unless he can run the gauntlet of his own profession. . . . I should like to see this principle of consulting the State Bar go farther than we have up to the present time."[79] As governor, Warren followed through by asking for public bar review of his nominees before sending them on to the Commission on Qualifications.

Fear of crime was a factor in California's pioneering turn to a form of merit selection. However, crime was not a sufficient condition for judicial reform. Except for Missouri, other states did not turn to professional panels and appointment in the Depression era. California had a number of unique factors that led to reform. Its crime wave was more severe than that of other states, and most significantly, a handful of lawyers and businessmen had the dynamic and creative political skills to overcome the Great

Depression's antielite headwinds. As his judicial reform campaign illustrates, Warren had brought together elite and populist politics in the
1930s and 1940s. As chief justice, Warren ran afoul of populist politics
when a crime wave drove a wedge between them in the mid-1960s. It was
this huge crime wave of the 1960s that put the Warren Court in a negative
light but helped spread Oakland prosecutor Warren's revival of appointment around the country.

"The ABA Plan"

Three years after California's success, the ABA adopted the Judicature
Society's plan as its official recommendation. In the 1910s, the ABA
poured its energy into opposing the movement for judicial recall (the removal of judges by popular referendum), and its leaders hailed its success
in limiting the judicial recall as one of their "great achievements."[80] Over
the 1920s and 1930s, the ABA and major urban bar associations had
focused more and more attention on the problems of judicial elections
and committed more resources to fixing those problems.[81] The ABA had
been assembling committees and disseminating reports to advise bar associations on how to educate the public, clean up the races, and set professional standards for the bench. In 1937, one scholar was nevertheless
"amazed" that the ABA had done so little on judicial selection for so
many years, because such efforts were low-profile.[82] However, in that
same year, the ABA focused on the issue more than before, perhaps because the fight over the New Deal focused new attention on judicial politics and judicial independence. The *American Bar Association Journal*
was publishing broad critiques of judicial elections and defenses of judicial appointments. One writer called for all judges in the United States to
be appointed as a rightful "aristocracy of learning." This lawyer argued
that the chief role for the judiciary was to check "the tyranny of democracy" and the "tyranny of dictatorship": " 'The few' restrained the am-
bition of 'the one' and the emotions of 'the many.' "[83] These labels may
have been a hyperbolic defense of the U.S. Supreme Court against Franklin Roosevelt and the New Deal, but they were even more likely a reference to fascism in Europe. Other articles that year more explicitly defended judicial independence against Roosevelt, but one by William J.
Donovan framed the issue in terms of the importance of protecting minority rights, focusing on racial, ethnic, and religious minorities, including Jews. "And when we see what has happened to minority religious and
racial groups in other countries today we realize that it is not too fantas-
tic to suppose that some future administration, in a time of great excite-

ment and popular feeling, might endeavor to curtail the religious liberties of certain of our citizens. If the Supreme Court can be enlarged [by court packing] to permit such curtailment, these citizens will of course be helpless."[84] The Nazis were already casting a shadow over these debates on American judicial independence.

In the same year, John Perry Wood, the chairman of the Committee on Judicial Selection and Tenure, proposed the new selection resolution in an ABA House of Delegates meeting. A former elected judge in California, Wood cited California's recent successes and called the plan "dual agency," referring to the nominating commission and the appointing governor as two separate agents of judicial selection. Wood contended that "elections drive away the qualified candidates, leaving the unqualified on the bench." He argued that an earlier reform of replacing conventions with direct primaries had failed: "The more direct the popular control, the more effectively are the judges 'delivered into the bonds of politics.' " Wood indicated his distaste for judicial elections of any kind—even the less competitive retention elections—but he acknowledged the political reality that the voters would demand some kind of popular control, and Wood believed that retention elections were the least bad option.[85]

Another Californian at the meeting, Arthur Brouillet, argued that these reform efforts would be futile, because organized labor fiercely opposed them. He noted that even though California voters adopted the statewide reforms in 1934, labor thwarted the efforts at city-based merit reforms in Los Angeles and San Francisco. Wood replied that the real problem had been that the Chamber of Commerce had overplayed its hand in those efforts by "foisting" its own design upon the voters, and thus it triggered a stronger backlash from labor. Wood described his own experiences persuading labor councils to support reform: "No body of people were so much in need of just and independent judges as the poor man who could not hire the best council." Ultimately, the resolution was adopted in a relatively close vote, forty-four to thirty-four.[86] It is not clear whether this narrow margin reflected disagreement only over the details of the plan, or over the bar's role in the plan, or more generally over appointment versus election. In either case, the bar's support for reform seemed to build. Thereafter, the *ABA Journal* published more articles criticizing judicial elections, proposing the nomination/appointment model, and trumpeting signs of progress.[87] It vacillated between calling it the "dual agency" plan, the AJS or Kales Plan, and sometimes the California model, but often enough, it simply focused on appointment over election.

The ABA and the California voters were not alone in their push for judicial independence during the Great Depression. Even though the U.S.

Supreme Court made a series of unpopular decisions in the mid-1930s, the general public did not support constitutionally permissible checks on the Supreme Court. In 1935 and 1936, the conservative majority on the U.S. Supreme Court had struck down one major New Deal program after another. In 1936, Franklin Roosevelt won reelection with 61 percent of the popular vote and all of the states except Maine and Vermont. The Democrats even extended their huge congressional majorities to a 76-to-17 advantage in the Senate and a 334-to-88 advantage in the House. The inescapable conclusion was that the voters had given Roosevelt a powerful mandate for the New Deal. In February 1937, Roosevelt proposed the Judiciary Reorganization Bill, also known as the "court-packing" plan. Under the plan, Roosevelt would appoint one new justice for every sitting justice over the age of seventy and a half. The Constitution did not fix the number of Supreme Court justices, and the number had fluctuated over time—often guided by political packing or unpacking. Presidents Thomas Jefferson, Andrew Jackson, Abraham Lincoln, and U.S. Grant each had increased the size of the Court for political advantage. Court packing was also a less aggressive proposal than many of the proposals in the nineteenth century or during the Progressive Era for federal judicial elections, judicial recall, or popular override. And yet the public response was hesitant and sometimes hostile.[88] Gallup polls showed an average of only 39 percent of the public supporting the plan, even after Roosevelt campaigned for the plan in fireside chats. Even the scholars who conclude that the plan was gaining support concede that the margin was "very, very close"— much closer than the election of 1936 just months before.[89] Justice Owen Roberts famously switched sides in 1937 to uphold major New Deal statutes, and thus "a switch in time saved nine," that is, the number of justices remained nine. If the public supported the New Deal so strongly, its opposition to court packing is a puzzle. It is possible that the public voted for Roosevelt rather than the New Deal, but that scenario is unlikely. More likely, the public strongly supported the New Deal, but even more strongly supported checks and balances against executive overreaching.

Even during the Great Depression, the public was often more committed to judicial independence than to achieving its own policy preferences. The economic crisis had increased the demand for presidential power and centralized authority, but the public still valued the separation of powers and federalism, which required an independent judiciary. The rise of fascism in Europe also tipped that balance. Hitler and Mussolini stirred anxieties about executive abuses of power and reaffirmed the importance of constitutional limits and strong courts. After World War II, Americans would confront these issues again, and would turn to judicial elections both as a New Deal lesson and as a check against authoritarianism.

The Missouri Plan

Today, the merit plan is known as the Missouri Plan, not the California Plan. At the prompting of California businessmen, Earl Warren had flipped the American Judicature Society's model, giving the governor the power to nominate and reducing the professional commission's role. In 1940, Missouri was the first state to enact the AJS and ABA model with the nominating commission leading the way. Together with some failed efforts in other states, Missouri offers more clues about the role of business versus labor, urban versus rural politics, urban elites, and anticrime rhetoric in the puzzle of merit's rise.

In 1938, advocates for merit selection were making progress in seven states, but almost all of them failed. Reformers in Michigan were able to put a limited merit plan on the ballot, with a nominating commission composed of three judges, three lay members appointed by the governor, and three lawyers chosen by the state bar.[90] The press initially supported the plan, but the American Federation of Labor, the Congress of Industrial Organizations, and the Detroit chapter of the liberal National Lawyers' Guild fought the plan. The state bar stayed on the sideline and did not fund the merit campaign. There is no record of that campaign framing merit selection as a solution to the Great Depression crime wave. The merit proposal lost 60 percent to 40 percent overall, with stronger support in urban areas. Wayne County (i.e., Detroit) voted against it by a 54 percent to 46 percent margin, while the rest of the state voted 63 percent to 37 percent against.

Ohio also voted on a merit plan for its appeals courts, with a nominating commission composed entirely of lawyers. Business interests and the Republican Party offered more support than they had in Michigan, but their coalition of groups included no law enforcement organizations, and there is no evidence that they offered any anticrime message.[91] Instead, their coalition was led by the bar association, the Chamber of Commerce, and the Ohio Bankers Association, and it left the distinct impression that the reform was mainly probusiness—not a winning argument in the fall of 1938. The Ohio bar was divided, because some lawyers had more connections through the political parties.

Meanwhile, the Democratic Party and the labor unions formed the Ohio League to Preserve Democracy and Elected Judiciary to lead their opposition. They attacked the merit plan as a step from democracy toward dictatorship, with direct and hyperbolic comparisons to Germany, Italy, and the Soviet Union. Voters rejected this merit proposal almost two to one.[92] It performed better in Cincinnati and Cleveland, but still lost in those cities 58 percent to 42 percent. In both Ohio and Michigan, urban voters were more favorable to merit plans than rural voters were, but the merit campaigns needed to run up large majorities in the cities to offset rural opposition. In the highly industrialized cities of Ohio and Michigan, the opposition of urban labor overcame the support of urban professionals and reformers.

By contrast, Missouri's merit plan succeeded in 1940. Missouri demographically was not so different from Michigan and Ohio. It had large cities and powerful party machines, but its unions were smaller and slightly more moderate.[93] The most significant difference was that Missouri had bigger political scandals over party machines and judges provoking statewide outrage. A galvanized state bar then campaigned simultaneously for criminal justice reform and merit selection. Missouri's bar association was savvy enough to frame merit selection as an anticrime and anticorruption measure. The Democrats had swept Missouri's elections during the Great Depression, so that they controlled 90 percent of the state senate and between 65 and 70 percent of the state house. By the late 1930s, all of the supreme court judges and intermediate appellate judges were Democrats. The party was so dominant in the mid-1930s that its primary voters could choose incompetent but well-connected nonpracticing lawyers, who would then win general elections. The *St. Louis Post-Dispatch*, a liberal-leaning paper, called one of these judges "a humiliation to the law and to the city" as he botched his duties dealing with electoral fraud.[94] Democratic party boss Thomas Pendergast ran Kansas City, and he was beginning to take over the entire state government. A *New York Times* columnist called him "the most powerful boss in America."[95] Pendergast had taken advantage of Prohibition with a gambling and alcohol racket, and he increased his wealth with corrupt government contracts for his concrete and construction business. It was rumored (but unsubstantiated) that Pendergast killed off his rivals and buried them in concrete underneath official state buildings. In a federal grand jury investigation of voting fraud, his thugs were accused of four murders and 200 assaults.[96] Pendergast had handpicked Harry Truman for a U.S. Senate seat in 1934, and then engineered the election of Governor Lloyd Stark. Governor Stark sought to distance himself from the Pendergast machine with more nonpartisan appointments, including James Douglas of St. Louis to fill out a term on the supreme court. Outraged, Pendergast fought Douglas's reelection bid in 1938, and Pendergast's candidate made it a relatively close race. Even though Douglas was reelected, the race underscored the power of party machines over the courts. A year later, Pendergast was convicted of tax evasion and election fraud, and momentum continued to build for political and judicial reform.[97]

At the same time, the most infamous of the "public enemies" in the 1930s marauded in the Midwest, and very often in Missouri. In the "Kansas City Massacre" of 1933, a crime gang killed three police officers in a brazen attempt to free an associate from police custody, a shocking event that played an important role in coining the phrase "war on crime" and in propelling J. Edgar Hoover's career in the FBI.[98] Bonnie and Clyde's gang had a shootout with the Kansas City police, in which Clyde's brother was shot in the head. "Pretty Boy" Floyd got his start in St. Louis (where he received his first felony conviction), then rose up through the Kansas City underworld. His most famous murders were in Kansas City, including the shooting of a federal agent. These high-profile criminals alarmed the public. The Missouri courts were overwhelmed with criminal cases, and with no space in jails, trial judges were swamped with difficult bond decisions. These questions required more experience and expertise than the existing partisan bench had.

The Missouri Bar Association grew exasperated with political corruption and incompetent docket management, and the state's lawyers unified to support merit selection. The bar association organized the Conference on Criminal Justice in February 1937, and the Missouri Institute for the Administration of Justice (the M.I.A.J.) emerged from this meeting as the face of the merit campaign. The Conference on Criminal Justice had gathered leading lawyers and law enforcement to address the state's rise in crime and its overloaded criminal docket. The M.I.A.J.'s mission was to pursue criminal law reform, civil law reform, and the merit plan simultaneously—and with lay leaders, not lawyers, making the case. The Missouri bar knew that the public, already skeptical of lawyers, would perceive a merit commission with its bar-selected members as self-serving. In announcing the M.I.A.J., the *Missouri Bar Journal* explained: "It is thought that much of the actual detail work will be done, or at least engineered by the lawyers. [But] with the aid of laymen, we think we can influence the Legislators and the voters of the state, to a greater extent, than acting solely as lawyers."[99] The M.I.A.J.'s president was a bank chairman and a former president of the St. Louis Chamber of Commerce, and its seven directors were all nonlawyers.

One of the M.I.A.J.'s founders was Rush Hudson Limbaugh, the grandfather of conservative talk radio's Rush Limbaugh. Limbaugh the Elder was truly self-made: born on a small farm, he worked his way through college and law school, hung a shingle, took small cases, served as a local prosecutor, and eventually became a leading trial lawyer in Missouri and a leader of the state Republican Party.[100] In 1931, he was the appointed prosecutor in the impeachment of the state treasurer, a Republican, on corruption charges, and he returned to criminal prosecution during World War II.[101] In the 1950s, he became president of the Missouri Bar Association and was a supporter of civil rights and integration of the bar.[102] Back in the 1930s, he helped found the M.I.A.J. to promote legal expertise. In an interview later in his life, Limbaugh talked about lawyers as "an essential part of a society and even more so today because of the complexity of life today. . . . [I]t is necessary for so many people in business or in any walk of life [to have help in] determining what their rights are everywhere. . . . The presence of a lawyer is almost as necessary as a teacher or a physician."[103] Limbaugh focused on the lawyer's role in assisting business, but also viewed all lawyers as public servants and public educators. Limbaugh joined forces with professors from Washington University's law school, as well as other lawyers, but they mostly served in the background behind the lay frontmen and frontwomen of the M.I.A.J.

As the M.I.A.J. began its campaign in the fall of 1937, the Conference on Criminal Justice announced that the M.I.A.J. was the best organization for "bringing about the adoption of the program."[104] The M.I.A.J.'s agenda included stricter setting of bond, with judges having powers of summary judgment on bond defaults, more efficient criminal trials, and more power for judges to set procedural rules. Later that fall, an M.I.A.J. official reiterated in a speech titled "Agenda for the M.I.A.J." that they were pursuing each of the Conference on Criminal Justice's proposals.[105] Then the bar president's farewell address in 1937 trumpeted the creation of the M.I.A.J. to address the state's "problem of Criminal law enforcement." The bar and M.I.A.J. would lobby and campaign together to "focus public attention on solving the crime problem." The M.I.A.J. was crucial in mobilizing public opinion: "I know of no more significant contribution this Association can make to the welfare of this State than by giving hearty support to the Institution [M.I.A.J.]."[106] The M.I.A.J. organized its first statewide conference in December 1937. The former police commissioner of St. Louis, a featured speaker, emphasized that a stronger bench was crucial for law enforcement, and judges needed to have more rule-making power over criminal law. Recounting his visit to England to study the English justice system, he found that their judges were more efficient and more expert—because they were "appointed for life, and they are out of politics."[107] The businessmen and law enforcement at the conference bemoaned the Missouri courts' docket mismanagement: One worried about delays on the civil docket; the other feared delays on the criminal docket. Joined together through the M.I.A.J., they agreed that merit selection would produce a less corrupt, more competent, more efficient, and more powerful state judiciary.

At the same time, the M.I.A.J. also targeted Missouri's cities as problems. Their major concern was the urban party machine, "which sits behind closed doors and fixes up the plan," turning judicial elections into corrupt appointments.[108] But they were also concerned about the cities' voters—who were not like the rural voter of "native birth" and "well-educated."[109] City machines practiced dirty politics by appealing to race and religion, they claimed, but in the country, "politics is clean."[110] It is important to note that St. Louis and Kansas City had rapidly growing black populations and ethnic minorities, similar to California's cities.[111] Merit selection allowed white elites to maintain control over the courts, against the growing voting strength of ethnic minorities, who were perceived to be tarnishing the party system and to be contributing to urban crime. It is not accidental that, in terms of trial courts, the M.I.A.J.'s plan mandated merit selection only for Jackson County (i.e., Kansas City) and the City of St. Louis, and allowed other counties to vote on whether to adopt the merit plan for their courts. The campaign again and again emphasized the corruption and dirty politics of these two cities, and distinguished the ignorant urban voter from the rural voter who knew all of the candidates.

Over the next two years, the M.I.A.J. built a campaign for criminal and civil procedure reforms first, and merit reforms second, as reflected in their archival records.[112] The M.I.A.J. proposals included giving judges more power to set bail and bond, to grant or refuse severances of criminal trials for joint defendants, to issue summary judgments, and to set procedural rules.[113] These successes established the M.I.A.J.'s credibility as a law-and-order organization focused on crime. Then it focused entirely on merit selection. The campaign never used the term "merit selection." Instead, it was the "non-partisan court plan." The plan had five parts:

1. A statewide Appellate Judicial Commission with seven members: one Missouri Supreme Court justice, three lawyers (one from each appellate district, elected by the district's bar members), and three lay members appointed by the governor. Each serves a six-year term. None of the commission members may hold public office (aside from the judges) or a position in a political party, nor may they collect a salary for their work on the commission.
2. For the Circuit Courts (i.e., trial courts) in the City of St. Louis and Kansas City (and any other judicial district opting into the merit plan by popular vote), a Circuit Judicial Commission consisted of five members: the presiding judge of the district's court of appeals, two lawyers chosen by the bar, and two lay

people chosen by the governor. They, too, may not hold public or party office, nor collect a salary.

3. Whenever there is a vacancy on an appellate court, the commission submits a list of three lawyers to the governor, who may appoint one from the list.

4. Each appointed judge serves a term until the next general election, at which point he or she may run in a retention election, with the following question on the ballot: "Shall Judge —— of the —— Court be retained in office? Yes. No. (Scratch one)."

5. If a majority vote "yes," the Supreme Court and intermediate Court of Appeals judges win twelve-year terms; the Circuit Court trial judges win six-year terms.[114]

The retention elections and long terms of twelve years were designed to give judges additional job security and insulate them from competition. The reform campaign continued to capitalize on surging antiboss sentiment after additional convictions of party hacks on vote fraud charges.[115] The leaders of the reform effort noted that all seven judges on the Missouri Supreme Court and all eighteen on the St. Louis Circuit Court were Democrats, and they warned of the dangers of one-party rule. The attacks on partisanship framed party politics not only as corrupt but also as criminal by alluding to organized crime, bribery, and fraud. Newspapers tended to refer to party bosses with the same images as crime bosses: partisan selection "permits political bosses to knife Judges who don't hitch with the machine and imposes 'handicaps' on Judges who want to do their duty."[116] Corrupt parties (i.e., Missouri's Democratic Party) "frequently sweep[] good men from the bench and carry[] unfit men to their seats," filling the bench with corrupt "political Judges who pay off party bosses for machine support."[117]

As the merit plan campaign heated up in 1939, the bar and the M.I.A.J. continued to fight for their law-and-order criminal reforms. The *St. Louis Post-Dispatch* ran editorials over the period of 1938–1942 in favor of changes in criminal law and in favor of merit reforms side by side.[118] The message was the same: Missouri courts needed to be more efficient in managing their dockets with more power in the courtroom. One editorial, entitled "Toward a Clean Judiciary," contended that the nonpartisan court plan would "free Judges from many political pressures, raise efficiency in the courts and attract candidates who will not now run for the bench because it means becoming involved in party politics, machine patronage and spoils."[119]

The Missouri bar and the M.I.A.J. adopted the same strategy as the California Committee's bypassing the partisan state legislature with a constitutional ballot initiative. Again, the turn to direct democracy to curtail direct democracy is ironic. Emphasizing judicial independence rather than professionalization, expertise, or merit, Missouri's reformers continued using the label "the Non-Partisan Court Plan." The St. Louis Bar Association and the Lawyers' Association of Kansas City actively supported the Missouri Bar Association. However, the Kansas City Bar Association and the St. Louis County Bar Association opposed it, probably because they were more connected to the urban Democratic machines. All of the major newspapers supported the plan, emphasizing the corruption of party politics.

Interestingly, Missouri labor was split. The AFL, which was among the more moderate and less political of the unions, opposed the merit plan, while the CIO, usually more active in electoral politics and further to the left, supported it. The AFL may have been more connected to Democratic machines, while the CIO was likely to have been an outsider to these machines. Thus it likely felt disadvantaged by the Pendergast Democratic Party machine, and preferred nonpartisanship over Pendergast's partisan corruption. The CIO was much smaller in Missouri than the AFL, but the split in labor organizations divided the opposition.[120] Labor unions were not as strong in Missouri as they were in the more industrialized states anyway, so the split was an extra advantage for the merit campaign. At the same time, all of the major Chambers of Commerce supported the plan with considerable resources—making strange bedfellows with the CIO. Joining them were the Missouri League of Women Voters and the Missouri Federation of Women's Clubs, just as these groups had been an important part of California's reform coalition out of their post-suffrage antipartisan, anticorruption, antipatronage mission.[121] Churches, the American Legion, the deans of Washington University School of Law and St. Louis University's law school, and countless civic groups also participated. Though the Republican Party had much to gain from reducing partisan control (i.e., Democratic control), it was relatively quiet, because the campaign depended on the message of nonpartisanship—and because the Republican Party itself was not popular in 1930s Missouri. The forces supporting the plan were much better organized and better funded, and took the leaders of the Democratic Party by surprise.

In 1940, Amendment Number Three passed 55 percent to 45 percent, again thanks to urban voters overcoming rural opposition. Of Missouri's 114 counties, 92 opposed the plan (over 80 percent).[122] The measure passed only because the urban voters of St. Louis and Kansas City voted for it overwhelmingly. The plan had exempted all of the trial judges in counties outside St. Louis and Kansas City and allowed them to opt into the merit plan. Still, rural voters rejected the merit plan—perhaps out of ideological opposition, perhaps out of fear of incremental spreading of merit plans, and perhaps out of simple ignorance of such fine print. Meanwhile, many urban and suburban voters embraced the merit plan, rejecting Pendergast and the urban machines that controlled their cities. The urban AFL members were outvoted by other urbanites. The crime wave surely added to the urban and suburban voters' support for more efficient, more expert, and less corrupt courts.

In terms of party politics, many Democrats voted for merit plans, even though the merit plan would reduce the party's control over judicial selection. Recall the theory that majority parties are more likely to turn to nonpartisan reforms and judicial independence if they fear losing power and are risk averse to being a minority party without judicial protection. This kind of risk aversion strategy may have been a factor shaping the Democrats' voting, but not a major factor. The Democrats had dominated Missouri politics throughout the 1930s, so that the appellate courts were entirely composed of Democrats. In 1940, they lost some seats in the legislature, so that their control of the state senate fell from 91 to 81 percent, and their control of the state house fell from 65 percent to 57 percent. Despite these losses, it was still clear that Democrats were winning local elections. The only branch the Republicans won in 1940 was the governorship in a very close vote. The nonpartisan court plan shifted a lot of power to the governor. If the Democrats were worried about the Republican Party's resurgence, it would have been odd for the Democrats to ignore their continuing success in legislative elections and all other statewide elections. Democratic voters were unlikely to have engaged in such a complicated and sophisticated political analysis when anticrime and anticorruption were simpler and more salient issues in 1940. California Republicans were facing a much more obvious threat from the emerging Democratic-Labor-Socialist coalition in 1934.

The 1940 election was not the end of the Missouri story. The Democratic legislative leadership alleged that the press and the bar association had manipulated the voters with "false and scurrilous propaganda." The Democratic Party proposed a constitutional amendment to repeal the Non-Partisan Court Plan (Proposition No. 3) with a vote on their Proposition No. 4 in November 1942. The promerit *St. Louis Post-Dispatch* attributed the repeal effort to the now-convicted Pendergast's "machine-courthouse ring," and also to the tort plaintiffs' bar, a "fringe of damage-suit lawyers," who had a financial interest in partisan judges.[123] Over the course of the twentieth century, the plaintiffs' bar and trial lawyers would play a bigger and bigger role in financing judicial elections, long before corporations got involved.

One leader of the repeal effort was the Lawyers' Association of St. Louis, a smaller bar organization that was more connected to the Democratic Party and represented the tort plaintiffs' bar. The Lawyers' Association of St. Louis called itself "A Committee of One Thousand Lawyers Against the Nazi Court Scheme" and labeled the merit plan a "Fascist Scheme" of corporate interests, insurance companies, railroads, and the press that supported those interests. The association asserted that "the so-called Non-Partisan Court Scheme is borrowed from Nazi Germany. . . . It is Fascism's Entering Wedge in America."[124] The Lawyers' Association of St. Louis's *Bench and Bar* took a promerit cartoon from the *St. Louis Post-Dispatch* and doctored it. The original portrayed a hand-labeled "Proposition No. 4" grasping at a judge with the caption "Trying to drag the courts back into politics." The doctored antimerit cartoon changed the label to "Nazis Reach for Courts," adding the caption: "In a Missouri court, a sinister, ever-present hand warns the Judge to please his fascist masters, or else—"[125]

The *St. Louis Post-Dispatch*'s editorial deplored allegations of fascism as "absurd and ridiculous," identifying such "hysterical propaganda" as proof that the repealers had no legitimate arguments of their own and instead resorted to hyperbole.[126] Under the heading "Propaganda That Backfires," the *Post-Dispatch* editors published a letter to the editor stating that although the repeal amendment may have had some appeal, "the fact that its sponsors are resorting to paper ruffianism is, without more, a sufficient reason for voting against it."[127]

In response to charges that the merit plan was undemocratic and even "fascist," its proponents reminded the public that the Founders established an appointed federal judiciary in order to protect democracy and the people's rights. A new system of appointment would take back power from special interests, especially "when events in Europe challenge us to make democracy work."[128] Merit supporters thus used the specter of fascism in their favor, albeit more subtly. The repeal effort failed, 64 percent to 36 percent, with a major shift county by county: 111 out of 114 counties voted to retain the merit plan. Rural voters may have learned more about the plan from more experience and from a more active campaign. It is also possible that the St. Louis trial lawyers and their absurd rhetoric alienated voters.

In the first year of the plan, voters removed a sitting judge from Kansas City, Marion Waltner, who owed his seat to the Pendergast machine, not the merit panel. Waltner is one of only two judges to lose a retention election in seven decades of Missouri's merit plan.[129] The Pendergast machine tried to unseat nonpartisan judges in the 1940s but fell far short.[130]

Merit selection since then has followed the governor's party. Democrats controlled the governorship for twenty-four of the next twenty-eight years, and they filled the courts with Democrats. Only two Republicans joined the Missouri Supreme Court in those years. In 1948, Democratic Governor Forrest Smith announced that he would not appoint a Republican if any Democrats were included on the merit commission's list. The commission promptly gave him three Republican names and no Democrats. The second Republican was the Democratic governor's law school classmate. Missouri's merit plan did not eliminate party politics or cronyism, but according to all accounts, the selection process became much less partisan, more open, and more based upon merit.[131] Around the country, newspapers and legal periodicals reported that in Missouri, the plan offered more job security, because the retention races were often uncontested, and voting patterns in them were less partisan.[132] They suggested that more job security was attracting better nominees and was producing a more independent judiciary. Studies have also indicated that labor's concerns were well founded. Business interests and their allies have claimed many more seats on the Missouri merit commission, and very few union allies have made it.[133]

California and Missouri are two pieces of the merit puzzle, helping explain its odd pattern and timing. Merit proponents would always face an uphill battle to convince voters to abandon their power to vote for judges, and all the more so during the Great Depression and its populist reaction against appointed judges and the legal profession. In this era, labor unions had increased their power in direct partisan elections, and they began winning judicial elections. In response, business interests changed their approach, from a strategy of winning partisan elections to a strategy of getting rid of partisan elections in favor of professional appointment. They saw the state bar association as an ally, and they turned out to be right. But business and the bar still needed a unique constellation of forces, timing, and rhetoric in order to persuade a skeptical public. In rural nonindustrial states, the political stakes were too low and not yet ripe for merit: Business was too weak to overcome rural populism. In urban industrial states, the political stakes were already too high and overripe: Business was strong, but labor unions, ethnic voting blocs, and the Democratic party machines had enough time to grow even stronger, and they fought off reform efforts. In rural-but-industrializing states, the climate was just right: Business had grown powerful enough to support merit, but unions and ethnic opposition had not yet grown strong enough to stop them. One more piece of this complicated political puzzle was an effective campaign to frame the advantages—and the urgency—of professionalization and expertise.

In both California and Missouri, anticrime propaganda played a surprising role in winning over the public. In the 1970s, the business-urban elite-bar coalition would turn again to anticrime or race to build a broader coalition and win the uphill battle for popular support. Once upon a time, crime was actually a winning issue for judicial independence from popular politics, rather than a winning issue for judicial accountability to popular politics. The relationship between crime and judicial selection is contingent and contestable. Judicial elections in the early twenty-first century fit a "populist anticrime" model, but during the crime waves of the 1930s and again in the late 1960s–1970s, merit reformers offered a "progressive anticrime" model. Anticrime rhetoric has been a powerful and flexible tool in American history, and one that has been exploited to serve other interests. Many merit reformers opportunistically turned to anticrime propaganda to serve business interests or professional interests. Today, business interests have shifted the anticrime rhetoric from campaigning against judicial elections in general to campaigning against particular judges in those elections. These battles over merit and anticrime in the 1930s and the 1960s–1970s show the early strategy for the modern Republican coalition to overcome the New Deal coalition by uniting probusiness Republicans, urban professionals, social conservatives, and voters who were anxious about crime. Business had harnessed anticrime fears in the 1930s and the 1960s–1970s as a simple and popular campaign message and an engine of reform. After that, business interests reversed their anticrime strategy: not to reform judicial elections, but to win them.

CHAPTER TEN

The Puzzling Rise of Merit

THE EMERGENCE of merit selection (initial selection by nominating panels including leaders of the state bar and other officials) during the Great Depression was a puzzle. Part of the answer was that business interests mobilized in response to the populist prolabor uprising in favor of elite selection. These interests were able to frame their probusiness reform as antipartisan, anticorruption, and most surprisingly, anticrime to win popular support.

The merit revolution from 1950 through the late 1970s presents a similar puzzle. The "Missouri Plan" (and later, the "merit plan") spread through nineteen states, mainly in the South, the Great Plains, and the Rockies. Meanwhile, nine other states adopted a major piece of the plan (the nomination panel half or the retention election half). How did elite judicial appointment by lawyers replace direct elections mainly in the regions that were most alienated by the appointed Warren Court, and during a broader cultural turn against intellectuals and professional expertise?

From the Progressive Era through the New Deal and World War II, technocratic expertise had been on the rise steadily in American government. In the 1950s, there was increasing populist resentment of this trend. This era began with McCarthyism's attack on the academy, experts, and the professional class as unpatriotic and potentially traitorous. In 1952, the Democratic presidential nominee Adlai Stevenson was mocked as an "egghead," and Eisenhower-Nixon prevailed with a populist, anti-intellectual campaign in both 1952 and 1956.[1] Richard Hofstadter captured the national mood, writing *Anti-Intellectualism in American Life* in 1962 and "The Paranoid Style in American Politics" in 1964. Both focused on Americans' deep distrust of professional elites and experts. Lawyers have never been very popular, but the profession was even less popular in the early 1950s.[2] As the Warren Court's civil rights revolution marched from desegregation to the rights of criminal defendants, skepticism about lawyers and judges erupted into violence in the South and outrage in other regions. Billboards screaming "Impeach Earl Warren!" went up all over highways. Appointed judges and judicial independence were not in style. Or so it seemed.

The timeline of merit plan adoptions (see Appendix G) offers a strange pattern of elite professional selection spreading from the Great Plains to the southeast into Dixie and west into the Rockies. Even though the list is full of rural states, these states were urbanizing and industrializing relative to other rural states, and the merit campaigns were led by urban professionals and urban interests, and supported more by urban voters.[3] Merit reform often targeted urban courts and urban problems, and sometimes exempted rural courts.[4]

The two theories that have been the best explanations for the spread of merit are still flawed. One is that the American Judicature Society (AJS) was "instrumental" in the merit campaigns.[5] A second is that the parties in these states were more worried about losing power than the parties in other states, which led them to hedge their bets with a more independent bench that could protect them later if they found themselves out of power.[6] From the 1950s through the 1970s, the AJS did not play the leading role, but more of a supporting role for the local leaders who had initiated these campaigns. Only after the state bar and local interests organized their own campaigns for merit did the AJS organize "Citizens Conferences" for reform. This role may have been very helpful, but there is little evidence that the AJS strategized and initiated this campaign from above more than the local bar, local civic leaders, and local businesses organized their campaigns on the ground. And while there may be some hint of partisan risk aversion in a handful of states in the late 1960s, the evidence mostly points away from this factor, because most of these states adopted merit while one party dominated the state legislature.[7]

Geographic contiguity—neighborly borrowing—played an important role in shaping merit's spread. Between 1958 and 1962, Missouri's neighbors to the north and west adopted the Missouri Plan (Kansas, Nebraska, and Iowa). After a pause of a few years, their neighbors in Colorado, Oklahoma, and then Idaho, Utah, Arizona, and Nevada followed. Some scholars have identified cascades, bandwagon effects, and horizontal federalism as ways of understanding the spread of ideas and institutions.

Geographic proximity can help ideas spread and get bandwagons rolling. It is certainly possible that the pattern of rural-but-urbanizing/industrializing states was merely a reflection of the plan spreading among Missouri's neighbors—which just happened to be rural but urbanizing. But then it is hard to explain why some neighbors adopted merit, while more urban and industrial neighbors (Illinois, for example) and more rural neighbors did not. And it is hard to explain how merit leaped to Indiana, but not to Michigan or to Ohio. The merit plan started in Missouri because of its relative balance of business interests, labor, and urban party machines. Merit's spread from Missouri took on the same rural-but-urbanizing pattern for the same reasons.

Just as in the Great Depression, business interests led the campaign for merit with the help of the bar, and the opposition came mainly from organized labor and urban party machines. The pioneer reforms in California and Missouri had already demonstrated that businesses were behind the merit campaigns, and that the merit plan benefited business interests. Merit succeeded in the states where business had grown powerful enough to support a campaign for merit selection, but also where labor and urban machines had not yet reached enough power to block those campaigns. Business interests in these states had to be strong enough to overcome rural voters' populism, and they were also motivated by the foreseeable growth of the labor vote and the growth of urban political machines, which would both challenge business interests in the near future. Thus, business groups in these states had a narrow window of opportunity. And they still required the help of a number of other factors in order to build political coalitions and take advantage of this window. Racial tension, scandal, and Cold War politics also created political opportunities. Business interests were necessary in the spread of merit selection: They developed the product. But business interests were not sufficient: They needed help marketing and selling that product. The public bought into the label of "merit" and the idea of judicial independence and the rule of law.

Corporate interests in state courts also shifted over the course of the twentieth century, from labor relations to tort litigation. In the first half of the twentieth century, business focused on labor litigation and labor unions' increasing success in judicial elections. In the second half of the century, labor issues receded in importance in state court as the federal government took over labor law and "preempted" state law.[8] Meanwhile, personal injury litigation and the increasing clout of trial lawyers became an enormous challenge for corporations. Between 1950 and 1959, tort damage awards in American courts increased from $1.8 billion to $5.4 billion, and they grew thereafter at an annual rate of almost

10 percent. As tort awards were increasing, the trial lawyers who represented the injured plaintiffs gained economic clout. As administrative alternatives threatened to take over and reduce those awards, trial lawyers organized and mobilized politically after World War II. In 1946, a handful of other workers' compensation lawyers formed the National Association of Claimants' Compensation Attorneys (NACCA). Melvin Belli, California's "King of Torts," a.k.a. "Tortious Maximus," joined the group in 1949, and the organization grew rapidly. By the mid-1950s, the defense bar was already getting nervous about the NACCA's lobbying and sharing litigation strategies.[9] By 1967, the NACCA had 22,000 members and renamed itself the American Trial Lawyer Association (ATLA). In court, personal injury lawyers had persuaded jurors to increase tort awards. Out of court, they lobbied against administrative reform and tort reform, helped elect sympathetic judges, and opposed merit selection.[10] For the same reasons that business interests had fought for merit for several decades, personal injury lawyers vehemently opposed merit selection. They believed that the merit plan was a form of bureaucratic tort reform that would be controlled by corporations and the elite bar, not the trial lawyers.[11] Trial lawyers were one of the most important sources of money in judicial elections for most of the twentieth century, and it is probably no accident that state judges expanded tort liability at the same time.[12] As tort damages exploded, corporate interests responded from the 1950s through the 1970s by focusing on merit reform, before they shifted strategies after 1980 to spending heavily to win judicial elections.

This chapter is not a comprehensive account of merit's spread over three decades and twenty-four states. Instead, it focuses on some key moments in merit's spread in a few of those states, points to some themes in its spread, and suggests that merit's puzzle had many interlocking pieces and few simple answers. It draws on contemporary newspaper accounts, bar publications, a new look at quantitative research on state party politics and other social science research, as well as the records from American military lawyers in Japan, to find some of those pieces and match them up. The underlying political force was corporate interests against labor and torts plaintiffs, and those forces took advantage of other factors to turn popular skepticism into popular support. In addition to the tort wars, two real wars—World War II and the Cold War—shaped the ideas of judicial independence and the rule of law. American lawyers reacted to World War II and fascism by asserting new arguments for judicial independence from executive abuses of power and from partisan politics. MacArthur's military lawyers established the next model of professional selection and retention elections in postwar Japan, turning to the legal profession as a defender of constitutional democracy against authoritarianism. Then the Cold War provided fodder for "rule of law" ideology and judicial independence, and it also led to the coining of the terms "meritocracy" and the "merit plan." After those events shaped the intellectual climate of the post–World War II era, the politics of race, ethnicity, and anticrime assisted businesses' campaigns for merit in several states. Specific scandals over a judge's election were sometimes the triggers, offering an opening for these larger political forces and interests to take advantage. At the time, the defenders of direct elections argued that the merit campaign was not simply a good government reform, but it had disturbing similarities to disenfranchisement. This period also illustrates the changing perceptions of judges and parties—and the need for their separation. Interest groups drove the campaigns for merit selection, but they relied heavily on the rhetoric of judicial independence and nonpartisanship to legitimate their reform efforts. That rhetoric resonated with the public as they voted for these reforms.

"The Bitter Lessons" of World War II: Germany, Japan, and Judicial Independence

Scholars have observed that World War II and the fight against fascism and totalitarianism changed Americans' attitudes toward individual rights and led to the expansion of judicial review to protect minorities.[13] The wars also shaped the legal profession's campaign for judicial independence and for increasing its role in judicial selection. In the American Bar Association's (ABA) debates over adopting the model of bar nomination commissions in 1937, various ABA leaders had argued that fascism and dictatorship had reminded Americans of the importance of judicial independence in defending individual rights and in protecting racial and ethnic minorities.[14] After the ABA vote and as war loomed, bar leaders and Supreme Court justices continued referring to the Nazis to highlight the importance of a strong legal profession and in promoting the ABA plan for judicial selection.[15] In 1938, Justice Stanley Reed addressed the ABA Section on Judicial Administration and the National Conference of Judicial Councils, the forerunners to the judicial nomination committees, and the future leaders of the merit campaigns. Justice Reed made references to authoritarianism and urged lawyers in private practice, not just public officials, to take a stronger stand against threats to American democratic values. Then, just two months before Pearl Harbor, the president of the ABA warned the gathered bar association leaders that war was unavoidable, and lawyers needed to contribute to President

Roosevelt's rallying cry for America to be "an arsenal of Democracy." To this end, he criticized judicial elections and mentioned that the ABA had been campaigning for its model of nonpartisan judicial selection with professional nominating commissions. "Removing judges from the political arena . . . would be a gift to any state, and to the country, in the cause of National Defense," because America's judges would be more inspiring on the homefront and overseas.[16] The speech was full of hyperbole, but the point was that the confrontation with Hitler gave the bar leadership ample fodder to press its case for a higher profile for lawyers.[17]

After the war, the leaders of the legal profession continued to frame their case for judicial independence—and for the bar's role in judicial selection.[18] In 1945, Justice Robert Jackson, just months before he served as prosecutor in the Nuremberg trials, referred to "the bitter lessons of this decade" in his call for an "independent judiciary" and "the rule of law."[19] Attorney General Tom Clark—soon to be Justice Clark—denounced "the mockery and travesty of the Nazi courts," and he called on the legal profession to stand guard "with open eyes" and protect civil rights.[20]

These experiences shaped the next state to adopt a version of the merit plan with retention elections—and it was not actually an American state. It was Japan after World War II, because American military lawyers drafted a new Japanese constitution under General Douglas MacArthur's supervision. These American lawyers had been shaped by two of the biggest crises in American history: the Great Depression and World War II. Some had been New Deal lawyers, and some had been anti–New Deal conservatives, but each drew lessons from the New Deal to support judicial elections. Most importantly, these lawyers illustrate how World War II and the fight against fascism had underscored the importance of judicial independence, the legal profession, and the rule of law. The military lawyers drew on the models from California and Missouri to establish a merit plan for Japan: initial selection by the legal profession and the cabinet, followed by retention elections.[21]

President Truman had ordered General MacArthur, the Supreme Commander of the Allied Powers (SCAP) in Japan, to take over the Japanese government and run the occupation and reconstruction. Under Japan's Meiji Constitution of 1890, the courts had not been a separate branch because they were placed under the direct control of the executive's Justice Ministry, and the Diet interfered with their jurisdiction. MacArthur's officers believed, among the many factors blamed for Japanese militarism, that the Meiji constitution's weak judiciary played a role in leaving the emperor, the military, and the bureaucracy unchecked.[22] MacArthur's team of about eighteen officers worked nonstop in secret hammering out a new constitution. The section on the judiciary received more time and energy than any other.[23] It was led by three American lawyers: Colonel Charles Kades, a former New Deal lawyer; Commander Alfred Hussey, a pro–New Deal Democrat;[24] and Lieutenant Colonel Milo E. Rowell, a conservative Republican business lawyer from California.[25]

Rowell believed that militarists were able to take over Japan because its courts had "neither dignity nor independence," merely serving as an instrument of the imperially appointed prosecutor, and subservient to the police.[26] Rowell wanted a strong court system that would be able to protect individual rights and to enforce the constitution. Rowell and Hussey started the chapter with a preamble-like opening: "A strong and independent judiciary is the bulwark of the people's rights."[27] They explicitly granted the Japanese courts the power of judicial review. The appointment process also departed from the U.S. Constitution, and more resembled the American merit plan. For supreme court justices, Rowell and Hussey gave the appointment power not to the prime minister, but to the Japanese cabinet as a whole. For lower court seats, they had the supreme court nominate at least two candidates, and the cabinet would pick one.[28] At that time, the Americans expected Japanese politics to generate multiple parties and compromise, and the constitution's parliamentary system would encourage coalition building in order to form a government. Hussey argued that multiparty pluralism was more "desirable" than two-party rule.[29] Because the drafters envisioned a cabinet assembled through compromise, they expected that the cabinet would make judicial appointments through compromise, too, much like the pluralist compromises on merit nomination commissions.[30]

Rowell and Hussey had both opposed judicial elections initially,[31] but Kades persuaded Rowell by drawing explicitly on California's model of retention elections, which Rowell had experienced as successful as a Californian.[32] Kades reminded them of the clash over the New Deal, and argued that regular elections were better than another constitutional crisis and a threat of court packing.[33] He persuaded Rowell that elections would bolster the courts' public legitimacy, making them strong enough to protect individual rights.[34] The committee emphasized relative judicial independence—independence from the executive branch—more than relative independence from the people. They concluded that executive abuses of power were a bigger concern than too much popular control.[35] Retention elections shifted power from the executive to the people, just as nineteenth-century Americans had done.

Just as California's retention elections were a model for the Japanese constitution, Missouri's merit plan became a model for its implementation.[36] After the ratification of the postwar constitution, MacArthur and his officers worked with the Japanese government to draft the Courts Act filling in the details of the judicial system.[37] For the selection of judges, the Courts Act provided for a professional "consultative committee," with eleven members drawn from the three branches of government, the bar, and the academy.[38] The idea was that the legal profession would be an additional check on the executive branch, and its inclusion in the selection process would help bolster civil society and judicial independence from the party in power. After 1947, Japanese governments continued consulting the Japanese bar on judicial appointments.[39]

Drawing from both the experience of the Great Depression and the New Deal, and the contrasting experience of fascism and world war, MacArthur's military lawyers faced difficult choices between judicial independence and judicial accountability. Because many of them had been New Dealers themselves, one might have expected that they would turn to judicial elections in favor of accountability. But they defended judicial elections explicitly in terms of judicial independence, as the means of separating the courts from the executive branch, the most dangerous branch of the authoritarian regimes. Similar to the American Revolutionaries of 1848, MacArthur's military lawyers contended that judicial elections would strengthen the legitimacy of the courts in the eyes of the public, allowing the judges to be bolder in standing up to authoritarian abuses and in defending the constitution. The Americans might have been exporting judicial elections, but they were also exporting judicial independence at exactly the same time. The Japan episode reflects how World War II changed attitudes toward executive power, political parties, courts, and the legal profession and helped lay a foundation for a puzzling domestic judicial transformation.

The Cold War, "Meritocracy," and Expertise

The Cold War also sparked a revival of "the rule of law" ideology. Once World War II ended, Americans refocused on separation of powers and federalism, and many were concerned with excessive executive power in the wake of fascism and the spread of Communism. Progressives and conservatives worked together to modernize and strengthen state governments, and that effort sparked a new interest in constitutional revision and judicial efficiency. Civic groups nationwide drafted model state constitutions and designs for modern judiciaries, and they circulated them.

These models included versions of merit selection by judges and/or the state bar.[40] Leading lawyers relied on the Cold War to make arguments in favor of the Missouri Plan. For example, Senator Alexander Wiley of Wisconsin wrote an article titled "A Free Judiciary: America's System Contrasted with the Soviets," primarily to endorse the Missouri Plan as part of the Cold War battle of ideas and institutions. His main point was to contrast the Soviet judiciary's lack of independence and its lack of professional training with Missouri's nonpartisan selection and the role of legal expertise.[41]

In the 1950s, the ABA and the legal profession expanded their efforts to help fight the ideological Cold War. In the mid-1950s, Charles S. Rhyne, a lawyer who often represented state and local governments against the federal government before the Supreme Court, had an idea: If labor unions had Labor Day, and if the Communists had May Day, the rule of law should have a Law Day. Anti-Communists had already tried to reclaim May 1 by declaring it "Loyalty Day" or "Americanization Day" since 1920s Red Scare and immigration anxieties. Rhyne explicitly sought to reclaim May 1 from the Communists by making it Law Day. In a speech years later, Rhyne explained, "The immediate inspiration for a May 1 celebration of law was directly related to the Cold War. For many years the American news media gave front page headlines and pictures to the Soviet Union's May Day parade of new war weapons. . . . My idea was to contrast the United States' reliance on the rule of law with the Soviet Union's rule by force."[42] Rhyne became president of the ABA and successfully persuaded President Eisenhower to proclaim May 1 "Law Day." In 1958, Eisenhower declared, "In a very real sense, the world no longer has a choice between force and law. If civilization is to survive it must choose the rule of law." The annual materials from the ABA promoting Law Day built on this founding merger of rule of law, loyalty, and anti-Communism. They also trumpeted "judicial independence" as the American way, the guarantee of American freedom and democracy.[43] These anti-Communists were rule-of-law conservatives finding new public support for judicial independence and the legal profession.

Civil service reform had been called the "merit system" since the 1910s, but the movement for professional judicial selection did not adopt the label "the merit plan" until 1958. The Cold War led to the coining of the term "meritocracy," and it also restored interest in the rule of law and judicial independence as concepts and as rhetoric. The Cold War produced McCarthyism and attacks on experts and elite lawyers, but in the years after Senator Joe McCarthy's demise, the Cold War led to the invention of the word "meritocracy."[44] The term "meritocracy" itself was coined in 1958 by Michael Young, a young leader in the British Labour Party. Young grew disillusioned with his party's paeans to merit and its neglect of deeper class inequality. He left Labour and wrote a dystopian futurist critique, in the guise of a sociology dissertation written in 2030 looking backward at Labour's agenda. He envisioned a world governed by IQ tests and by a test-prep industry. Once the tests created a perception of equal opportunity, there would be no more support for social welfare for the undeserving, unmeritorious poor. In the end, Young's future world of intelligentsia power becomes a polarized society that collapses in revolt.[45] Young described this future as "rule not so much by the people as by the cleverest people," but he stumbled around in search of a name for it. He considered "aristocracy," Greek for "rule by the best," but its modern connotation was hereditary privilege. Then Young thought up "meritocracy" and published his book *The Rise of the Meritocracy* in 1958, and his neologism caught on.[46] Young had predicted that the United States was too committed to social equality and leveling, and too suspicious of intellectuals to adopt such a testing-based system. In fact, America was already on its way. The Americans who were building the standardized educational testing regime quickly took notice of the book and were amused.[47] They believed they were building a meritocracy that was more reliable, more stable, and more popular than the one Young predicted. In the midst of the Cold War, the concept of meritocracy was the West's reply to the Communists' equality argument: Capitalism simultaneously could offer liberty, equality, and efficiency through merit-based systems.

In 1958, the same year Young published *The Rise of the Meritocracy,* the Nebraska Bar Association introduced the name "merit plan," interchangeably with "the Missouri plan" and "the ABA plan."[48] By 1961, the Nebraska State Bar Association referred to the plan exclusively as "the Merit Plan,"[49] and this new packaging spread throughout the country. The "merit system" had been the name for the good-government reforms of civil service hiring and promotion since the Progressive Era and the New Deal, in contrast with party patronage, corruption, incompetence, and inefficiency. The label "merit" emphasized the professional bar's participation in the nominating commissions, but curiously, it obscured the lay participation, even though one might have imagined that lay participation would have made the proposals more palatable. For example, Nebraska's nominating commissions are composed of four lawyers elected by the Nebraska State Bar Association and four nonlawyers appointed by the governor, plus one supreme court justice who acts as a nonvoting chair. No more than two lawyers and two nonlawyers may belong to the same political party. The proponents of this reform might have emphasized nonpartisanship, bipartisanship, and a balance between professional and lay leadership. Instead, they emphasized "merit."

In the 1930s, "Curb Crime" captured the mood in California, and the label "nonpartisan" had captured the mood in Missouri. In the late 1950s and early 1960s, "merit" captured a national perspective, connecting equality of opportunity to nonpartisan expertise. These Cold War ideological shifts set the stage for merit's spread.

Alabama, Race, and Reaction in 1950

In 1950, Birmingham, Alabama, was the first American jurisdiction to adopt nominating commissions and appointments since Missouri had in 1940. Birmingham shows how business interests were the main force for merit, but they built support by using other political opportunities (in this case, race). Their switch came before the Warren Court and the height of the civil rights era, but even so, it offers an explanation for why southern states would turn to merit plans during and after the Warren Court. The spark was Big Jim Folsom and the fears he instilled among wealthy white Alabamans of a potential interracial revolution at the ballot box. As an upstart populist Democratic governor in the 1940s and 1950s, Folsom tried to unite blacks and poor whites against the conservative white establishment. Birmingham's Old South (hardline segregationists) and its New South (big business and the rising professional class) together fought back in part by taking judicial selection away from Folsom and from the masses, and giving it to the conservative legal establishment.

After two losing congressional campaigns as a "wet" anti-Prohibition candidate, Folsom served as a delegate to the 1944 Democratic National Convention as an avid supporter of left-wing Henry A. Wallace, a pro–civil rights northerner with socialist sympathies. Two years later, at age thirty-eight and with no official experience, he ran for governor with a neighborly door-to-door campaign. He was the only World War II veteran in the field, and after his wife died in childbirth, Big Jim's story as a widower raising two small children made him all the more sympathetic. At six-foot-eight, he was known as "the little man's big friend." He also became known as "Kissin' Jim," because at the end of each campaign rally, he'd kiss all the pretty young women in the audience and announce that this particular town had the prettiest girls in all of Alabama. While the four other candidates appealed to local party bosses, Folsom ran against the party bosses, promising a "mother's spring cleaning" of all of Alabama's political corruption.[50]

He announced his "People's Program," which included the repeal of the poll tax and reapportionment of the legislature, both of which would increase the power of poor whites. He was the only candidate to endorse labor's organizing and collective bargaining power and to call for the expansion of Social Security. All the other candidates supported increased liquor regulation or prohibition, but Folsom replied, "Liquor has been a problem for two thousand years, and wiser men than I have failed to find a solution."[51] Truth be told, liquor was a personal problem for Big Jim, as all of Alabama would find out later when he appeared drunk on television.

The four establishment candidates ignored Big Jim and focused all of their attacks on each other, so it was a shock when Big Jim won the first round of the Democratic primary with 28.5 percent of the vote, and then won the high-turnout runoff with 58.7 percent, winning more votes than any other candidate for Alabama state office ever had received before. The shocked Democratic establishment accused him of being "a direct threat to orderly, well-directed government" and of being in the pocket of "the communist fringe," the Congress of Industrial Organizations (CIO), and the NAACP. But the Democratic nomination guaranteed his win in the general election. His raucous inauguration filled the streets of Montgomery with poor whites from all over Alabama and drew comparisons to Andrew Jackson's boisterous inauguration.[52]

Big Jim's win was primarily due to poor whites turning out to vote in droves, but there was another threat looming in the late 1940s: black enfranchisement. In *Smith v. Allwright* in 1944, the U.S. Supreme Court struck down the all-white primary as unconstitutional.[53] In response, Democratic Party leaders in Alabama sought other ways to disfranchise black voters. In 1946, they led the ratification of a constitutional amendment, called the "Boswell Amendment," giving local voting registrars complete discretion to assess the qualifications of those registering to vote. The NAACP challenged the Boswell amendment in federal court, and the white establishment worried that judicial scrutiny might jeopardize all of their voting restrictions against both black voters and poor whites. Folsom's upset win exacerbated those fears. He was actually no radical and no integrationist—at least not in 1946. But as he clashed with white conservatives, he relished provoking the establishment and recognized a political opportunity to broaden his support. Folsom focused on appointing voter registrars to each county board who shared his agenda of expanding suffrage. He instructed the registrars to apply the state voting rules fairly, without regard to race. Folsom's appointees started registering more black voters, and Folsom threatened resistant county boards with prosecution by his attorney general or by Truman's Justice Department. The malapportioned and reactionary legislature fought back by appealing directly to the voters with a constitutional amendment in early 1948, but the voters rejected it in a big win for Folsom.[54] The state constitution barred a governor from serving consecutive terms, so he invested his political capital in his slate of candidates for the 1950 election, and he kept his eye on returning to power in 1954. But he did not back down from civil rights. He shook hands with black supporters at some of his rallies, much to Dixiecrat dismay.[55] In his Christmas 1949 address to the state, he challenged his audience:

> It is time to ask questions about our inner self. . . . Our Negroes who constitute 35% of our population in Alabama—are they getting 35% of the fair share of living? Are they getting adequate medical care . . . ? Are they provided with sufficient professional training . . . ? Are the Negroes being given their share of democracy, the same opportunity of having a voice in the government under which they live? As long as the Negroes are held down by deprivation and lack of opportunity, the other poor people will be held down alongside them.[56]

At the same time, federal courts were also striking down various walls of Alabama's segregation. District Judge Clarence Mullin declared Birmingham's segregationist zoning laws unconstitutional in 1947, which led to bombings of black homes near white areas. In 1949, another federal district judge struck down the Boswell amendment, leading to a rush of black voter registration.[57] State judge Horace Wilkinson wrote in an alarmist article to the state bar that "our problem bluntly stated is to prevent a fusion of the races," claiming that the NAACP had a plan for mass registration in 1949. Arguing for the creation of a separate Democratic Party upholding white supremacy, he wrote, "We are splotched with a bloc of Negro votes in Birmingham, Mobile, and other places. We need to clear the political complexion of our Party."[58]

Birmingham, the second largest city in the South, was the center of the backlash against Folsom. Birmingham was the industrial capital of the New South, a new economy of manufacturing, big business, and a rising professional class.[59] Civil rights were literally explosive in Birmingham, as noted by the shameful nickname "Bombing-ham" for the fifty bombings after the federal court's zoning ruling up to the infamous church bombing of 1963 that killed four young girls.[60] In 1948, when the Dixiecrats revolted from Truman and the national Democrats, they chose Birmingham for their convention. Bull Connor arose in Birmingham politics in the

1940s and 1950s as a hardline segregationist before earning national infamy as the Birmingham public safety commissioner who used fire hoses, attack dogs, and even a tank against civil rights protesters. Martin Luther King Jr. wrote his famous "Letter from a Birmingham Jail" and later called Birmingham "the most segregated city in America."[61]

Blacks were about one third of both the state population and Birmingham's population. If they could vote, and if some poor whites continued to support Folsom, they could potentially overturn Jim Crow in Alabama.[62] The president of the Alabama Bar, a prominent Dixiecrat leader, feared registration of blacks in urban areas where they might already meet existing voting requirements more easily than rural blacks and be less susceptible to poverty and intimidation as obstacles to voting.[63] As Folsom continued to fight to open voter registration, Birmingham's New South lawyers and businessmen lined up with the Old South segregationists to block him.[64] Judges in Alabama were technically elected, but in practice many judges were appointed by the governor because judges sometimes timed their retirement to trigger appointments rather than elections. A 1949 study showed that 40 percent of Alabama judges had been appointed initially.[65] This ongoing practice meant that Jim Folsom and other potentially progressive governors could appoint integrationist, antibusiness judges. The Alabama State Bar first sponsored a plan to replace the state's partisan elections with the Missouri Plan. However, state legislators had more invested in local party machines and more to lose by giving control to the bar, so they forced the bar to compromise on a plan limited to Jefferson County (i.e., Birmingham), and limited to vacancies.[66] Aside from vacancies, judges would run in partisan elections, so the effect of the amendment was to eliminate the governor's power to appoint unilaterally. The proposed Jefferson County Judicial Committee, consisting of two members of the bar, two laypeople, and one Jefferson County circuit judge, would send a list of three names to the governor for each appointment.[67] The bar representatives would be elected by the Birmingham bar membership, and the two laypeople would be selected by Jefferson County's legislative delegation.[68] Thus, the governor would have no control of the committee, and he would be limited to the choices of the legislature, the bar, and the bench.

Folsom denounced the amendment for partial merit selection in Alabama as a "scheme" by "corporate lawyers" to promote their own interests.[69] In fact, it is likely that some of the Alabama bar did not care about Folsom's views on race, but they simply were taking advantage of racial fears to take judicial selection back from the voters and from the party machines. The Birmingham Post-Herald was not a particularly segregationist newspaper, but it endorsed the amendment enthusiastically, because of its conservative economic interests and because of "New South" identification with expertise and professionalism. Amendment 3 passed statewide by a vote of 53 percent to 47 percent.[70] Jefferson County voters approved the plan by a margin of almost two to one.[71] In the same election, Folsom's handpicked candidate was defeated, but four years later, Folsom won back the governorship. Just thirteen days after Folsom had won the Democratic nomination in May 1954, the Supreme Court decided *Brown v. Board of Education*.[72] Folsom's Democratic nomination made his election a foregone conclusion, but *Brown* also sealed the fate of his second term. Folsom's emerging biracial "people's program" never regained its foothold, swept away by massive resistance and white supremacy.[73] No other southern state adopted merit selection in the 1950s or 1960s, but several southern states turned to merit in the early 1970s. The question was why Democratic politicians would give up their secure party control over the courts. Alabama of 1950 gives us a hint: When black voter registration and federal court decisions shake white Democrats' confidence in their voting power, merit selection becomes an alternative to black suffrage.

Birmingham foreshadows the spread of merit in the South in the 1970s. The primary forces for merit were business and the bar, just as they had been in Birmingham in 1950. Merit selection started in the southern periphery or border states, and even though it never took hold in most of Dixie, it still made inroads against the odds of post-*Brown* populism. These successes were chiefly due to the New South reemerging from the turbulent desegregation fights of the 1960s. Professionals, moderates, and growing businesses—the core of what was known as "the New South"—led the campaigns for merit, opposed mostly by Democratic Party insiders and state legislators. Editorials, letters to the editor, and endorsements in southern newspapers were overwhelmingly on the side of merit selection, as they had been in other merit campaigns from the 1950s through the 1970s. Professionals and businesses were invested in modernizing the South and moving from Jim Crow to a more integrated economy, so to speak. Although the New South's interests were the main factor promoting merit selection in Dixie, the Old South and black suffrage played a role, too.

Florida and Tennessee were the first two southern states to adopt the merit plan in the 1970s, and both reflect a combination of Old and New South. In Florida (as in most of the South), the Democrats had dominated all the branches of government for decades. Thus, it is not surprising that frustrated Florida Republicans embraced the merit plan. The bar associations and many civic groups like the League of Women Voters also supported the plan, just as they had in other states. But more surprising was the support of many Democrats, even though merit seemed to run against their partisan interests.[74] "New South" Democrats like Florida Governor Reubin Askew and state legislator (and later U.S. senator) Bill Nelson led the merit effort as part of a modernization program.[75] Bill Nelson said, "What we want to do is eliminate judges, particularly in a big geographic area, having to raise campaign contributions, putting them in the position of having to go to lawyers who practice in front of them for endorsements, help, and money."[76] New South professionals were trying to transform the South's image from corrupt provincialism to good government. Tennessee's effort to adopt the new system was similarly bipartisan, led by the Tennessee Bar Association.[77]

But in both Florida and Tennessee, in addition to the New South voices, there are echoes of Birmingham circa 1950, with an "Old South" political factor below the surface. Just as the expansion of black suffrage in Alabama in 1950 triggered the first postwar merit plan in Birmingham as a tool of retaining white control, the Voting Rights Act shaped the expansion of the merit plan in the early 1970s. The impact of the Voting Rights Act was initially slow, but in the early 1970s it began to reshape the voting rolls. Tennessee and Florida were the southern states with the most progress in registering black voters.[78] Even if statewide white voters might have maintained large majorities, black voters in Democratic primaries would reshape nomination battles. The crucial issue in judicial selection was the control of trial and intermediate courts, where concentrated black voting populations would have been most potent and most able to align with more progressive urban whites. Cities in Tennessee and Florida had rapidly growing black populations and black voters, and often growing Hispanic populations. As 1950s Birmingham illustrated, white Democrats were risk averse not about interparty competition, but about intraparty and interracial competition. Black suffrage would transform local judicial races in many southern cities, unless judicial selection could be taken away from the voters. Thus, it is not as surprising that the Warren Court and the Voting Rights Act of 1965 revived white southerners' interest in judicial appointments over elections, as well as in elite lawyers' power over the ballot. What was merit for some was disempowerment for others. The merit campaigns in the 1960s and 1970s were a complex mix of coalition politics around the country, but Birmingham's 1950 campaign highlights the role of race and racism in merit's rise.

Breaking the Ice: Alaska, 1955–1956

Alaska was the first state to adopt merit selection for all of its courts, and its turn to merit was part of its campaign for statehood and business investment in the 1950s. Alaskan leaders had a major challenge: They needed to win congressional support for Alaska's bid for statehood. Alaska was perceived as a vast and ungovernable wilderness requiring federal control, and unsuited for self-government. It was also thought to be more appropriate for military control, because it was the closest American territory to the Soviets. But most significantly, partisan politics blocked its statehood. Alaskan voters were solidly Democratic, and at that time, Eisenhower was president and Republicans controlled the Senate. National Republicans knew that Alaskan statehood was against their own self-interest. Alaskan leaders understood that nonpartisan appointment was a public statement to a national audience and to Republicans that Alaskans intended to govern responsibly with nonpartisanship. Judicial independence was important in Alaska not because of internal party competition, but precisely because of its lack of internal competition. Merit selection was also a way to attract business, reassuring potential investors that Alaska was not the Wild West and that it had respect for the rule of law.

An important step in the statehood campaign was a constitutional convention in the winter of 1955–1956. Alaskan lawyers traveled to the Lower 48 to interview politicians and academics about constitutional design, part of an overall strategy to build national approval. Alaska reflects a larger pattern of local organizers taking the lead in reform, drawing from the documents and ideas published by national organizations.[79] The national organizations were remote and reactive in these campaigns, not immediate and proactive. One theory suggests that merit selection was the product of powerful state bar associations, but this theory certainly does not apply to Alaska (or in many of the early merit adopters). The Alaska bar did not even exist in any organized way until the state constitutional convention was announced. Alaska's territorial legislature established the Alaska Bar Association in 1955 in anticipation of the convention and as part of the professionalism strategy for statehood. The bar's Statehood Committee put forward its case for judicial independence in its call for a convention: "The challenge is great because in the judiciary rests the ultimate protection of the fundamental rights of persons traditionally guaranteed by our American federal and state constitutions; only a well-designed judiciary can efficiently and fairly perform this guardianship function." The Statehood Committee asserted that a consensus had formed among "practicing attorneys, judges, legal theorists and laymen" for structuring courts, and cited the Missouri Plan as a model.[80] Delegates portrayed lawyers as guardians of "the people's rights" and of democracy, not threats to democracy.[81]

In drafting the constitution, the convention generally followed the model constitutions offered by national civic organizations, particularly the model offered by the National Municipal League, based in New York.[82] The model's commentary extolled the importance of judicial independence and federalism in defense against "demagogue[s]." The National Municipal League proposed a nominating "Judicial Council" made up of sitting judges, bar-selected lawyers, laypeople appointed by the governor, and the chair of the legislature's judiciary committee. Similar to the old Kales proposal for the American Judicature Society, the National Municipal League plan would have the chief justice be elected by the voters, and instead of the governor, the chief justice would have the power to appoint judges from the council's nomination list.[83] In the end, the convention departed from this model's specifics, and instead it followed the Statehood Committee's program and a model closer to the Missouri Plan, in which the chief justice was not elected by the people, and the governor retained appointment power.[84] The judicial council, the constitution's name for the nominating body, consisted of seven members: three attorneys appointed by the state bar's governing body for staggered six-year terms, three non-lawyers appointed by the governor and confirmed by the legislature for staggered six-year terms, and the chief justice of the state supreme court.[85] The governor would appoint one nominee from the judicial council's list.[86] Each judge would face a retention election on a nonpartisan ballot three years after being appointed, and then every ten years thereafter.[87] Because the state constitution limited the governor to one four-year term, almost always one lay member of the council (and even two or all three) lay members had been appointed by an earlier governor, not the sitting governor making the selection from the council's list. Ten-year terms were relatively long for state judges around the country, indicating that the delegates were pursuing general judicial independence by increasing job security. Delegates discussed the problem of campaign finance in partisan elections, and they believed that retention elections would not draw much money.[88]

After the judiciary committee drafted this proposal, its chairman sent the proposal to Alaska's federal officials and other officials around the country for their comments. It was an effort to seek feedback, but it was also an effort to advertise Alaskans' commitment to judicial independence, nonpartisanship, and modernization.[89] Delegates predicted that every law school in the country would study Alaska's constitution, and they would conclude that Alaska has "the most progressive and most modern and up-to-date system of selecting the judiciary of any state."[90] One delegate admitted: "We have an end product to sell. We had better make that [constitution] pretty liberal if we are going to get into the Union."[91] In this case, liberal meant open and modern, as well as protective of individual rights. But it was also classically liberal, in the free market sense: attracting a market of investors, whose property rights would be protected by an independent judiciary. The legal profession would protect popular democracy, as well as business and investment. Alaska's voters ratified the constitution in April 1956 by more than two to one. The convention delegates spent more of their energy selling their constitution not to the voters but to a national audience as "typifying the best and most modern principles of efficient judicial administration" and "a guarantee of a strong, fearless, and independent judiciary."[92] Congress admitted Alaska as a state two years after ratification.

Part of Alaska's turn to merit was the cold state's Cold War, reflecting a national interest in the rule of law generally and in bipartisan stability on the Soviet border. But more significantly, Alaskans were simply trying to break the ice with Congress and national elites in a public relations battle. The territory needed political support in Washington and investment by out-of-state businesses. Whereas partisan elections emerged in the mid-nineteenth century in part because of localism, Alaska illustrated the increasing importance of a national audience, a national market, and national investors—all of which had a strong interest in judicial independence rather than local accountability and parochialism.

Kansas, the Right to Work, and a Dog That Didn't Bark

After Alaska, the next state to adopt bar nomination and retention elections was Kansas, and again, business interests were at the heart but were using other political events to create an opening for their judicial reforms. In fact, because Alabama's adoption has been overlooked and because observers get confused about the timing of Alaska's adoption,[93] Kansas has been perceived as the state that revived the Missouri Plan after almost two decades of inaction. The official story that Kansans tell about this decisive moment is about a scandal: the infamous "triple switch" of 1956–1957. The sitting governor, Fred Hall, was relatively unpopular and had lost the Republican Party nomination. In his last months in office, Governor Hall sought a new job.[94] When the chief justice of the supreme court, William Smith,[95] suddenly was hospitalized and decided to resign in the final days of Governor Hall's term, Hall decided that he wanted that job. Governor Hall kept Justice Smith's resignation a secret, and called his lieutenant governor John McCuish, who was also being hospitalized for high blood pressure.[96] Two days later, Hall and McCuish visited Chief Justice Smith in the hospital, and then, with their wives dressed in formal attire, went to the state capitol building, where Hall announced Smith's resignation and promptly resigned. That resignation turned Lieutenant Governor McCuish into Governor McCuish, and he then appointed former Governor Hall to the now vacant chief justice seat, all within a matter of minutes in January 1957.[97]

Kansans claim that the "triple switch" led to the merit plan one year later.[98] But this story by itself has some holes. The triple switch most obviously highlighted a problem with appointments. If the scandal had been the major cause of reform, it would have made more sense if the reform focused on the particular problem of shady vacancy appointments, and the reform might have replaced vacancy appointments with expedited direct judicial elections. As it turned out, Kansas's reforms went far beyond the vacancy problem. Kansas newspapers denounced the triple-switch as "the culmination of a deal in deepest secrecy."[99] But the merit plan's nomination commission and governor's appointment added no transparency, and the commission's selection process would be less transparent than elections. The newspapers also predicted that one result from the switch would likely be that "there would be a renewed effort to enact a constitutional amendment to take the state courts out of politics."[100] But the public's problem in the triple switch appears to have been with *backroom* politics, and they would have preferred more *popular* politics. Presumably, an expedited election might not take much longer than the procedures of merit nomination. Instead of having a nominating commission send names to the governor, it could put those names before the voters for a quick election. But Kansas's merit reform gave more power to the governor and less power to the voters than ever before. Another twist is that the reform lengthened the terms of Kansas Supreme Court justices from four to six years. By itself, the triple-switch scandal would have created pressure for shorter terms because of a spike in populism and because more frequent elections might reduce the number of interim appointments. Instead, the reforms led to more general judicial independence, not just a shift in relative independence. Something else was going on in Kansas.

Kansas borders Missouri, and the Kansas bar had been paying attention to the successes of the Missouri Plan for years. In August 1954—two and a half years before the triple switch—the *Kansas Bar Journal* called for a constitutional amendment to adopt the ABA plan/Missouri Plan.[101]

The Kansas bar repeated this endorsement in almost every issue of its journal, and often reported on its organizational meetings promoting this plan in 1955 and 1956, while Governor Hall was still unpopular, but before he had lost his party nomination.[102]

One might have expected the Kansas bar to have been buzzing about *Brown v. Board of Education,* particularly because the named defendant in the consolidated cases was the Board of Education of Topeka, *Kansas.* But Kansas lawyers let other states fret about desegregation. The *Kansas Bar Journal* published one relatively balanced note on segregation,[103] nothing at all like the bombastic rhetoric of the *Alabama Lawyer* in 1950. There are no signs of backlash against the Warren Court that would have dragged down the Kansas bar's plan to revive appointments and to increase judicial independence. Opposition to *Brown* was the dog that didn't bark. The lack of complaints about *Brown* suggests that the Warren Court backlash was not very strong outside the Old South; that the NAACP legal strategy to focus on segregation in border states was working, producing legal victories with less political backlash; and that Kansas lawyers seemed to be less opportunistic about race than Alabama lawyers. In Alabama, the Birmingham bar used race and Jim Crow to promote their corporate and political power. In Kansas, lawyers did not cite *Brown* either in favor of or against merit selection.

The issue that was far more pressing than desegregation was business versus labor. Kansas's judicial reform amendment was on the same ballot with a right-to-work amendment that would reduce the power of labor unions. One major issue was the "closed shop" versus "the right to work." Under the National Labor Relations Act, employers and unions could create a "closed shop," requiring all employees to be dues-paying members of the union. Right-to-work statutes and amendments prohibited contracts that required union membership and the payment of union dues before or after hiring. Right-to-work amendments first passed in the South during World War II, in Florida and Arkansas. They spread through the Great Plains next, to Nebraska and South Dakota in 1946, as well as to Arizona. The year 1947 was a big one: amendments passed in Iowa, North Dakota, Texas, Tennessee, Georgia, North Carolina, and Virginia. That year, the Taft-Hartley Act rolled back some federal protections of unions and abolished the closed shop but permitted a "union shop," an agreement that required new employees to join the union after their hire. The act also explicitly recognized the right of states to adopt right-to-work laws that mandated "open shops," that is, no requirement that employees belong to a union. In the early 1950s, five more states in the South and the Rockies joined. The Chamber of Commerce targeted Kansas and five other states in 1958. A right-to-work bill passed both houses of the Kansas legislature in 1956, but prolabor Republican Governor Hall vetoed it (making him unpopular with Republicans and leading to his defeat and the notorious triple switch). This fight dominated that election cycle, making judicial reform a side issue.

In 1955, the Kansas bar's journal published an article enthusiastically supporting right-to-work amendments.[104] Instead of spending time on racial discrimination, the journal focused on labor's closed shop as a problem of discrimination. According to the article's interpretation of Kansas law, the legislation also would have the effect of making union strikes illegal if their goal was a closed shop or a union shop—a rule that could be grounds for disrupting or enjoining many future strikes.[105] The proposed Kansas legislation would offer injunctive remedies and would outlaw these limitations as misdemeanors punishable by a $500 fine. The article defended the bill's constitutionality and suggested that it would be an effective tool against labor "since it strikes at the maintenance of union membership."[106]

The Kansas Chamber of Commerce and other business groups poured resources into the right-to-work campaign, while they supported the judicial reform amendment. The debate over the judiciary was relatively civil, but the right-to-work campaign was described by one observer as "Armageddon."[107] One letter to the editor offered signs of a spillover of nastiness from the labor campaign to the court campaign. A reader mocked labor's support for partisan elections by noting that they already were used to "the Hitler and Stalin method in selecting officers" anyway—a trifecta comparison of totalitarianism, party bosses, and corrupt union leadership.[108]

The triple switch was crucial in creating public outrage that could be channeled in support of a proposal that voters otherwise might have rejected. Indeed, many state papers linked the triple switch with coverage of the state bar's campaign for the merit plan. Thirty state senators quickly endorsed the merit plan, and despite its two previous failures in the state legislature, just two months after the triple switch the state legislature voted overwhelmingly to submit the merit plan to the voters via a constitutional amendment. Although there was "no overwhelming enthusiasm for the proposal" itself, "widespread disgust over the manner of [the] appointment" fueled the amendment.[109] One major Kansas newspaper noted that populist outcries might have worked to kill the plan "except for the fact that the Triple Switch was still on [voters'] minds."[110]

Amendment 1, the judicial selection amendment, passed with 60 percent of the vote, and Amendment 3, the right-to-work amendment, passed with 57 percent. It is worth noting that in the same year, right-to-work amendments failed in California, Colorado, Ohio, and Washington by wide margins and in Idaho by a narrow margin. In 1958, right-to-work legislation also failed in Kentucky, Louisiana, Maryland, and Rhode Island.[111] One lesson is that a state had to be industrialized enough for business to invest heavily in both merit selection and right-to-work, but not quite industrialized enough so that labor would not yet be big and organized enough to beat those efforts at the polls.

One surprising feature of the campaign for judicial reform in Kansas, Iowa, and Nebraska between 1958 and 1962 is the limited role of direct involvement by national reform organizations, such as the ABA and the AJS. The bar journals in all three states generously credited all of the local and state organizations and leaders who helped push through the constitutional amendments, but they make few references to outside help beyond an occasional regional meeting of the ABA on this topic.[112] This could have been a deliberate erasure so that each state bar could portray the reforms as home-grown, not carpetbagging. But the AJS would have had an interest in telling its subscribers and donors about its direct on-the-ground role in success—and yet it offered no such story. One member of the Nebraska bar credited an AJS Citizens' Conference held in Nebraska in 1960 for turning around the merit plan after it had faced opposition in the legislature, but even so, this AJS conference followed a few years of local efforts.[113]

The spread of merit was more horizontal than vertical. National organizations disseminated models and pamphlets, but the state bar and local leaders mobilized these campaigns. In a clear sign of horizontal federalism, Missouri's plan educated its neighbor Kansas, and Kansas in turn sparked its neighbors Iowa and Nebraska. Nebraska (and not a national organization) coined the term "merit plan" that spread rapidly and horizontally east and west. Only several years after these victories did the AJS start planning Citizens' Conferences in states where state and local leaders had already begun the reform efforts. The conferences certainly played an important role in supporting reform, but apparently not in initiating direct efforts.

From California and Missouri in the 1930s through the wave of merit in the 1950s–1970s, state bar associations organized the campaign initially, but then turned the campaign over to the lay leaders, such as police officials, university presidents, newspaper editors, and the League of Women Voters. The bar leadership stepped behind the scenes, along with the national organizations.[114]

Stumbles in Illinois and Pennsylvania

After the initial success of merit in the late 1950s and early 1960s, the merit campaign stalled through the mid-1960s. Two failed attempts illustrate the challenges facing merit plans in industrialized states with large cities, especially in the mid-1960s. At an earlier stage of development, business had more strength relative to labor and urban machines, but in states that had more advanced industry and urbanization, the combined strength of unions, the Democratic Party, and urban ethnic opposition overcame the business campaign for merit. The first was Illinois's campaign. In the early 1950s, a consensus had formed that Cook County courts were a mess of backlogs, delays, and patronage. The Chicago Bar Association and the Illinois Bar Association proposed a merit plan, with support from the media and civic organizations. In 1953, the Republican-dominated state senate voted for it overwhelmingly. Then the Chicago Democratic machine and organized labor mobilized against it, and the state house defeated it. Downstate leaders feared that the bar association would take the courts away from local politics and would give them to more centralized urban professionals.[115] Opponents trotted out class-based arguments, saying a list of reform supporters "read like a page out of Dun and Bradstreet or the social register of the Gold Coast." Democrats suspected that the plan was a Republican plot to reverse the Democrats' control of the courts.[116] With the defeat of merit, Illinois courts still needed reform desperately. Reformers compromised by dropping the merit commissions and keeping partisan elections, and focused instead on longer terms for judges and unopposed retention elections after the initial partisan election. In 1962, this new nonmerit amendment sailed through both houses, and barely passed 50 percent of all ballots cast. If merit had been on the ballot, unions and Chicago bosses would have killed it.[117]

A similar story played out in 1968 in Pennsylvania. For years, the state bar had been calling for a new constitutional convention, and the legislature called one for February 1968. The bar offered a model constitution, including a merit plan for judicial selection. Opponents argued that merit proposals were the secret agenda of "special interest law firms"[118] and "would have denied voters the right to select judges by the democratic process."[119] The convention went back and forth on the proposal, but deleted it from the final proposed constitution. After this defeat, the League of Women Voters fought for a second chance for the merit plan as a separate referendum scheduled a year later, in the spring of 1969. The opponents of reform reacted with bitter and sexist condemnation. One delegate called the League of Women Voters "the most insidious lobbyists of the convention. . . . They don't have the intellectual honesty to register as lobbyists, and, as typical women, if they don't have their way, they make threats. . . . They are the League of Women Vultures, not the League of Women Voters. They want to pick off the skin and bones of politicians, but they don't have the courage to run for political office themselves."[120] Other delegates loudly applauded these attacks.

The League of Women Voters and other women's groups were just as important in the 1960s–1970s campaigns as they were in California and Missouri in the 1930s. In the 1920s and 1930s, these groups had emerged from suffrage continuing with the same ideological commitments and political strategies: nonpartisanship, anticorruption, antipatronage. They also adopted a campaign for more equal opportunity through merit reform in civil service hiring and promotion.[121] In the 1960s and 1970s, the league was more highly educated with more advanced degrees and more professionals than before, so they would be even more favorable to professional expertise.[122] The league also more strongly supported civil liberties in response to McCarthyism, and increased its efforts in public education about the Bill of Rights in the 1950s.[123] This new agenda tied the organization more to judicial independence. Jim Crow and civil rights issues were thornier for the national organization because the southern states' leagues pushed for neutrality. Instead, the League of Women Voters focused on issues that touched on race more tangentially: anticorruption urban reforms, welfare policy, and merit reforms against hiring discrimination.[124] Merit campaigns were extensions of some of these issues. Later in the 1960s and 1970s, the crime wave might also have prompted these mainly white, middle-class suburban women to embrace the progressive anticrime case for merit. For example, the Tennessee League endorsed merit selection and called for increased coordination of law enforcement officials against crime.[125] It is possible that the urban crime wave increased the league's interest in judicial efficiency.[126]

In Pennsylvania, race and ethnicity shaped the debate over merit. Merit's supporters explicitly campaigned on the themes of "getting judges out of politics" and "stopping the party bosses and corruption."[127] But merit's opponents saw another motivation under the surface. The state NAACP opposed the plan because it would reverse the progress of minorities on the bench.[128] Herbert Sheinberg, a Jewish lawyer in Pittsburgh, wrote in a letter to the editor:

> [The merit plan] is simply a substitution of one form of politics for another. . . . Minority groups beware of this proposed plan! Politicians are acutely sensitive to the racial, religious and ethnic background of the voters. A slate of highly qualified candidates has always been chosen by our parties

with the voter appeal in mind. . . . The so-called merit plan provides a vehicle for the elimination of this delicate balance of racial, religious and ethnic groups that have provided us with responsible leadership through the years. . . . Wake up, voters of Pennsylvania, before one of your cherished rights of citizenship is forever taken from you.[129]

There is merit, so to speak, in this complaint. From the beginning, merit campaigns had coincided with rising black or ethnic minority voting power, and the white legal establishment had led the campaigns. Unlike in earlier campaigns, Pennsylvania's opponents of the merit plan—Democrats, labor, the Philadelphia party machine, and black voters—were strong enough to defeat the plan in a relatively close vote in May 1969.[130]

No merit plans passed between 1962 and 1966. One might say that in the height of the civil rights era, active direct democracy was in, and elite appointment was out. But even more important were geography, demography, and industry. The politics of labor and big cities posed structural challenges to merit proposals in general, and all the more so in the mid-1960s. In Illinois and Pennsylvania just as in the earlier campaigns in California, Missouri, and Kansas, the same coalitions emerged on both sides: urban and suburban middle-class professionals, business, and Republicans in favor; Democratic machines, ethnic groups, and labor opposed. Whereas this was a winning formula in the Great Plains and Rocky Mountain states, it fell short in the Great Lakes and the Northeast. In both Illinois in 1964 and Pennsylvania in 1968, the voters approved yes-or-no retention elections, but rejected the nominating panel (with or without bar influence), so that the parties retained their power over initial appointment. Here we can find some explanations for the rise of merit in the rural-but-urbanizing states, but not in more urban or more rural states.

Crime Can Be Curbed Again

The 1970s have been called "the Golden Age of Paranoia,"[131] and Richard Nixon perfected the politics of populist resentment, a lawyer who attacked the legal profession and expertise. The 1970s were years of backlash against appointed judges and legal elites, and yet merit plans continued to spread. One factor (among others) was that business groups had a renewed issue as part of their campaign: anticrime. The most dramatic crime wave in American history struck between the late 1960s through the 1970s. In a handful of states, a new campaign for law and order, echoing Earl Warren's "Curb Crime" campaign in 1934 and even preceding Nixon's "law and order" campaign in 1968, helped restart the merit plan.

In the 1960s, the Warren Court triggered a backlash against judicial independence in many parts of the country, in part because the public blamed a massive crime wave on the Warren Court's liberalization of criminal procedure rights. In the United States between 1960 and 1970, violent crime almost tripled, murders doubled, rapes more than doubled, and robberies almost quadrupled.[132] The wave continued into the 1970s, as violent crime doubled again between 1970 and 1980. Crime was not limited to the big cities. It struck every region in the country, and crime rates doubled or tripled over the 1960s even in the relatively rural states that adopted the merit plan between 1967 and 1977.[133] The crime wave tracks the merit wave from 1967 to 1980 almost exactly.

Adding to middle America's fear of chaos were a series of riots in American cities, from the Watts Riots in the summer of 1965 to a series of riots in the summers of 1966 and 1967, and then in April 1968 after Martin Luther King's assassination. Increasingly vocal antiwar demonstrations triggered a conservative backlash in the late 1960s. Even before 1968, many parts of middle America had already turned against the Democrats. After the Democrats' 1964 landslide, Republicans recovered some congressional seats in 1966 and reclaimed several rural state legislatures. In 1966, Colorado and Utah flipped from Democratic control to Republican control, and each also adopted the merit plan. Utah's flip was particularly dramatic: In 1964, Democrats controlled both houses of the legislature, but in 1966, Republicans won an 82 percent majority of the state senate and an 86 percent majority of the state house. Those Republicans then turned to the merit plan. Similarly, in Indiana, the state senate flipped from a Democratic majority of 58 percent to a Republican majority of 70 percent in 1968, and then adopted a merit plan. The party risk-aversion theory may apply to these states: Republicans opted for more judicial independence because they had been out of power for so long that they had learned the importance of nonpartisan courts, and they knew the tables could turn again. However, more states that adopted merit did not have flips in partisan control, and many states that did have party flips did not turn to merit, suggesting that partisan risk aversion was not a driving force overall.[134]

The crime wave was not the primary factor driving merit campaigns, but it was an additional influence that helped elites win popular support for an elite-oriented reform. In 1967, the President's Crime Commission addressed the spike in crime, and explicitly recommended that states adopt merit selection plans as one of several solutions.[135] Over the next few years, experts in criminal justice made similar links between the crime wave and the need for merit selection to produce judges more qualified to handle the crisis.[136]

In Colorado, the main slogan for the passage of merit in 1966 was the usual "take the judges out of politics." Opponents raised the usual fear that "the effect [would] be a change from popular politics to Bar Assn. politics," but voters seemed not to care.[137] Liberals had been hoping to build on the 1964 landslide, and they proposed an amendment to abolish the death penalty. But instead of liberals marching forward, they collided with a conservative resurgence. The death penalty opponents lost badly. During the merit campaign, Colorado newspapers were filled with references to the national and state crime waves.[138] Conservatives attacked the Warren Court with such claims as "our streets have been taken over by hoodlums and murderers as the Supreme Court ties the hands of our law enforcement officers."[139] However, they did not attack the Warren Court for being appointed or politically unaccountable. Supporters of the death penalty were the loudest voices of the 1966 election campaign, and their arguments spilled over into the other fall campaigns. In his successful reelection campaign, Governor John Love announced plans to form a state bureau of crime investigation, using professionalization to address the crime wave.[140] Judges running for office campaigned in terms of progressivism and professionalism to manage their dockets efficiently and process criminal cases more quickly.[141] Utah's merit campaign followed Colorado's success, coinciding with a focus on the crime wave and a focus on creating a more efficient, professional judiciary.[142]

Southern states also had their own crime waves. Between 1969 and 1971, Tennessee witnessed the largest two-year increase in the rates of violent crime, such as murder, aggravated assault, burglary, and especially forcible rape, in at least a decade.[143] Florida experienced a similarly sharp increase in violent crime rates, which more than tripled in the fifteen years leading up to that state's merit selection amendment.[144] Southern newspapers pitched judicial reform and merit selection as one way to address the crime wave. A 1972 *Tampa Tribune* editorial argued that the state's antiquated courts were so inefficient that they had to free "men accused of violent crime," and therefore a modernized and less political court was necessary.[145] In Kentucky, supporters of merit emphasized the rising crime problem and argued that merit panels and nonpartisan elections would produce a bench that could tackle crime.[146] Again, reformers pitched judicial independence and professionalization, rather than political accountability, as an answer to the crime wave.

The crime wave also played a role in New York's partial adoption of merit at the height of the crisis. The New York bar had been calling for merit reforms for decades, laying the groundwork for change, but it could not win on its own without significant help. New York is a good example of merit's complicated political balance of business and urban politics: business and urbanization had generated strong support for merit, but they also produced strong unions, ethnic diversity, and strong urban party machines opposed to merit.

The turning points were the judicial elections of the early 1970s. In 1967, New York had opened up its election laws to permit a candidate access to the primary ballot to challenge the party favorites. This change led to upsets and upheaval against the party establishment, especially in judicial elections. In 1972, Nannette Dembitz challenged the Democrats' selection of Henry Martuscello in the primary and won an upset by a large margin, becoming the first female nominee for New York's high court. Martuscello ran in the general election for the Liberal Party and divided the vote, giving the Republican Hugh Jones the victory. In 1974, Harold Stevens, the first African American on the Court of Appeals after being appointed to fill a vacancy, was running for a full term. Jacob Fuchsberg, a rich personal-injury trial lawyer with no judicial experience, challenged Stevens in the primary and spent huge amounts of his own money. The Democratic Party and the Association of the Bar of New York fought against Fuchsberg. The bar association had rated him as "not qualified" when he ran in 1973, and in his race against Stevens, it took the unusual step of campaigning against him, drawing attention to his unscrupulous trial tactics.[147] Fuchsberg pulled off the upset in a divisive primary and the general election, in which Stevens switched to the Republican ticket. This contest was a warning that the legal establishment and party leaders were losing control over judicial elections. Around the same time, the lower courts were embroiled in a corruption scandal about the manipulation of judicial retirements to protect patronage, and the scandals continued for a few years.[148]

Hugh Carey was elected governor in the same election as Fuchsberg's win, and when Carey took office, he immediately called for the end to judicial elections and for a turn to merit selection. He also called for an end to primary challenges in judicial races, a proposal labeled "the Fuchsberg Bill."[149] Newspapers supported Carey's proposals by continuing to attack Fuchsberg.[150] In between his election and the adoption of merit, Fuchsberg was investigated for financial improprieties on the bench.[151] Another key event was the near-bankruptcy of New York City in 1975. Governor Carey and Mayor Abraham Beame navigated the city through the crisis, but even though the city survived, the crisis underscored the problem of partisan incompetence and the need for nonpartisan expertise. Corporations, major law firms, and the bar association organized the campaign and enlisted other civic organizations to mobilize support.[152] Otherwise, most New York City voters supported the call for merit.[153] The head of the New York

League of Women Voters, who lobbied for merit reform, said that the bar was able to fundraise so successfully because the bar's establishment feared "nontraditional" judges like Fuchsberg who could take advantage of the electoral reforms and ruin the reputation of the Court of Appeals.[154] Like earlier leaders of the League of Women Voters, she also may have believed that merit selection would be more open to female candidates than party politics, but women's groups were split on this question.

One group opposed to merit reforms was the judges on the lower courts. Over one hundred judges established the Ad Hoc Committee for the Preservation of an Elected Judiciary, and they attacked merit reforms as "elitist and undemocratic."[155] Of course, they also knew that partisan elections had put them on the bench and merit committees might threaten their job security or advancement. The other vocal opponents of merit were the trial lawyers and black organizations. The NAACP warned that merit committees would reduce the number of minority judges. Merit advocates pointed out that popular elections had just hurt a black incumbent, but minority organizations witnessed how Stevens and other minorities were rising up in the party system, and Stevens had party support as he came close to winning. They were skeptical that the white establishment bar association would be an improvement. They saw a future of judicial elections as more favorable than bar appointment.

"Merit" also carried a new political connotation in the context of intensifying debates over race and affirmative action. Earlier, the label "merit" had been used to distinguish good government from party patronage and to contrast American equality of opportunity with socialism. By the 1970s, it was also used to critique racial affirmative action. In New York, a campaign for merit signaled a combined critique from Republicans and white moderate Democrats of the Democratic Party's urban political machine and its minorities gaining clout. Upstate voters who, like other rural voters in other states, had been skeptical of giving up their right to vote on judges were more likely to be persuaded by this message. Race helps explain why some New York labor unions broke with union tradition and endorsed the merit amendment.[156]

Race also intensified another factor in favor of merit selection: the urban crime wave peaking in the mid-1970s. Anticrime again was not the most important force for merit reforms, but it provided another way to frame the issue for broader support. New York's leading politicians championed merit selection as an anticrime strategy in the brutal summer of 1977—the summer of Son of Sam and "The Bronx Is Burning." New York City voters gave the plan a large enough majority to overcome its upstate shortfall.[157] Politicians offered merit selection as an explicit solution to the crime problem. In the debates before the 1977 election that decided the judicial reform amendment, mayoral candidates, including Mario Cuomo, answered a debate question about the crime wave by suggesting merit selection as one solution.[158] In 1978, the *New York Times* reported that Mayor Ed Koch "presented his new judicial-selection procedure as a fulfillment of a campaign promise to make 'open and prompt selection of judges based on merit alone.' Such a process 'is essential to turn our criminal-justice system around.'"[159] Interestingly, Koch framed his merit/professional nomination process as more transparent and open to the public than the partisan nomination process of smoke-filled rooms. Governor Hugh Carey echoed the same message in the *New York Times,* promising that merit selection would decrease crime and would make New Yorkers' homes and streets safer.[160]

As in the 1930s, urban leaders and urban voters drove the wave of adoptions from 1967 to 1977. Over 60 percent of the legislative sponsors of merit plans in the 1960s and 1970s were from urban areas, which is even more disproportionate than it appears considering that the urban population of most of these states was relatively small.[161] Crime was a part of the reason that these states swung decisively in favor of merit.

In the various stages of judicial development, economic interests drove the design and redesign of judicial selection. The rise and spread of merit is a key example. The relationship between business and labor shaped the strange regional path of merit. In rural-but-industrializing states, business interests had grown strong enough to organize merit campaigns, but industry and urbanization had not yet produced unions or city machines that could block businesses' efforts. These powerful conditions set the stage for merit. But merit reforms spread only incrementally in the 1950s and early 1960s. Merit's success depended upon another factor: opportunistic leadership. The American bar sold itself as good soldiers in the Cold War, contrasting Communism with democracy, the rule of law, and judicial independence—the values that described the mix of nomination, appointment, and election in the merit plan. And the Nebraska bar helped develop an effective marketing strategy with the new label "merit." Big Jim Folsom may have been a dynamic leader, but the Alabama bar and businesses were even more opportunistic in taking advantage of racial anxieties in establishing probusiness merit reforms. Alaska's enterprising delegates used merit as a marketing strategy. In Kansas, a scandal over judicial appointments was an opportunity on which business and the bar capitalized by steering the reaction toward merit appointment, instead of more obvious antiappointment responses. Geography and economics set the stage for reform, but it was a handful of creative political actors in particular states who made the difference.

Business had its own self-interest in merit reforms, but it was able to use the rhetoric of judicial independence to legitimate its efforts and build public support. On the one hand, the rise of merit selection is the story of successful propaganda. Business had harnessed anticrime fears in the 1930s and the 1960s–1970s as a simple and popular campaign message and an engine of reform. After that, business interests reversed their anticrime strategy: not to reform judicial elections, but to win them.

But the ideas of judicial independence and the rule of law were not merely campaign rhetoric. For merit to spread, these ideas had to be sincere, because many key actors in merit's spread chose judicial independence over their more direct political interests. In Missouri, Oklahoma, Maryland, Tennessee, Florida, Kentucky, Nevada, and Hawaii, Democrats generally had controlled or even dominated state elections, but they were willing to surrender their upper hand in judicial elections to nonpartisan bar leaders—even if they had reason to suspect that the bar was hostile to parts of the Democratic base. In Kansas, Iowa, Nebraska, Idaho, Vermont, Wyoming, and South Dakota, Republicans similarly had a lock on the electoral process, but they also turned over their power to bar leadership, even if many of these rural heartland Republicans had reason to believe that professional elites had different values. Many party leaders helped usher in merit selection against their immediate party interests, perhaps because business and economic interests were even stronger. But even more strikingly, in almost all of the states adopting merit plans, the voters themselves went to the polls to give up their right to vote for judges. One might explain all of these choices by suggesting that their partisan interests were trumped by other kinds of interests, such as economic interests, racial anxieties, fear of crime, or other political interests. Nevertheless, the campaigns for merit so consistently emphasized fairness, equal justice, and judicial independence, that it would be hard to dismiss the entire movement as insincere. The consistent theme in these campaigns was "getting the courts out of politics" and fostering a more professional and independent judiciary. Even if some merit entrepreneurs may have designed these campaigns cynically, the party regulars and the general public who supported those campaigns were persuaded to abandon a long tradition of direct partisan democracy in favor of a new experiment with obvious downsides and political risks. One could say that business interests hoodwinked them. Or one could say that enough of the party leadership and the general public cared sincerely about the ideas of fairness, justice, and judicial independence that, when combined with other political and economic factors, they were willing to move from direct democracy to professional expertise and "merit." In some ways, the turn to merit was an unusual move, but it was consistent with an ongoing and evolving commitment to judicial independence over the course of American history.

CHAPTER ELEVEN

Judicial Plutocracy after 1980

N THE MID-TWENTIETH CENTURY, judicial elections were "sleepy" and "low key" with relatively inexpensive campaigns.[1] This period followed labor's increasing success in winning these elections in the early twentieth century, and it coincided with business interests shifting their efforts from winning judicial elections to reforming judicial elections. Judicial races were often unopposed.

Something changed around 1980. After spending their capital (political and financial) on campaigns for merit reforms, businesses returned to trying to win judicial elections outright, and they did so by capitalizing on socially conservative issues and by pouring money into key races. Trial lawyers and other interests that had already been invested in judicial elections responded by spending more and doubling down. Judicial elections changed from local to national, drawing national political operatives on more national hot-button issues and drawing national attention. The increasing power of political advertising made it easier for local and national groups to challenge incumbents, and the expense of this advertising required incumbents and challengers to raise more money. This transformation is illustrated by the end of Rose Bird's judicial career in California and by the beginning of Karl Rove's political career in Texas and Alabama judicial races.

Rose Bird and California

California had been the first state to return to appointments and to adopt a merit-style judicial commission and retention elections. Earl Warren and his "Curb Crime" team had proposed that a nominating commission (the chief justice of the supreme court, an intermediate appellate judge, and the attorney general) would provide the governor with a list of candidates. Recall that the businessmen's Commonwealth Club persuaded Warren to switch the order, so that the governor would send a candidate for confirmation by this same panel, called the Commission on Qualifications. The ball would be in the governor's court, so to speak.

After the switch back to appointment in 1934, both Republican and Democratic governors generally appointed left-leaning justices, so that the California Supreme Court was legendarily liberal from the 1940s through the early 1980s. Republican governors Earl Warren and Goodwin Knight (who had been a judge known for performing marriages and issuing divorces for the Hollywood stars) were moderates, and as it turned out, they appointed a total of only two justices in sixteen years (1942–1959). Liberal Democrats Culbert Olson, Pat Brown, and Jerry Brown appointed nineteen justices in their twenty years as governor, including Roger Traynor, who served for thirty years as one of the most influential state judges in the twentieth century. This partisan imbalance on the number of appointments illustrates another problem with appointments generally: the timing of retirements and replacements can be manipulated.

Ronald Reagan tried to push the court to the right, especially on the death penalty, but he had only three appointment opportunities in his eight years, and of those three, one wound up writing two controversial decisions striking down the state death penalty as unconstitutional in the 1970s.[2] Reagan's second appointee was a moderate,[3] and his one conservative illustrates the significance of the governor going first in California nominations. William Clark, Reagan's right-hand man, had not finished either college or law school. In fact, he dropped out of Loyola Law School because of poor grades. Reagan was still able to appoint Clark to lower courts and then to the state supreme court. At the Commission of Qualifications stage, the Reagan-appointed chief justice, Donald Wright, voted against Clark for being unqualified, but the attorney general and the intermediate appellate judge gave Clark a two-to-one confirmation.[4] It is highly unlikely a nominating commission would have sent Clark's name to Reagan if the commission had the lead in the process.

The California Supreme Court was famously leading the fight against the death penalty, but it was even more of a national leader in expanding tort liability in favor of victims and consumers against corporate defendants. In the 1940s, the California Supreme Court wrote several landmark pro-plaintiff decisions that every first-year law student reads today: inferring liability without direct evidence in products liability and medical malpractice;[5] and inferring causation, even against a defendant that cannot have caused the injury.[6] The California judges then waged a tort revolution in the 1960s and 1970s in products liability, emotional distress, property owner liability, psychiatrists' liability for their patients' violence, and other major doctrinal changes favoring consumers over business and insurance.[7] Those precedents spread nationally and transformed American tort law.

California lawyers had also led a revolution in personal injury law and damage awards. In the 1950s, tort awards tripled in size, and they continued growing rapidly through the rest of the century. As tort awards were increasing, tort plaintiffs' lawyers gained economic clout. At the same time, they perceived a threat from another legal development: the rise of administrative alternatives to the tort system from which they were prospering. Labor lawyers earlier had founded the National Association of Claimants' Compensation Attorneys (NACCA), which actually focused on one such administrative alternative to tort law: the workers' compensation system. But the trial lawyers took over the organization and changed its focus to defend the torts system from reform. Melvin Belli, California's "King of Torts," and other California lawyers led this fight. In 1956, NACCA voted to include all personal injury lawyers. In the 1960s, NACCA's leadership began a campaign they called "The Big Push," a national effort to increase membership and broaden their coalition of plaintiffs' lawyers. Its membership grew from 500 in 1956, to about 5,000 in 1961, to about 22,000 in 1967, when the group renamed itself the American Trial Lawyers Association (ATLA). The California chapter of ATLA was a national leader, spreading tactical trial advice about how to increase jury awards, and sharing strategic political advice on how to fight tort reform, how to elect sympathetic judges, and how to oppose merit reform.[8]

Even before "the Big Push," the defense bar recognized NACCA as a major threat. The corporate defense bar took notice and blamed "Mr. Belli and his cohorts."[9] One reason business interests continued to favor merit selection is that they recognized how NACCA/ATLA helped pro-plaintiff judges win elections. Trial lawyers were one of the most important sources of money in judicial elections for most of the twentieth century.[10] Personal injury lawyers spent their larger and larger war chests on opposing merit judicial reform. Corporations understood that the state bar associations' traditional leadership was skeptical of the personal injury lawyers and was more favorable to business. For the same reasons why business interests had fought for merit for several decades, personal injury lawyers vehemently opposed merit selection. They believed that the merit plan was a form of bureaucratic tort reform that would be controlled by corporations and the elite bar, and not the trial lawyers.[11]

At the height of California's two-front fight for criminal defendants and against tort defendants, liberal Governor Jerry Brown appointed Rose Bird, his state secretary of agriculture with no judicial experience, to be chief justice in 1977. Bird was born in Arizona, but after her father left the family, her mother moved to New York. She grew up in poverty, but went on to graduate from Long Island University and then received her law degree magna cum laude from Berkeley. She became the first female clerk for the Supreme Court of Nevada, the first female lawyer for the Santa Clara public defender's office, and the first female cabinet member in California as Jerry Brown's secretary of agriculture.[12] She supported Cesar Chavez, the farm labor activist, and she fought for the passage of the Agriculture Labor Relations Act, which guaranteed farm workers the right to unionize. Her prolabor efforts sealed her antagonistic relationship with California businesses.[13] Her nomination for chief justice was opposed by most Republicans, and it appeared that the Commission on Qualifications might reject her when the acting chief justice announced his opposition because she had never been a judge before. Then the moderate Republican attorney general voted for her, giving her a two-to-one majority.[14]

Bird faced her retention election just one year later, and Republicans organized the strongest campaign against a California judge in the era of retention elections. Agribusiness was waiting for this election, and it had more fodder when Bird voted along with the majority (and wrote separately to concur) that when the legislature had increased sentences for crimes involving "great bodily injury," the legislature had not intended to include all rapes automatically for those enhanced sentences.[15] She squeaked by with 52 percent of the vote, while no other supreme court justice before then had received less than 62 percent of the vote. In a seemingly cynical move, the supreme court had delayed releasing its decision striking down the "use a gun, go to prison" law until after the 1978 election. A subsequent investigation into this delay was inconclusive on Justice Bird's ethical conduct.[16] Over the next few years, there were several unsuccessful attempts to recall her.[17] More tort controversies only turned up the heat. In the 1980s, Bird voted with the majority to establish market share liability, a leap in extending liability when there is no proof of causation.[18]

In 1982, four judges were up for retention elections, and three were liberal "Jerry's judges": Cruz Reynoso, Allen Broussard, and Otto Kaus. In the same election, Republican Attorney General George Deukmejian was running against Democratic Los Angeles Mayor Tom Bradley to succeed Jerry Brown, and Deukmejian also ran against Jerry's judges and their obstruction of the death penalty. Even though a "No" campaign against these judges was underfunded and disorganized, the elections were about as close as Rose Bird's: Kaus received 57 percent, Broussard 56 percent, and Reynoso 52 percent (the same as Bird in 1978).[19] The conservative justice, Frank Richardson, sailed through with 76 percent, more consistent with the large majorities before 1978.

In 1986, three of Jerry's judges were back on the ballot: Cruz Reynoso again, Joseph Grodin, and Rose Bird. Most Republican candidates that year presented a united message against California's liberal judges, and Deukmejian led the campaign vocally. Three organizations assisted in the "Vote No" campaign. The first was "Crime Victims for Court Reform," managed by political consultant Bill Roberts, who ran Governor Deukmejian's 1982 campaign.[20] Its advertising put the spotlight on families of crime victims, but it was funded by agricultural interests, like the Farm Bureau Federation and the Western Growers Association.[21] Oil and gas companies and insurance and real estate interests also funded the organization.[22] A second group was "Californians to Defeat Rose Bird," sponsored by Republican antitax activists Paul Gann and Howard Jarvis, who were known for co-writing Proposition 13, which dramatically reduced California's property taxes in 1978. Bird had issued a dissent arguing that their Proposition 13 violated the state's equal protection clause.[23] A third group was the "Bird Watchers Society," which was sponsored by Congressman William Dannemeyer and other Republican politicians.

The campaigns against the chief justice focused primarily on her rulings in capital punishment cases. The death penalty was a powerful political issue, as demonstrated by 71 percent of the electorate voting for the state's Death Penalty Initiative in 1978. As the 1986 campaign highlighted the most heinous crimes, polls showed that support for the death penalty had risen to 83 percent.[24] Bird's critics pointed out she had voted to overturn death sentences in all fifty-six death penalty cases that came before her. In fifty-three of those fifty-six cases, she commanded a majority.[25] Families of victims told their stories in long radio ads, TV ads, and widely circulated pamphlets.[26] Newspaper ads also featured these grieving family members, and asked, "Are you tired of living in fear of crime?"[27] The Crime Victims for Court Reform (CVCR) released a district attorney's "box score" saying that she ruled for the prosecution in only 12 percent of cases.[28] Critics claimed she made prosecutors' jobs harder by changing the rules regarding exclusion of evidence, suppressing admissions or confessions by criminals, and creating new rights for criminals and defendants.[29] Former Governor

Pat Brown said, "Those polls are so overwhelmingly in favor of the death penalty that any politician, no matter how qualified he may be otherwise, if he opposes the death penalty, he's done for. People want vengeance; they want blood."[30]

While crime and the death penalty were the main message, conservatives also emphasized that Bird was antibusiness. Deukmejian directly appealed to businesses to donate to the cause multiple times.[31] Governor Deukmejian was quoted as saying that Bird "has certainly made it more onerous and more burdensome and more expensive for business to operate in California."[32] When questioned on this assertion, his press secretary, Larry Thomas, clarified it in a phone interview and said, "It isn't so much a single decision, but it is a collective impression of the business people who have talked to the governor that the court has a history of activist decisions that make the business climate in the state far from stable."[33]

In the end, the "No" groups spent between $7.5 million and $10 million against Bird. Other groups also organized against her, like the California Organization of Police and Sheriffs and pro-life groups. As Bird became a political liability for the Democratic Party, Republican candidates spent millions linking their Democratic opponents to Bird. Four of the biggest Republican spenders spent $2 million on commercials linking their opponents to Bird.

Bird raised millions for her own campaign, and she had some outside support, particularly from the National Organization for Women (NOW).[34] However, she refused to ally herself too closely with Democratic leadership for fears of impropriety and confirming the Republicans' allegation of her partisanship. She disdained having to campaign for her job. Her TV commercials were dry appeals for judicial independence, in stark contrast to the emotional and effective advertisements against her featuring crime victims pleading for justice.[35] She also blocked the formation of an independent committee that would have defended all six justices, insisting on running her own inept campaign.[36] Furthermore, Democrats avoided mentioning her, or even turned on her to avoid getting dragged down by her.[37]

On election day, Bird received only 34 percent for retention, Reynoso received 40 percent, and Grodin received 43 percent. These abysmal percentages were unheard of in retention elections.[38] The anti-Bird campaign then inspired similar campaigns in other states to oust justices, specifically challenging liberal judges in Ohio, New Jersey, and North Carolina. According to Keith Clark, a businessman heading the campaign against North Carolina's chief justice, "The Bird race helped inspire this campaign."[39]

Texas, Alabama, and Karl Rove

Before Rose Bird's defeat, Texas judicial elections were a prime example of the sleepy era. In 1976, Don Yarbrough was an obscure young lawyer who said that he ran for the state supreme court because God told him to. He won the Democratic nomination and then the general election because voters thought he was either Don Yarborough, former candidate for governor, or Ralph Yarbrough, the two-term U.S. senator. After a few months on the bench, Yarbrough resigned when he was charged and convicted for perjury. He jumped bond, but eventually was captured in the Virgin Islands and brought back to prison. In 1978, an unknown plaintiff lawyer, Robert Campbell, won his race for the state supreme court because University of Texas running back Earl Campbell had just won the Heisman Trophy, and the name Campbell had a good ring to Texas football fans.[40] These problems of name recognition continued even in the more competitive era. In the 1990s, someone named Gene Kelly challenged a much more qualified and endorsed candidate in a Texas judicial primary without campaigning—and he won. In the general election, his opponent (future U.S. Senator John Cornyn) barely prevailed after spending almost all of his funds on advertisements declaring, "He's Not That Gene Kelly."[41]

Competitive elections were rare, in part because Texas had as much an appointive system as an elective one in actual practice. As in many parts of the country, judges would resign instead of waiting for the end of their terms, so that the governor would be able to appoint a new judge for the vacancy. Many of these judges opposed judicial elections in general, or in this particular circumstance, they trusted the governor more than the electorate, or they wanted to spare their replacements from the extra stress and work of running for office. They still had to run in the next general election, but as the incumbent, it was usually easier to raise funds, campaign, and have higher name recognition.

From 1940 to 1962, about two thirds of Texas's trial and appellate judges had been initially appointed by the governor, and this rate was more or less consistent through the 1970s. However, by the 1990s, that number had shrunk to two fifths of appellate court judges and half of district court judges.[42] Judicial elections were increasingly contested and competitive. In Texas and around the country, fewer judges were colluding to undermine judicial elections. One likely explanation was an increase in two-party competition. In the mid-twentieth century, many states were dominated by one party or the other. In presidential elections, Republicans had the advantage of Cold War politics, but in state and local elections, Democrats retained the New Deal coalition's advantage on domestic and economic issues. In particular, Democrats dominated the South, so the only potential competition was in the Democratic primary. An aging Democratic judge might prefer to give his Democratic governor the power to appoint his replacement, rather than trigger a primary battle. Once there was more party parity and divided government, a retiring judge from one party did not want the governor from the opposing party to flip his seat, and preferred to give the voters a chance to keep his seat in the same party.

One turning point in Texas was in 1978. A Republican, William Clements, was elected governor for the first time since Reconstruction, a signal of a more competitive two-party system in the state and in the South. After 1978, a Democratic judge approaching the end of his term would avoid giving Clements the advantage of choosing the new judge, and would opt for a shot at a Democrat winning the seat. At the same time, Republicans were emboldened to challenge more state and local offices, including judicial races, and they realized that they could overcome the Democrats' built-in advantages of incumbency and party identification by spending a lot more money on these races.

The tort wars transformed Texas judicial elections, just as they had in California. In the 1970s, Texas plaintiff lawyers had been winning more money in tort cases, and with that war chest, the Texas Trial Lawyers Association and individual trial lawyers invested that money right back into the judicial system to support pro-plaintiff Democratic judges. As a result, Texas courts ruled in favor of tort plaintiffs against corporate defendants more and more.[43] In 1980, Texas had the first judicial race in the country to exceed $1 million in spending, driven by tort law.[44] Between 1980 and 1986, campaign spending in contested appellate races increased 250 percent. In these years, donations from trial lawyers, ranchers, and other interests over $100,000 became common.[45]

It was this climate that produced the infamous *Pennzoil v. Texaco* case. In 1984, Texaco interfered with Pennzoil's deal to buy Getty Oil. Pennzoil sued Texaco, and its brash Houston lawyer Joe Jamail immediately donated $10,000 to Houston trial judge Anthony Farris, a friend of Jamail's, as soon as the assignment was announced. Texaco filed a motion for Judge Farris to recuse himself, but the judge rejected the motion. Scholars noted that even though Pennzoil had a relatively weak case, it went on a sudden winning streak with Judge Farris, culminating in a $10.5 billion jury verdict ($7.5 billion in compensatory damages, $3 billion in punitive damages).[46] As Texaco appealed the jury verdict, Jamail donated $355,000 to the Texas Supreme Court's justices, and Texaco's lawyers made smaller donations. Lo and behold, the Texas Supreme

Court declined to review the verdict, and after losing its appeal to the U.S. Supreme Court, Texaco declared a strategic bankruptcy.[47] Jamail reportedly earned between $330 million and $420 million for his contingency fee, a nice net profit over his hundreds of thousands in donations to judges.[48] The case received national media coverage, including *60 Minutes* airing a stinging piece titled "Justice for Sale?"

In the wake of the *Pennzoil* case, Chief Justice John Hill teamed up with the speaker of the Texas house and the lieutenant governor to propose a merit plan. They called it "the Texas Plan," both because they wanted a more populist name than "merit" and because fiercely proud and independent Texans would not be enthusiastic about following "Missouri's" plan.[49] Hill's plan was attacked from every direction. Trial lawyers liked the old system and did not want any changes. On the opposing side, Republicans and business interests were watching the polls, and even if they had lost elections in the past, they saw a growing opportunity to win direct elections themselves. If Jamail and Pennzoil could spend and win for one oil company against another, corporations could spend and win for their broader interests and fight back in the tort wars. Labor, women, and minorities had begun to see gains in partisan elections, and they worried that the elite male bar associations would reverse the diversity. These groups and the trial lawyers put enough pressure on the Democrats to oppose the merit plan, too, and the plan died.[50] Frustrated, Chief Justice Hill resigned in 1987 to attract attention to the crisis and to promote his merit proposal, but to no avail.

By 1988, a different reform campaign mobilized: "Clean Slate '88." In 1987, the Texas Supreme Court had nine Democrats and no Republicans, with a solid pro-plaintiff majority. As luck would have it, six seats on the Texas Supreme Court would be on the ballot. Clements, the Republican governor, had recently appointed Tom Phillips to be the youngest chief justice (thirty-nine years old) in Texas history. As an interim appointment, Phillips was on the ballot that November, and he hired another young gun to run his race: the thirty-eight-year-old Karl Rove.

Rove moved to Texas to work for a Republican state legislator, and at that time, Democrats held almost every statewide office and a nine-to-one advantage in the legislature. In 1978, Rove worked on George W. Bush's unsuccessful congressional campaign and on Clements's successful campaign for governor. Then Rove took the lead for Phillips in coordinating the Republican challengers in a unified "Clean Slate '88" campaign. Their well-financed campaign focused on tort reform and populist themes. In a memo to Phillips, Rove wrote, "No Republican has won by running as an establishment candidate. Our party's candidates have won by appearing as champions of the little man and not the big boys."[51] Rove targeted trial lawyers for jeopardizing jobs for average Texans, and he promised corporate donors that a Republican court would limit compensation for injured employees and consumers and would put caps on damage awards.[52]

Of the six seats on the ballot, "Clean Slate" Republicans won three, and conservative pro-defendant Democrats won two more seats by echoing Rove's attacks on trial lawyers and tort reform themes. The 1988 campaign was the end of the pro-plaintiff Texas Supreme Court, and it was the beginning of the Republican takeover of the court. Ten years later, the court had nine Republicans and no Democrats, and Republicans held unanimous control thereafter. The decline of southern Democrats and the rise of southern Republicans was common from the 1980s and 1990s, but the sudden flip of the Texas judiciary in 1988 was particularly remarkable, and Rove pulled off a similar flip in Alabama in the 1990s.

In 1994, the Business Council of Alabama hired Rove to run a slate of judicial candidates with the same message as Clean Slate '88. Alabama previously had been an example of the "low-key" era of judicial elections, and no Republican had served on the Alabama Supreme Court in more than one hundred years. But that was before Rove's arrival. The tort wars were the substance of the campaigns. Alabama courts had an image of being a forum for Alabama residents to sue national or international corporations and win millions from Alabama jurors. The most infamous example was *BMW v. Gore*. Dr. Ira Gore had bought a new BMW for $40,000 and discovered that its paint had been damaged in transit and it had been repainted at a cost of $601. BMW's policy was if its repair to a new car had cost more than 3 percent of the car's suggested retail price, it would sell the car on the market as "used." In this case, BMW's repair was about 1.5 percent, so it did not disclose the damage or the repair. Dr. Gore claimed that the actual damage was $4,000 and that BMW had sold about 1,000 cars with similar damage. Gore asked for $4 million in damages, and an Alabama jury agreed to every penny. In August 1994, as the judicial campaigns were in full swing, the Alabama Supreme Court reduced the award, but still gave Gore $2 million—an amount that still astonished the public for a single car paint job.[53] After the election, the U.S. Supreme Court ruled in a landmark decision that even the reduced punitive damage award was "grossly excessive," and sent the case back for either a new trial or a lower award.[54]

Throughout the summer of 1994, Rove's Republican candidates reminded voters that the Democratic incumbents had been soliciting donations from the trial lawyers that had cases before them. The American Trial Lawyers Association and personal injury lawyers indeed had been heavily invested in Alabama judicial elections, which contributed to Alabama's massive damage awards. The Republican challengers repeated Rove's catch-phrases "jackpot justice" by "wealthy personal-injury lawyers" as they toured the state.[55] Both the campaign and the underlying solicitation problem drew national media coverage.

A number of journalists and academics report some disturbing allegations about Rove's behind-the-scenes tactics in Alabama. Mark Kennedy, the incumbent Democrat, had served as a juvenile and family court judge, and had helped create the Children's Trust Fund of Alabama to help abused children. This reputation was Kennedy's strongest asset, and his campaign ads showed him talking about his children's advocacy while holding children's hands. A former Rove campaign staffer working for Republican Harold See, a University of Alabama law professor, told a reporter that they had spread a rumor that Kennedy was a pedophile. "It was our standard practice to use the University of Alabama to disseminate whisper-campaign information. That was a major device we used for the transformation of this stuff. The students at the law school are from all over the state, and that's one of the ways that Karl got the information out—he knew the law students would take it back to their home towns and it would get out." The rumor spread, but Kennedy was able to squeak out a win over See by 1 percent. Still, Kennedy was so shaken by the 1994 campaign and what he called its "collateral damage" that he did not run again. His campaign manager explained, "What Rove does is try to make something so bad for a family that the candidate will not subject the family to the hardship. Mark [Kennedy] is not your typical Alabama macho, beer-drinkin', tobacco chewin', pickup-drivin' kind of guy. He is a small, well-groomed, well-educated family man, and what they tried to do was make him look like a homosexual pedophile. That was really, really hard to take."[56]

Two years later, Rove worked for See again in a challenge to Democratic incumbent Kenneth Ingram. According to a campaign staffer, Rove thought See had stalled, so he ordered flyers with nasty attacks not against Ingram, but against See. "I was told, 'Do not hand it to anybody, do not tell anybody who you're with, and if you can, borrow a car that doesn't have your tags.' So I borrowed a buddy's car [and drove] down the middle of the street. . . . I had hefty bags stuffed full of those rolled-up pamphlets, and I'd cruise the designated neighborhoods, throwing these things out with both hands and literally driving with my knees."[57] The trick was to mislead the public into thinking Ingram had resorted to mudslinging first, making the incumbent appear scared of See, and allowing Rove to go negative against Ingram without the blame of going negative first. See defeated Ingram, and afterward Ingram sighed, "They just beat you down to your knees."[58] Now that attack ads and sound bites are so common in judicial races, judges around the country report that their colleagues worry about getting assigned controversial cases in election years. Some find ways to shift their docket from criminal cases to civil cases in their election years.

In 1994, the Alabama Supreme Court was entirely composed of Democrats. By 2004, it was entirely Republican. Alabama is a prime example of the explosion of campaign spending at the start of the twenty-first century. Alabama's 2004 supreme court campaigns cost a total of $7.5 million, and its 2006 campaigns increased to over $13 million. Around the country, judicial elections had cost a total of $60 million in direct campaign donations in the 1990s. In the 2000s, that cost rose more than threefold to $200 million. In 2004, the seventeen most expensive judicial elections cost a total of $47 million in direct contributions. In 2006, the eleven most expensive elections cost a total of $39 million. Among many other factors, the *Bush v. Gore* litigation in 2000 may have led to more partisan spending on state courts. The Florida Supreme Court's Democratic majority had ruled in favor of Gore twice, reminding both parties that federal elections can be decided in state court.

The bare-knuckled campaign tactics have been spreading along with the campaign cash. Wisconsin has become a particularly vicious battleground on both sides. Judge Louis Butler had authored major decisions against lead paint manufacturers and doctors, and was targeted by conservatives in 2008.[59] Michael Gableman, his opponent with almost no appellate practice experience, ran ads showing Butler, the state's first black justice, side by side with a picture of Reuben Lee Mitchell, who is also black. An alarmed woman's voice-over says, "Louis Butler worked to put criminals on the street, like Reuben Lee Mitchell, who raped an eleven-year-old girl with learning disabilities. Butler found a loophole. Mitchell went on to molest another child. Can Wisconsin families feel safe with Louis Butler on the Supreme Court?"[60] Butler had not ruled in Mitchell's case, but had represented him as a lawyer twenty years earlier as a state public defender. Butler won a lower court appeal, but the state supreme court ruled that the trial error had been harmless and did not free him. Only after serving his full sentence, Mitchell committed another crime. After Gableman defeated Butler narrowly, the state's judicial commission found that Gableman's ad was so intentionally misleading that it rose to the level of a lie. It requested the state supreme court to discipline him. The court's three liberals agreed, but the three conservatives did not, leaving the court deadlocked.[61]

Also in 2008, Diane Hathaway, a Michigan Democrat, ran ads attacking Chief Justice Cliff Taylor for sleeping on the bench. Taylor had written the Michigan Supreme Court decision upholding the statutory damage caps for personal injuries, and personal injury lawyers responded by financing Hathaway's challenge.[62] Right after winning by nine points, she gave a partisan victory speech announcing that her new four-vote majority "would undo a great deal of the damage that the Republican-dominated court has done. Not only will we not neglect our duties. We will not sleep on the bench."[63] With vitriol spilling into a 2010 tort decision undoing a tort precedent, the justices accused each other of "being mean-spirited," acting on "spectacular hubris," engaging in "doctrinal destruction" and "obvious manipulation" of facts, and "having contempt for the common law and common sense."[64] The total spending in the two 2008 races exceeded $10 million. The Republican challenger in Wisconsin and the Democratic challenger in Michigan in 2008 were also helped by lucky timing. Wisconsin's judicial election was on April 1 (appropriately enough), an off-cycle election with low turnout. Michigan's judicial election was on November 4, 2008, with Barack Obama on the ballot. Michigan Democrats turned out in droves, voted party-line all the way down the ballot, and swept the state races. It is worth noting that both Wisconsin and Michigan have formally "nonpartisan" judicial elections, but the campaigns are in fact as partisan, expensive, and aggressive as the partisan elections, if not more so.

An Alternative: Merit Selection

There is a stark pattern in these races: *All* of the million-dollar races between 2000 and 2009 were the partisan or nonpartisan kind. None of the retention elections came close to that level of spending, and in particular, the merit-plan retention elections had almost no money at all.[65] From 2000 to 2008, only the New Mexico merit-plan retention election and a quasi–merit retention election in California cost more than $100,000.[66]

One reason that merit-selected judges had raised little money is that retention elections offer strong job security, and thus these judges very rarely face organized and well-financed opposition. And one reason potential opponents decide not to invest in challenges is that it is so difficult to defeat incumbents. Between 1 percent and 2 percent of judges running in retention elections have been defeated, while incumbents in partisan elections are defeated in 23 percent of their races and incumbents in nonpartisan elections are defeated in roughly 8 percent to 9 percent of their races. By comparison, 5 percent to 6 percent of incumbent congressmen were defeated over the same time period.[67]

Judges in merit selection states tend to face a built-in competitive disadvantage because they run in retention elections without necessarily having any background in campaigning. Usually the first election they have ever run in is their retention election. They have no experience campaigning, fundraising, or hiring a political staff to help with those challenges. Even with this structural disadvantage, merit plan judges almost always win overwhelmingly and unopposed. The retention election system reduces the incentives for a judge's opponents to invest in her defeat because those opponents do not choose the replacement. In merit systems, a multimember pluralist commission fills the seat. If these interests do not control the merit commissions and the governorship as well, they have little reason to expect much return on their investment in defeating the incumbent. And perhaps merit selection produces better judges who get reelected more easily. There is anecdotal evidence that merit commissions nominate candidates with more judicial experience, but academic studies are mixed or inconclusive about whether merit selects more experienced candidates or produces better judges, in part because it is hard to quantify judicial quality.[68]

Yet Rose Bird was famously defeated in a retention election. But that retention election proves the rule. In every other merit plan state, the professional commission nominates a list of candidates, and the governor is limited to that list. However, in California, the governor nominates one specific candidate, and the professional commission simply approves or disapproves that candidate. This unusual design was a last-minute backroom switch in 1934 from young Earl Warren's pro-professional standard plan to the Commonwealth Club's probusiness reordering. Fifty-two years later, that switch made a big difference in the political calculus of Rose Bird's opponents.

The actor or actors who have the first crack at nominations control the process. In California, businesses knew that if they could defeat the three liberals, they would give Republican Governor Deukmejian control over three judicial nominations, and they were confident that Deukmejian would support their interests. The California judicial commission simply would rubber-stamp his nominees. The corporate money spent on defeating those three judges was a very wise investment. In other states, political interests have much less confidence that a multimember commission drawn from very different groups will serve their interests, and thus, it is less wise to pour their political capital into those merit plan retention elections.

The merit plan is structurally insulated from modern hardball politics, but that certainly was not former Tennessee Justice Penny White's experience. So far, Tennessee and Nebraska in 1996 and Iowa in 2010 have been exceptional in merit retention elections.[69] Interest groups may have found partisan and nonpartisan elections to be the low-hanging fruit, and in the future, they may start to target retention elections where there is a vulnerable incumbent and a more favorable governor and nominating commission. After all, many of these interests had been slow in shifting their focus from reforming judicial elections in the mid-twentieth century to winning them at the end of the century. Business interests also may have been slow in expanding their campaigns to merit states, and merit states may be a future battleground.[70] In 2010, there were signs that aggressive hot-button campaigning and interest group spending are coming to merit retention elections. In 2010, out-of-state organizations spent almost $1 million to unseat three Iowa judges who had ruled in favor of gay marriage.[71] Money also poured in against Florida and Colorado merit-selected judges in the same election, and a Kansas judge faced a well-organized challenge from prolife groups, but all of those incumbents survived.

Beyond the future vulnerability of retention elections to increased spending, the merit plan has other flaws. Studies show that governors sometimes manipulate the commissions from the outside, the judges on the merit commissions can manipulate the bar commissioners, and the bar commissioners influence the lay members.[72] But this news should not be shocking. Politics and influence inevitably find their way into any system of judicial selection. Another question is diversity. Studies in the 1970s, '80s, and '90s showed that the merit plan tended to produce a less diverse bench in terms of race, ethnicity, and sex.[73] Some advocates of merit selection were motivated by preventing the bench from becoming more diverse ethnically, racially, and ideologically. A New York judge once offered this critique in song at a bar association dinner in the 1960s:

> Oh the Old Missouri Plan
> Oh the Old Missouri Plan
> When Wall Street lawyers all judicial candidates will scan
> If you're not from Fair Old Harvard
> They will toss you in the can
> Oh the Old Missouri Plan
> Oh the Old Missouri Plan
> It won't be served with sauerkraut nor sauce Italian
> And spaghetti they will ban
> There'll be no such dish
> As gefilte fish
> Oh the Old Missouri Plan[74]

However, other studies find merit systems gradually becoming more diverse, and sometimes even more diverse than elected systems.[75] When the bar was more homogenous, nominating commissions reflected that homogeneity. As the bar has diversified, so have nominating commissions and the nominees they offer. Merit plans also tend to produce more pro-business judges and fewer pro-union judges, and this pattern was true even when unions were politically stronger and more invested in state courts.[76] There was a reason why businesses campaigned for merit reforms for so much of the twentieth century.

Plutocracy, however, is expanding into merit's territory. Business interests have begun to campaign against the merit plans that they had fought to establish over the course of the twentieth century. Even in Missouri—home of the Missouri Plan—as well as in other states, corporate interests are campaigning to scrap the merit plan and go back to partisan elections. In Missouri, the organization "Show Me Better Courts" (a riff of Missouri's motto) says that it will be "putting the people—not special interest groups or elite legal industry associations—in charge of Missouri's judiciary."[77] Funded by business groups, "Show Me Better Courts" and other anti-merit-plan groups argue that trial lawyers have captured the nominating commissions and install judges who push personal injury awards higher and drive businesses out of the state.[78] The merit plan has its own insider supporters, the Missouri Bar Association and other bar organizations, fighting back to keep their seats on the nominating panel. These campaigns are simply part of a larger pattern: economic interests find ways of playing by the existing rules of judicial selection to win, and when they stop winning, they campaign to change the rules.

We could walk away from this historical tour of American courts shaking our heads cynically and conclude that judicial selection just doesn't matter. Politicization and corruption are inevitable, and reformers are often biased, manipulative, and disingenuous. A number of political scientists and hard-core legal realists believe that law is nothing but politics by other means and we should not pretend otherwise. They believe judges should play by the same rules as other politicians, they are relatively satisfied with judicial democracy, and they generally are skeptical of arguments for judicial independence from public opinion.[79]

But over the history of judicial selection reforms and campaigns, the general public has not shared this skepticism. In fact, these campaigns more often than not have reflected a commitment to general judicial independence, not just relative independence and judicial accountability. The leaders of the reform efforts and the voting public have endorsed the separation of judges from regular politics, even if politics in some form cannot be eliminated. In this particular moment in American history, the two biggest threats to judicial independence are money and job insecurity. A switch from elections to governors' appointments probably would not increase job security unless term lengths were also extended significantly. The nineteenth century revealed the flaws of appointment's patronage, cronyism, and capture. Of the most realistic models, merit selection (circa 2000–2009) turns out to address both the problems of money and job security. The merit plan is not perfect, and it does not eliminate politics from judicial selection. For several decades, merit plans seem to have produced less diversity on the bench than other systems.[80] It is not surprising that bar leadership has tended to replicate itself, and it is not surprising that political parties offered diversity earlier than bar elites did. However, as the bar has become increasingly diverse, so too have the nominations by the bar leadership on merit commissions.[81]

There are plenty of unpleasant stories cloaked under the label "merit," and we should not ignore that history. The primary reason often given for "merit" selection is that it produces better judges, but the jury is still out on that claim, and it is likely a hung jury, considering how difficult it is to define and measure merit.[82] The case for the merit system actually does not hinge on producing the most "merit." The merit system's most concrete advantages are that it shifts the balance to judicial independence from the influence of party politics and money and that it has produced more job security for its judges. The problem of judicial plutocracy has been more limited to partisan and nonpartisan competitive elections. In the 1990s and 2000s, relatively little money went into retention elections, and even less was spent in the states with both merit selection and retention elections. However, it is also likely that well-funded interests have only been slow in turning their sights on merit states' retention elections, and those states may be the next battleground for expensive campaigns, more defeated judges, and weakened state courts. In 2010, national organizations spent almost $1 million to defeat three pro-gay-marriage justices in Iowa, and money poured into the merit retention races in Colorado and Florida, though the judges survived those challenges. Business groups are also challenging the Missouri Plan in Missouri itself, hoping to use a referendum to overturn the state's merit plan.[83] These developments suggest that the battleground is expanding, and that plutocracy is spreading into meritocracy's territory.

It is inevitable that big spending and partisanship will invade the merit system from time to time, but it would be a mistake to overlook the contrast between merit systems and competitive election systems. The advocates of merit reforms campaigned in favor of more job security and less political competition, and their reforms generally delivered as advertised. Only 1 percent or 2 percent of judges running in retention elections have been defeated, far lower than the other election modes. This pattern is not accidental. It reflects the stated intentions of the merit reformers in the 1930s and in the 1950s–1970s.[84] Retention elections create a safety valve for popular participation and a mechanism for preserving judicial accountability, but without threatening judges as acutely as competitive elections.

Merit selection reflects an ongoing cycle of institutional design, corruption, reform, new corruption, and new reform. On the one hand, the cycling goes back and forth between appointment, elections, and appointments again.[85] But it is also accurate to describe these developments as synthesis, driven by evolving notions of politics, separation of powers, and judicial independence. In the late eighteenth century, appointments during good behavior were designed to separate judges from the political branches. In the mid-nineteenth century, corruption and capture led states to adopt direct elections in order to separate the courts from the political branches even more decisively. In the twentieth century, the partisanship and corruption of direct elections led to a hybrid of appointment and election. But it was not sufficient to return to the old system of governors appointing judges. The twentieth century witnessed the increasing power of the experts and the professions, and they presented an opportunity for a new model of separating the powers by creating a nominating commission. These commissions were a new mini-branch, partly drawn from the other branches (lay leaders appointed by the governor and legislators), partly drawn from the courts (sitting judges), and partly drawn from civic leaders outside the government (the leaders of the bar). By dividing the commission among so many different groups and bases of power, it is much harder for any one group to control the process or to predict how the commissions will select new judges. As a result, opposition groups have less incentive to campaign against incumbents. Many interest groups and businesses had pushed for merit reforms, but once they had a new winning strategy in judicial elections in the 1980s, they shifted their resources to win judicial elections, and it is probably no coincidence that that the spread of merit slowed to a halt since then. Even though the merit system has been very different from partisan and nonpartisan elections in the past, there are signs that these differences are blurring. The 2010 defeat of the three Iowa judges who had ruled in favor of gay marriage may be a harbinger of money spilling over into merit. In a high-profile fight over explosive social issues, some groups will be sufficiently motivated by punishing the incumbents, expressing their outrage, and deterring other judges in other states. Such groups are not necessarily focused on who the replacements will be. Some regard hotly competitive retention elections as a hallmark of judicial accountability and public engagement. Others might seek new ways to bolster merit's insulation judges from direct political pressure.

Politics usually overwhelms institutional machinery, but sometimes well-designed machinery can withstand political pressure. Judicial selection is a delicate balance between diffused and concentrated power. When the people elect the judge, the power is too diffuse, because voters with too little knowledge of the candidates are too easily swayed by the parties and the special interests that step into that vacuum. In traditional appointments, governors have concentrated power and dominate the selection of judges.[86] Federal judicial selection also has reflected this concentrated power of presidents and interests. Appointments can be even more vulnerable to cronyism, patronage, and self-dealing than partisan elections. In both elections and appointments, an individual or a narrow set of interests can wield enormous power.

The merit plan strikes a balance between concentration and diffusion. It improves upon traditional elections and traditional appointments, more than just a compromise between the two. In contrast with other methods, it adds a thicker layer of insulation from the political parties with a new set of veto points. The governor and the parties do not get the first crack at selecting judges. Instead, a bipartisan commission of lawyers, judges, and public officials must agree. Merit may not be "nonpolitical," but it is multipolitical or pluralistic, and it furthers the separation of powers by creating a different selection mechanism from the party-controlled elections for the other branches. Even though changes between selection systems usually shift only relative independence from one political force to another, merit selection increases general judicial independence by insulating judges from concentrated power, from parties, and from the pressures of big campaign financing.

At the same time, the rising number of high-profile defeats in merit retention elections and the emergence of major spending in those elections are a sign that the merit system is becoming more competitive. For those who prefer more competitive judicial elections with more publicity, this may be a welcome sign. Those who want to preserve more judicial independence and less competition might reject all forms of judicial elections, but they might also consider merit's historical track record as an opportunity for new reform. Whether one prefers accountability or independence, both sides might consider five areas of reform that are illuminated by this history. First, retention elections allow for more adjustment of reelection thresholds. Second, the nominating commissions can be adjusted to produce more accountability or more independence. Third, judges' term lengths can be made longer or shorter. Fourth, recusal rules can address the influence of money on the courts. Fifth, there are other mechanisms for checking the courts that could either enhance judicial elections or replace judicial elections.

First, retention elections allow for a solution that is not as workable in competitive elections: changing the threshold for winning. For example, two states require judges to win 57 percent or 60 percent of the "yes" vote in their retention elections.[87] This tweak illustrates how retention elections offer more options for winning thresholds, and these examples are tweaks in favor of competition and accountability by making it harder for judges to win. Reformers who want to protect judicial independence might reverse this threshold change, requiring 60 percent of voters to vote "no" in order to remove a judge. With this change, retention elections would be more like impeachment than a competitive election. Kentucky's chief justice compared running for office to a root canal: "You feel better when it's over but you realize there is something positive in the process. By running for office[,] judges . . . have an opportunity to learn what real people are doing on a daily basis and what they are thinking."[88] Even with a 60 percent threshold, retention elections would still encourage judges to explain their role in a democracy and to listen to the public's concerns. But they would be less likely to weigh those concerns over their sense of justice. The merit-plan judges in Tennessee, Nebraska, and Iowa would have survived a 60 percent "no" threshold, but Rose Bird would not have. Still, if a judge has lost over 60 percent, the voters inevitably will find some other way of checking the courts. A retention election is a safety valve in those cases.

A second solution would be to abandon the retention campaigns entirely, and rely solely on merit appointment and reappointment. A few states send their merit-selected judges back to the nominating commissions for renomination, rather than out to the voters to campaign.[89] However, this reform would face an uphill battle politically. Merit reforms prevailed in the mid-twentieth century in part because they preserved voter input.[90] The populist hill is easier to climb if the commissions are designed to reflect the general public and to appear more nonpartisan. Most panels are designed to balance representation from the bar, the governor's representatives, and the legislature's representatives, plus a member or two from the judiciary. This design reflects the separation of powers, but not the separation of parties.[91] It reflects the balancing of institutions, but not real politics. Most states have no provisions to mandate bipartisan balance on these commissions. In a state where one party has narrowly won the governorship and the legislature, that party will usually dominate the merit commission and can convert the formally nonpartisan panel into a partisan machine in practice. Unsurprisingly, some merit commissions have played partisan politics to skew lists in favor of their party and to force opposing governors' hands.[92] Beyond the mandate for multibranch membership, there could also be a mandate for more bipartisan balance on these commissions. Instead of creating slots for the governor's appointees and the legislature's appointees, commissions could reserve the lay seats for a balance of Democrats and Republicans. Such a balance might encourage bipartisanship in practice and might be more appealing to a public that likes the label of "bipartisanship." Supermajority voting rules, requiring more than just bare majorities and party-line votes in forming slates of nominees, might foster consensus, compromise, and bipartisanship, even if there is a risk of obstructionism.[93]

In addition to bipartisanship, other adjustments in the commissions' composition might promote real nonpartisanship and popular participation. Many states balance the lawyers and judges on the merit commissions with lay members appointed by the governor and the legislature. There is something strange about this structure: the judges have to face the voters eventually in retention elections, but the general public's ostensible representatives on the commissions never actually face the voters. They are very often partisan insiders. Instead of politicians appointing lay members, voters might elect them directly. The nominating commissions would reflect a better balance of elite and nonelite, insiders and outsiders. Bar leaders and judges would meet with directly elected officers, not the middle-men and middle-women of the partisan elected officials. Such changes to merit commissions' membership might generate more public support for replacing retention elections with more popular commissions. In fact, they could be rebranded from "merit" commissions to "popular" commissions or "public" commissions. This reform might be appealing to both proponents of accountability or general independence, if they are seeking more deliberation with the public, replacing the partisan appointees to the commissions.

If reformers proposed the election of some number of nominating commissioners (let's say one third), the public might embrace this outlet for participation and accountability, and they might accept the replacement of retention elections with merit reappointment. The commissioner elections might be equally noisy, but the judges themselves would be separated from the campaign trail and from campaign finance. The public might be even more accepting if the commissions were more transparent.

If the public might select some commissioners more directly, the commissions might also be delivered more directly to the public. Some of the backlash against merit stems from its secrecy and the insider politics of the professional bar. Nominating panels' deliberations could be more open to the public. Even as the U.S. Chamber of Commerce has invested more in contesting judicial elections, it continues to support merit selection.

The Chamber's Institute for Legal Reform has proposed "best practices" for merit selection, including more transparent nominating commission meetings with more disclosure of the members' interests and more public participation.[94]

A third area of reform is term length. It is the simplest mechanism: Americans turned to shorter terms in the early nineteenth century to increase accountability, and then to longer terms in the late nineteenth century to increase independence. During Reconstruction, a series of corruption scandals triggered a reform movement for lengthening judges' terms. Of course, longer terms might have insulated some corrupt judges, but the reformers' theory was that more general judicial independence from political pressure would insulate judges from corrupting influences. A California Supreme Court justice once said, "There's no way a[n elected] judge is going to be able to ignore the political consequences of certain decisions, especially if he or she has to make them near election time. That would be like ignoring a crocodile in your bathtub. . . . You know it's there, and you try not to think about it, but it's hard to think about much else while you're shaving."[95] One scholar underscored the point: "The ability to ignore the crocodile doubtless depends on how long before you have to take a bath."[96] The Model Code of Judicial Conduct states: "Deference to the judgments and rulings of courts depends upon public confidence in the integrity and independence of judges . . . [which] depends in turn upon their acting without fear or favor."[97] Fear and favor are not limited to judicial elections. A judge approaching reappointment has the same fear of the governor or the legislature, and must maintain favor. One scholar criticized judicial elections for creating a "majoritarian difficulty," putting political pressure on judges to follow public opinion instead of the law.[98] Indeed, a growing number of studies show that elected judges decide cases more in line with local public opinion than appointed judges do.[99] However, the "majoritarian difficulty" is more a product of short terms than of the mode of judicial selection. Judges who are popularly elected to life terms might be "majoritarian" in getting on the bench, but they would be insulated from the ongoing majoritarian difficulty, just like federal judges. Appointed judges serving short terms would face a powerful majoritarian challenge if they wanted to be reappointed. The nineteenth century demonstrated that appointments are no less political than elections, as governors used their appointment powers for political gain. In some states, merit-selected judges are appointed to the bench for about a year or two, and then run in one retention election to win a longer term of between eight and twelve years.[100] Those who favor judicial independence might support this design, but then give judges even longer terms after retention, so that judges are scrutinized briefly, and then are more insulated thereafter. Those who favor accountability might not want too short an initial term, so that voters have more of a judge's record to evaluate before the first retention election.

A fourth area of reform is regulating money itself. It might seem at first that campaign finance regulations and limits on campaign speech would be possible solutions. However, the U.S. Supreme Court has made a series of decisions allowing more freedom for independent political advertising uncoordinated with the candidate and more freedom for direct corporate campaign spending.[101] Some have argued that judicial campaigns should be treated differently than other campaigns under the First Amendment, but the Supreme Court was skeptical of this argument in *Republican Party v. White*.[102] The Supreme Court has also exacerbated the problem by freeing corporations to spend on campaigns in *Citizens United*. In his dissent in that case, Justice Stevens warned, "At a time when concerns about the conduct of judicial elections have reached a fever pitch, the Court today unleashes the floodgates of corporate and union general treasury spending in these races."[103] Some states had not limited corporate spending in the first place, so *Citizens United* has little effect there, but in states that had been trying to contain the flood, the U.S. Supreme Court possibly has accelerated corporate and union spending, and *White* probably prevents the states from treating the financing of judicial elections differently from the financing of other elections. Another solution might be public funding for judicial elections, but only three states offer public funding, and this funding has been too stingy to attract candidates and deter explosion of spending. Merit selection offers a solution to the problem of campaign finance without regulation, because there has been less money in retention elections in the first place.

There is a way to address the problem of money without regulating campaign finance or campaign speech directly and without running afoul of the First Amendment. The answer is to rely on the Fourteenth Amendment's due process clause instead, because due process requires judicial recusal and disqualification under some circumstances. In *Caperton v. Massey*, the West Virginia case discussed in the Introduction, the U.S. Supreme Court ruled that judges must recuse themselves from the cases of major political donors and supporters.[104] The dissenters raised legitimate questions about the limits and manageability of this rule, but it turns out the rule is workable, and it even has the distinct advantage of disincentivizing spending without regulating the spenders or the speech.[105] Instead, it regulates the judges once they are presiding on the bench, not on the campaign stump. As long as the U.S. Supreme Court or the state courts take this issue seriously, then judges will be risk averse and recuse themselves more often, and that in turn will make donors risk averse in spending. Instead of benefiting from campaign spending, the donor runs the risk of each additional dollar triggering recusal or disqualification on appeal. The marginal cost of each donation quickly exceeds the marginal benefit. The *Caperton* due process rule depends on strict disclosure rules for direct and indirect campaign spending, so that litigants know whether they have a *Caperton* claim in the first place. Whereas the *Citizens United* decision has created a legislative impasse over disclosure, the courts could construct their own post-*Caperton* rules on disclosure through discovery. Sunlight is the best disinfectant. If *Caperton* motions include disclosure and discovery rules, judicial elections will remain more transparent than the politics of appointment and reappointment. Following *Caperton*, several states tightened their recusal and disclosure rules for campaign contributions. For example, New York's state judicial board required judges to recuse themselves from any case involving a party or firm that had donated more than $2,500.[106] The American Bar Association called for states to adopt similar rules that were more restrictive than the U.S. Supreme Court's *Caperton* rule.[107] The U.S. Supreme Court has focused attention on the issue, but it is unlikely to hear many cases on recusal, because the Justices hear so few cases each year, and the lower federal courts generally have no jurisdiction over civil proceedings in state court. Only the state legislatures and state courts can manage and enforce these rules on a regular basis. If the states do not make a serious effort, recusal will only be a band-aid solution at best, a façade inducing complacency at worst.

A fifth area of reform is finding alternative ways to check the courts. Advocates of judicial accountability might embrace the model of "independent judges, dependent judiciary."[108] The judges themselves can be insulated from removal or attack, but the public can still have a means to override some judicial decisions. Instead of voting judges out of office, voters might focus instead on the substance of their rulings through constitutional amendment and legislative override, just as many progressives had suggested in the 1910s. The recall of judicial decisions, popular or legislative override, and judicial supermajority voting rules were ways of checking and balancing the courts without attacking the judges. Even if Teddy Roosevelt's proposal for the recall of decisions was unwieldy or unlikely, another form of that idea is alive and well in state politics: the constitutional amendment overriding court decisions. The relative ease of the state amendment process has given the states more flexibility to alter judicial selection (for example, to adopt merit selection). It also has given the public a chance to channel its opposition to court decisions. Af-

ter the Massachusetts Supreme Judicial Court ruled in favor of gay marriage, many states reacted by amending their constitutions to define
marriage as between one man and one woman. The California Supreme
Court triggered the same response. One can agree or disagree with the
courts or the voters on the merits of gay marriage, but the big picture lesson is that the constitutional amendment process gave voters an opportunity to react directly to the substance of court decisions, without punishing the judges themselves. The same is true in the tort wars. Some state
judges have struck down tort reform, such as damage caps, on constitutional grounds.[109] In those same states, the prodefense interests could
pass constitutional amendments allowing for damages caps instead of
unseating judges. And on other tort issues, either the trial lawyers or corporations could achieve their goals through simple legislation. If voters
and politicians channel their energy in the constitutional amendment
process, they are fulfilling a more traditional role in a democracy's separation of powers: law making and constitution making. Then the judges
can fulfill their role: applying the law to individual cases. Take the death
penalty as an example: Judges can apply criminal law and the rules for
the death penalty to individual cases when looking closely at the facts of
guilt and innocence. If the public and the politicians disagree with those
rulings, they can change the law through constitutional and statutory
revision—and overcoming the appropriate hurdles for making such
changes—instead of punishing individual judges for their legal decisions.
This separation of law-making and law-applying powers does not remove political pressure, but it gives judges a little more space to examine
the facts and apply the law fairly when one party is unpopular or lacks
economic and political capital. Some observers have described the federal government's "democratic deficit" because of how hard it is to attain
a two-thirds majority in both houses of Congress and then three-quarters
of the states to amend the federal constitution. On top of that, the federal
judges serve for life. By contrast, the states have a democratic surplus: it
is far easier to revise state constitutions, and to vote judges in and out of
office. Giving state judges more job security and more independence
would be one way to reduce the democratic surplus and balance the state
judicial "budget."

It may not be surprising that the American public has valued judicial
accountability. But it is intriguing that the American public has a long
history of valuing judicial independence at the same time. The modern
models of judicial selection reflect both values. All systems of judicial selection are vulnerable to politics, whether popular politics, partisan politics, or elite politics. But some systems are more vulnerable to financial

pressure and job insecurity than others. Merit selection offers a balance between judicial accountability and independence, with more reason to expect a degree of protection from the influence of money and partisan competition. We also have reason to believe that these models will continue to evolve, as the understandings of separation of powers and the relationship between law and politics also evolve.

Conclusion:
Interests, Ideas, and Judicial Independence

THERE ARE NOW FOUR BASIC FORMS of judicial selection, each descended from the four stages of judicial development over American history, and each striking a different balance of judicial independence and judicial accountability. The age of judicial aristocracy produced the federal system of executive appointment and life tenure, and a few states in New England have hung on to this first model.[1] The age of judicial democracy produced the second model, competitive elections, whether partisan or nonpartisan. Over half of the states rely primarily on partisan or nonpartisan elections, and the age of judicial plutocracy has taken over this system.[2] There is little meaningful difference between the partisan and nonpartisan versions, except for less helpful ballots and more ignorant voting in the nonpartisan races. A third form is an unsuccessful mix of aristocracy and democracy: judicial appointment to terms of a few years, and judges in those states must "run" for reappointment behind the scenes.[3] Finally, judicial meritocracy is a synthesis of executive appointment, popular elections, and modern expert bureaucracy, with a new version of separation of powers and judicial independence.[4] About twenty states use merit selection in some form.

State judicial elections seem deeply ingrained, despite their flaws. "So powerful is the curb of incessant responsibility" to the voters, Thomas Jefferson once wrote approvingly, that there would "hardly ever [be] an instance of change" away from judicial elections.[5] In 1877, a federal judge in Iowa lamented this same fact: "Popular elections have brought the judicial office into direct connection with party politics and all the bad methods and influences of faction. [But] I do not believe that the law for popular election of judges can be changed. Popular privileges, once granted, are not likely to be surrendered."[6] Ex-Confederate leader Robert Toombs that same year echoed the same view even more colorfully: "It is easy to take the route to hell, but few people ever returned from it."[7] (For Toombs, hell meant the inclusion of ex-slaves and poor whites.)

True, judicial democracy has been entrenched in American life since the American revolutions of 1848. But Jefferson and Toombs were not entirely correct. In the twentieth century, many states significantly reformed judicial elections, switching to a combination of professional or "merit" appointment and retention elections designed to be nonpartisan and less competitive. There are few other episodes in American history when the public went to the polls to surrender their own power to vote. And it is also unusual to find episodes in which both political parties have tolerated the loss of their power and patronage with limited benefit in return. One might have thought that judicial accountability is an inevitable and overwhelming force in a democracy, because public opinion, the parties, and elected officials would not allow the judiciary—"the least dangerous branch"—to obstruct their interests or clash with their values. However, it turns out that the value of judicial independence has been a surprisingly robust, resilient, and popular value from the colonial era to the present. In each stage of judicial development, reformers framed their proposals in terms of judicial independence from a particular political threat, and this rallying cry won enough public support to overcome inertia and even to persuade the public to surrender some of its power.

Much of the scholarship and discussion about judicial selection by historians, political scientists, law professors, pundits, and the public emphasizes the role of politics and interests. For example, historians over the last century have debated to what extent economics and interests controlled the Federal Convention of 1787. At the risk of oversimplifying that debate, the delegates had a general interest in national commerce and private property, which contributed, among other factors, to the Constitution's protection of judicial independence. Another example is the theory that political actors choose judicial independence (for example, the switch from partisan elections to merit selection) when they foresee losing political power, and thus political parties act out of risk aversion. Judicial independence, according to this view, is a form of insurance protecting a group's interests against rival groups rising to power.[8] This book, as the first comprehensive, archival study of state judicial selection over American history, certainly confirms some of these assumptions about political interests. On the one hand, political and economic interests drove each stage of judicial selection. But on the other, ideas about judicial independence shaped the debates and the path of reform.

The rise of judicial elections in the 1840s was a reaction to an economic and fiscal crisis. Elected judges would be more independent from the other branches, more responsive to the people, escape the grasp of party patronage machines, enforce the constitution, and limit spending. Many leaders of this movement rallied against crony capitalism, supported free markets, and took early steps toward laissez-faire constitutionalism. The shift to nonpartisan elections in the Progressive Era loosely reflected an opposing economic vision favoring regulation. Once corporate interests discovered that labor was beginning to win judicial elections, they sought to change the rules and drove the rise of professional or "merit" selection over the twentieth century. In some states in this era, such as Alaska and some southern states, leaders believed that the merit plan would be more attractive to investors and commerce for assuring a more reliable enforcement of contracts and commitments (consistent with some leading theories about the sources of judicial independence).[9] But when businesses learned they could win judicial elections in the 1980s, it is no surprise that the spread of merit fizzled, and that money flowed into partisan and non-partisan elections. It is striking how what would later become the keystones of modern American conservatism played critical roles in the two major revolutions in judicial selection. Judicial democracy arose in the mid-nineteenth century as the outgrowth of fiscal conservatism, moral opposition to public debt, the Jacksonian vision of capitalism, and nascent laissez-faire. Judicial meritocracy arose in the mid-twentieth century as a combination of business interests and anticrime "law and order."

At each stage, economic interests set the agenda, but they emphasized ideas about judicial independence. The consistent concept over time has been that judges are fundamentally unlike other political officers, and they should be separated from politics in order to act as judges. Change results primarily because the perceptions of politics change over time. The conception of judging might also change, but the core distinction between law and politics survives. The advocates of judicial elections in New York in 1846 contended that elections would promote judicial independence and judicial power. New Yorkers argued that judicial elections would allow judges to rise above politics, gain confidence, and channel "natural" law from "God himself." Supporters in other states argued that judicial elections would foster "an independent judiciary," and that American voters would reject judges who made "political" decisions, and would select only the "honest, impartial, decided, and fearless." They had faith that voters would support "better men," "more independent men," judges with "honesty and integrity" to rise above "fear, favor, or affection" in order to decide cases in accordance with "the law." These arguments may have been naïve, and they even may have been disingenuous, but these were the public arguments that the reformers of the 1840s and 1850s emphasized in support of judicial elections.[10]

After the Civil War, a new set of state conventions lengthened judges' terms, and the goal was not just relative independence, but also general judicial independence, to insulate judges from political pressure generally. During the Progressive Era and the New Deal, critics of the courts proposed major checks on the courts, and yet the public rejected most of them, even if they disagreed with the courts' rulings. The turn to nonpartisan elections and merit selection in the twentieth century were both pitched as separating judges from politics. Business had its own self-interest in merit reforms, but it needed to rely heavily upon the rhetoric of judicial independence to convince a skeptical public and to legitimate their work. These leaders called for reforms with the slogan "Get Judges out of Politics!" It is possible that these leaders' support for judicial independence was only rhetoric. If so, the question remains why they devoted so much effort to framing their reforms in these terms at each stage. Apparently, the general public either wanted or needed this framing, perhaps because a significant portion of the American public has a sincere commitment to judicial independence. The principles of fairness and the separation of law from politics help explain why so many Americans in the twentieth century voted to scale back their power to vote for judges when they ratified merit reforms, even if those votes were mixed with other motives.

These episodes also suggest that judicial independence guided some key political leaders, because they supported these reforms even though the changes went against their immediate political interests. In the 1840s and 1850s, many state conventions adopted judicial elections with bipartisan support, even where one party dominated statewide elections. Judicial appointments gave majority parties a decisive advantage, because they would win the governorship consistently and monopolize the appointment process. Judicial elections would reduce this advantage by allowing more local control over judicial selection, giving the minority party a chance to win more seats in their strongholds. Nevertheless, a significant number of majority party leaders supported the change. Similarly, merit selection spread mostly in states with a dominant political party, and again, a significant number of those leaders were willing to hand over their partisan control to a relatively insulated professional commission. In both cases, there were many factors to explain their departure from their immediate partisan interests, but considering their public emphasis on the value of judicial independence, it would not be a stretch to imagine that some of these leaders sincerely believed their own propaganda.

Neither ideas nor interests by themselves can explain the evolution of American judicial politics, but it was ideas and interests bouncing off of each other. Particular interests and powerful groups might have been a driving force at each stage, but they also needed to frame their arguments in broader terms of judicial independence in order to legitimate their proposals. The ideas of fairness, justice, and the rule of law were crucial for public opinion. Even when ideas and economics set the stage for legal reforms as preconditions and precipitants, these campaigns succeeded when specific events made these issues seem urgent and triggered the change in judicial design. Historical change is not simple; it is usually the constellation of many forces, big and small.

The adoption of partisan judicial elections in the nineteenth century and then their partial rejection/reformation in the twentieth century *both* were the result of a widespread commitment to the idea of judicial independence. This seeming paradox is possible because judicial independence is often a relative concept, and the understandings of judicial independence have changed over time. Relatedly, the perceptions of "good" and "bad" politics have also changed over time. Americans have embraced the notion of making judges independent of "corrupting" politics, while making the courts accountable to some idealized concept of democracy. Each set of reforms also reflected changing perspectives on the separation of powers. In the eighteenth century, life tenure first separated judges from imperious monarchs, as well as from the other political branches and from factions. Meanwhile, the political appointment process was an acceptable form of politics. In the mid-nineteenth century, perceptions changed: appointments were viewed as corrupting, and political parties became a necessary way to mobilize the masses against threats to democracy. Timing was crucial: the economic crisis and the wave of conventions coincided with the success of the second two-party system generating unprecedented voter participation. At that moment, direct elections were designed to separate judges from corrupt governors and incompetent legislatures, to harness the political parties' power to strengthen the courts, and to bolster the judges' enforcement of constitutional limits. The next few decades exposed more of the flaws of partisan elections: the insider politics of party bosses and special interests and the public politics of campaigning that clashed with an evolving notion of the judge's proper role. In the late nineteenth century, longer terms were the means of separating judges from parties and special interests. Then, in the twentieth century, nonpartisan elections were an attempt to insulate judges from the parties, and merit commissions were a more successful attempt, a new kind of "branch" mixing representatives from the other branches and from civic society. The "merit" plan replaced one kind of insider politics with another (the bar association and professional expertise), and it was designed to reduce the public spectacle of judges campaigning. These stages of judicial reform are good examples of "concrete negation" and synthesis, as the legal system develops in reaction to specific crises and builds on past efforts more than cycling back to earlier forms.[11] Most reforms succeeded in insulating the courts from one set of evils, but they often exposed courts to new political forces—sometimes unwittingly, sometimes wittingly. Again, the distinction between "general" and "relative" judicial independence is vital. Some stages achieved more general independence: life tenure and salary protections at the Founding, longer terms during Reconstruction, and merit selection's increased job security. Other stages focused on relative independence. In the nineteenth century, judicial elections made judges more independent from the other branches of government, but more accountable to the people. Parties and special interests then found a way to retain their influence under either system. Judicial review (whether in the boom of the 1840s–1850s or today) might represent judicial independence from the legislature or public opinion, but it also might reflect the influence of parties or special interests. Another example of relative judicial independence is the merit plan shifting power from the parties and the voters to the professional bar and to governors. No matter how one designs a system of judicial selection, politics of one sort or another inevitably figure out that new system. The test for reformers is to learn from past flaws, but the pitfall for reformers is that they often fight the last war, not the next one.

Thomas Jefferson was wrong. The American public has demonstrated again and again that it shares the aspirations of the rule of law, fairness, and judicial independence. Sometimes the people will surrender, in Jefferson's words, their "incessant" control when reformers have appealed to these principles. Judicial selection may be inevitably political, but this history shows that the American public perceives that there should be a separation of law and politics (even if the definition of these ideas shifts), and this history shows that calls for judicial independence have been powerful and successful. Even though the term "rule of law" has been used for particular agendas and interests over the course of American history, it is still a vital aspiration in a legal system. Both liberal and conservative thinkers conclude that the "rule of law" depends upon impartiality, equal and consistent treatment, the protection of general fundamental principles protected from arbitrary power, and the separation of law from politics. Both the aspiration and the appearance of impartiality and nonpartisanship are crucial for the courts to work. Beginning in the colonial period, Americans have experienced on-going cycles of corruption and reform, and the reforms reflect a synthesis of appointment and elections, expertise and democratic accountability. In the context of nineteenth-century corruption, judicial elections had a clear logic as a good-government reform, based on an image of robust elections with informed voters selecting based on honesty, integrity, a commitment to constitutional principles, and an understanding of the legal system. Unfortunately, the practice of judicial elections has not lived up to these hopes. When judicial elections are quiet and under the radar, the voters are ignorant of the candidates, and the elections have problems with democratic legitimacy. Now that many judicial elections are as competitive as other elections, their politicization, partisanship, intense fundraising, and massive spending on negative, simplistic, and often misleading advertising raise new questions about their legitimacy in a judicial system. At the start of the twenty-first century, we face a new crisis in judicial politics and special interests. If we have learned from history, it is also a new opportunity for redeclaring judicial independence.[12]

APPENDIXES

NOTES

ACKNOWLEDGMENTS

INDEX

Appendix A:
Judicial Elections Timeline

	For Elections		*Against Elections*
1777	Territory of Vermont for lower courts		
—			
1812	Georgia for "inferior" courts		
—			
1816	Indiana for circuit courts		
—			
1832	**Mississippi** (C)		
1833			
1834			Missouri (A), Tennessee (C)
1835	Georgia for superior courts (A)		North Carolina (C)
1836	Michigan for circuit courts (C)		
1837		**PANIC**	
1838			Pennsylvania (C)
1839		**SECOND PANIC**	
1840		**DEPRESSION**	
1841		**DEPRESSION**	
1842		**DEPRESSION**	Rhode Island (C)
1843		**DEPRESSION ENDS**	
1844	Iowa for lower courts (C)		New Jersey (C)
1845			Texas (C), Louisiana (C), Missouri (C)
1846	**New York** (C), **Wisconsin** (C)		
1847	**Illinois** (C)		
1848–1850	**Pennsylvania** (A)		
1848	Arkansas for circuit courts (A)		
1849	**California** (C)		

(continued)

	For Elections	Against Elections
850	Kentucky (C), Michigan (C), Missouri (A), Ohio (C), Texas (A), Virginia (C) Alabama (A), Connecticut (A), and Vermont (A) for circuit courts	
851	Maryland (C), Indiana (C)	New Hampshire (C)
852	Louisiana (C)	
853	Tennessee (A), Florida (A)	Massachusetts (C)
857	Minnesota (C), Iowa (C)	
858		
859	Oregon (C)	
860		
861	Kansas (C)	

Notes: The left column of the timeline shows states that adopted judicial elections, and the right column shows states that did not. All state conventions after 1812 are included and are indicated as (C). The timeline also indicates with (A) when a state adopted an amendment that changed its court system—in the left column when the amendment adopted some form of judicial elections, and in the right column when the amendment reformed the state's courts without adopting judicial elections. States listed in **bold** adopted judicial elections for all of their courts.

Appendix B:
State Supreme Court Cases Declaring State Laws Unconstitutional

	1780–1789	1790–1799	1800–1809	1810–1819	1820–1829	1830–1839	1840–1849	1850–1859	1860–1864
New Hampshire	1	–	–	1	1	1	1	2	0
Massachusetts	4	–	1	2	0	1	0	3	1
Rhode Island	1	–	–	–	–	–	–	2	0
Connecticut	0	0	0	0	3	2	1	0	1
New York[1]	0	0	0	5	6	4	6/13*	32*	14*
New Jersey	1	1	1	2	0	1	0	1	1
Pennsylvania	–	1	0	0	0	0	7/1*	7*	11*
Delaware	–	0	0	0	1	0	2	0	0
Maryland	–	0	0	0	2	4	4	1*	1*
Virginia	4	1	0	1	1	0	0	0*	0*
North Carolina	1	1	2	3	0	1	0	5	1
South Carolina	–	1	0	0	0	0	0	0	0
Georgia	–	–	–	–	–	–	3	3	0
Vermont 1791		–	0	2	6	3	0	2	1
Kentucky 1792		–	5	2	8	4	2	3*	2*
Tennessee 1796		–	0	2	1	12	6	2/11*	1*
Ohio 1803			1	–	0	0	2	11*	1*
Louisiana 1812				0	0	0	4	2/12*	1*
Indiana 1816				–	1	0	1	28*	13*
Mississippi 1817				–	1	1*	2*	1*	1*
Illinois 1818				–	0	1	1	5*	5*
Alabama 1819					1	2	1	4	1
Maine 1820					2	0	0	4	1
Missouri 1820					1	3	1	8*	4*
Appointed total	12	5	10	20	35	39	42	30	7
Elected total[1]	0	0	0	0	0	1	16	119	54
California[2] 1850								21*	14*

Notes: For a full list of cases and state-by-state graphs, see Shugerman, "Economic Crisis and the Rise of Judicial Elections and Judicial Review: Appendices." http://papers.ssrn.com/sol3/papers.cfm?abstract_id=1542870. This chart aggregates only states that had entered the Union by 1821 to prevent skewing the results.

– = under 50 total reported cases for the decade

* = the court was elected for most (usually all) of the decisions in this decade

1. For a description of New York's complicated mix of elected and appointed courts, see Shugerman, "Economic Crisis and the Rise of Judicial Elections and Judicial Review: Appendices."

2. California is not included in the totals to avoid skewing the 1850s total higher.

Appendix C:
Total Reported Cases by Decade (on Westlaw and Lexis)

	1780–1789	1790–1799	1800–1809	1810–1819	1820–1829	1830–1839	1840–1849	1850–1859
New Hampshire	0	0	0	130	439	678	1014	1311
Massachusetts	6	4	481	976	770	1204	1464	2202
Rhode Island	0	0	0	0	1	10	26	301
Connecticut	171	338	176	298	376	374	399	595
New York	0	166	870	966	1183	1497	1408	993
New Jersey	1	139	144	207	366	605	561	706
Pennsylvania	0	283	394	748	1085	1447	2131	2534
Delaware	0	211	77	104	88	274	295	211
Maryland	25	134	142	156	292	343	390	708
Virginia	29	346	429	581	536	589	592	570
North Carolina	4	223	252	408	522	903	1625	1971
South Carolina	48	203	386	519	841	1041	1257	1019
Georgia	0	0	0	0	0	0	520	1982
Vermont 1791		19	132	103	328	777	966	1028
Kentucky 1792		24	471	835	1606	1283	997	891
Tennessee 1796		3	142	341	230	817	958	1231
Ohio 1803			0	0	250	452	729	969
Louisiana 1812				391	1107	1360	2584	2274
Indiana 1816				22	181	342	695	1373
Mississippi 1817				15	82	258	1095	1178
Illinois 1818				3	103	194	718	1317
Alabama 1819					341	907	2351	2024
Maine 1820					451	805	1339	1686
Missouri 1820					273	418	1013	1834

Appendix D:
State Judicial Review, 1780–1864

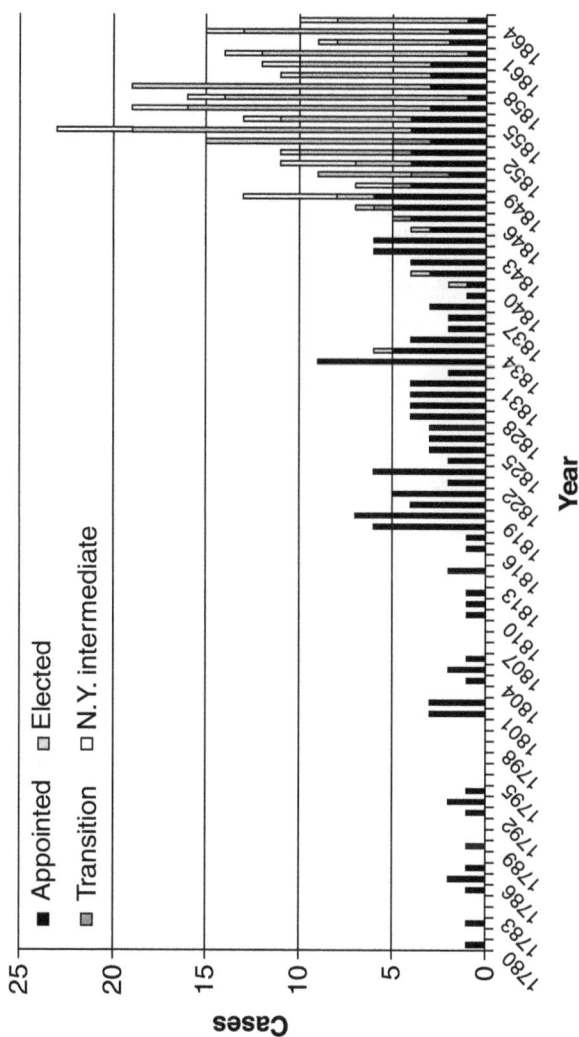

Appendix E:
Subject Matter of State Supreme Court
Cases of Judicial Review

	1780–1799	1800–1809	1810–1819	1820–1829	1830–1839	1840–1849	1850–1859	1860–1864
Judicial power; separation of powers; jurisdiction	1		6	6	5	17	39	14
Other separation of powers							2	
Takings/eminent domain			3	1	5	7	18	2
Internal improvement/ roads/public works					1	5	4	3
Banks; monopolies; corporations				2	3	5	9	3
Taxes/public debt			1	2	1	2	16	7
Legislative procedure (single subject rule; title; etc.)						3	22	6
Ex post facto/ retroactive laws	1	2	6	4	2	9	13	6
Impairing obligations of contract/private debt		1	4	15	17	5	24	15
Vested property rights	2	1	4	4	1	8	16	3
"Law of the land"/ due process/freedom of contract	1				2		6	2
Special or partial laws					5	1	3	
Right to jury trial	5	5	1	4	2	2	10	4

(continued)

	1780–1799	1800–1809	1810–1819	1820–1829	1830–1839	1840–1849	1850–1859	1860–1864
Criminal procedure				1			4	4
Appointment and removal		1		2	1	4	7	2
Liquor prohibition			1			3	14	2
Referenda						2	5	
Marriage and divorce				1	2	2	2	
Married women's property						5	4	1
Bastardy/incest			1					1
Interstate commerce/federal commerce clause		1	1			1		1
Slavery/race			1	1	3	3	6	
Religious freedom						1		
School laws					1		4	2
Bear arms				1		1		
Voting/election Law								2
Local government/districting	1				1	2	7	2
Attorney fees/bar						2	2	1
Currency					2			
Anti-dueling					1			
Native Americans					1			1

Notes: Not all cases fit cleanly into one category or another, and some cases cover more than one category, so this list is both over- and underinclusive. Again, California is not included to avoid skewing the totals. For short descriptions case by case, see Shugerman, "Economic Crisis: Appendices," http://papers.ssrn.com/sol3/papers.cfm?abstract_id=1542870.

Appendix F:
States Adopting and Rejecting *Rylands*

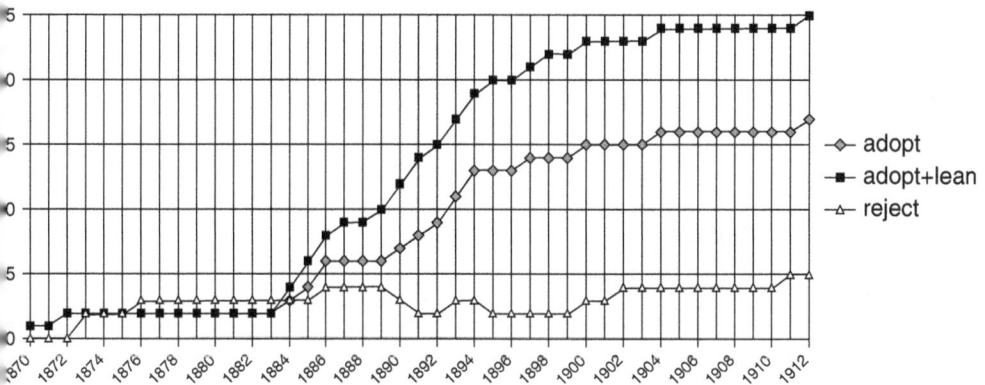

The line marked by squares on data points is the total number of states adopting *Rylands*, leaning toward it, or adopting a similar rule.

The Johnstown Flood was on May 31, 1889. Note the rapid rise of adoptions from 1889 to 1900, especially the line marked by diamonds for explicit adoptions.

The pattern of adoption starting in the mid-1880s, before the Johnstown Flood, is attributable to a few factors that were addressed in an earlier article, "The Floodgates of Strict Liability."[1] First, disastrous California floods in the early 1880s led to the state's adoption of *Rylands* in 1886. Some of those floods related to hydraulic mining, and two other states adopting in the 1880s were mining states (Nevada in 1885 and Colorado in 1887). Second, upper midwestern states were the majority of the other adopting states in the 1880s (Michigan and Wisconsin in 1884, Illinois in 1885 and 1887, and Iowa in 1886). In the 1880s, this region's population and industry were growing rapidly, and the region's political trends had recently shifted toward agrarian populism and against industry.

Appendix G:
Timeline for the Adoption of Merit Selection

1934	California
1935	
1936	
1937	
1938	
1939	
1940	Missouri
1941	
1942	
1943	
1944	
1945	
1946	
1947	
1948	
1949	
1950	Alabama (Birmingham)
1951	
1952	
1953	
1954	
1955	
1956	Alaska
1957	
1958	Kansas
1959	

(continued)

1960		
1961		
1962	**Iowa, Nebraska**	
1963		
1964		(Illinois: retention only)
1965		
1966		
1967	**Colorado, Oklahoma, Utah**	Vermont: merit appointment; Idaho (interim only)
1968		(Pennsylvania: retention only)
1969		
1970	**Indiana**	
1971	**Tennessee**	
1972	**Florida, Wyoming**	
1973		
1974	**Arizona**	Kentucky (interim only)
1975		
1976	**Maryland**	Nevada
1977		(New York; Washington, D.C. merit appointment)
1978		(Hawaii, merit appointment)
1979		
1980	**South Dakota**	

Notes: Bold states on the left follow the basic merit plan of merit selection *and* retention elections. States on the right-hand side adopted a limited aspect of the merit plan. This timeline does not include merit plans adopted by executive order, because they were more temporary, and governors often used them to boost the appearances of a governor's nominations without truly constraining themselves.

Appendix H:
Partisan Balance during Merit Campaigns: Judicial Independence as Partisan Strategy

The partisan risk-aversion thesis was offered based upon a very general quantitative study. Andrew Hanssen, in "Learning about Judicial Independence," 33 *Journal of Legal Studies* 431 (2004), suggested that there was a pattern of states with party parity turning to nonpartisan merit plans because of risk aversion: the majority party was willing to sacrifice short-term control of the courts in favor of long-term insurance against being out of power. He states that states adopting merit plans had a party in power controlling 64 percent of the legislative seats, on average. That number for the states not adopting merit was 72 percent, suggesting that the party in power in those states had less to worry about. Hanssen calculated state-by-state partisan balance by aggregating partisan affiliation in the state legislatures over three decades. I focus on the eight years around the time the state adopted a merit plan, because that timeframe is a more realistic view of political actors' strategic horizon.

On closer examination state by state, the thesis does not find much support in the 1950s, 1960s, or 1970s. In the 1930s, California Republicans may have had reason to worry about losing power and may have shifted in favor of nonpartisan reforms as a result. In 1950, Alabama Democrats had more to worry about in terms of intraparty interracial competition, which fits the general thesis. The same may be true of the other southern states adopting merit plans in the early 1970s. However, the state-by-state numbers for the partisan balance in the 1960s and 1970s undercut the claim more generally. States with a dominant party firmly retaining power adopted merit plans, while states with party reversals in power tended not to adopt merit plans. Of the merit states, the only ones with any party reversals of power in the years around the adoption of merit were Colorado, Utah, Indiana, and Arizona, and even in those states, only one house of the legislature flipped, and it did so only once.

Illinois and Pennsylvania had much closer party balance than the merit states, and yet those two states failed to adopt merit selection. They limited their reform to the addition of retention elections following initial partisan elections. The states that did not adopt any aspect of merit selection generally had more switches in party control over the 1960s and 1970s. Eight of those states were dominated by Democrats throughout the era (mostly southern states);[1] eleven others had complete reversals in control.[2] Even though the partisan risk-aversion thesis may have played some role in some states, it is difficult to see a strong pattern confirming the partisan risk aversion generally.

In the table below, the asterisk denotes the year the merit reform was adopted.

Partisan Balance of State Legislature at the Time of Adopting Merit Plan

	Upper House (R, D)	Lower House (R, D)
California 1930	36, 4 (90% R)	73, 7 (91% R)
California 1932	35, 5 (88% R)	55, 25 (69% R)
California 1934*	31, 8 (80% R)	42, 37 (53% R)
California 1936	25, 15 (63% R)	33, 47 (59% D)
Missouri 1936	3, 31 (91% D)	45, 105 (70% D)
Missouri 1938	3, 31 (91% D)	52, 98 (65% D)
Missouri 1940*	6, 28 (81% D)	65, 85 (57% D)
Missouri 1942	17, 17 (50%)	95, 55 (63% R)
Missouri	1940: 14–1 Democrats in Congress	
Kansas 1954	35, 5 (88% R)	89, 36 (71% R)
Kansas 1956	32, 8 (80% R)	83, 42 (66% R)
Kansas 1958*	32, 8 (80% R)	69, 56 (55% R)
Kansas 1960	32, 8 (80% R)	82, 43 (66% R)
Alaska 1958 (1959*)	2, 18 (90% D)	5, 33 (87% D)
Alaska 1960	7, 13 (65% D)	18, 20 (53% D)
Alaska 1962	5, 15 (75% D)	20, 20 (50%)

	Upper House (R, D)	Lower House (R, D)
Iowa 1958	33, 17 (66% R)	59, 49 (55% R)
Iowa 1960	35, 15 (70% R)	78, 30 (72% R)
Iowa 1962*	38, 12 (76% R)	79, 29 (73% R)
Iowa 1964	38, 12 (76% R)	82, 26 (76% R)

Nebraska (nonpartisan legislature, but strongly Republican)

Illinois 1960	31, 27 (53% R)	89, 88 (50% R)
Illinois 1962	35, 23 (60% R)	90, 87 (51% R)
Illinois 1964*	33, 25 (57% R)	59, 118 (67% D)
Illinois 1966	38, 20 (66% R)	99, 78 (56% R)
Colorado 1964	20, 15 (57% R)	24, 41 (65% D)
Colorado 1966 (1967*)	20, 15 (57% R)	38, 27 (58% R)
Colorado 1968	24, 11 (69% R)	38, 27 (58 % R)
Colorado 1970	21, 14 (60% R)	38, 27 (58% R)
Oklahoma 1964	7, 41 (85% D)	21, 78 (79% D)
Oklahoma 1966 (1967*)	10, 38 (79% D)	25, 74 (75% D)
Oklahoma 1968	10, 38 (79% D)	23, 76 (77% D)
Oklahoma 1970	9, 39 (81% D)	21, 78 (79% D)
Idaho 1964	25, 19 (57% R)	42, 37 (53% R)
Idaho 1966 (1967*)	22, 13 (63% R)	38, 32 (54% R)
Idaho 1968	22, 13 (63% R)	38, 32 (54% R)
Idaho 1970	21, 14 (54% R)	41, 29 (59% R)
Utah 1964	12, 15 (56% D)	30, 39 (57% D)
Utah 1966 (1967*)	23, 5 (82% R)	59, 10 (86% R)
Utah 1968	20, 8 (73% R)	48, 21 (70% R)
Vermont 1964	24, 6 (80% R)	115, 35 (77% R)
Vermont 1966 (1967*)	22, 8 (73% R)	96, 54 (64% R)
Vermont 1968	22, 8 (73% R)	93, 55 (63% R)
Pennsylvania 1964	27, 22 (55% R)	93, 116 (56% D)
Pennsylvania 1966	27, 22 (55% R)	103, 99 (51% R)
Pennsylvania 1968*	27, 23 (54% R)	95, 108 (53% D)
Pennsylvania 1970	27, 23 (54% R)	90, 113 (56% D)
Indiana 1966	21, 29 (58% D)	66, 34 (66% R)
Indiana 1968	35, 15 (70% R)	73, 27 (73% R)
Indiana 1970*	29, 21 (58% R)	53, 46 (53% R)
Indiana 1972	29, 21 (58% R)	73, 27 (73% R)

(continued)

	Upper House (R, D)	Lower House (R, D)
Maryland 1966	8, 35 (82% D)	24, 118 (83% D)
Maryland 1968	8, 35 (82% D)	25, 117 (82% D)
Maryland 1970*	10, 33 (77% D)	21, 121 (85% D)
Maryland 1972	10, 33 (77% D)	21, 121 (85% D)
Maryland 1976*	8, 35 (81% D)	25, 117 (82% D)
Tennessee 1968	13, 20 (61% D)	49, 49 (50% D)
Tennessee 1970 (1971*)	13, 19 (59% D)	43, 56 (57% D)
Tennessee 1972	13, 19 (59% D)	43, 56 (57% D)
Tennessee 1974	12, 20 (62% D)	34, 63 (65% D)
Florida 1968	16, 32 (67% D)	42, 77 (65% D)
Florida 1970	15, 33 (69% D)	38, 81 (68% D)
Florida 1972*	14, 25 (64% D)	43, 77 (64% D)
Florida 1974	12, 27 (69% D)	34, 86 (72% D)
Wyoming 1968	19, 11 (63% R)	46, 16 (74% R)
Wyoming 1970	19, 11 (63% R)	40, 20 (67% R)
Wyoming 1972*	19, 11 (63% R)	40, 20 (67% R)
Wyoming 1974	17, 13 (57% R)	44, 17 (72% R)
Arizona 1970	17, 13 (60% R)	34, 26 (57% R)
Arizona 1972	18, 12 (60% R)	34, 26 (57% R)
Arizona 1974*	18, 12 (60% R)	38, 22 (63% R)
Arizona 1976	12, 18 (60% D)	33, 27 (55% D)
Kentucky 1974	8, 30 (79% D)	22, 78 (78% D)
Kentucky 1976	8, 30 (79% D)	23, 77 (77% D)
Nevada 1972	7, 13 (65% D)	22, 18 (55% R)
Nevada 1974	6, 14 (70% D)	15, 25 (63% D)
Nevada 1976*	3, 17 (85% D)	9, 31 (78% D)
Nevada 1978	3, 17 (85% D)	5, 35 (88% D)
New York 1974	37, 21 (64% R)	80, 68 (54% D)
New York 1976	34, 26 (57% R)	62, 88 (59% D)
New York 1977*	36, 21 (63% R)	58, 87 (60% D)
New York 1980	35, 25 (58% R)	64, 86 (57% D)
Hawaii 1974	8, 17 (68% D)	16, 35 (69% D)
Hawaii 1976	7, 18 (72% D	16, 35 (69% D)
Hawaii 1978*	7, 18 (72% D)	10, 41 (80% D)
Hawaii 1980	7, 18 (72% D)	9, 42 (82% D)

	Upper House (R, D)	Lower House (R, D)
South Dakota 1976	16, 19 (54% D)	37, 33 (53% R)
South Dakota 1978	23, 12 (66% R)	48, 22 (69% R)
South Dakota 1980	24, 11 (69% R)	48, 22 (69% R)
South Dakota 1982	25, 10 (71% R)	49, 21 (70% R)

Notes: Data based on Carl Klarner, "State Partisan Balance, 1959–2004," *State Politics and Policy Quarterly* (2006), www.ipsr.ku.edu/ SPPQ/journal_datasets/klarner.shtml. Accessed July 16, 2009; Walter Dean Burnham, "Partisan Division of American State Governments, 1834–1985" (electronic database, available at Harvard and MIT).

Hanssen also discusses "administration costs" (the procedural requirements for passing reform either by constitution or statute) and the age of the state, but these factors are weak. Almost all of the early merit states and most of the merit states overall had been in the Union for a century or more and required constitutional amendments, not merely statutes.

For a more general theory about party competition and judicial independence, see F. Andrew Hanssen, "Learning about Judicial Independence," 33 *Journal of Legal Studies* 431 (2004). See also Mark Ramseyer, "The Puzzling (In)Dependence of Courts: A Comparative Approach, 23 *Journal of Legal Studies* 721 (1994); Matthew Stephenson, "'When the Devil Turns . . .': The Political Foundations of Independent Judicial Review," 32 *Journal of Legal Studies* 59 (2003).

Notes

Introduction

1. And for the Sake of the Kids, "McGraw," http://www.youtube.com/watch ?v=HpVTVg56gic&feature=related. A follow-up ad defended these claims. "McGraw Wrong Again," http://www.youtube.com/watch?v=kzCSMqVM ZjI&feature=related. The script is also available at http://www.ncjudges .org/media/news_releases/11_11_04.html.
2. Adam Liptak, "Judicial Races in Several States Become Partisan Battlegrounds," *N.Y. Times,* Oct. 24, 2004; "Court Race Goes Negative: Benjamin Opens Campaign with Ads Attacking McGraw," *Charleston Daily Mail,* Aug. 25, 2004. See also Deborah Goldberg et al., *The New Politics of Judicial Elections, 2004 Report* at p. 4, at http://www.gavelgrab.org/wp-content/ resources/NewPoliticsReport2004.pdf.
3. Caperton v. A. T. Massey Coal Co., Inc., 129 S. Ct. 2252 (2009).
4. Id., 2263–64.
5. Id., 2266 (internal quotation omitted).
6. Avery v. State Farm Mut. Ins. Co., 835 N.E.2d 801 (Ill. 2005).
7. Justice at Stake 2004 report, at 19, http://www.justiceatstake.org/files/New PoliticsReport2004.pdf.
8. People v. Miller, 725 N.E.2d 48 (Ill. App. 2000).
9. *New Politics of Judicial Elections, 2004.*
10. Adam Liptak, "Judicial Races in Several States Become Partisan Battlegrounds," *N.Y. Times,* Oct. 24, 2004.
11. Id.
12. James Sample, "The Campaign Trial," Mar. 6, 2006, slate.com.
13. Avery v. State Farm, 547 U.S. 1003 (2006).
14. John Fund, "Wisconsin's Judicial Revolution," *Wall St. Journal,* Apr. 5, 2008; Patrick Marley, "Gableman Team Suggests Ethics Complaint Is Harassment,"

Wisconsin Journal-Sentinel, July 8, 2009; Ryan J. Foley, "Supreme Court Deadlocks in Gableman Ethics Case," *Wisconsin State Journal,* July 1, 2010; Justice at Stake, "2000–2008 Worst Judicial Campaign Ads," http://www .youtube.com/watch?v=4Du_WEHjMMw; "She Said," *Detroit Free Press,* Dec. 10, 2008, p. 2A; "Editorial: A Misleading Ad," *Milwaukee Journal-Sentinel,* Mar. 29, 2011; see also http://www.youtube.com/watch?v=sWif64wiTjY.

15. Crocker Stephenson, Cary Spivack, and Patrick Marley, "Justices' Feud Gets Physical," *Milwaukee Journal-Sentinel,* June 25, 2011; Eric Kleefeld, "Disorder in the Court: How Wisconsin Justice Became So Divisive," talkingpoints memo.com, June 30, 2011.
16. State v. Odom, 928 S.W.2d 18 (Tenn. 1996). See Traciel V. Reid, "The Politicization of Retention Elections: Lessons from the Defeat of Justices Lanphier and White," 83 *Judicature* 68, 70–71 (1999); Michael Dann and Randall M. Hansen, "Judicial Retention Elections," 34 *Loy. L.A. L. Rev.* 1429, 1431–37 (2001).
17. Penny J. White, et al., "Breaking the Most Vulnerable Branch: Do Rising Threats to Judicial Independence Preclude Due Process in Capital Cases?" 31 *Colum. Human Rights L. Rev.* 123, 140 (1999).
18. Varnum v. Brien, 763 N.W.2d 862 (2009).
19. Sandhya Somashekhar, "Opponents of Same-Sex Marriage Target Iowa Judges," *Wash. Post,* Aug. 26, 2010. Iowa Ethics and Campaign Disclosure Board, Campaign Disclosure Reports, at https://webapp.iecdb.iowa.gov /PublicView/?d=IndepExpend%2f2010; Campaign for Working Families at http://www.cwfpac.com/about.php.
20. Mike Glover, "Gay Marriage Foes Back Push to Oust Iowa Justices," *AP Daily Press,* Oct. 25, 2010.
21. Matthew Streb, *Running for Judge: The Rising Political, Financial and Legal Stakes of Judicial Elections,* 7 (2007).
22. Nine states that select judges by gubernatorial appointment are Connecticut, Delaware, Hawaii, Maine, Massachusetts, New Hampshire, New Jersey, Rhode Island, and Vermont. New York's lower-court judges are elected, but not its judges on its highest court, the court of appeals. South Carolina and Virginia use legislative appointment.
23. See, for example, *Justice at Stake Campaign, The New Politics of Judicial Elections* 2006, at 15 (2006), available at http://www.justiceatstake.org/me dia/cms/NewPoliticsofJudicialElections2006_D2A2449B77CDA.pdf; *Justice at Stake Campaign, The New Politics of Judicial Elections 2004,* at 19 (2004), available at http://www.justiceatstake.org/media/cms/NewPoliticsReport2004 _83BBFBD7C43A3.pdf.
24. *Justice at Stake Campaign, The New Politics of Judicial Elections, 2000–09: Decade of Change* (2010); Justice at Stake Campaign, Candidate Fund-Raising in Supreme Court Races by Rank, 2000–2008, http://www.justiceatstake.org /media/cms/JAS_20002008CourtCampaignExpenditur_63951A4654869 .pdf (last visited Jan. 31, 2010); *Justice at Stake Campaign, Money and Elections,* http://www.justiceatstake.org/issues/state_court_issues/money__elections .cfm (last visited Jan. 31, 2010).

25. Justice Paul Pfeifer, quoted in Adam Liptak and Janet Roberts, "Campaign Cash Mirrors High Court's Rulings," *N.Y. Times,* Oct. 1, 2006.

26. See Chapter 11 for citations of these studies.

27. Adam Liptak, "Looking Anew at Campaign Cash and Elected Judges," *N.Y. Times,* Jan. 29, 2008, A14; Adam Liptak and Janet Roberts, "Campaign Cash Mirrors a High Court's Rulings," *N.Y. Times,* Oct. 1, 2006, A1.

28. The American Bar Association's Model Code of Judicial Conduct has a long-standing rule against personal solicitations. A.B.A. Model Code of Conduct, Canon 7.B(2) (1972); A.B.A. Model Code of Conduct, Rule 4.1(A)(8) (2007). Norman Redlich, *Standards of Professional Conduct for Lawyers and Judges* (1984). More states have adopted the rule in their own codes.

29. U.S. Constitution, art. III, § 1.

30. Judith Resnik, "'Uncle Sam Modernizes His Justice': Inventing the Federal District Courts of the Twentieth Century for the District of Columbia and the Nation," 90 *Geo. L. J.* 607 (2002). See Karen Donovan, "Shareholders' Advocates Protest Justice's Removal," *National L. J.,* June 6, 1994, at B1; Diana B. Henriques, "Top Business Court Under Fire," *N.Y. Times,* May 23, 1995, at D1; Richard B. Schmitt, "Delaware Governor Picks Trial Judge for Supreme Court," *Wall St. Journal,* May 26, 1994, at B7; Jan Hoffman, "A Prominent Judge Retires, Objecting to the Governor's Litmus Test," *N.Y. Times,* Dec. 14, 1997, at 49; Peter Lewis, "Rice Won't Reappoint Judge Who Ruled Girl Enticed Attacker," *Seattle Times,* Oct. 10, 1990, at A1.

31. John Blume and Theodore Eisenberg, "Judicial Politics, Death Penalty Appeals, and Case Selection," 72 *S. Cal. L. Rev.* 465 (1999).

32. Fred R. Shapiro, "Quote . . . Misquote," *N.Y. Times,* July 27, 2008, Magazine at 16 (quoting *Daily Cleveland Herald,* Mar. 29, 1869) (attributing this quip to John Godfrey Saxe and noting its frequent misattribution to Otto von Bismarck).

33. Amalia D. Kessler, "Marginalization and Myth: The Corporatist Roots of France's Forgotten Elective Judiciary," 58 *Am. J. Comp. L.* 679 (2010); Mary L. Clark, "Judges Judging Judicial Candidates," 114 *Penn St. L. Rev.* 49 (2009); Adam Liptak, "Rendering Justice, with One Eye on Re-election," *N.Y. Times,* May 25, 2008. In addition to France, the other countries with such a civil service and testing system are the Czech Republic, Germany, Italy, Japan, Poland, Portugal, Spain, and Turkey. Chart, *N.Y. Times,* May 25, 2008.

34. The only other nations that elect even a small number of judges are Switzerland, Japan, and France, and these countries narrowly limit the scope of the elections. Steven P. Croley, "The Majoritarian Difficulty: Elective Judiciaries and the Rule of Law," 62 *U. Chi. L. Rev.* 689, 691 n.3 (1995); Kessler, "Marginalization and Myth."

35. "O'Connor Celebrates IJA and the Judiciary," IJA Rep. (Dwight D. Opperman Inst. of Judicial Admin. at NYU Sch. of L.), Winter 2006–7, at 2, available at http://www.law.nyu.edu/institutes/judicial/newsletters/newsletter5.pdf. See, for example, Paul J. DeMuniz, "Politicizing State Judicial Elections: A Threat to Judicial Independence," 38 *Willamette L. Rev.* 367, 387–88 (2002).

36. Alexis de Tocqueville, *Democracy in America* 269 (J. P. Mayer ed., George Lawrence trans., 1969) (1835). Those three states were Mississippi, Indiana, and Georgia.

37. Croley, "The Majoritarian Difficulty," 722; Caleb Nelson, "A Re-Evaluation of the Scholarly Explanations for the Rise of the Elective Judiciary in Antebellum America," 37 *Am. J. Legal Hist.* 190, 207 (1993).

38. For similar observations on particular stages of judicial elections, see Kermit L. Hall, "The Judiciary on Trial: State Constitutional Reform and the Rise of an Elected Judiciary, 1846–1860," at 45 *The Historian* 337 (1983); James A. Henretta, "The Rise and Decline of 'Democratic-Republicanism': Political Rights in New York and the Several States, 1800–1915," in *Toward a Usable Past* 50, 72–77 (Paul Finkelman and Stephen E. Gottlieb eds., 1991); F. Andrew Hanssen, "Learning About Judicial Independence: Institutional Change in the State Courts," 33 *J. Legal Stud.* 431 (2004). Caleb Nelson offers a mixed account, including the conclusion that judicial elections were meant to "hobble" the courts. Caleb Nelson, "A Re-Evaluation of the Scholarly Explanations for the Rise of the Elective Judiciary in Antebellum America," 37 *Am. J. Legal Hist.* 190, 207 (1993). This book elaborates, refines, and clarifies their interpretations while also challenging some of them.

39. See Robert. W. Gordon, "Critical Legal Histories," 36 *Stan. L. Rev.* 57, 103–13 (1984).

40. John Hart Ely, *Democracy and Distrust: A Theory of Judicial Review* (1980); Tom Ginsburg, *Judicial Review in New Democracies: Constitutional Courts in Asian Cases* 18 (2003); Ran Hirschl, *Towards Juristocracy: The Origins and Consequences of the New Constitutionalism* (2004) (arguing that elites align in "hegemonic preservation," rather than in competition with each other); Mark Ramseyer, "The Puzzling (In)Dependence of Courts: A Comparative Approach, 23 *J. Legal Stud.* 721 (1994); Matthew C. Stephenson, "'When the Devil Turns . . .': The Political Foundations of Independent Judicial Review," 32 *J. Legal Stud.* 59 (2003).

41. Gordon Wood, *The Creation of the American Republic: 1776–1787*, at 626 (1998 ed.).

42. Kenneth Stampp, *The Peculiar Institution: Slavery in the Antebellum South* (1956).

43. David Garland, *Peculiar Institution: America's Death Penalty in an Age of Abolition* (2010).

44. *Proceedings of the Constitutional Convention of the State of Georgia Held in Atlanta*, 1877, pp. 223–24 (Robert Toombs).

45. Lawrence Stone, *The Causes of the English Revolution 1529–1642*, at vii (1972). Stone's preconditions are more materialist, whereas I use the term to include ideology and intellectual trends.

1. Declaring Judicial Independence

1. Jefferson to Samuel Kercheval, July 12, 1816, in *The Writings of Thomas Jefferson* 15:34 (Andrew A. Lipscomb et al. eds., 1903).

2. Charles H. McIlwain, *The High Court of Parliament and Its Supremacy: An Historical Essay on the Boundaries between Legislation and Adjudication in England* 47–48, 71, 109, 119 (1910); J. H. Baker, *An Introduction to English Legal History* (2d ed. 1979).

3. Christine A. Desan, "Constitutional Commitment to Legislative Adjudication in the Early American Tradition," 111 *Harvard L. Rev.* 1469–70 (1998); J. W. Gough, *Fundamental Law in English Constitutional History* 41–47 (1955).

4. See "Judicial Action by the Provincial Legislature of Massachusetts," 15 *Harvard L. Rev.* 208–18 (1901); Mary Patterson Clarke, *Parliamentary Privilege in the American Colonies* 49–52, 117 (1943); Oliver Morton Dickerson, *American Colonial Government, 1696–1765: A Study of the British Board of Trade and Its Relation to the American Colonies, Political, Industrial, Administrative* 198–99 (1912); Carl Becker, *The History of Political Parties in the Province of New York, 1760–1776* 39 (1909); Gordon S. Wood, *The Creation of the American Republic, 1776–1787* 159 (1969); Desan, "Constitutional Commitment," 1495–1503; Leonard Levy, *Legacy of Suppression: Freedom of Speech and Press in Early American History* 20–23, 66–67 (1960). The General Assembly of Virginia had appellate jurisdiction until a royal order in 1682, but it and other colonial assemblies retained the power to grant new trials and revise judgments. Erwin C. Surrency, "The Courts in the American Colonies," 11 *Am. J. Legal History* 253, 261 (1967).

5. Wood, *Creation of the American Republic,* 154–55; see also Mary Patterson Clarke, "The Assembly as a Court," chap. 2 in Clarke, *Parliamentary Privilege;* Edward S. Corwin, "The Progress of Constitutional Theory between the Declaration of Independence and the Meeting of the Philadelphia Convention," 30 *American Historical Review* 513 (1925); Surrency, "Courts in the American Colonies," 260–61.

6. Surrency, "Courts in the American Colonies," 261.

7. Wood, *Creation of the American Republic,* 154.

8. Wesley W. Horton, *The Connecticut State Constitution: A Reference Guide* (1993); John D. Cushing, ed., *The Earliest Laws of the New Haven and Connecticut Colonies, 1639–1673* (1977); Dwight Loomis and J. Gilbert Calhoun, eds., *The Judicial and Civil History of Connecticut* (1895); David Mars and Fred Kort, *Administration of Justice in Connecticut, 1637–1957* 20–24 (1963); Robert J. Taylor, *Colonial Connecticut: A History* (1979).

9. *Bonham's Case,* 77 Eng. Rep. 646 (1610). On the debate about whether *Bonham's Case* in fact stood for judicial review of legislation or was consistent with legislative supremacy, see Gough, *Fundamental Law in English Constitutional History* (supporting the case for judicial review); R. H. Helmholz, "Bonham's Case, Judicial Review, and the Law of Nature," 1 *Journal of Legal Analysis* (2009).

10. J. H. Baker, *An Introduction to English Legal History* 144–45 (1979) (citing Acts of the Privy Council, 1615–1616).

11. Id.

12. Id.; Baker, *Introduction to English Legal History,* 145.

13. Joseph H. Smith, "An Independent Judiciary: The Colonial Background," 124 *U. Penn. L. Rev.* 1105–10 (1976).
14. Act of Settlement, 1701, 12 & 13 Will. 3, c. 2.
15. Barbara Aronstein Black, "Massachusetts and the Judges: Judicial Independence in Perspective," 3 *Law and History Review* 106–7 (1985).
16. F. W. Maitland, *The Constitutional History of England* 312–13 (1908); T. F. T. Plucknett, *A Concise History of the Common Law* 61 (2010).
17. Wood, *Creation of the American Republic,* 160; Black, "Massachusetts and the Judges," 108–09; Richard Ellis, *The Jeffersonian Crisis: Courts and Politics in the Young Republic* 6–7 (1971); Mary L. Volcansek and Jacqueline Lucienne Lafon, *Judicial Selection: The Cross-Evolution of French and American Practices* 19–20 (1988).
18. Scott Douglas Gerber, *The Origins of an Independent Judiciary, 1606–1787* (2010).
19. Plucknett, *Concise History,* 61–62.
20. John Locke, *The Second Treatise of Civil Government* §§ 143, 144, 150, 159 (1690).
21. Montesquieu, *Of the Laws Which Establish Political Liberty, with Regard to the Constitution,* chap. 6 in bk. 11 of *The Spirit of the Law* 157 (Anne M. Cohler trans. and ed., 1989).
22. William Blackstone, *Commentaries on the Laws of England* 1:259–60; 3:23–24 (1765).
23. John Adams, "Thoughts on Government (1776)," in *The Works of John Adams, Second President of the United States* 5:189, 198 (Charles Francis Adams ed., 1851).
24. Smith, "Independent Judiciary," 1121.
25. Id., 1122 (citing Bernard Bailyn, ed., *Pamphlets of the American Revolution, 1750–1776* 256–72 [1965]).
26. Id., 1125–28.
27. Benjamin Franklin, "The Causes of the American Discontents before 1768," in 5 *The Writings of Benjamin Franklin* 84 (Albert Henry Smyth ed., 1906).
28. Virginia Constitution of 1776; Willi Paul Adams, *The First American Constitutions: Republican Ideology and the Making of the State Constitutions in the Revolutionary Era* 267 (1980).
29. Donald S. Lutz, "The First American Constitutions," in *The Framing and Ratification of the Constitution* 73 (Leonard Levy and Denis Mahoney eds., 1987).
30. W. P. Adams, *First American Constitutions,* 267–68.
31. These states were Delaware, Evan Haynes, *The Selection and Tenure of Judges* 106 (2005); Maryland, id., at 115; Massachusetts, id.; New Hampshire, id. at 121; New York, id. at 123; North Carolina, id. at 124; South Carolina, id. at 128; and Virginia, id. at 133. Only four of those eight states adopted the model of executive appointment with legislative consent. These states were Maryland, id. at 115; Massachusetts, id.; New Hampshire, id. at 121; and New York, id. at 123. The other four chose legislative election

with no role for the governor. These states were Delaware, id. at 106; North Carolina, id. at 124; South Carolina, id. at 128; and Virginia, id. at 133.

32. Scott Gerber, *A Distinct Judicial Power* 327 (2011). Virginia and North Carolina granted judges "good behavior" tenure and limited removal to impeachment. New York did, too, but also had a mandatory retirement age of 60. South Carolina's 1790 constitution dropped the removal by address option, leaving only impeachment.

33. Id., 121–22, 127.

34. Id., 108, 127–28.

35. Gerber, *A Distinct Judicial Power,* 329; Haynes, *Selection and Tenure,* 105; *Charter of Connecticut* (1662).

36. Gerber, *Distinct Judicial Power,* 327. Virginia, Maryland, Massachusetts, North Carolina, Pennsylvania, and Delaware were the six protecting judicial salaries.

37. Wood, *Creation of the American Republic,* 161; see also Martha Andes Ziskind, "Judicial Tenure in the American Constitution: English and American Precedents," *Supreme Court Review* 138–47 (1969).

38. Corwin, "Progress of Constitutional Theory," 514; John Phillip Reid, *Legislating the Courts: Judicial Dependence in Early National New Hampshire* (2009).

39. Max Farrand, *Records of the Federal Convention of 1787,* at 119 (1911).

40. Id., 120.

41. Id.

42. U.S. Constitution, art. II, § 2; art. III, § 1.

43. Larry Kramer, *The People Themselves: Popular Constitutionalism and Judicial Review* 75 (2004).

44. "The Federalist No. 78," in *The Federalist Papers* 437 (Isaac Kramnick ed., 1987).

45. Id., 440.

46. Id., 437.

47. Id., 441.

48. Id., 442.

49. Gordon Wood, *The Creation of the American Republic: 1776–1787,* at 626 (1998 ed.). Jack Rakove refers to the Federalists' "aristocratic conception of politics," but notes that they "subverted" it with their use of democratic rhetoric during the ratification debates. Jack Rakove, *Original Meanings: Politics and Ideas in the Making of the Constitution* 133 (1996). But generally, Rakove points to instances when the Federalists objected to attacks of "aristocracy." Rakove, *Original Meanings,* 276–77.

   There has been over a century of debate on the economic interpretations of the American constitution. Among a number of different priorities, including building national and military strength and a robust civic republic, the Federalists sought to protect private property and commercial development. See Charles Beard, *An Economic Interpretation* (1913); Robert A. McGuire, *To Form a More Perfect Union: A New Economic Interpretation of the U.S. Constitution* (2003); Jennifer Nedelsky, *Private Property and the Limits of American Constitutionalism: The Madisonian Framework and Its Legacy* 22–25, 73–75 (1990); but see Max Edling, *A Revolution in Favor of Government: The Origins of the U.S. Constitution and the Making of the American State* (2003); Forrest McDonald, *We the People: The Economic Origins of the Constitution* (1992); Robert E. Brown, *Charles Beard and the Constitution* (1956). See also Stephen L. Elkin, *Reconstructing the Commercial Republic: Constitutional Design after Madison* 19–50 (2006) (viewing Madison as balancing propertied classes and lower classes).

50. Gordon Wood, *The Radicalism of the American Revolution* 323(1991).
51. See James Wilson in the Pennsylvania Ratification Debates, 4 *The Founders' Constitution* 139 (Philip B. Kurland and Ralph Lerner eds., 1987) ("I believe that public happiness, personal liberty, and private property, depend essentially upon the able and upright determinations of independent judges"). For later Federalists, see 1 St. George Tucker, *Blackstone's Commentaries* (1803), editor's app. at 354 (The Constitution seeks to secure judicial independence to protect the "life, liberty, [and] property of the citizens of America"); 1 James Kent, *Commentaries on American Law* (1826), at 273 (noting the importance of judicial independence for the preservation of "personal security[] and private property").
52. Id.
53. John Fabian Witt, *Patriots and Cosmopolitans: Hidden Histories of American Law* 63–69 (2007); see also Bernard Bailyn, "The Democracy Unleashed," *Ideological Origins of the American Revolution* 272–301 (1967) (2d ed. 1992).
54. James Madison, *Notes of Debates in the Federal Convention of 1787* (1987), at 73 (Gerry), 235 (Morris), 250 (Mason), 402 (Butler), 413 (Mason), 427 (Madison), 450–53 (Mason, Mercer, and Gerry), 584 (Randolph), 651 (Mason).
55. Hamilton, Speech of 18 June 1787, in Farrand, *Records*, I:299. See also id. at 288–89, 309–10; Daniel Hulsebosch, *Constituting Empire*, 235.
56. Madison, *Notes*, 251.
57. This quotation is according to John Lansing's notes, in James H. Hutson, ed., *Supplement to Max Farrand's Records of the Federal Convention of 1787*, at 142 (1987).
58. James Kent to Nathaniel Lawrence, 9 Nov. 1787, in Merrill Jensen, *The Documentary History of the Ratification of the Constitution*, 14:75; see also Robert R. Livingston, in Elliott, *Debates*, 2:277–78; Daniel Hulsebosch, *Constituting Empire*, 233.
59. Herbert J. Storing, *What the Anti-Federalists Were For: The Political Thought of the Opponents of the Constitution* 2:44 (1981).
60. Hartz, *Liberal Tradition in America*, 102–06; Hulsebosch, *Constituting Empire*, 238.
61. Daniel Hulsebosch, "A Discrete and Cosmopolitan Minority: The Loyalists, the Atlantic World, and the Origins of Judicial Review," 81 *Chicago-Kent Law Review* 825, 865 (2006).

62. Bruce Mann, *Republic of Debtors* 81–94 (2002).
63. John Bach McMaster and Frederick D. Stone, *Pennsylvania and the Federal Constitution, 1787–88,* at 280 (1888); Storing, *What the Anti-Federalists Were For,* 51.
64. James Madison, "The Federalist No. 51," in *The Federalist Papers;* Storing, *What the Anti-Federalists Were For* 2:48–49, 52 (citing Federalist Farmer IV, 2.8.58; [Maryland] Farmer II, 5.1.30); Saul Cornell, *The Other Founders: Anti-Federalism and the Dissenting Tradition in America* 30, 52, 69, 71, 107, 134, 151–52 (1999); Saul Cornell, "Aristocracy Assailed: The Ideology of Backcountry Anti-Federalism," *Journal of American History* 76, no. 4 (Mar. 1990).
65. Cornell, *Other Founders.*
66. Brutus, "XI: The Supreme Court: They Will Mould the Government into Almost Any Shape They Please," *New York Journal,* Jan. 31, 1788, repr. in Herbert J. Storing, ed., *The Complete Anti-Federalist* 2:129–30 (1981).
67. U.S. Const., art. VI; Kramer, *People Themselves.*
68. Brutus, "XI: The Supreme Court," repr. in Storing, *Complete Anti-Federalist,* 2:130.
69. Brutus, "XV: The Supreme Court: No Power Above Them That Can Controul Their Decisions, or Correct Their Errors," *New York Journal,* Mar. 20, 1788, reprinted in Storing, *Complete Anti-Federalist,* 2:372–73.
70. See Jackson Turner Main, *The Anti-Federalists: Critics of the Constitution, 1781–1788* 156 (2004).
71. Brutus, "XV: The Supreme Court," in Storing, *Complete Anti-Federalist,* 2:374.
72. Id., 377–78 (emphasis in original).
73. Brutus, "XVI," repr. in Storing, *Complete Anti-Federalist,* 188.
74. See Main, *Anti-Federalist,* 156.
75. 4 *Worcester Magazine* 243 (1788).
76. Volcansek and Lafon, *Judicial Selection,* 50–69.
77. Pa. Const. of 1790, art. 5, §§ 2, 4.
78. Horton, *Connecticut State Constitution.*
79. Connecticut Const. of 1818, art. 5, § 3.
80. Peter J. Galie, *The New York State Constitution* (1991).
81. James Pfander and Jonathan L. Hunt, "Public Wrongs and Private Bills: Indemnification and Government Accountability in the Early Republic," 85 *N.Y.U. L. Rev.* 1862 (2010).
82. Connecticut would turn back to electing lower court judges in 1850, in the middle of the wave of adoptions. See Kermit L. Hall, "The Judiciary on Trial: State Constitutional Reform and the Rise of an Elected Judiciary, 1846–1860," 45 *Historian* 337 (May 1983); Jon C. Blue, "Judicial Tenure in Connecticut: How It Was Gained and How It Was Lost, 1818–1863," 20 *Quinnipiac Law Review* 152–53 (2000).
83. See, for example, James Wilson in the Pennsylvania Ratification Debates, 4 *The Founders' Constitution* 139 ("I believe that public happiness, personal

liberty, and private property, depend essentially upon the able and upright determinations of independent judges").

84. See Jed Handelsman Shugerman, "*Marbury* and Judicial Deference," 5 *Univ. of Pennsylvania Journal of Constitutional Law* 58 (2003). See also John Phillip Reid, *Legislating the Courts: Judicial Dependence in Early National New Hampshire* (2008); Richard Ellis, *The Jeffersonian Crisis: Courts and Politics in the Young Republic* (1971).

2. Judicial Challenges in the Early Republic

1. See, for example, Philip Hamburger, *Law and Judicial Duty* (2008); Larry Kramer, *The People Themselves: Popular Constitutionalism and Judicial Review* (2004); William Treanor, "Judicial Review Before *Marbury*," 58 *Stan. L. Rev.* 455 (2005).
2. Mary Sarah Bilder, "The Corporate Origins of Judicial Review," 116 *Yale L. J.* 502 (2006).
3. Kramer, *People Themselves*; Barry Friedman, *The Will of the People*, 33–38 (2009).
4. Friedman, *Will of the People*, 31–33, 41–43.
5. Keith Whittington, "Judicial Review of Congress before the Civil War," 97 *Geo. L. J.* 1257 (2009); Mark Graber, "Naked Land Transfers and American Constitutional Development," 53 *Vanderbilt L. Rev.* 73 (2000).
6. 1 H. & J. 236 (Md. 1802).
7. Robert Lowry Clinton, *Marbury v. Madison and Judicial Review*, 76–77, 76 n.95 (1989); Paul S. Clarkson and R. Samuel Jett, *Luther Martin of Maryland* 200 (1970); Charles G. Haines, *The American Doctrine of Judicial Supremacy* 106–08 (1914); Sylvia Snowiss, "The Marbury of 1803 and the Modern Marbury," 20 *Const. Commentary* 231, 241 (2003); William M. Meigs, "The Relation of the Judiciary to the Constitution," 19 *American L. Rev.* 185 (Mar.–Apr. 1885): 185; James B. Thayer, "The Origin and Scope of the American Doctrine of Constitutional Law," 7 *Harvard L. Rev.* 140 (1893). For court decisions crediting *Whittington* as a foundation for the doctrine of judicial review, see, for example, Attorney General of Maryland. v. Waldron, 426 A.2d 929 (Md. 1981); Perkins v. Eskridge, 366 A.2d 21 (Md. 1976); Murphy v. Yates, 348 A.2d 837, 848 & n.9 (Md. 1975); Jones v. Freeman, 146 P.2d 564 (Okla. 1943). But see Richard E. Ellis, *The Jeffersonian Crisis: Courts and Politics in the Young Republic* 244 (1971).
8. *Whittington*, 1 H. & J. at 244.
9. Brutus, "XV: The Supreme Court: No Power above Them That Can Controul Their Decisions, or Correct Their Errors," *N. Y. Journal*, Mar. 20, 1788, reprinted in Herbert J. Storing, *What the Anti-Federalists Were For: The Political Thought of the Opponents of the Constitution* 2:377–78 (1981) (emphasis in original).
10. Deuteronomy 4:34, 7:19, 11:2, 26:8; see also Exodus 6:6, Psalms 136:12.

11. The conspiracy to kill Caesar began when Caesar had engineered his appointment for life. Cassius Dio, *Roman History*, 44.8.4.

12. Kramer, *People Themselves*, 3–6.

13. Susan Dunn, *Jefferson's Second Revolution* 209–10 (2004).

14. Id.; James Roger Sharp, *The Deadlocked Election of 1800: Jefferson, Burr, and the Union in the Balance* (2010); Bruce Ackerman, *The Failure of the Founding Fathers: Jefferson, Marshall, and the Rise of Presidential Democracy* (2005).

15. Ellis, *Jeffersonian Crisis*; John Philip Reid, *Legislating the Courts* (2008).

16. Jed Shugerman, "Marbury and Judicial Deference," 5 *University of Pennsylvania Journal of Constitutional Law* 58 (2003).

17. An Act to Provide for the More Convenient Organization of the Courts of the United States, ch. 4, 2 Stat. 89 (1801) [hereinafter the Judiciary Act of 1801].

18. An Act to Repeal Certain Acts Respecting the Organization of the Courts of the United States; and for Other Purposes, ch. 8, 2 Stat. 132 (1802) [hereinafter the Repeal Act]; An Act to Amend the Judicial System of the United States, ch. 31, 2 Stat. 156 (1802).

19. Marbury v. Madison, 5 U.S. (1 Cranch) 137 (1803).

20. Stuart v. Laird, 5 U.S. (1 Cranch) 299 (1803).

21. Maryland Constitution, XL, XLVII, LX, Declaration of Rights, XXXIII.

22. Maryland Constitution of 1776, Declaration of Rights, art. XXX.

23. *Whittington*, 1 H. & J. 236, 249 (1802).

24. C. Ashley Ellefson, *The County Courts and the Provincial Courts in Maryland, 1733–1763*, at 43, 51, 133 (1990).

25. L. Marx Renzulli, Jr., *Maryland: The Federalist Years* 187 (1972); Norman K. Risjord, *Chesapeake Politics, 1781–1800*, at 517–19, 544–45 (1978).

26. Ellis, *Jeffersonian Crisis*, 243–44; An Act for the Better Administration of Justice in the Several Counties of the State, §§ II, V (1796), in William Kilty, ed., *The Laws of Maryland*, vol. 2 (1800).

27. Id. § IV, ch. XLIII. Section XVIII limits the way justices may be replaced. There was no time limit on the term of office held during good behavior, so the office was for life

28. *Whittington*, 1 H. & J., 239.

29. Id.

30. "'Fellow Citizen,' To Mr. Wright of the Senate of the United States," *Washington Federalist*, Feb. 9, 1802. In the summer of 1801, a Federalist sympathizer observed that the Federalists had made the judiciary a polarizing partisan issue. William Pinkney to Ninian Pinkney, July 21, 1801, in William Pinkney, ed., *The Life of William Pinkney* 38–39 (1853).

31. Renzulli, *Maryland*, 220, 226–27; "'Fellow Citizen,' To Mr. Wright of the Senate of the United States," *Washington Federalist*, Feb. 9, 1802.

32. "From Annapolis," *Baltimore American*, Nov. 13, 1801.

33. Ellis, *Jeffersonian Crisis*, 243–44; Clarkson and Jett, *Luther Martin*, 198.

34. *Maryland Gazette*, Jan. 14, 1802; Kilty, *Laws of Maryland*, ch. XLIII.

35. The two other Republican appointees were William Clagett and Richard Sprigg. Sprigg had served in the U.S. House of Representatives as a Republican in the 1790s. Renzulli, *Maryland*, 188.
36. *Whittington*, 1 H. & J. 236, 239 (Md. 1802). The term "disseised" is used in the context of the assize of novel disseisin, referring to the seizing of another's property.
37. Id., 236.
38. *Pittsfield Sun* (Mass.), reprinted in *Independent Chronicle* (Boston), Sept. 6, 1802. See also *Gazette of the U.S.* (Phila.), Jan. 25, 1802; *U.S. Chronicle* (Providence), Feb. 11, 1802; "A Marylander," *Washington Federalist*, Dec. 31, 1801; *National Intelligencer* (Washington, D.C.), Dec. 30, 1801; *Baltimore Democratic Republican*, June 24, 1802. One indication of the obvious importance of this trial was the prominence of Whittington's counsel: two Federalist congressmen, Luther Martin, one of the framers of the Constitution, and Robert Goodloe Harper, one of the leaders of the Federalist Party. Clarkson and Jett, *Luther Martin*, 200–01.
39. *U.S. Chronicle*, Feb. 11, 1802 (emphasis in original). See also "Fellow Citizen," *Washington Federalist*, Feb. 9 and Feb. 15, 1802; *Gazette of the U.S.*, Jan. 25, 1802; "Fellow Citizen," *Washington Federalist*, Feb. 15, 1802.
40. "A Marylander," *Washington Federalist*, Dec. 31, 1801.
41. 11 *Annals of Congress* 108–09 (1802).
42. Id., 110.
43. Edward C. Papenfuse et al., *A Biographical Dictionary of the Maryland Legislature, 1635–1789*, at 291 (1985). See also "Judge Gabriel Duvall," *Marlborough Gazette*, Gabriel Duvall Papers, Library of Congress, Washington, D.C.; *Baltimore American*, July 1, 8, 9, 15, 16, Aug. 19, 20, 1800; *Maryland Gazette*, Aug. 14, 1800; Renzulli, *Maryland*, 216; *Maryland Gazette*, Sept. 11, 1800.
44. *Baltimore American*, July 1, 1800; Risjord, *Chesapeake Politics*, 559. Duvall amassed 2,379 votes to Chase's 774 votes (approximately). *Maryland Gazette*, Nov. 20, 1800.
45. James Haw et al., *Stormy Patriot: The Life of Samuel Chase* 6 (1980).
46. Id.
47. Papenfuse et al., *Biographical Dictionary*, 213–16; Jane S. Elsmere, *Justice Samuel Chase*, 36, 44, 128, 233 (1980); Haw, *Stormy Patriot*, 149, 207–08.
48. *American & Commercial Daily Advertiser* (Baltimore, Md.), Feb. 2, 1801.
49. Papenfuse et al., *Biographical Dictionary*, 273–74.
50. *Pittsfield Sun* (Mass.), reprinted in *Independent Chronicle* (Boston), Sept. 6, 1802.
51. Id.
52. Repeal Act, ch. 8, 2 Stat. 132 (1802); An Act to Amend the Judicial System of the United States, ch. 31, 2 Stat. 156 (1802).
53. John Rutledge to James A. Bayard, Mar. 26, 1802, Collery Collection, Historical Society of Delaware, Wilmington, Del.
54. Probably hearing this same message from Ross, Gouverneur Morris noted in his diary on April 5 that "Mr. Ross calls to tell me he is advised that the

Chief Justice is disposed to go quite as far as we could wish." Diary of Gouverneur Morris, Apr. 5, 1802, in Gouverneur Morris Papers, Library of Congress, Washington, D.C. Holt mistakenly cites this passage to April 6 of the diary. See Wythe Holt, "'If the Courts have firmness enough to render the decision': Egbert Benson and the Protest of the 'Midnight Judges' Against Repeal of the Judiciary Act of 1801," in Wythe Holt and David A. Nourse, *Egbert Benson, First Chief Judge of the Second Circuit (1801–1802)*, at 10 (1987) (describing the Federalist plans as "buoyed by the report from Richmond").

55. Chief Justice John Marshall to Justice William Paterson, Apr. 5, 1802, in *The Papers of John Marshall* 6:106 (Charles F. Hobson ed., 1990).

56. Justice Samuel Chase to Justice William Paterson, Apr. 6, 1802, William Paterson Papers, MSS Room (Lenox), New York Public Library, New York, N.Y.

57. Justice Samuel Chase to Chief Justice John Marshall, Apr. 24, 1802, reprinted in George Lee Haskins and Herbert A. Johnson, *Foundations of Power: John Marshall, 1801–15*, at 174–75 (1981):

> But by neither of these modes, nor by any other (as Mandamus or Quo Warranto) could remedy be obtained. This *defect* of remedy to obtain a Right (which Justice abhors) will induce every Judge of the Supreme Court to act with the greatest caution; and he must, in my judgement, decline to execute the office of a Circuit Judge, if he apprehends, that he shall, thereby, violate the Constitutional Rights of the Circuit Judges.

58. James A. Bayard to Richard Bassett, Apr. 24, 1802, Bayard Papers, Maryland Historical Society, Baltimore, Md.; James A. Bayard to Alexander Hamilton, Apr. 25, 1802, in *The Papers of Alexander Hamilton* 25:613–14 (Harold C. Syrett ed., 1977); Diary of Gouverneur Morris, Apr. 24, 1805, Gouverneur Morris Papers, Library of Congress, Washington, D.C.

59. Holt, "If the Courts," 110–11.

60. Haskins and Johnson, *Foundations of Power*, 177 (citing a letter from William Cushing to William Paterson, May 29, 1802, Miscellaneous Manuscripts, William Cushing, New-York Historical Society, New York, N.Y.).

61. Id.

62. *Whittington*, 1 H. & J. 236, 241–42 (Md. 1802).

63. Id., 243. See also id. at 246.

64. Id., 246.

65. Id. See Caleb Nelson, "Judicial Review of Legislative Purpose," 83 *N.Y.U. L. Rev.* 1784 (2010) for a reference to *Whittington* and judicial review of intent.

66. *Whittington*, 1 H. & J. at 248.

67. Id., 249.

68. See *Washington Federalist*, Dec. 21, 22, 29, 1801; Jan. 7, 9, 12, 19, 28; Feb. 4, 10, 20; and Mar. 19, 22, 31, 1802. For the identification of Lucius Junius Brutus as Cranch, see William Cushing, *Initials and Pseudonyms* 42 (1885).

69. Lucius Junius Brutus, "No. 10," *Washington Federalist*, Feb. 4, 1802.

70. Lucius Junius Brutus, "No. 12," *Washington Federalist*, Mar. 19, 1802 (citing Harcourt v. Fox, 1 Shower's Parliamentary Cases 516 [1693]). The following

information in the paragraph is from this *Washington Federalist* article, unless otherwise noted.

71. Id.

72. Lucius Junius Brutus, "No. 14," *Washington Federalist*, Mar. 31, 1802 (emphasis in original).

73. 10 U.S. 87 (1810).

74. 17 U.S. 518 (1819).

75. Id., 249–50. Chase noted only one exception to this rule, the case of elegit, a judgment of debt, damages, or forfeiture. He explained that it bore no similarity to Whittington's case, and thus there was no way for the court to extend the writ by equity.

76. 2 William Blackstone, *Commentaries*, 120–21.

77. Sir Frederick Pollock and Frederic William Maitland, *The History of English Law Before the Time of Edward I*, 2:134 (1895).

78. Id.

79. Whittington v. Polk, at 251 (Duvall, J., dissenting).

80. Carroll Bond, *The Court of Appeals of Maryland: A History*, 78–79, 88–89 (1928).

81. The Maryland Constitution required two successive legislative assemblies to vote to amend the constitution, with the second vote following a new election. Maryland Constitution of 1776, Sec. LIX.

82. Roger Griswold to Oliver Wolcott, Mar. 5, 1801, Oliver Wolcott Papers, Connecticut Historical Society, Hartford, Conn.

83. John Randolph to Joseph Nicholson, July 25, 1802, in Shippen Papers, Library of Congress, Washington, D.C.

84. Letter from Charles Carroll to Robert Goodloe Harper, June 15, 1802, Robert Goodloe Harper Papers, Maryland Historical Society, Baltimore, Md.

85. *Baltimore Democratic Republican*, June 22 and 24, 1802; *Maryland Gazette*, June 24, 1802; *Washington Federalist*, June 30, 1802.

86. "Read! Assize of Novel Disseisin," *Baltimore Democratic Republican*, June 24, 1802.

87. *National Intelligencer* (Washington, D.C.), June 14, 1802; "Judiciary," *Baltimore Democratic Republican*, June 24, 1802.

88. *Pittsfield Sun*, reprinted in *Independent Chronicle*, Sept. 6, 1802.

89. Id.

90. *Washington Federalist*, June 30, 1802.

91. Friedman, *Will of the People*, 64 (citing *Republican Watch-Tower*, May 21, 1803).

92. Mark Graber, "Establishing Judicial Review: *Marbury* and the Judicial Act of 1789," 38 *Tulsa L. Rev.* 627 (2003).

93. Albert Beveridge, *The Life of John Marshall* 3:153 (1944); Clinton, *Marbury and Judicial Review*, 102–03; Donald Dewey, *Marshall versus Jefferson: The Political Background of* Marbury v. Madison, 135–36 (1970); Haines, *American Doctrine of Judicial Supremacy*, 232; Haskins and Johnson, *Foundations of Power*, 215–17; Robert G. McCloskey, *The American*

Supreme Court, 43–44 (1960); Charles Warren, *The Supreme Court in United States History*, 1:231–32 (1922). One suggestion is that the lay press failed to understand the complexities of the decision. Another suggestion is that state courts, like the Maryland General Court, had already announced the doctrine of judicial review, so *Marbury* was no big news. However, if writers understood that the U.S. Supreme Court was now adopting this doctrine as a direct challenge to the Republicans, then this would have been very big news. Clinton, *Marbury and Judicial Review*, 102–03.

94. For more on *Laird*, see Haskins & Johnson, *Foundations of Power*, 180–81; Bruce Ackerman, *The Failure of the Founding Fathers*, 179–86 (2005).

95. Maryland Constitution of 1776, sec. LVI.

96. U.S. Constitution, Article III, Sec. 1.

97. Haskins and Johnson, *Foundations of Power*, 215–17; Friedman, *Will of the People*, 63.

98. Susan Low Bloch, "The *Marbury* Mystery: Why Did William Marbury Sue in the Supreme Court?" 18 *Const. Commentary* 607 (2001).

99. William W. Van Alstyne, "A Critical Guide to *Marbury v. Madison*," 1969 *Duke L.J.* 1, 15; Robert J. Pushaw, Jr., "Justiciability and Separation of Powers: A Neo-Federalist Approach," 81 *Cornell L. Rev.* 393, 446–47 (1996); Edward S. Corwin, *The Doctrine of Judicial Review* 7–9 (1914); David P. Currie, "The Constitution in the Supreme Court: The Powers of the Federal Courts, 1801–1835," 49 *U. Chicago L. Rev.* 646, 653 (1982); Akhil Reed Amar, "*Marbury*, Section 13, and the Original Jurisdiction of the Supreme Court," 56 *U. Chi. L. Rev.* 443, 453–64 (1989). But see Louise Weinberg, "Our *Marbury*," 89 *Va. L. Rev.* 1235 (2003); James E. Pfander, "*Marbury*, Original Jurisdiction, and the Supreme Court's Supervisory Powers," 101 *Colum. L. Rev.* 1515, 1539–46 (2001).

100. Ellis, *Jeffersonian Crisis*, 244.

101. Maryland Constitution of 1776, Sec. LIX.

102. Haw et al., *Stormy Patriot*, 215.

103. Id.

104. Ellis, *Jeffersonian Crisis*, 244.

105. Id., 245.

106. Id., 102–07.

107. William Cushing to Samuel Chase, June 11, 1802, Cushing Papers, Massachusetts Historical Society, Boston, Mass.

108. Friedman, *Will of the People*, 67; Haskins and Johnson, *Foundations of Power*, 238–45.

109. Haskins and Johnson, *Foundations of Power*, 245.

110. In addition to the boycott question, it is possible that the justices might have shifted course on *Stuart v. Laird*. As late as December 1802, Federalists speculated that there would be two dissents in *Stuart v. Laird*—presumably Marshall and Chase. Sen. William Plumer to Livermore, Dec. 12, 1802, Plumer Papers, Library of Congress, Washington, D.C: "It is said Chief Justice Marshall has over-ruled a plea to the jurisdiction of the Circuit Court in Virginia, without deciding whether the repeal of the Judiciary law was

constitutional. A writ of l___ [original illegible] is bro't [brought] & it is said the Supreme Court will, with two dissenting votes, confirm the decision." Given a few changes of events, it is possible that Justice Chase might at least have followed through with dissents, especially if he had been emboldened by the Maryland court.

111. Jesse Higgins, *Sampson against the Philistines, or the Reformation of Lawsuits* (1805).
112. Ellis, *Jeffersonian Crisis*, 177.
113. Id., 153–56.
114. Ohio Constitution of 1803, art. 3, § 8.
115. Rutherford v. M'Fadden, (Ohio 1807), in *Ohio Unreported Judicial Decisions—Prior to 1823*, at 71 (1952)
116. Donald F. Melhorn, *"Lest We Be Marshall'd": Judicial Powers and Politics in Ohio, 1806–1812* (2003), appendix C (quoting "Articles of Impeachment Against George Tod," Ohio Senate, Seventh General Assembly, Journal, 54–55 [1809]).
117. William B. Neff, *Bench and Bar of Northern Ohio* 52 (1921).
118. Ellis, *Jeffersonian Crisis*, 164.
119. Id., 165, 170, 181.
120. Id., 181.
121. Beadleston v. Sprague, 6 Johns. 101 (N.Y. S. Ct. Jud., 1810); Dash v. Van Kleeck, 7 Johns. 477 (N.Y. S. Ct. Jud., 1811); Roosevelt v. Cebra, 17 Johns. 108; 1819 N.Y. Lexis 118 (N.Y. S. Ct. Jud., 1819); People v. Platt, 17 Johns. 195; 1819 N.Y. Lexis 143, October, (N.Y. S. Ct. Jud., 1819); Post v. Riley, 18 Johns. 54; 1820 N.Y. Lexis 50 (N.Y. S. Ct. Jud., 1820); People v. Foot, 19 Johns. 58 (N.Y. 1821) (appointment powers of the Council of Appointment); In re Wendell, 19 Johns. 153; 1821 N.Y. Lexis 51 (N.Y. S. Ct. Jud., 1821) (debt, obligations of contract).
122. Hulsebosch, *Constituting Empire*, 270–71.
123. Jack Peltason, "Missouri Plan for the Selection of Judges," *University of Missouri Studies* 20, no.2 (1945): 11–12 (quoting the *Missouri Republican*, June 26, 1822).
124. Id., 14 (quoting the *Missouri Republican*, May 22, 1822).
125. Amendment of 1822 to the 1820 Constitution, art. 1, § 7.
126. Amendment of 1834–35 to the 1820 Constitution, art. 2, § 1.
127. Theodore Ruger, "'The Question which Convulses a Nation': The Early Republic's Greatest Debate About the Judicial Review Power," 117 *Harv. L. Rev.* 826 (2004); Kramer, *People Themselves*, 151–52.
128. Nelson v. Allen, 9 Tenn. 360, 1830 WL 883, 1 Yer. 360 (Tenn. 1830) (1813 statute: obligations of contracts); Marr v. Enloe, 9 Tenn. 452, 1830 WL 901, 1 Yer. 452 (Tenn. Ct. Err. & App., 1830) (1824 and 1827 statutes: unequal taxation); State Bank v. Cooper, 10 Tenn. 599, 1831 WL 1032, 24 Am. Dec. 517, 2 Yer. 599 (Tenn. 1831) (1829 statute: creation of a special court for the determination of suits commenced by the Bank of the State of Tennessee against its officers, is unconstitutional as a partial law, violating right to jury trial, and not "law of the land" under Tennessee Constitution); Tate's Ex'rs

v. Bell, 12 Tenn. 202, 1833 WL 1093, 26 Am. Dec. 221, 4 Yer. 202 (Tenn. 1833) (1829 act authorizing executors to revive a judgment is a partial law; separation of powers); Lowry v. McGhee, 16 Tenn. 242, 1835 WL 943, 8 Yer. 242 (Tenn. 1835) (1820 act, in allowing bank note for debt payments, violates U.S. Const. art. 1, § 10, which prohibits any State making anything but gold and silver coin a tender in payment of debts).

129. Wally's Heirs v. Kennedy,10 Tenn. 554, 1831 WL 1023, 24 Am. Dec. 511, 2 Yer. 554 (Tenn. 1831) (striking down a statute barring suits by Cherokee "reservees"); Cornet v. Winton's Lessee, 10 Tenn. 142 (1826); Blair v. Path-killer's Lessee, 10 Tenn. 406 (1830).

130. Timothy Heubner, "Judicial Independence in an Age of Democracy, Sectionalism, and War, 1835–1865," in *The History of the Tennessee Supreme Court*, 61–74 (James W. Ely, Jr. ed., 2002).

131. Shugerman, "Economic Crisis and the Rise of Judicial Elections and Judicial Review," 123 *Harvard L. Rev.* 1061 (2010).

132. See Evan Haynes, *The Selection and Tenure of Judges* (2005), at 108 (Georgia: three-year terms); id. at 110 (Indiana: seven-year terms); id. at 121 (New Jersey: seven-year terms); id. at 125 (Ohio: seven-year terms); id. at 127–28 (Rhode Island: at pleasure of the legislature); id. at 132 (Vermont: one-year terms); Connecticut adopted one-year terms for lower court judges in 1818. Id. at 105–06.

133. Alabama switched to six-year terms, Amendment of 1830, art. 5, § 13. Tennessee switched judicial tenure from good behavior to twelve years for supreme court judges and eight years for the lower courts. Tennessee Constitution of 1835, art. 6, §§ 3, 4. Arkansas adopted eight-year terms for supreme court judges and four-year terms for circuit court judges. Arkansas Constitution of 1836, art. 6, § 7. Pennsylvania switched from good behavior to fifteen-year terms for supreme court justices and ten-year terms for the court of common pleas in 1838. Pennsylvania Constitution of 1838, art. 5, § 2. Florida adopted five-year terms for its judges in 1838, but it did not become a state until 1845. Florida Constitution of 1838, art. 5, §§ 11, 12. Only Georgia, Indiana, Mississippi, and Michigan adopted judicial elections on any level from 1810 to 1844.

134. *Whittington*, 1 H. & J. 236, 243 (Md. 1802).

135. 10 U.S. (6 Cranch) 87 (1810). See Chapter 3, "Judicial Elections as Separation of Powers."

136. Kramer, *People Themselves*, 174 (citing Pennsylvania mobilizing its militia after United States v. Peters (9 U.S. (5 Cranch) 115 (1809); Virginia contesting Martin v. Hunter's Lessee, 14 U.S. 304 (1816) and Cohens v. Virginia, 19 U.S. 264 (1821); Kentucky rejecting Green v. Biddle, 21 U.S. 1 (1823); and Ohio staging a bank war over M'Culloch v. Maryland, 17 U.S. 316 (1819), leading to Osborn v. Bank of the United States, 22 U.S. 738 (1824).

137. 31 U.S. (6 Pet.), 515, 541 (1832). See Chapter 3, "Judicial Elections as Separation of Powers."

138. R. Kent Newmyer, *The Supreme Court under Marshall and Taney* 83–92 (1968); Hampton Carson, *The History of the Supreme Court of the United*

States I:242 (1904); Charles G. Haines, *The Role of the Supreme Court in American Government and Politics, 1789-1835,* at 590 (1944).

139. G. Edward White, *The Marshall Court and Cultural Change, 1815-1835,* 191-94.

140. Fletcher v. Peck (1810); Martin v. Hunter's Lessee (1816); McCulloch v. Maryland (1819); Sturges v. Crowninshield (1819); Dartmouth College v. Woodward (1819); Cohens v. Virginia (1821); Gibbons v. Ogden (1824).

141. Donald M. Roper, "Judicial Unanimity and the Marshall Court—A Road to Reappraisal," 9 *Am. J. Leg. History* 118 (1965).

142. Keith Whittington, "Judicial Review of Congress Before the Civil War," 97 *Geo. L. J.* 1257 (2009). Mark Graber, "Naked Land Transfers and American Constitutional Development," 53 *Vand. L. Rev.* 73 (2000). Graber found a number of decisions by federal courts limiting congressional power in land transfers—often erring by legislative oversight rather than by deliberate intent. Graber acknowledges that these cases were not technically invalidating legislative measures and did not cite specific constitutional texts. Whittington admirably unearthed several decisions in which the Marshall Court limited statutes, but these opinions are often cursory or ambiguous. See U.S. v. Cantril, 8 U.S. 167 (1807) (one-sentence opinion); Hodgson v. Bowerbank, 9 U.S. 303 (1809) (one-sentence opinion); Jackson v. Twentyman, 27 U.S. 136 (1829) (unsigned, four-sentence opinion with no citation of a constitution clause); Reynolds v. M'Arthur, 27 U.S. 417 (1829) (longer opinion on vested property rights and retrospective legislation); Parsons v. Bedford, 28 U.S. 433 (1830) (jury trial and Seventh Amendment); U.S. v. Percheman 32 U.S. 51 (1833) (vested property case); U.S. v. Phelps, 33 U.S. 700 (1834). Whittington acknowledges that the U.S. government won more of these property claim cases than it lost. Whittington, "Judicial Review," 97 *Geo. L. J.* 1302-03. For pre–Marshall Court judicial review, see U.S. v. Yale Todd (unpublished, 1794); Mossman v. Higginson, 4 U.S. 12 (1800) (arguably statutory interpretation and constitutional avoidance doctrine, not judicial review).

143. Friedman, *Will of the People,* 72.

3. Judicial Elections as Separation of Powers

1. Thomas Jefferson to Samuel Kercheval, July 12, 1816, in *The Writings of Thomas Jefferson,* 15:34 (Andrew A. Lipscomb et al. eds., 1903).

2. Dr. Thomas Young, "To the Inhabitants of Vermont," 1777, in *Vermont Voices, 1609 through the 1990s: A Documentary History of the Green Mountain State,* 67 (J. Kevin Graffagnino, Samuel B. Hand, and Gene Sessions eds., 1999).

3. Robert E. Shalhope, *Bennington and the Green Mountain Boys: The Emergence of Liberal Democracy in Vermont, 1760-1850* 171 (1996).

4. Vermont Territorial Constitution of 1777, ch. 2, § 18; ch. 2, § 27.

5. Shalhope, *Bennington and the Green Mountain Boys,* 97, 170. On localism and law, see Laura Edwards, *The People and Their Peace: Legal Culture and the Transformation of Inequality in the Post-Revolutionary South* (2009).

6. Id., 95.

7. Id.
8. Ira Allen, *The Natural and Political History of the State of Vermont, One of the United States of America* (1798), reprinted in *Ethan and Ira Allen: Collected Works*, 3:1–146 (J. Kevin Graffagnino ed., 1992); Michael A. Bellesiles, *Revolutionary Outlaws: Ethan Allen and the Struggle for Independence on the Early American Frontier* 108–09, 135, 170 (1993).
9. Allen, *History of Vermont*, in *Ethan and Ira Allen: Collected Works*; Bellesiles, *Revolutionary Outlaws*, 178–79.
10. Vermont Constitution of 1786, ch. 2, § 9.
11. Georgia Const., 1812 Amendment, art. 3, § 4. Some sources suggest that Georgia began electing lower court judges in 1777 or 1793. Albert Berry Saye's *A Constitutional History of Georgia* (1948) states that although many sources are in error on the topic, no judicial elections occurred under the Constitution of 1777. There is also no evidence in the records or the contemporary newspapers of judicial elections in the 1790s. Evan Haynes, *The Selection and Tenure of Judges* 108 (1944); William Bacon Stevens, *A History of Georgia* 2:303 (1859); Warren Grice, *The Georgia Bench and Bar* 1:3 (1931); Melvin Hill, *The Georgia State Constitution: A Reference Guide* 5 (1994).
12. Stephen Burbank and Barry Friedman, *Judicial Independence at the Crossroads: An Interdisciplinary Approach* 9, 19–20 (2002).
13. Stevens, *History of Georgia*, 2:478.
14. 10 U.S. (6 Cranch) 87 (1810).
15. Congressional Research Service, *The Constitution of the United States: Analysis and Interpretation* (Johnny H. Killian, George A. Costello, and Kenneth R. Thomas eds., 2004).
16. Saye, *Constitutional History of Georgia*, 144.
17. Ulrich Bonnell Phillips, *Georgia and State Rights*, 91–93 (1902).
18. Saye, *Constitutional History of Georgia*, 166 (quoting the *Augusta Chronicle*, Sept. 16, 1795). Emphasis in original.
19. Id., 167.
20. John D. Barnhart, *Indiana to 1816: The Colonial Period*, 272–73 (1971).
21. Id., 273, 276.
22. Id., 276.
23. Logan Esarey, *A History of Indiana*, 1:156–59 (1915).
24. Id.; Leander J. Monks, ed., *Courts and Lawyers of Indiana*, 1:19 (1916).
25. Barnhart, *Indiana*, 307.
26. Monks, *Courts and Lawyers*, 1:20, 47.
27. Id., 1:47; Lewis B. Ewbank and Dorothy L. Riker, eds., *The Laws of the Indiana Territory, 1809–1816*, 65, 68 (1934).
28. Monks, *Courts and Lawyers*, 1:48.
29. Ewbank and Riker, *Laws*, 65–70; Monks, *Courts and Lawyers*, 1:49–50.
30. Barnhart, *Indiana*, 334–36.
31. Id., 347.
32. Id., 362; Patrick Baude, "Indiana's Constitution in a Nation of Constitutions," in *The History of Indiana Law*, 23 (David J. Bodenhamer and Randall T. Shepard eds., 2006).
33. Barnhart, *Indiana*, 323.

34. Id., 349–50.

35. Id., 351–52.

36. John D. Barnhart, "Southern Influence," "The Southern Influence in the Formation of Indiana," 33 *Indiana Magazine of History* 262–65 (1937).

37. Baude, "Indiana's Constitution," 23.

38. Monks, *Courts and Lawyers,* 1:52; Barnhart, *Indiana,* 267–70, 453; Indiana Constitution of 1816, art. 5, § 4, available at http://www.in.gov/history /6008.htm; "Friday Morning," Journal of the Convention of the Indiana Territory, June 21, 1816 (Indianapolis, 1912), available at http://www.in.gov/ history/6117.htm.

39. Stephen Duncan to Levin Wailes, Sept. 14, 1832, in Wailes Papers (BLC Box 1, Z 76), Mississippi Department of Archives and History, Jackson, Miss.

40. http://uselectionatlas.org/USPRESIDENT/GENERAL/pe1832data.html.

41. Alabama and Virginia in 1830, Missouri in 1834 and 1845, Georgia and Tennessee in 1835, Arkansas and Michigan in 1835, Maryland in 1837, Florida and Pennsylvania in 1838, New Jersey in 1844, and Texas in 1845. In 1835, Michigan limited its elections to lower court judges and appointed its supreme court.

42. Christopher J. Olsen, *Political Culture and Secession in Mississippi,*17–37 (2000).

43. Henry S. Foote, *Casket of Reminiscences,* 266–67 (1874).

44. Edmund Morgan, *Inventing the People,* 183–85 (1988).

45. Robert V. Haynes, "The Formation of the Territory," in *A History of Mississippi* 183 (Richard Aubrey McLemore ed., 1973).

46. D. Clayton James, *Antebellum Natchez,* 110–12 (1968).

47. Edwin Arthur Miles, "Jacksonian Democracy in Mississippi," in *James Sprunt Studies in History and Political Science* 42 (1960): 33.

48. *Journal of the Convention of the Western Part of the Mississippi Territory, Begun and Held at the Town of Washington, on the Seventh Day of July, 1817;* Dunbar Rowland, "Mississippi's First Constitution and Its Makers," 6 *Publications of the Mississippi Historical Society* 79–90 (1902); W. Magruder Drake, "Mississippi's First Constitutional Convention," 18 *Journal of Mississippi History* 79–110 (1956).

49. "Judicial Selection and Tenure in Mississippi," 43 *Mississippi Law Journal* 90–101 (1943).

50. W. Magruder Drake, "The Framing of Mississippi's First Constitution," 29 *Journal of Mississippi History* 318–20 (1967).

51. John Ray Skates Jr., *A History of the Mississippi Supreme Court, 1817– 1948,* 21–66, 125–218 (1973); *Biographical and Historical Memoirs of Mississippi,* I:111–27 (1891); D. Clayton James, *Antebellum Natchez,* 101– 61 (1968).

52. James, *Antebellum Natchez,* 112.

53. Charles S. Sydnor, *Slavery in Mississippi* (1965).

54. J. F. H. Claiborne, "A Trip through Piney Woods," 529, cited in Miles, *Jacksonian Democracy in Mississippi,* 32.

55. Sir Charles Lyell, *A Second Visit to the United States of North America,* 161–62 (1849).

56. Robert Lowry and William H. McCardell, *A History of Mississippi* (1978); James, *Antebellum Natchez*, 116.
57. Harry v. Decker and Hopkins, *Walker's Mississippi Reports* (June term, 1818), 36.
58. Mississippi v. Jones, June Term, 1820, *Walker's Mississippi Reports*, p. 83.
59. Jacob Wheeler, *A Practical Treatise on the Law of Slavery* (1837); William Goodell, *The American Slave Code in Theory and Practice* (1853).
60. Paul Finkelman, *An Imperfect Union*, 181–82, 195–96, 207 (1981).
61. John Bettersworth, "The Homefront, 1861–1865," in *A History of Mississippi*, I:508 (Richard A. McLemore ed., 1973); Sydnor, *Slavery in Mississippi*, 178, 186, 212; *Pearl River* (Mississippi) *Advocate*, Feb. 12, 1831.
62. "The Legislature," *Natchez Gazette*, Jan. 22, 1825 (citing U.S. Constitution, art. I, § 10; Mississippi Constitution [1817]).
63. Id.
64. *Natchez Gazette*, Jan. 22, 1825; *Jackson Southern Luminary*, Jan. 26, 1825.
65. *Natchez Gazette*, Jan. 22, 1825.
66. "Judicial Selection," 90, 100–01. Eugene C. Barker, "The Influence of Slavery in the Annexation of Texas," 11 *Mississippi Valley Historical Review* 28 (1924) (Judge Child had been a Natchez lawyer).
67. *Woodville Republican*, July 23, 1825.
68. *Biographical and Historical Memoirs of Mississippi*, 114.
69. James, *Antebellum Natchez*, 114; Dunbar Rowland, "Mississippi's First Constitution," 92–95.
70. J. F. H. Claiborne, *Mississippi as a Province, Territory and State* 479 n.* (1964).
71. Miles, *Jacksonian Democracy in Mississippi*, 34–35; Porter L. Fortune, "'The Formative Period' in *A History of Mississippi*, 259 (Richard Aubrey McLemore ed., 1973).
72. W. Magruder Drake, "Mississippi's Constitutional Convention of 1832," 23 *Journal of Southern History* 357 (1957); Robert E. May, *John A. Quitman, Old South Crusader*, 51 (1985).
73. Sean Wilentz, *The Rise of American Democracy*, 314 (2005).
74. May, *Quitman*, 30.
75. Id., 36; Wilentz, *Rise of American Democracy*, 427.
76. Cherokee Nation v. Georgia, 30 U.S. 1 (1831).
77. Jill Nogren, *The Cherokee Cases*, 117 (1996).
78. Worcester v. Georgia, 31 U.S. (6 Pet.), 515, 541, 543–46 (1832).
79. Natchez *Mississippi Gazette*, Apr. 6, 1832 (emphasis in original).
80. *Natchez Gazette*, Apr. 23, 1832.
81. Id., Apr. 27, 1832 (emphasis in original).
82. Sen. George Troup, "Georgia and the Supreme Court," *Vicksburg Mississippian*, Apr. 16, 1832; "Georgia and the Supreme Court," *Vicksburg Mississippian*, Apr. 16, 1832.
83. Drake, "Mississippi's Constitutional Convention of 1832," at 356, 359.
84. Henry Foote, *Vicksburg Mississippian*, Feb. 20, 1832.
85. Id., Mar. 19, 1832 (emphasis in original).
86. *The Natchez*, July 14, 1832.

87. Those three delegates who served both in 1817 to 1832 were Dougall McLaughlin, Joseph Johnson, and Gerard Brandon. Brandon voted to keep judicial appointments, while McLaughlin and Johnson voted for elections.

88. *Biographical and Historical Memoirs of Mississippi* (1891, 2 vols.).

89. May, *Quitman,* 53; Drake, "Mississippi's Constitutional Convention of 1832," 358, 360–61.

90. Drake, "Mississippi's Constitutional Convention of 1832," 357.

91. *Natchez Courier,* May 4, 1832.

92. May, *Quitman,* 59–62.

93. Christopher J. Olson, *Political Culture and Secession in Mississippi,* 27 (2000).

94. John A. Quitman to Eliza Quitman, Oct. 1832, in Quitman Papers, Mississippi Department of Archives and History, Jackson, Miss.

95. Drake, "Mississippi's Constitutional Convention of 1832," at 367.

96. Foote, *Casket of Reminiscences,* 348.

97. May, *Quitman,* 57.

98. James D. Lynch, *Bench and Bar of Mississippi,* 194 (1881); Dunbar Rowland, *Courts, Judges, and Lawyers of Mississippi,* 89; Henry S. Foote, *The Bench and Bar of the South and Southwest,* 63 (1876).

99. James, *Antebellum Natchez,* 119.

100. Rowland, *Courts, Judges, and Lawyers of Mississippi,* 77–80.

101. *Journal of the Proceedings of the Convention to Form a Constitution for the Government of the State of New Jersey* 129 (1844).

102. *Fragments of the Debates of the Iowa Constitutional Conventions of 1844 and 1846,* at 105 (Benjamin F. Shambaugh ed., 1900) (Elijah Sells).

103. William Penn Clark, "To the Electors of Muscatine, Johnson, and Iowa Counties," *Iowa Standard,* New Series, vol. I, no. 10, Aug. 19, 1846 (emphasis in original).

104. Miles, *Jacksonian Democracy in Mississippi,* 25.

105. Gerard Magliocca, *Andrew Jackson and the Constitution: The Rise and Fall of Generational Regimes,* 76–78 (2007).

106. Groves v. Slaughter, 40 U.S. (15 Pet.) at 486, 489.

107. Id., at 485.

108. Wilentz, *Rise of American Democracy,* 315.

109. Haynes, *Selection and Tenure of Judges,* 101–35.

110. Jacob Katz Cogan, "Imagining Democracy: Popular Sovereignty from the Constitution to the Civil War," 156 n.59 (Nov. 2002) (unpublished Ph.D. dissertation, Princeton University) (listing Alabama, Connecticut, Delaware, Georgia, Kentucky, Maine, Maryland, New York, Ohio, Pennsylvania, Vermont, and Virginia adopting the direct election of executive and mixed executive/judicial officials, including justices of the peace and court clerks, by the early 1830s).

111. Edwin Surrency, "The Courts in the American Colonies," 11 *Am. J. of Legal History* 347 (1967).

112. Vermont Constitution of 1793, ch. II, § 9; Ohio Constitution of 1803; Georgia Constitution, Amendment of 1812; Indiana Constitution of 1816,

art. V, § 12; New York Constitution, Amendment of 1826; Tennessee Constitution of 1834, art. VI, § 15; Arkansas Constitution of 1836, art. VI, § 15–17;
Pennsylvania Constitution of 1838, art.VI, § 7. Rhode Island had its justices
of the peace elected in 1842, and New Jersey in 1844. Michael Ellis, "The
Origins of the Elected Prosecutor," 121 *Yale L. J.* (forthcoming 2012).
113. Alexander Keyssar, *The Right to Vote,* app. tbl. A.9 (2000).
114. Wilentz, *Rise of American Democracy.*
115. Harry L. Watson, *Liberty and Power,* 232 (rev. ed. 2006).
116. Larry Kramer, *The People Themselves* 202 (2004); Lee Benson, *The Concept
of Jacksonian Democracy* (1961); Daniel Walker Howe, *What Hath God
Wrought: The Transformation of America 1815–1848* (2007); Marvin Meyers,
The Jacksonian Persuasion (1957); Wilentz, *Rise of American Democracy.*
117. Watson, *Liberty and Power,* 232. For a critique of the view that high voter
turnout meant widespread and deep political engagement, see Glenn C.
Altschuler and Stuart Blumin, *Rude Republic: Americans and Their Politics
in the Nineteenth Century* (2000). For a critique of this critique, see Sven
Beckert, "Involved Disengagement? Reconsidering the Golden Age of Participatory Democracy," 28 *Reviews in American History* 560 (2000).
118. Albert Burton Moore, *History of Alabama,* 118–21 (1934).
119. Jones v. Watkins, 1 Stew. 81; 1827 Ala. LEXIS 45 (Ala. 1827); Moore, *History
of Alabama,* 120–21.
120. Moore, *History of Alabama,* 120; Malcolm Cook McMillan, *Constitutional
Development in Alabama, 1798–1901: A Study in Politics, the Negro, and
Sectionalism,* 149 (1955).
121. McMillan, *Constitutional Development in Alabama,* 50, 121.
122. Id. (quoting Huntsville *Southern Advocate*).
123. Moore, *History of Alabama,* 120–21; William Garrott Brown, *A History
of Alabama* (1900); Thomas Perkins Abernethy, *The Formative Period in
Alabama, 1815–1828* (1965); Virginia Van der Veer Hamilton, *Alabama:
A History* (1984).
124. 31 U.S. 515 (1832).
125. Alexander Keyssar, *The Right to Vote* (2000).
126. Harold Joseph Counihan, *North Carolina 1815–1836: State and Local
Perspectives on the Age of Jackson,* 131–32 (1971); Thomas E. Jeffrey, *State
Parties and National Politics: North Carolina, 1815–1861,* 62–63 (1989).
127. Walter F. Pratt, "The Struggle for Judicial Independence in Antebellum
North Carolina: The Story of Two Judges," *Law and History Review,* vol.
4, no. 1 (1986): 131–32.
128. Id., 129–59.
129. Id., 131.
130. Id., 147.
131. See Martin Brinkley, "Supreme Court of North Carolina: A Brief History,"
http://www.aoc.state.nc.us/www/copyright/sc/facts.html.
132. Hoke v. Henderson, 15 N.C. (4 Dev.) 1 (1833); Pratt, "Struggle for Judicial
Independence," 148–58.
133. Pratt, "Struggle for Judicial Independence," 158–59.

134. Pennsylvania Constitutional Convention, *Proceedings and Debates of the Convention of the Commonwealth of Pennsylvania*, Reported by John Agg V: 77 (1837); Russell Henry Kistler, *The Evolution of the Constitution of Pennsylvania, 1643–1838* (master's thesis, Lehigh University, 1943), 172–73, 229, 240–41; Roy H. Akagi, "The Pennsylvania Constitution of 1838," 48 *Pennsylvania Magazine of History and Biography* 301–333 (1924); Charles McCool Snyder, *The Jacksonian Heritage: Pennsylvania Politics, 1833–1848*, 96–107 (1958).

135. Rosalind L Branning, *Pennsylvania Constitutional Development*, 24–25 (1960); Sylvester K. Stevens, *Pennsylvania: Birthplace of a Nation* (1964).

136. Haynes, *Selection and Tenure of Judges*, at 108 (Georgia: three-year terms); id. at 110 (Indiana: seven-year terms); id. at 121 (New Jersey: seven-year terms); id. at 125 (Ohio: seven-year terms); id. at 127–28 (Rhode Island: at pleasure of the legislature); id. at 132 (Vermont: one-year terms).

137. Id. at 101 (Alabama: six-year terms in 1830); id. at 102 (Arkansas: four- and eight-year terms in 1836); id. at 107 (Florida: five-year initial terms in 1838); id. at 115 (Maine: seven-year terms in 1839, and Michigan: seven-year terms in 1836); id. at 117 (Mississippi: four- and six-year terms in 1832); id. at 130 (Tennessee: eight- and twelve-year terms in 1835).

4. Panic and Trigger

1. *Report of the Debates and Proceedings of the Convention for the Revision of the Constitution of the State of New York*, 671–72 (William G. Bishop and William H. Attree reporters, Albany, *Albany Atlas* 1846) [*New York Report*]; *Debates and Proceedings in the New-York State Convention for the Revision of the Constitution*, 493 (S. Croswell and R. Sutton reporters, Albany, *Albany Argus* 1846) [*New York Debates and Proceedings*].

2. Peter Temin, *The Jacksonian Economy*, 113–47, 154, 157 (1969); James Roger Sharp, *The Jacksonians versus the Banks: Politics in the States After the Panic of 1837*, at 27 (1970); Peter L. Rousseau, "Jacksonian Monetary Policy, Specie Flows, and the Panic of 1837," 62 *J. Econ. Hist.* 457 (2002); John Joseph Wallis, *What Caused the Crisis of 1839?* (Nat'l Bureau of Econ. Research, Working Paper No. H0133, 2001).

3. John Lauritz Larson, *Internal Improvement*, 78, 136–41 (2001); George Rogers Taylor, *The Transportation Revolution, 1815–1860* (1952).

4. Charles W. McCurdy, *The Anti-Rent Era in New York Law and Politics, 1839–1865*, 32–33, 58, 75, 77, 104, 129 (2001); Larson, *Internal Improvement*, 203, 209–14, 221; John Joseph Wallis, "Constitutions, Corporations, and Corruption: American States and Constitutional Change, 1842–1852," 65 *J. Econ. Hist.* 211, 214 n.3 (2005); Peter J. Galie, *Ordered Liberty*, 96 (1996); 1 A. K. McClure, *Old Time Notes of Pennsylvania*, 57–65 (1905); 2 Theodore Calvin Pease, *The Frontier State, 1818–1848*, at 198–99, 205, 212–16 (1922); Janet Cornelius, *Constitution Making in Illinois, 1818–1970*, at 27 (1972).

5. Tony A. Freyer, *Producers versus Capitalists*, 35 (1994); Gerald Leonard, *Invention of Party Politics: Federalism, Party Politics, and Constitutional*

Development in Jacksonian Illinois, 156–57 (2002); Daniel Walker Howe, *What Hath God Wrought: The Transformation of America, 1815–1848* (2007).

6. Edward J. Balleisen, *Navigating Failure*, 126 (2001); Bruce H. Mann, *Republic of Debtors*, 3 (2002); P. G. M. Dickson, *The Financial Revolution in England*, 33 (1967); J. G. A. Pocock, *The Machiavellian Moment*, 478–83 (1975); Edmund Morgan, *Inventing the People: The Rise of Popular Sovereignty in England and America* (1988); James H. Hutson, "Country, Court, and Constitution: Antifederalism and the Historians," 38 *Wm. & Mary Q.* 337, 356–60 (1981); Lance Banning, *The Jeffersonian Persuasion*, 200–01 (1978); *The Constitutional Debates of 1847*, at 406–07; Cornelius, *Constitution Making in Illinois*, 27; Steven H. Steinglass and Gino J. Scarselli, *The Ohio State Constitution*, 25 (2004); James Warner Harry, *The Maryland Constitution of 1851*, at 15–16 (1902); McCurdy, *Anti-Rent Era*, at 77.

7. *New York Debates and Proceedings*, 549–73. There were only roll call votes for the districting and structure of judicial elections. See id., at 544 (elections only on general ticket); id., at 546 (elections by districts); id., at 549 (selection of chief judge); id., at 550, 556 (mix of general statewide and districted elections—the ultimate winner); id., at 562, 564 (term length); id., at 573 (qualifications for the bench). The convention reporters Croswell and Sutton were affiliated with the *Albany Argus*, the Hunker newspaper. Another report was produced by William G. Bishop and William H. Attree, who were associated with the *Albany Atlas*, the Barnburner newspaper. *Report of the Debates of the Convention for the Revision of the Constitution of the State of New York* (William G. Bishop and William H. Attree, reporters, 1846) [hereinafter *New York Report*].

8. *New York Debates*, 587.

9. Oliver Wolcott, quoted in Lee Benson, *The Concept of Jacksonian Democracy*, 3 (1961).

10. Herbert D. A. Donovan, *The Barnburners*, 10, 31–47 (1925); DeAlva Stanwood Alexander, *A Political History of the State of New York*, 53–57 (1969) (1909); Jonathan H. Earle, *Jacksonian Antislavery & the Politics of Free Soil, 1824–1854*, 62 (2004); 3 Jabez D. Hammond, *The History of Political Parties in the State of New-York*, 696 (4th ed. 1850); McCurdy, *Anti-Rent Era*, 122–23; Sean Wilentz, *The Rise of American Democracy: Jefferson to Lincoln*, 530–32, 591–92 (2005); James A. Henretta, "The Birth of American Liberalism: New York, 1820–1860," in *Republicanism and Liberalism in America and the German States, 1750–1850*, 165, 174 (Jürgen Heideking and James A. Henretta eds., 2002); Gustavus Myers, *The History of Tammany Hall*, 140 n.1 (2d ed. 1917); L. Ray Gunn, *The Decline of Authority*, 183 (1988), Richard Hofstadter, *Anti-Intellectualism in American Life*, 169 (1963).

11. Donovan, *Barnburners*, 33 (quoting 1 *Life of Thurlow Weed*, 534 [1883]).

12. Glenn C. Altschuler and Jan M. Saltzberger, *Revivalism, Social Conscience and Community in the Burned-Over District* (1983).

13. James A. Henretta, "The Strange Birth of Liberal America: Michael Hoffman and the New York Constitution of 1846," 77 *N.Y. Hist.* 151, 165, 167–68, 175 (1996).

14. Donovan, *Barnburners,* at 32–33, 111, 117; Arthur M. Schlesinger Jr., *The Age of Jackson,* 191–92 (1945).
15. See Gunn, *Decline of Authority,* at 183.
16. Daniel J. Hulsebosch, *Constituting Empire,* 259–73 (2005); Marvin Meyers, *The Jacksonian Persuasion,* 244 (1957).
17. Meyers, *Jacksonian Persuasion,* 184; Jabez D. Hammond, *The History of Political Parties in the State of New York, from the Ratification of the Federal Constitution to December, 1840* (1842).
18. Nathaniel H. Carter and William L. Stone, *Reports of the Proceedings and Debates of the Convention of 1821,* at 318–19 (1821).
19. Id., at 318–321.
20. Meyers, *Jacksonian Persuasion,* 186; Carter and Stone, *Reports of the Proceedings and Debates of the Convention of 1821,* 333–37.
21. *New York Debates* (1821), 321–22.
22. Hulsebosch, *Constituting Empire,* 270–71.
23. Id., 203 (citing Resolutions of Marshall County, *Sangamo Journal,* Sept. 6, 1839); Larry Kramer, *The People Themselves: Popular Constitutionalism and Judicial Review,* 202 (2004).
24. Wilentz, *Rise of American Democracy,* 487.
25. Id., 498.
26. See generally Lee Benson, *The Concept of Jacksonian Democracy* (1961); Howe, *What Hath God Wrought*; Meyers, *Jacksonian Persuasion*; Harry L. Watson, *Liberty and Power: The Politics of Jacksonian America,* 232 (rev. ed. 2006).
27. McCurdy, *Anti-Rent Era,* xiii.
28. Donovan, *Barnburners,* 44; Gunn, *Decline of Authority,* 183; McCurdy, *Anti-Rent Era,* 223–28, 266–70; Henry Christman, *Tin Horns and Calico: A Decisive Episode in the Emergence of Democracy,* 134–48 (1975); Thomas Summerhill, *Harvest of Dissent,* 73–80 (2005).
29. Taylor v. Porter, 4 Hill 140 (N.Y. 1843).
30. McCurdy, *Anti-Rent Era,* 198–206, 254–56.
31. Donovan, *Barnburners,* at 10, 20, 27–28, 34–35, 58–59; 3 Jabez D. Hammond, *Political History of the State of New York,* 696 (1852).
32. *A History of Constitutional Reform in the United States* (pt. 2), 18 *Democratic Rev.* 403, 403 (1846).
33. For example, 1 *United States Magazine and Democratic Review,* at i (1838).
34. Gunn, *Decline of Authority,* 183.
35. Id., 173; Galie, *Ordered Liberty,* 100.
36. Letter by Michael Hoffman, "On Reforms Necessary in the Body of Law, in the Written Pleadings, and in the Practice of the Courts" (Mar. 21, 1846), in *Constitutional Reform in a Series of Articles Contributed to the Democratic Review,* 63, 69–70 (Thomas Prentice Kettell ed., 1846) [hereinafter Hoffman, 1846 Letter].
37. Wallis, "Constitutions, Corporations, and Corruption," 231.
38. Convention of Friends of Constitutional Reform, *Address and Draft of a Proposed Constitution Submitted to the People of the State of New-York,*

art. IV, § 1, at 3 (1837); Hammond, *Political History*, 539; *A History of Constitutional Reform in the United States* (pt. 2), at 405.

39. McCurdy, *Anti-Rent Era*, at 192–94.
40. Wilentz, *Rise of American Democracy*, 376; David Grimsted, "Rioting in Its Jacksonian Setting," *American Historical Review*, vol. 77, no. 2 (1972), 376.
41. New York Supreme Court decision, cited in Alden Chester, *Legal and Judicial History of New York* (1911).
42. *New York Herald*, Apr. 20, 1846; *Albany Evening Atlas*, Apr. 22, 1846.
43. *Albany Evening Atlas*, Apr. 25, 1846; Apr. 21, 1846.
44. *New York True Sun*, Apr. 3, 1846.
45. Id.
46. *Albany Evening Atlas*, Mar. 9, 1846.
47. Id.; *N.Y. Morning News*, May 29, 1846.
48. *Albany Evening Atlas*, Apr. 29, 1846.
49. Philip L. Merkel, "Party and Constitution Making: An Examination of Selected Roll Calls from the New York Constitutional Convention of 1846," app. 1, pp. 2–3 (May 2, 1983) (unpublished graduate seminar paper, University of Virginia) (on file with the Harvard Law School Library); Meyers, *Jacksonian Persuasion*, 264 (identifying Conrad Swackhamer with the Radicals); *Alb. Argus*, Apr. 4, 17, 21, 24, 25, May 4, 1846; *Alb. Evening Atlas*, Apr.–May, 1846; *N.Y. Daily Herald*, Apr. 18, 1846; *N.Y. Daily Trib.*, Apr. 5, 11, 20, 22, 30, May 1, 2, 8, July 3, 1846.
50. *The New Constitution of New York*, 9 *Law Rep.* 481, 481–82 (1847).
51. N.Y. Const. of 1846 art. III, § 16; art. V, § 3, § 8; art. VII, §§ 6–14; art. VIII, § 1, reprinted in *The Federal and State Constitutions, Colonial Charters, and Other Organic Laws of the United States* 1351, 1357, 1362–63 (Ben Perley Poore ed., 2d ed. 1878); Galie, *Ordered Liberty*, 100–10.
52. N.Y. Const. of 1846, art. V, § 8.
53. Gunn, *Decline of Authority*, 188–89; Henretta, "Strange Birth of American Liberalism."
54. *N.Y. Report*, at 513 (Campbell White, Hunker).
55. "Reorganization of the Judiciary," *N.Y. Evening Post*, 1846; Merkel, "Party and Constitution Making," 23; "Constitutional Reform," *The United States Magazine and Democratic Review*, December 1843, 571; "History of Constitutional Reform in the United States," *The United States Magazine and Democratic Review*, June 1846, at 414; "Constitutional Reform," *The United States Magazine and Democratic Review*, June 1846, 569.
56. James D. Folts, *Duely and Constantly Kept, A History of the New York Supreme Court, 1691–1847, and an Inventory of Its Records (Albany, Utica, and Geneva Offices)*, 1–2 (1991).
57. Id., 1–7.
58. *New York Debates*, 482 (William Wright); id., at 501–02.
59. *Albany Evening Journal*, Mar. 23, 1846; *Albany Evening Journal*, Apr. 11, 1846.
60. *New York Debates*, 456.
61. Id., 503.

62. *New York Report*, 141.

63. Id., 770.

64. See id., 178 (Alvah Worden, Whig); id., 187 (John Hunt, Barnburner).

65. See, for example, id., 181 (Robert Morris, Barnburner); id., 188 (Ambrose Jordan, Anti-Rent Whig); id., 199 (Henry Nicoll, Barnburner); id., 204 (Richard Marvin, Whig); id. 237 (Charles Kirkland, Whig).

66. See id., 141 (George Patterson, Whig); id., at 575 (Charles Kirkland, Whig).

67. Id., 595 (Richard Marvin, Whig).

68. Id., 651 (Amos Wright, Whig).

69. Id., 613 (Conrad Swackhamer, Barnburner) (emphasis in original).

70. James A. Henretta, "The Strange Birth of Liberal America," 175 (quoting Letter from Michael Hoffman to Azariah Flagg (Aug. 9, 1842) (emphasis in original).

71. Letter by Michael Hoffman, "On a Reorganization of the Judiciary of the State of New York" (Sept. 12, 1845), in *Constitutional Reform in a Series of Articles Contributed to the Democratic Review*, at 58, 59, 69 (1845) [hereinafter Hoffman, 1845 Letter]; Hoffman, 1846 Letter, at 69–70.

72. *New York Report*, 671–72; *New York Debates and Proceedings*, 493.

73. *New York Report*, 671–72; *New York Debates*, at 492 (Michael Hoffman, Barnburner) ("[If judges] were not elected by the sovereign body, [New Yorkers] would look in vain for judges to stand by the constitution against the encroachments of power [by the other branches]").

74. *New York Report*, 671–72; *New York Debates*, at 492.

75. *New York Report*, 404.

76. *New York Debates*, at 411–12 (Alvah Worden, Whig); id., 540 (James Tallmadge, Whig).

77. Id., 483–84 (William B. Wright, Anti-Rent Whig); *New York Report*, at 645 (Ira Harris, Anti-Rent Whig).

78. McCurdy, *Anti-Rent Era*, 198–206, 254–56.

79. *New York Debates*, at 645 (Ira Harris, Anti-Rent Whig).

80. *New York Debates*, at 371 (Charles Ruggles, Hunker).

81. *New York Debates*, at 852.

82. "Elective Judiciary," 22 *U.S. Democratic Rev.* 199, 199 (1848).

83. Galie, *Ordered Liberty*, 110. The voters rejected the Barnburners' separate constitutional proposal to extend black suffrage.

84. *New York Herald*, May 22, 23, 1847; *Albany Evening Journal*, Apr. 29, June 3, 1847.

85. *Albany Argus*, May 1, 4, 12, 22, 25, 1847.

86. *Albany Evening Journal*, May 20, 1847.

87. *Argus*, June 5, 1847.

88. Id., June 7, 1847.

89. *New York Herald*, July 1847.

90. Merkel, "Party and Constitution Making," at 2–6, 30; Donovan, *Barnburners*, at 117.

91. N.Y. *Const. of 1846*, art. VI, § 24.

92. Charles M. Cook, *The American Codification Movement: A Study of Antebellum Legal Reform* (1981); Robert W. Gordon, "The American Codifica-

tion Movement: A Study of Antebellum Legal Reform," 36 *Vanderbilt L. Rev.* 431 (1983) (book review); Lawrence Friedman, *A History of American Law,* 340–44; Morton Horwitz, *The Transformation of American Law, 1870–1960,* 117–19 (1992).

93. Gordon, "American Codification Movement," 441–45.
94. Caleb Nelson, "Re-Evaluation," 193. See, for example, *Journal of the Proceedings of the Convention to Form a Constitution for the Government of the State of New Jersey* 129 (1844). *Fragments of the Debates of the Iowa Constitutional Conventions of 1844 and 1846,* at 105 (Benjamin F. Shambaugh ed., 1900) (Elijah Sells).
95. *The Convention of 1846,* at 291 (Milo M. Quaife ed., 1919); Milo M. Quaife, *The Movement for Statehood: 1846–47,* at 37–41 (1918); Ray A. Brown, "The Making of the Wisconsin Constitution" (pt. 1), 1949 *Wis. L. Rev.* 648, 657; and (pt. 2), 1952 *Wis. L. Rev.* 23, 59; Edward P. Alexander, "Wisconsin, New York's Daughter State," *Wis. Mag. Hist.,* Sept. 1946, at 11, 24–25.
96. *Constitutional Debates of 1847* [Illinois], 477, 505, 749.
97. 2 *Debates of the Maryland Reform Convention to Revise the State Constitution,* 540, 548, 557, 569–71, 585 (1851).
98. *Pennsylvanian,* June 14, 1847; id., June 12, 1847; id., June 11, 1847; id., June 8, 1847; id., June 2, 1847; id., June 1, 1847; id., May 28, 1847.
99. See Owen C. Coy and Herbert C. Jones, *California's Constitution,* 15 (1930).

5. The American Revolutions of 1848

1. Sean Wilentz, *The Rise of American Democracy: Jefferson to Lincoln,* 602–32 (2005); Daniel Walker Howe, *What Hath God Wrought: The Transformation of America 1815–1848,* 792–836 (2007).
2. Charles Breunig, *Age of Revolution and Reaction, 1789–1850,* at 259–66, 272–76 (2d ed. 1977); Mike Rapport, *1848: Year of Revolution* 65, 79–91, 99–100, 135–36, 335–40 (2008); Priscilla Robertson, *Revolutions of 1848,* at 99, 129, 139, 232, 268, 325–30 (1952); Tim Roberts, "The United States and the European Revolutions of 1848," in *The European Revolutions of 1848 and the Americas,* 76 (Guy Thomson ed., 2002).
3. G. Alan Tarr, *Understanding State Constitutions,* 111 (2000); John Joseph Wallis, "Constitutions, Corporations, and Corruption: American States and Constitutional Change, 1842–1852," 65 *J. Econ. Hist.* 211, 212 (2005); John Joseph Wallis, Richard E. Sylla, and Arthur Grinath III, "Sovereign Debt and Repudiation: The Emerging-Market Debt Crisis in the U.S. States, 1839–1843," at 26–27 (Nat'l Bureau of Econ. Research, Working Paper No. 10753, 2004), available at http://ssrn.com/abstract=590763. States revising their constitutions between 1844 and 1853 were New Jersey, Louisiana (twice), Missouri, New York, Illinois, Kentucky, Ohio, Michigan, Virginia, Maryland, Indiana, and Tennessee. New states were Iowa, Texas, Wisconsin, and California. Evan Haynes, *The Judicial Selection and Tenure,* 101–35 (1944); Wallis, "Constitutions, Corporations, and Corruption," at 219 tbl.2.
4. Howe, *What Hath God Wrought,* 793.
5. "An Elective Judiciary," 7 *Pa. L. J.* 247, 249 (1848).

6. Louis Hartz, *Economic Policy and Democratic Thought*, 26 (1948).
7. See Merrill D. Peterson, *Democracy, Liberty, and Property: The State Constitutional Conventions of the 1820s*, at xiii–xvi (1966).
8. Kermit L. Hall, "Mostly Anchor and Little Sail: The Evolution of American State Constitutions," in *Toward a Usable Past*, at 388, 401; Tarr, *Understanding*, 133; Edward L. Widmer, *Young America: The Flowering of Democracy in New York City* (1998); Howe, *What Hath God Wrought*, 829.
9. Hartz, *Economic Policy*, 314–15.
10. Alexis de Tocqueville, *Democracy in America*, 89 (J. P. Mayer ed., George Lawrence trans., 1969) (1835).
11. Tarr, *Understanding*, 112 (quoting Kermit L. Hall, *The Magic Mirror* 103–04 [1989]).
12. 2 *Report of the Debates and Proceedings of the Convention for the Revision of the Constitution of the State of Indiana*, 1346 (H. Fowler ed., 1850) [hereinafter *Indiana Report*] (remarks of delegate Daniel Read).
13. Tarr, *Understanding*, at 98.
14. Wallis, "Constitutions, Corporations, and Corruption," 213–19, 230–33, 238; Tarr, *Understanding*, 98, 118–19.
15. Jacob Cogan, "Imagining Democracy: Popular Sovereignty from the Constitution to the Civil War," 203 (PhD diss., Princeton University) (citing H.R. Rep. No. 141 [1852]). *Dred Scott* prompted some northerners to call for an amendment establishing federal judicial elections.
16. *Some Objections to a Joint Resolution Recommending to the People of Pennsylvania an Elective Judiciary*, 37–38 (1849).
17. *Illinois Debates of 1847*, at 466 (remarks of delegate Archibald Williams).
18. See, e.g., Samuel M. Smucker, *Popular Arguments in Favor of an Elective Judiciary*, 5, 27 (1850).
19. *The Illinois Constitutional Debates of 1847*, at 461–62 (remarks of delegate David Davis).
20. Id., at 752 (remarks of delegate John Dement).
21. Id., at 466 (remarks of delegate Archibald Williams); "The New Constitution—The Tendency of Its Power," *Wkly. Nw. Gazette* (Galena, Ill.), Sept. 17, 1847, at 2.
22. 2 *Indiana Report*, 1808–09 (remarks of delegate Judge Borden).
23. *Report of the Debates and Proceedings of the Convention for the Revision of the Constitution of the State of Kentucky*, 173 (R. Sutton reporter, 1849) [hereinafter *Kentucky Report*] (remarks of delegate Ninian Gray); id., at 268 (remarks of delegate James Guthrie); id., at 409 (remarks of delegate Philip Triplett). See Kermit L. Hall, "Judiciary on Trial: State Constitutional Reform and the Rise of an Elected Judiciary, 1846–1860," 45 *The Historian* 350 n.62 (1984) (citing R. D. Turnbull, "To the People of Brunswick, Lunenberg, Nottoway and Dinwiddle," *Richmond Enquirer*, June 28, 1850, at 3–4); 2 *Debates and Proceedings of the Maryland-Reform Convention to Revise the State Constitution* 501 (1851); Va. Const. of 1850, art. VI, § 11, in 2 Benjamin Perley Poore, *The Federal and State Constitutions, Colonial Charters, and Other Organic Laws of the United*

States 1933 (1878); Margaret Nelson, *A Study of Judicial Review in Virginia, 1789–1928*, at 31 (1947).

24. Samuel Medary, *The New Constitution* (1849).
25. "The Carbonari," *New Constitution*, Sept. 8, 1849, at 289, 293–94; "Change of the State Constitution," *New Constitution*, July 21, 1849, at 177, 184; "The Convention," *New Constitution*, Sept. 8, 1849, at 289, 303–04; "The Discovery of America by the Northmen," *New Constitution*, Oct. 6, 1849, at 353, 362; "Europe—The Debates on Hungary in England—On the Press in France—The Fate of Italy," *New Constitution*, Sept. 1, 1849, at 273, 276; "Germany, in 1849," *New Constitution*, Aug. 4, 1849, at 209, 214; "Radicalism," *New Constitution*, Sept. 22, 1849, at 321, 327–28.
26. K., "Necessity of a New Constitution," *New Constitution*, Sept. 8, 1849, at 289, 292 (emphasis in original).
27. "The New Constitution," *New Constitution*, Sept. 8, 1849, at 289, 302.
28. "The Constitutional Convention," *New Constitution*, June 9, 1849, at 81, 95; "Election of Judges by the People," *New Constitution*, Oct. 20, 1849, at 385, 395 (hailing New York's "more pure [and] able Judiciary").
29. "Constitutional Reform in Missouri," *New Constitution*, July 28, 1849, at 193, 193; "The Constitutions of the Different States," *New Constitution*, July 21, 1849, at 177, 185–88; "Convention Law of New York," *New Constitution*, June 8, 1849, at 81, 92; "Election of Judges," *New Constitution*, Aug. 25, 1849, at 257, 271–72; "Election of Judges," *New Constitution*, July 21, 1849, at 177, 190–91; "Election of Judges by the People," *New Constitution*, June 8, 1849, at 81, 91; "Indiana—Her New Constitution," *New Constitution*, Sept. 8, 1849, at 289, 289; "The States—Their Constitutions, &c," *New Constitution*, May 5, 1849, at 1, 8.
30. "Revision of the State Constitution," *New Constitution*, June 23, 1849, at 113, 118; "Constitutional Reform," *New Constitution*, Sept. 29, 1849, at 337, 349.
31. "Reform," *New Constitution*, Nov. 17, 1849, at 401, 405.
32. "Ordinance of July 13, 1787," *New Constitution*, May 19, 1849, at 33, 47.
33. "Biennial Sessions of the Legislature," *New Constitution*, June 2, 1849, at 65, 68.
34. "The New Constitution Assuming Shape," *New Constitution*, Aug. 25, 1849, at 257, 268 (original italics).
35. *New Constitution*, May 5, 1849, at 1.
36. "Constitutional Reform," *New Const.*, Sept. 29, 1849, reprinted in *Medary*, supra note 22, at 337, 349 (reprinting an article from the *Findlay Democratic Courier*); "Revision of the State Constitution," *New Const.*, June 23, 1849, reprinted in *Medary*, supra note 22, at 113, 118 (reprinting an article from the *Ohio Patriot*).
37. "The Constitutional Convention," *New Constitution*, June 9, 1849, at 81, 95.
38. "Madison," Letter to the Editor, *New Constitution*, June 23, 1849, at 113, 116 [hereinafter Madison Letter I]; "Madison," Letter to the Editor, *New Constitution*, July 21, 1849, at 177, 189 [hereinafter Madison Letter II].

39. Veto, reprinted in Medary, *The New Constitution*, at 206.
40. "The New Constitution Assuming Shape," Aug. 25, 1849, reprinted in Medary, *The New Constitution* at 257, 268 (reprinting an article from the *St. Clairsville Gazette*), (emphasis omitted).
41. "Election of Judges," 8 *Am. L. J.* 481, 481 (1849).
42. 1 *Report of the Debates and Proceedings of the Convention for the Revision of the Constitution of the State of Ohio, 1850–1851*, at 86 (J. V. Smith reporter, 1851) [hereinafter *Ohio Report*] (remarks of delegate J. Milton Williams); "Constitutional Reform in Ohio," *New Constitution*, Aug. 18, 1849.
43. 2 id., at 217 (remarks of delegate James W. Taylor).
44. 1 *Report of the Debates and Proceedings of the Convention for the Revision of the Constitution of the State of Ohio, 1850–1851*, at 562 (remarks of delegate Joseph Vance). Similar sentiments were also expressed in Indiana. See 2 *Indiana Report*, at 1808–09 (remarks of delegate James W. Borden).
45. 2 *Official Report of the Debates and Proceedings in the State Convention, Assembled May 4th, 1853, to Revise and Amend the Constitution of the Commonwealth of Massachusetts* 771 (1853) (remarks of delegate Edward L. Keyes). Kermit Hall cites Keyes in this speech as also claiming that judicial elections will "energize" judges and make them "independent" and "on par" with the other branches, Hall, "Judiciary on Trial," at 350, and other legal academics have quoted this passage from Hall, see, for example, F. Andrew Hanssen, "Learning About Judicial Independence: Institutional Change in the State Courts," 33 *J. Legal Stud.* 447 (2004). However, I can find no record of this passage in the Massachusetts Debates or elsewhere.
46. See, for example, *N. Am. & U.S. Gazette* (Phila.), Oct. 12, 1847, at 2.
47. See, for example, "The Election of Judges," *Pennsylvanian,* Oct. 5, 1850, at 2.
48. Cogan, "Imagining Democracy," at 212 (quoting *Debate in the House of Representatives on the Proposed Amendment to the Constitution, Remarks of Mr. Biddle of Philadelphia, February 8, 1850, Pa. Telegraph*, Feb. 20, 1850).
49. "An Elective Judiciary," *Baltimore Sun*, June 4, 1851 (excerpted in Stephen B. Presser and Jamil S. Zainaldin, *Cases and Materials on Law and Jurisprudence in American History*, 413 (2006).
50. "Election of Judges," 8 *Am. L. J.* 481, 481 (1849) (emphasis in original).
51. Greenough v. Greenough, 11 Pa. 489, 495 (1849) (emphasis in original).
52. Id.
53. *New York Report,* at 671.
54. Caleb Nelson, "A Re-Evaluation of the Scholarly Explanations for the Rise of the Elective Judiciary in Antebellum America," 37 *Am. J. Legal Hist.* 190, 207, 224 (1993). For a fuller discussion of Nelson's interpretation, see Jed Handelsman Shugerman, "Economic Crisis and the Rise of Judicial Elections and Judicial Review," 123 *Harv. L. Rev.* 1061 (2010).
55. See Shugerman, "Economic Crisis," for more details.
56. Renée B. Lettow, "New Trial for Verdict Against Law: Judge-Jury Relations in Early Nineteenth-Century America," 71 *Notre Dame L. Rev.* 505, 508

(1996); see also Stephen C. Yeazell, Essay, "The Misunderstood Consequences of Modern Civil Process," *Wis. L. Rev.* 631, 641–42 (1994).

57. Lettow, "New Trial," 507–08.

58. Id., at 522, 527–29.

59. See Maxwell Bloomfield, *American Lawyers in a Changing Society, 1776–1876,* at 136–90 (1976); Maxwell Bloomfield, "Law vs. Politics: The Self Image of the American Bar (1830–1860)," 12 *Am. J. Legal Hist.* 306 (1968); see also Alfred S. Konefsky, "The Legal Profession: From the Revolution to the Civil War," in 2 *Cambridge History of Law in America* 68 (Michael Grossberg and Christopher Tomlins eds., 2008).

60. *Wisconsin Convention of 1846,* at 286 (remarks of delegate Charles M. Baker).

61. Cogan, "Imagining Democracy," 212 (quoting "Debate in the House of Representatives on the Proposed Amendment to the Constitution, Remarks of Mr. Biddle of Philadelphia," February 8, 1850, *Pa. Telegraph,* Feb. 20, 1850).

62. Smucker, *Popular Arguments in Favor of an Elective Judiciary,* 5, 27 (1850); see also "An Elective Judiciary," *Baltimore Sun,* June 4, 1851 (excerpted in Presser and Zainaldin, *Law and Jurisprudence,* 413).

63. *New York Report,* at 645 (remarks of delegate Ira Harris).

64. Id., at 290.

65. "The Election of Judges," 3 *Western L. J.* 423, 423 (1851).

66. Id., at 426.

67. 1 *Ohio Report,* at 691 (remarks of delegate J. McCormick); *Kentucky Report,* at 408–09 (remarks of delegate Philip Triplett in reply to delegate Nathan Gaither, id. at 404).

68. Tom Ginsburg, *Judicial Review in New Democracies: Constitutional Courts in Asian Cases,* 18 (2003); Mark Ramseyer, "The Puzzling (In)Dependence of Courts: A Comparative Approach," 23 *Journal of Legal Studies* 721 (1994); Matthew C. Stephenson, "'When The Devil Turns . . .': The Political Foundations of Independent Judicial Review," 32 *J. Legal Stud.* 59 (2003); Hanssen, "Learning About Judicial Independence," 431.

69. Missouri, Indiana, Illinois, Virginia, and Arkansas. Jed Handelsman Shugerman, Chart of State Partisan Balance (Jan. 2010) (unpublished chart, on file with the Harvard Law School Library) (based on W. Dean Burnham, Partisan Division of American State Governments, 1834–1985, http://dx .doi.org/10.3886/ICPSR00016).

70. Georgia, North Carolina, Connecticut, Rhode Island, Delaware, and New Jersey. See id.

71. *The Constitutional Debates of 1847,* at 483 (remarks of delegate Onslow Peters).

72. See, for example, *New York Debates,* at 480, 484.

73. Smucker, *Popular Arguments in Favor of an Elective Judiciary,* 4–5.

74. Glenn C. Altschuler and Stuart M. Blumin, *Rude Republic: Americans and Their Politics in the Nineteenth Century* (2000).

75. Gerald Leonard, *The Invention of Party Politics, Federalism, Popular Sovereignty, and Constitutional Development in Jacksonian Illinois,* 1–17 (2002).

76. Richard Hofstadter, *The Idea of a Party System,* 40 (1969).

77. Leonard, *Invention,* 10–11.

78. Id., 35–47.

79. Bray Hammond, *Banks and Politics in America from the Revolution to the Civil War* (1957); Leonard, *Invention*; John Joseph Wallis, "The Concept of Systematic Corruption in American History," in *Corruption and Reform,* 23 (Edward L. Glaeser and Claudia Goldin eds., 2006).

80. Leonard, *Invention,* 156–61.

81. Smucker, *Popular Arguments in Favor of an Elective Judiciary,* 4–5.

82. Stephen Skowronek, *Building a New American State,* 24 (1982).

83. Hall, "Judiciary on Trial," 342–43, 348.

84. Charles W. McCurdy, *The Anti-Rent Era in New York Law and Politics, 1839–1865,* 157–58, 257, 261, 266 (2001); Philip L. Merkel, "Party and Constitution Making: An Examination of Selected Roll Calls from the New York Constitutional Convention of 1846," app. 1, at 2–3, 6 (May 2, 1983) (unpublished graduate seminar paper, University of Virginia) (on file with the Harvard Law School Library).

85. See Merkel, "Party and Constitution Making," app. 1; see also *New York Debates,* at vii–viii (listing delegates by profession).

86. New York's consensus for judicial elections was so dominant that the convention never needed a roll call vote on the basic issue of elections versus appointments. Pennsylvania's legislative votes were more than two-to-one in favor of judicial elections. "Some Objections to a Joint Resolution Recommending to the People of Pennsylvania an Elective Judiciary," 8 (1849). Most states had similar margins in favor of judicial elections. The proposals failed in Massachusetts and New Hampshire, where New England culture seems to have been a bulwark against the populist wave.

87. For more on Hall's thesis, see Jed Handelsman Shugerman, "Economic Crisis and the Rise of Judicial Elections and Judicial Review," 123 *Harv. L. Rev.* 1061 (2010).

88. Id., at 585–86 (remarks of delegate Ansel Bascom); id., at 756–57 (remarks of Levi S. Chatfield).

89. Ky. Const. of 1850, art. IV, § 8; Md. Const. of 1851, art. IV, § 4.

90. Ind. Const. of 1851, art. VII, § 21; Md. Const. of 1851, art. IV, § 31; N.Y. Const. of 1846, art. VI, § 8.

91. *New York Report,* at 780 (remarks of delegate Henry C. Murphy, Hunker).

92. See, for example, *The Constitutional Debates of 1847,* at 464; *New York Report,* at 483, 586–87, 756–57, 607–09.

93. *New York Report,* at 581–82 (remarks of delegate William G. Angel); id., at 607 (remarks of delegate Enoch Strong).

94. See, for example, "The New Constitution of New York," 9 *Law Rep.* 481 (1847).

95. "Election of Judges," 9 *Am. L. J.* 378 (1850); see also "Election of Judges," 8 *Am. L. J.* 481, 482–83 (1849).

96. Robert Cover, *Justice Accused,* 144 n.* (1975).

97. Prigg v. Pennsylvania, 16 U.S. (Peters) 539 (1842).

98. Id., 625–33.
99. Thomas D. Morris, *Free Men All: The Personal Liberty Laws of the North, 1780–1861*, at 114 (1974). See Paul Finkelman, *An Imperfect Union* (1981).
100. Kermit Hall, "The Judiciary on Trial," 351. Hall also cites an Indiana delegate making this argument, but it does not appear in the text.
101. Id.; Nelson, "Re-evaluation," 194 (citing Edward Keyes and Rodney French in the Massachusetts Debates).
102. Morris, *Free Men All,* 117 (citing *Pennsylvania Freeman,* Mar. 11, 1847; Pennsylvania Abolition Society Minutes, 3:520–22).
103. *Pennsylvania Session Laws of 1847,* at 206–08.
104. Edward Needles, *An Historical Memoir of the Pennsylvania Society for Promoting the Abolition of Slavery,* 104–07 (1848) (discussing the society's activities from 1843 to 1848).
105. A. K. McClure, *Old Time Notes of Pennsylvania,* 111–20 (1905); George P. Donehoo, *Pennsylvania: A History,* 2:1388–93 (1926).
106. "Some Objections to a Joint Resolution Recommending to the People of Pennsylvania an Elective Judiciary," 8 (1849).
107. Helen Catterall, ed., *Judicial Cases Concerning American Slavery and the Negro,* 1:372–74, 283–84 (1926–1937) (Rachel v. Emerson, 1845; Orchard v. David, 1846; Mullins v. Wall, 1848).
108. Lowell H. Harrison, *The Antislavery Movement in Kentucky,* 42 (1978).
109. Id., 47.
110. Id., 49–50.
111. Id., 56.
112. Id., 52–53.
113. Steven A. Channing, *Kentucky: A Bicentennial History,* 107 (1977).
114. Harrison, *Antislavery Movement,* 56.
115. James P. Gregory, "The Question of Slavery in the Kentucky Constitutional Convention of 1849," *Filson Club History Quarterly* 23 (1949): 92–93.
116. Id., 93.
117. George L. Willis, Sr., "History of Kentucky Constitutions and Constitutional Conventions," *Register of the Kentucky Historical Society,* vol. 28, no. 85 (1930), 315–16.
118. Carl R. Fields, "Making Kentucky's Third Constitution, 1830–1850" (Ph.D. diss., University of Kentucky, 1951), 242 (citing *Kentucky Statesman,* Nov. 7, 1849 and Nov. 10, 1849).
119. Id., 228, 242, 338.
120. *Report of the Debates and Proceedings of the Convention for the Revision of the Constitution of the State of Kentucky, 1849,* 231ff. (1849).
121. Catterall, *Judicial Cases,* 1:399–400; 404–06.
122. H. Robert Baker, *The Rescue of Joshua Glover: A Fugitive Slave, the Constitution, and the Coming of the Civil War* (2004).
123. William J. Evitts, *A Matter of Allegiances: Maryland from 1850 to 1861,* at 47 (1974); Christopher Wildenhain, "Reforming Slavery on the Maryland Court of Appeals" (history thesis, Brown University, 2007).

124. John F. Phillips, "The Lawyer in Missouri One Hundred Years Ago," *Missouri Historical Review* 13.4 (July 1919). Christopher Phillips and Jason L. Pendleton eds., *Union on Trial: The Political Journals of Judge William Barclay Napton, 1829–1883*, 101–03, 487–88 (2005); Gerald T. Dunne, *The Missouri Supreme Court: From Dred Scott to Nancy Cruzan*, 48 (1993).

125. *Debates and Proceedings of the Minnesota Constitutional Convention* [of 1857] (1857) (Remarks of Mr. Setzer).

126. Baker, *Rescue of Joshua Glover;* Abelman v. Booth, 62 U.S. 506 (1859).

127. Wildenhain, "Reforming Slavery," 21; Lawrence Friedman, *A History of American Law*, 324 (1973); Carroll Taney Bond, *The Court of Appeals of Maryland, a History*, 159 (1928); Anita Aidt Guy, *Maryland's Persistent Pursuit to End Slavery, 1850–1864* (1997); Jennifer Caughey, "Conscription during the Civil War: The Curious Tale of How Politics and an Election Shaped the Fate of Conscription's Constitutionality" (seminar paper, Harvard Law School 2008).

128. "Objections to a Resolution Recommending to the People of Pennsylvania an Elective Judiciary," 26–31 (1849).

129. Larry Kramer, *The People Themselves*, 164, 200 (2004) (identifying judicial elections as an example of popular constitutionalism); David Pozen, "Judicial Elections as Popular Constitutionalism," 110 *Colum. L. Rev.* 2047 (2010).

6. The Boom in Judicial Review

1. See Appendix E, "Subject Matter of State Supreme Court Cases of Judicial Review."

2. There are a few examples of countermajoritarian theories during the Founding, such as James Madison, Alexander Hamilton, and James Iredell during the Convention and Ratification debates or in letters, but these were not judicial decisions. See Robert J. Steinfeld, "The Early Anti-majoritarian Rationale for Judicial Review," in 2 *Transformations in American Legal History: Essays in Honor of Morton Horwitz* 143 (2010). A small number of state judges made such arguments over the next few decades, but those cases were isolated. William E. Nelson, Commentary, "Changing Conceptions of Judicial Review: The Evolution of Constitutional Theory in the States, 1790–1860," 120 *U. Pa. L. Rev.* 1166 (1972).

3. My friend Matthew Lindsay has raised some helpful questions about linking this era to the laissez-faire constitutionalism of the *Lochner* era. "In Search of Laissez-Faire Constitutionalism," *Harvard Law Review Forum* 55 (2010). First, I do not claim that the elected judges of the 1840s–1850s produced full-blown *Lochner*ism, but that they played a role and marked a shift toward laissez-faire constitutionalism. I agree with Lindsay that other forces, such as antislavery and emancipation, the Reconstruction amendments, and industrialization played major roles. However, emphasizing some factors should not mean dismissing other factors. By itself, the explo-

sion of state judicial review against regulation and state action with respect to property and the economy helped lay a foundation for the *Lochner* era. Lindsay suggests that the 1840s–1850s ideology was anti–class legislation and anticorruption, reflective of the Jacksonian era, and not a broader free market ideology. However, free market ideology usually includes the critique that state action distorts the market because of special interests, corruption, and bias. Some scholars link the attack on "class legislation" to the later *Lochner* jurisprudence. Howard Gillman, *The Constitution Besieged* (1993). In the 1840s–1850s, that attack became bolder and broader. Moreover, several key leaders of the movement for judicial elections in the 1840s adhered to broader free market ideas, such as the Barnburner leader Michael Hoffman and other New York convention delegates, and such as the writers in *The New Constitution,* discussed below. See, for example, James A. Henretta, "The Strange Birth of Liberal America: Michael Hoffman and the New York Constitution of 1846," 77 *N.Y. History* 151, 153 (1996); *New York Report* at 513 (remarks of delegate Campbell White). Lindsay distinguishes the vested rights doctrine in the 1840s–1850s cases from the substantive due process cases of the *Lochner* era, but many scholars have identified vested rights doctrine as a forerunner or even a category of substantive due process; see, for example, John Harrison, "Substantive Due Process and the Constitutional Text," 83 *Va. L. Rev.* 493, 498–500 (1997); James W. Ely Jr., "The Oxymoron Reconsidered: Myth and Reality in the Origins of Substantive Due Process," 16 *Constitutional Commentary* 315, 338–342 (1999). Furthermore, substantive due process in defense of liberty interests against general economic regulation developed in the 1850s, beyond the standard vested rights decisions that had blocked transfers of physical property. See Wynehamer v. People, 13 N.Y. 378 (1856), discussed below.

4. Leigh Peters-Fransen, a remarkable research assistant, and I searched for the words "Constitution," "constitutional," and "unconstitutional" in each state database from 1790 to 1865, to find successful and unsuccessful constitutional challenges to statutes. I then added these cases to existing studies of particular state courts, like New York. See Jed Handelsman Shugerman, "Economic Crisis and the Rise of Judicial Elections and Judicial Review: Appendices and List of State Judicial Review Cases, 1780–1865" (Jan. 27, 2010), available at http://papers.ssrn.com/sol3/papers.cfm?abstract_id= 1542870. This comprehensive list builds on a handful of intensive studies of judicial review in the 1780s. See Philip Hamburger, *Law and Judicial Duty* (2008); Larry Kramer, *The People Themselves* (2004); William Michael Treanor, "Judicial Review Before *Marbury,*" 58 *Stanford L. Rev.* 455 (2005). For a much more complete list of antebellum federal judicial review precedents that challenges the notion that *Marbury* and *Dred Scott* were the only two examples, see Keith E. Whittington, "Judicial Review of Congress Before the Civil War," 97 *Georgetown L.J.* 1257 (2009). For other studies of judicial review in the antebellum era, see Don E. Fehrenbacher, "Constitutions and Constitutionalism in the Slaveholding South," 19–23,

92 nn.70–74, 93 nn.75–79, 94 nn.80–84 (1989); and William E. Nelson, Commentary, "Changing Conceptions of Judicial Review: The Evolution of Constitutional Theory in the States, 1790–1860," 120 *U. Pa. L. Rev.* 1166 (1972). See also Edward Corwin, "The Extension of Judicial Review in New York: 1783–1905," 15 *Michigan L. Rev.* 281 (1917) and Margaret V. Nelson, *A Study of Judicial Review in Virginia, 1789–1928* (1947).

5. For more details, see Jed Handelsman Shugerman, "Economic Crisis and the Rise of Judicial Elections and Judicial Review," 123 *Harv. L. Rev.* 1061, 1119 (2010).

6. See Morton Horwitz, *The Transformation of American Law, 1780-1860*, at 259–61 (1977).

7. One reason for the shift from the prodebtor, prolegislation class fight in the 1820s to the middle-class antilegislation framing of the 1840s may have been the Bankruptcy Act of 1841, which was passed in the midst of the post-Panic depression. The act's federalization of many creditor-debtor issues may have meant there was less reason to fight on these terms in the state legislatures, state courts, and state constitutional conventions. See Edward J. Balleisen, *Navigating Failure* 101–18 (2001). But this theory is only a partial explanation.

8. See Louis Hartz, *Economic Policy and Democratic Thought, 1776–1860* (1948); Richard Hofstadter, *The American Political Tradition and the Men Who Made It* (1948).

9. See Appendix C (listing numbers of reported cases by state and decade). For more on this question, see Shugerman, "Economic Crisis and the Rise of Judicial Elections and Judicial Review," 1116–17, 1148.

10. For more on this question, see Shugerman, "Economic Crisis," 1117–19.

11. Aker v. State, 5 Ind. 193, 193–94 (1854) (citing Maize v. State, 4 Ind. 342 [1853]). See Appendix E.

12. See Wynehamer v. People, 13 N.Y. 378 (1854); see also People v. Toynbee, 20 Barb. 168 (N.Y. Gen. Term 1855); Wood v. Brooklyn, 14 Barb. 425 (N.Y. Special Term 1852); James W. Ely Jr., "The Oxymoron Reconsidered: Myth and Reality in the Origins of Substantive Due Process," 16 *Constitutional Commentary*, 315, 338–342 (1999).

13. Kramer, *The People Themselves*, 57–72. Kramer cites judicial elections as an example of popular constitutionalism, id., at 164, 200.

14. William Nelson, "Changing Conceptions of Judicial Review," 1179–80.

15. Id., at 1180–85.

16. 1 Max Farrand, *Records of the Federal Convention of 1787*, at 135 (1911) (rev. ed. 1966); see Robert J. Steinfeld, "The Early Anti-majoritarian Rationale for Judicial Review," in *Transformations in American Legal History: Essays in Honor of Morton Horwitz*, 2:143 (2010).

17. *The Federalist* No. 78, at 438 (Alexander Hamilton) (Isaac Kramnick ed., 1987).

18. Corwin, "Extension of Judicial Review in New York," 306–13.

19. See Shugerman, "Economic Crisis"; but see Matthew Lindsay, "In Search of Laissez-Faire Constitutionalism," 123 *Harv. L. Rev. Forum* 55 (2010).

20. People ex rel. Fountain v. Bd. of Supervisors, 4 Barb. 64, 72 (N.Y. Gen. Term 1848).
21. Id., at 72.
22. Id., at 73.
23. See Thorne v. Cramer, 15 Barb. 112, 117 (N.Y. Gen. Term 1851).
24. Id., at 118.
25. Id., at 119.
26. Bradley v. Baxter, 15 Barb. 122, 126 (N.Y. Gen. Term 1853). The author of *Bradley* was Judge Daniel Pratt, a Democrat. See *New York State Government—1853, Wkly. Herald,* Jan. 1, 1853, at 3.
27. *Bradley,* 15 Barb. at 126.
28. Id.
29. See Thomas M. Cooley, *Treatise on the Constitutional Limitations Which Rest upon the Legislative Power of the States in the American Union,* 358–59 (3d ed. 1874).
30. See Charles Grove Haines, "Judicial Review of Legislation in the United States and the Doctrines of Vested Rights and of Implied Limitations on Legislatures" (pt. 1, 2, and 3), 2 *Texas L. Rev.* (1924); Edward S. Corwin, *The Twilight of the Supreme Court: A History of Our Constitutional Theory,* 375 (1934); Melissa Saunders, "Equal Protection, Class Legislation, and Color Blindness," 96 *Mich. L. Rev.* 245, 263 (1997); see also John Harrison, "Substantive Due Process and the Constitutional Text," 83 *Va. L. Rev.* 493, 498–500 (1997).
31. 13 N.Y. 378 (1856).
32. 13 N.Y. at 396.
33. 13 N.Y. at 433–34.
34. James W. Ely Jr., "The Oxymoron Reconsidered: Myth and Reality in the Origins of Substantive Due Process," 16 *Constitutional Commentary* 315, 338–342 (1999). See also Raoul Berger, *Government by Judiciary,* 178 (1975) (commenting that *Wynehamer* was the "locus classicus of substantive due process" and had "fashioned" the doctrine); John Hart Ely, *Democracy and Distrust,* 18 (1980); but see Ryan Williams, "The One and Only Substantive Due Process Clause," 120 *Yale L. J.* 408 (2010).
35. *Wynehamer,* 13 N.Y. at 390.
36. See De Chastellux v. Fairfield, 15 Pa. 18 (1850).
37. Id., at 20.
38. Id.
39. See Ervine's Appeal, 16 Pa. 256, 268 (1851).
40. Id. (quoting Greenough v. Greenough, 11 Pa. 489 [1849]).
41. *Greenough,* 11 Pa. at 495.
42. William A. Porter, *An Essay on the Life, Character and Writings of John B. Gibson,* 102 (1855).
43. See Cincinnati Gas Light & Coke Co. v. Bowman, 12 Ohio Dec. Reprint 147 (Super. Ct. Cincinnati 1855).
44. Id., at 157–58.
45. Beebe v. State, 6 Ind. 501, 527 (1855) (Stuart, J., concurring).

46. People v. Gallagher, 4 Mich. 244, 267 (1856) (Pratt, P. J., dissenting).
47. Griffith v. Comm'rs of Crawford County, 20 Ohio 609, 623 (1851).
48. There are three cases from southern states in the 1830s. See Jones' Heirs v. Perry, 18 Tenn. (10 Yer.) 59, 61 (1836); Wally's Heirs v. Kennedy, 10 Tenn. (2 Yer.) 554, 557 (1831); Goddin v. Crump, 35 Va. (8 Leigh) 120, 151 (1837).
49. Rice v. Foster, 4 Del. (4 Harr.) 479, 487 (1847). Delaware was more of a "border state" than a traditional slave state.
50. See Sadler v. Langham, 34 Ala. 311, 321 (1859); State v. Moss, 47 N.C. (2 Jones) 66, 68 (1854); see also Wiley v. Parmer, 14 Ala. 627, 630–31 (1848). One possible exception to majoritarian reasoning is the Arkansas Supreme Court explaining in 1853 that, even though the state constitution had no clause requiring just compensation for lands taken for public use, such a requirement must be implied. The court explained that just compensation was necessary for protecting "the minority against the majority." Ex parte Martin, 13 Ark. 198, 207 (1853).
51. William E. Nelson, "The Impact of the Antislavery Movement upon Styles of Judicial Reasoning in Nineteenth Century America," 87 Harv. L. Rev. 513, 514, 528–29, 538–39 (1974).
52. See, for example, Jones v. Robbins, 74 Mass. (8 Gray) 329, 338–41 (1857); Opinion of the Judges of the Supreme Court, 30 Conn. 591, 593–94 (1862).
53. For more information on the subject matter of cases over these decades, see Appendix E.
54. See, for example, "The Constitutional Convention," The New Constitution, June 9, 1849; "Constitutional Reform," New Const., Aug. 11, 1849, reprinted in Medary, The New Constitution, at 225, 236, 238 (reprinting an article from the Louisville Chronicle); "Reasons Why the People Should Vote for a Convention to Amend the Constitution of Ohio," New Const., Sept. 15, 1849, at 305, 316 (reprinting an article from the Cadiz Sentinel).
55. Michael F. Holt, The Political Crisis of the 1850s, at 107 (1978).
56. Id., at 103.
57. Id., at 132–34.
58. "To the Democracy of Albany County and the State," Daily Alb. Argus, May 1, 1847.
59. See, for example, Daily Alb. Argus, May 25, 1846.
60. See New York Herald, July 1, 1847; Albany Evening Journal, June 8, 9, 1847; "Judicial Election," Daily Alb. Argus, June 8, 1847.
61. See, for example, Alb. Evening J., April 29, May 20, June 2, 3, 5, 8, 1847; Daily Alb. Argus, May 1, 4, 12, 22, 25, June 5, 7, 8, 1847; N.Y. Herald, May 22, 23, 1847.
62. See Jed Handelsman Shugerman, "The Twist of Long Terms: Judicial Elections, Role Fidelity, and American Tort Law," 98 Geo. L. J. 1349 (2010).
63. See Thomas P. Roberts, Memoirs of John Bannister Gibson, 134–37 (1890).
64. David K. Watson and Moses M. Granger, "The Judiciary of Ohio," in 5 History of Ohio, 85, 135–36 (Emilius O. Randall and Daniel J. Ryan eds., 1912).
65. Lee Benson, The Concept of Jacksonian Democracy: New York as a Test Case, 144, 165, 342–43 (1961).

66. Andrew L. Kaufman, "The First Judge Cardozo: Albert, Father of Benjamin," 11 *J. L. & Religion* 271, 283–84 (1994).

67. Id., at 285, quoting Letter from Albert Cardozo to John R. Brady (July 26, 1866).

68. Id. (quoting Letter from Albert Cardozo).

69. Id., at 284.

70. Andrew Kaufman, *Cardozo* (1998).

71. For more on Comstock, see Thomas M. Kernan, "George Franklin Comstock," in *The Judges of the New York Court of Appeals,* 57, 58 (Albert M. Rosenblatt ed., 2007).

72. Kernan, "Comstock," 58–59.

73. Id., at 58.

74. Id., at 58–59.

75. George Franklin Comstock, "Let Us Reason Together" (1864), reprinted in 2 *Union Pamphlets of the Civil War,* 873, 876 (Frank Freidel ed., 1967).

76. Id. at 879 (emphases omitted).

77. 1 *History of the Republican Party in Ohio,* at 89–90, 97.

78. 2 *Harvard Memorial Biographies,* 237 (1867) (biography of William Yates Gholson Jr.).

79. William B. Neff, *Bench and Bar of Northern Ohio,* 60 (1921).

80. Proslavery Democrats won the presidential elections of 1852 and 1856, and in Congress, they held the upper hand in the mid-1850s.

81. N.Y. Const. of 1846, art. VI, § 4. Ill. Const. of 1848, art. V, § 3; Ky. Const. of 1850, art. IV, § 4; Mich. Const. of 1850, art. VI, § 2; Va. Const. of 1850, art. VI, § 10; Md. Const. of 1851, art. IV, §§ 4, 9; Ind. Const. of 1851, art. VII, §§ 2, 3.

82. Of the judges offering countermajoritarian justifications, more came from districted courts (New York, Indiana, and Michigan) than from statewide seats (Pennsylvania and Ohio).

83. See generally Maxwell Bloomfield, *American Lawyers in a Changing Society, 1776–1876,* at 136–90 (1976); Paul D. Carrington, *Stewards of Democracy,* 47–67 (1999); Alexis de Tocqueville, *Democracy in America,* 263–70 (J. P. Mayer ed., trans. by George. Lawrence, 1969). Edwards, *People and Their Peace.*

84. See Laura J. Scalia, *America's Jeffersonian Experiment: Remaking State Constitutions 1820–1850,* at 31–75 (1999).

85. See Kramer, *People Themselves,* 161–64; Alfred S. Konefsky, "The Legal Profession: From the Revolution to the Civil War," in 2 *Cambridge History of Law in America,* 68–105 (Michael Grossberg and Christopher Tomlins eds., 2008).

86. Fred R. Shapiro, "Quote . . . Misquote," *N.Y. Times,* July 27, 2008, Magazine at 16 (quoting *Daily Cleveland Herald,* Mar. 29, 1869) (attributing this quip to John Godfrey Saxe and noting its frequent misattribution to Otto von Bismarck).

87. Holt, *Political Crisis,* 136–38.

88. William Forbath, *Law and the Shaping of the American Labor Movement,* Appendix A: Labor Legislation in the Courts, 1885–1910, 177–92 (1991).

89. Edward Corwin, "The Extension of Judicial Review in New York," 15 *Mich. L. Rev.* 281, 307–13 (1917).
90. Congressional Research Service, *The Constitution of the United States: Analysis and Interpretation* (Johnny H. Killian, George A. Costello, and Kenneth R. Thomas eds., 2004), 2163–87.
91. Id.
92. See, for example, Hartz, *Economic Policy and Democratic Thought*; Oscar Handlin and Mary Flug Handlin, *Commonwealth: A Study of the Role of Government in the American Economy: Massachusetts, 1774–1861* (1947); Harry N. Scheiber, "Government and the Economy: Studies of the 'Commonwealth' Policy in Nineteenth Century America," 3 *Journal of Interdisciplinary History* 135 (1972).
93. William Novak, *The People's Welfare* (1996).
94. Carter Goodrich, *Government Promotion of American Canals and Railroads, 1800–1890* (1960); Horwitz, *Transformation of American Law.*
95. Jerry Mashaw, *Creating the Administrative Constitution* (2011).
96. Novak, *People's Welfare,* 238–39. But Horwitz contends that formalist limits on common-law changes emerged in the 1850s, too.

7. Reconstructing Independence

1. See, for example, Steven P. Croley, "The Majoritarian Difficulty: Elective Judiciaries and the Rule of Law," 62 *U. Chicago L. Rev.* 689, 691 (1995). David E. Pozen, "The Irony of Judicial Elections," 100 *Columbia L. Rev.* 100 (2008). There is new evidence that judicial elections were more competitive in the mid-twentieth century than modern commentators had thought in terms of contested elections and close elections, but not yet evidence of aggressive campaigning as individual candidates relative to the turn of the twenty-first century. See Herbert Kritzer, "Competitiveness in State Supreme Court Elections, 1946–2009," 8 *J. Emp. Legal Stud.* 237 (2011).
2. Pozen, "Irony of Judicial Elections," 102.
3. "Objections to a Resolution Recommending to the People of Pennsylvania an Elective Judiciary," 26–31 (1849).
4. Lawrence Friedman, *A History of American Law,* 280 (3d. ed. 2005).
5. Kermit L. Hall, "*Progressive* Reform and the Decline of Democratic Accountability: The Popular Election of State Supreme Court Judges, 1850–1920," 9 *Am. Bar Found. Res. J.* 345, 354–55, 357 & tbl. 1 (1984). Turnout in off-year nonpresidential elections has been about 40 percent in recent years. See United States Elections Project: 2006 General Election Turnout Rates, http://elections.gmu.edu/Turnout_2006G.html (last visited Mar. 16, 2010); United States Elections Project: 2002 General Election Turnout Rates, http://elections.gmu.edu/Turnout_2002G.html (last visited Mar. 16, 2010).
6. *Smull's Legislative Hand Book and Manual of the State of Pennsylvania* (1882–1902) (archived at Harvard University, Yale University, the University of Pennsylvania, and the State Library of Pennsylvania in Harrisburg).

7. *Smull's Legislative Hand Book and Manual of the State of Pennsylvania,* 554 (1894); *Smull's Legislative Hand Book and Manual of the State of Pennsylvania,* 618–19 (1900).

8. Those five were the elections of 1880, 1887, 1888, 1892, and 1901. See *Smull's Legislative Hand Book and Manual of the State of Pennsylvania,* 271–72 (William P. Smull ed., 1881) [hereinafter *Smull's* 1881]; *Smull's Legislative Hand Book and Manual of the State of Pennsylvania,* 401–02 (1888) [hereinafter *Smull's* 1888]; *Smull's Legislative Hand Book and Manual of the State of Pennsylvania,* 410–11 (1889); *Smull's Legislative Hand Book and Manual of the State of Pennsylvania,* 490–91 (1893); *Smull's Legislative Hand Book and Manual of the State of Pennsylvania,* 624–25 (1902).

9. *Smull's Legislative Hand Book and Manual of the State of Pennsylvania,* 412–14 (John A. Smull ed., 1878); *Smull's Legislative Hand Book and Manual of the State of Pennsylvania,* 693–94 (1883) [hereinafter *Smull's* 1883].

10. Friedman, *History of American Law,* 280 (citing 8 *Albany L. J.* 18 [July 5, 1873]).

11. Barry Friedman, *The Will of the People,* 154–55 (2009).

12. Id.

13. George Edwards, "Why Justice Cooley Left the Bench: A Missing Page of Legal History," 33 *Wayne L. Rev.* 1563 (1987).

14. "Proceedings of the Convention: Balloting for Supreme Judge," *Phila. Inquirer,* Aug. 23, 1877, at 1.

15. "Wheels within Wheels: Complicated Local Politics," *Phila. Inquirer,* Mar. 22, 1882, at 2.

16. "The Convention," *Phila. Inquirer,* May 11, 1882, at 1.

17. Id.

18. Id.; "In Philadelphia: How the Nominations Were Received—Expressions of Opinion," *Phila. Inquirer,* May 11, 1882, at 1; "The Work of the Convention," *Phila. Inquirer,* May 11, 1882, at 4; "The Independents: Their Approaching Convention," *Phila. Inquirer,* May 18, 1882, at 2; "Getting Interesting: A Ticklish Political Outlook," *Phila. Inquirer,* May 29, 1882, at 2; "Young Republicans Indorsing the Regular Ticket," *Phila. Inquirer,* June 28, 1882, at 2; "A Few of the Republican Leaders Discussing the Political Situation," *Phila. Inquirer,* July 1, 1882, at 2.

19. "Independent Judges: The Uprising of the People for a Free Bench," *Balt. Sun,* Oct. 19, 1882, at 1.

20. Id. (reproducing the remarks of J. Hall Pleasants).

21. *Smull's Legislative Hand Book and Manual of the State of Pennsylvania* (1882).

22. "The Westmoreland Judgeship," *Pittsburgh Com. Gazette,* Oct. 24, 1889.

23. "The Thirty-Fifth Judicial District," *Pittsburgh Com. Gazette,* Oct. 30, 1889.

24. John Fabian Witt, *The Accidental Republic,* 157, 281 n.22 (2004) (quoting "First Round for Warner," *N.Y. Herald,* June 12, 1894).

25. "Disgraceful Scene," *Rochester Union & Advertiser,* June 12, 1894.

26. Witt, *Accidental Republic,* at 158, 281 n.23 (quoting "Seventh Judicial District," *N.Y. Times,* Sept. 15, 1894).

27. Witt, *Accidental Republic*, 166–78; Ives v. South Buffalo Railway, 94 N.E. 436 (N.Y. 1911).

28. Glenn C. Altschuler and Stuart M. Blumin, *Rude Republic: Americans and Their Politics in the Nineteenth Century*, 220–22 (2000).

29. Kevin Hill, "South Carolina: Defining Power, Defining People," and James E. Anderson, "The Texas Constitution: Formal and Informal," in *The Constitutionalism of the American States*, 348, 370 (George E. Connor and Christopher W. Hammons eds. 2008).

30. Republicans opted for appointments in Louisiana (1864), Mississippi (1868), South Carolina (1868), Florida (1868), Texas (1869), and Virginia (1870), and elections in Alabama (1868), Georgia (1868), and North Carolina (1868), and for Arkansas Supreme Court justices, but not lower court judges (1868). Evan Haynes, *Judicial Selection and Tenure*, 102, 107, 109, 113, 117, 124, 129, 131, 133 (1944).

31. Id., 103, 107, 109, 117.

32. 1 James Bryce, *American Commonwealth*, 507 (1888) (3d ed. 1905).

33. Id., 104, 115.

34. Renée Lettow Lerner, "From Popular Control to Independence: Reform of the Elected Judiciary in Boss Tweed's New York," 15 *Geo. Mason L. Rev.* 109 (2007).

35. Haynes, *Judicial Selection and Tenure*, 104, 119, 123, 127, 135.

36. Thomas Schaller, "Pioneer and Outlier: Maryland Constitutionalism," in *The Constitutionalism of American States*, at 100 (2008).

37. "The Constitution of the State of Maryland [1864]" (1865), 44–45 [art. 4, §3].

38. "The Debates of the Constitutional Convention of the State of Maryland [1864]," vol. 2 (1864), 1177.

39. 3 *Debates of the Constitutional Convention of the State of Maryland [1864]*, at 1388 (Mr. Sands).

40. Id., 1386, 1391.

41. Id., 1525–27, 1528.

42. Lettow Lerner, "From Popular Control to Independence," 116–18, 120, 123, 127–30, 145–46, 157–58.

43. Id., 132.

44. Id., 132, 136–38.

45. 3 *Proceedings and Debates of the Constitutional Convention of the State of New York*, 2365 (1868).

46. Id.

47. Id., 2359.

48. Id., 2373.

49. Id., 2382.

50. Lettow Lerner, "From Popular Control to Independence," at 143–44, 156–59.

51. Id., 157 (citing D. B. Eaton, *Should Judges Be Elected? Or the Experiment of an Elective Judiciary in New York* [1873]).

52. Id.

53. 4 *Debates of the Convention to Amend the Constitution of Pennsylvania,* 486 (1873).
54. See Mahlon H. Hellerich, "The Origin of the Pennsylvania Constitutional Convention of 1873," 34 *Penn. Hist.* 158 (1967).
55. Id., 162.
56. Id., 166, 170, 177, 185. The other two were preserving "stability . . . against sudden changes by the legislature, actuated by politics or corrupt motives," and strict regulation of the money raised and spent by cities. Id.
57. See 3 *Debates of the Convention to Amend the Constitution of Pennsylvania,* 637–779 (recording days eighty-seven through eighty-nine); 4 id., 3–489 (recording days ninety through one hundred).
58. 3 id., 729.
59. 3 id., 742, 776.
60. 3 id., 706.
61. 3 id., 748. See also 3 id., 753, 771; 4 id., 23.
62. 4 id., 21.
63. 3 id., 691, 706, 749; 4 id., 33.
64. See 4 id., 486.
65. 1 E. B. Willis and P. K. Stockton, *Debates and Proceedings of the Constitutional Convention of the State of California* 8 (1880).
66. 1 id., 78, 94, 102, 111–12, 113, 119, 132, 141, 144.
67. Id. (McFarland).
68. 2. id., 961 (McFarland); 2 id., at 961 (Tinnin).
69. 2 id., 960 (Eagon). See also id. (Smith).
70. 3 id.,1514.
71. This section is drawn from Jed Handelsman Shugerman, "The Twist of Long Terms," 98 *Georgetown L. J.* 1349 (2010); Jed Handelsman Shugerman, "A Watershed Moment: Reversals of Tort Theory in the Nineteenth Century," 2 *J. Tort L.* (2008) [hereinafter Shugerman, "Watershed Moment"]; Jed Handelsman Shugerman, "Note: The Floodgates of Strict Liability: Bursting Reservoirs and the Adoption of Fletcher v. Rylands in the Gilded Age," 110 *Yale L. J.* 333 (2000) [hereinafter Shugerman, "Floodgates"].
72. See David McCullough, *The Johnstown Flood,* 36, 41–42, 203, 224–25, 237, 241, 264 (1968); "Disaster, Disaster, Disaster," 17–18 (Douglas Newton ed., 1961); "The Broken Dam," *Pittsburgh Com. Gazette,* June 4, 1889; "The Club Is Guilty," *N.Y. World,* June 7, 1889; "The Dam Defective," *Pittsburgh Com. Gazette,* June 5, 1889; "That Fatal Dam: An Expert Engineer Says It Was in Every Respect of Very Inferior Construction," *Pittsburgh Com. Gazette,* June 8, 1889; "From the St. Louis Republic," *Pittsburgh Com. Gazette,* June 5, 1889; *Johnstown Trib.,* July 8, 1889; "Report of the Committee on the Cause of the Failure of the South Fork Dam," 24 *Transactions Am. Soc. Civ. Engineers,* 431, 456–57 (1891); Willis Fletcher Johnson, "History of the Johnstown Flood," 266–80 (1889).
73. Note, "The Law of Bursting Reservoirs," 23 *Am. L. Rev.* 643, 646–47 (1889). Thomas A. Woxland and Patti J. Ogden, *Landmarks in American*

Legal Publishing, 48 (1989); Erwin C. Surrency, *A History of American Law Publishing,* 192 (1990).

74. Rylands v. Fletcher (1866) 1 L.R. Exch. 265, 279 (Exch. Ch.).

75. Rylands v. Fletcher (1868) 3 L.R.E. & I. App. 330, 338-39, 342 (H.L.).

76. See A. W. B. Simpson, "Bursting Reservoirs," 13 *J. Leg. Studies* 209, 251-64 (1984); Jed Handelsman Shugerman, "The Twist of Long Terms." For original research establishing that Holmes actually endorsed *Rylands* and was favorable to strict liability, see David Rosenberg, *Hidden Holmes* (1995). For more on *Rylands*'s significance in Anglo-American history, see Clare Dalton, "Losing History: Tort Liability in the Nineteenth Century and the Case of *Rylands v. Fletcher,*" 29-73; Kenneth Abraham, "*Rylands v. Fletcher:* Tort Law's Conscience," in *Torts Stories,* 207 (Robert Rabin and Stephen Sugarman eds., 2003).

77. Losee v. Buchanan, 51 N.Y. 476, 486-87 (1873).

78. Brown v. Collins, 53 N.H. 442, 446, 450-51 (1873).

79. Marshall v. Welwood, 38 N.J.L. 339, 341 (1876), overruled by State Dept. of Envtl. Prot. v. Ventron Corp., 468 A.2d 150, 157 (N.J. 1983).

80. Pa. Coal Co. v. Sanderson, 6 A. 453 (Pa. 1886). See Shugerman, "Watershed Moment," for more discussion of *Sanderson* and other related cases.

81. Shugerman, "Floodgates," 340-41.

82. See, for example, Friedman, *History of American Law,* 409-27; Morton J. Horwitz, *The Transformation of American Law, 1780-1860,* at 85-108 (1977); G. Edward White, *Tort Law in America,* 3-19 (1980).

83. See Charles O. Gregory, "Trespass to Negligence to Absolute Liability," 37 *Va. L. Rev.* 359, 381-88 (1951); William K. Jones, "Strict Liability for Hazardous Enterprise," 92 *Colum. L. Rev.* 1705, 1706-11 (1992); Virginia E. Nolan and Edmund Ursin, "The Revitalization of Hazardous Activity Strict Liability," 65 *N.C. L. Rev.* 257, 257-60 (1987); Robert Rabin, "The Historical Development of the Fault Principle: A Reinterpretation," 15 *Ga. L. Rev.* 925, 961 (1981).

84. See, for example, Richard A. Epstein, *Cases and Materials on Torts,* 139-43 (9th ed. 2008).

85. "Law of Bursting Reservoirs," 23 *Am. L. Rev.* at 647.

86. Id.

87. Nathan Daniel Shappee, "A History of Johnstown and the Great Flood of 1889: A Study of Disaster and Rehabilitation," 412 (1940) (unpublished Ph.D. dissertation, University of Pittsburgh), available at http://www.access padr.org/u?/acacc-jtf,394; "Against South Fork Club," *Johnstown Wkly. Democrat,* July 24, 1891, at 6; "A Flood Damage Suit," *Johnstown Trib.,* May 9, 1894, at 1; "Against the Fishing Club," *Johnstown Trib.,* Nov. 1, 1893, at 1; *Johnstown Trib.,* June 18, 1891, at 1.

88. "An Old Case Heard From," *Johnstown Trib.,* June 26, 1897, at 1; "Johnstown Flood Suit Recalled," *Johnstown Trib.,* Nov. 23, 1896, at 1; "South Fork Club Suits," *Johnstown Wkly. Democrat,* May 18, 1894, at 3; "The South Fork Cases," *Johnstown Trib.,* Feb. 24, 1892, at 1; "The South Fork Club Suits," *Johnstown Trib.,* Feb. 23, 1892; "The South Fork Fishing Club," *Johnstown Wkly. Democrat,* June 19, 1891, at 1; "The South Fork

Fishing & Hunting Club in Court," "The South Fork Suit," *Johnstown Trib.,* Dec. 15, 1891, at 1; see Shappee, "History of Johnstown and the Great Flood of 1889," and McCullough, *Johnstown Flood.*

89. Pa. Coal Co. v. Sanderson, 6 A. 453, 460–63 (Pa. 1886).
90. Id., at 462–63.
91. Id., at 459.
92. Robb v. Carnegie Bros., 22 A. 649 (Pa. 1891).
93. Robb v. Carnegie Bros., 145 Pa. 324, 336 (1891).
94. Id., at 324.
95. Robb, 22 A. at 650–51. The reversing judges were Clark, Green, and Paxson.
96. Id.
97. Id.
98. Id., at 651.
99. Id.
100. See Shugerman, "Twist of Long Terms."
101. Id., app. A; Shugerman, "Floodgates," at 334–35 and n.9; Appendix F.
102. See Shugerman, "Floodgates"; "Twist of Long Terms"; John T. Cumbler, *Northeast and Midwest United States: An Environmental History,* 138–41 (2005).
103. This finding confirms Peter Karsten's suggestion that judicial elections may have led state courts to favor plaintiffs in tort suits in the late nineteenth century. Peter Karsten, *Heart versus Head: Judge-Made Law in Nineteenth-Century America,* 288–91 (1997).

8. The Progressives' Failed Solutions

1. Lochner v. New York, 198 U.S. 45 (1905).
2. Adair v. United States, 208 U.S. 161 (1908); Employers' Liability Cases, 207 U.S. 463 (1908); Coppage v. Kansas, 236 U.S. 1 (1915); Hammer v. Dagenhart, 247 U.S. 251(1918); Knickerbocker Ice Co. v. Stewart, 253 U.S. 149 (1920); Eisner v. Macomber, 252 U.S. 189 (1920); and Adkins v. Children's Hospital, 261 U.S. 525 (1923).
3. State ex rel. Schwartz v. Ferris, 53 Ohio St. 314 (1895); State v. Gardner, 58 Ohio St. 610 (1898); Hibbard v. State, 65 Ohio St. 574 (1901); State ex rel. Ward v. Hubbard, 12 Ohio Cir. Dec. 87 (1901); City of Cleveland v. Clements Brothers Construction Co., 67 Ohio St. 197, 65 N.E. 885 (1902); Harmon v. State, 66 Ohio St. 249 (1902); State of Ohio ex rel. Knisely v. Jones, 66 Ohio St. 453 (1902); State ex rel. Yaple v. Creamer, 97 N.E. 602 (1912); Ives v. South Buffalo Railway Co., 201 N.Y. 271; 94 N.E. 431 (1911).
4. Steven H. Steinglass and Gino J. Scarselli, *The Ohio State Constitution: A Reference Guide,* 35 (2004).
5. Robert Marion LaFollette, *LaFollette's Autobiography: A Personal Narrative of Political Experiences,* 209 (1920); Hermann Hagedorn, ed., *National Edition: Works of Theodore Roosevelt,* vol. 17 (1926), 5–22 (Roosevelt's Aug. 31, 1910, speech).

6. Theodore Roosevelt, "A Charter for Democracy," in *Proceedings and Debates of Ohio Constitutional Convention of 1912* (Feb. 21, 1912): 383–87; Hermann Hagedorn, ed., 16 *Works of Theodore Roosevelt*, 206; William G. Ross, *A Muted Fury: Populists, Progressives, and Labor Unions Confront the Court, 1890–1937*, 134 (1994).

7. Roosevelt, "Charter for Democracy," 383–87.

8. Address of Gov. Johnson of California, in *Proceedings and Debates of Ohio Constitutional Convention of 1912* (Feb. 29, 1912): 547.

9. William Jennings Bryan, "The People's Law," in *Proceedings and Debates of Ohio Constitutional Convention of 1912* (Mar. 12, 1912): 666–67.

10. Ellen Torelle, ed., *The Political Philosophy of Robert LaFollette as Revealed in His Writings and Speeches*, 178, 404 (1975).

11. James B. Weaver, *A Call to Action*, 67–135, 74–75 (1892); Walter Clark, "Is the Supreme Court Unconstitutional?" *Independent*, Sept. 26, 1907, p. 726; Barry Friedman, *The Will of the People: How Public Opinion Has Influenced the Supreme Court and Shaped the Meaning of the Constitution* (2009); J. Allen Smith, *The Spirit of American Government*, 65–124 (1907); Louis B. Boudin, "Government by Judiciary," *Political Science Quarterly* 26 (June 1911).

12. John R. Vile, ed., *Encyclopedia of Constitutional Amendments, Proposed Amendments, and Amending Issues, 1789–1995*, at 371 (1996); Ross, *Muted Fury*, 94–95.

13. Elizabeth Sanders, *The Roots of Reform: Farmers, Workers, and the American State, 1877–1917* (1999).

14. Roosevelt, "Charter for Democracy," 383–87; Daniel Rodgers, *Atlantic Crossings: Social Politics in a Progressive Age* (1998); Leon Fink, *Progressive Intellectuals and the Dilemmas of Democratic Commitment* (1998); Glenda Gilmore, ed., *Who Were the Progressives?* (2002); Michael McGerr, *A Fierce Discontent: The Rise and Fall of the Progressive Movement in America, 1870–1920* (2003); Charles Postel, *The Populist Vision* (2007).

15. Arthur Schlesinger Jr., 2 *History of American Presidential Elections*, 1847 (1971).

16. Ross, *Muted Fury*, 36.

17. William Forbath, *Law and the Shaping of the American Labor Movement*, 136 (1991), citing Samuel Gompers, "Government by Injunction," 4 *American Federationist*, 82 (1897).

18. Forbath, *Law and the Shaping of the American Labor Movement*, citing Gompers, "Labor Organizations Must Not Be Outlawed," *American Federationist*, Mar. 1908, 180–190; Samuel Gompers, "To Organized Labor and Friends," *American Federationist*, Mar. 1908, 192, 193.

19. Forbath, *Shaping of the American Labor Movement*; James Gray Pope, "Labor's Constitution of Freedom," 106 *Yale L. J.* 941 (1997); but see Julie Green, *Pure and Simple Politics: The American Federation of Labor and Political Activism* (1998).

20. Norman Pollack, *The Just Polity: Populism, Law and Human Welfare, 1880–1920*, 64 (1987).

21. Barry Friedman, *The Will of the People*, 183 (2009).
22. 47 Cong. Rec. 3964–65; *Collected Works of William Howard Taft: Presidential Messages to Congress*, 155 (David Henry Burton ed., 2002).
23. Ross, *Muted Fury*, 151.
24. Forbath, *Law and the Shaping of the American Labor Movement*.
25. John Fabian Witt, *The Accidental Republic*, 166–78 (2004); Ives v. South Buffalo Railway, 94 N.E. 436 (N.Y. 1911).
26. John Ferejohn and Larry Kramer, "Independent Judges, Dependent Judiciary," 77 *NYU L. Rev.* 962 (2002).
27. Roosevelt, "Charter for Democracy," 384.
28. Patricia O'Toole, *When Trumpets Call: Theodore Roosevelt After the White House*, 147–49 (2005).
29. People v. Max, 70 Colo. 100, 198 P. 150 (1921), ruling that another section of the amendment violated the U.S. Constitution and that the amendment was nonseverable, so that the whole amendment was invalid.
30. The seven amendments appear as the following sections of the Ohio Constitution: art. II, § 33; art. II, § 34; art. II, § 35; art. II, § 37; art. II, § 40; art. VIII, § 6; and art. XVIII.
31. Jed Shugerman, "A 6-3 Rule," 37 *Ga. L. Rev.* 893 (2003). See also Katherine B. Fite and Louis Baruch Rubenstein, "Curbing the Supreme Court," 35 *Mich. L. Rev.* 762 (1937).
32. Jonathan L. Entin, "Judicial Supermajorities and the Validity of Statutes," 52 *Case W. Res. L. Rev.* 441 (2001).
33. Bryan, "People's Law," 666–67.
34. *Proceedings and Debates of Ohio Constitutional Convention of 1912*, at 143.
35. Id., 1028–30.
36. Ohio Const. art. IV, § 2 (repealed 1968).
37. Entin, "Judicial Supermajorities," 451–52.
38. N.D. Const. art. IV, § 89 (reenacted as N.D. Const. art. VI, § 4 in 1976).
39. Neb. Const. art. V, § 2.
40. James Bryce, *The American Commonwealth*, 353 (1906).
41. Robert Cushman, "Non-Partisan Nominations and Elections," 106 *Annals Am. Acad. Pol. & Soc. Sci.* 83 (1923).
42. Kermit L. Hall, *The Magic Mirror: Law in American History*, 368–69 (1989); Simeon Eben Baldwin, *The American Judiciary*, 330 (1905).
43. See B. Friedman, *Will of the People*, 183 (citing a study by the National Economic League led by William Howard Taft).
44. Gilbert E. Roe, *Our Judicial Oligarchy*, 14 (1912) (citing Gov. Aldrich).
45. Herbert M. Kritzer, "Law Is the Mere Continuation of Politics by Different Means: American Judicial Selection in the Twenty-First Century," 56 *DePaul L. Rev.* 423, 429 (2006).
46. Larry C. Berkson and Rachel Caufield, *Judicial Selection in the United States: A Special Report*, 2 (American Judicature Society 2004); Larry Berkson, Scott Bellter, and Michelle Grimaldi, *Judicial Selection in the United States: A Compendium of Provisions*, 4 (1980).

47. Ohio Rev. Code Ann. § 3505.04.
48. *Proceedings and Debates of Ohio Constitutional Convention of 1912*, at 1051–52.
49. Id., 1925–26.
50. Id., 1239.
51. Id., 1244.
52. Id., 1239.
53. Id.
54. Id., 1242, 1923.
55. Id., 1923–24.
56. Id.,1924.
57. Id., 1927, 2113.
58. See Ohio Const. art. V, § 7 (1912).
59. Frances R. Aumann, "Selection of Judges in Ohio," 5 *U. of Cincinnati L. Rev.* 413 (1931).
60. 103 Ohio Laws 476 (1913). See also 106 Ohio Laws 542 (1915); Aumann, "Selection of Judges in Ohio," 413 n.19.
61. Walter T. Dunmore, "Cleveland Bar's Influence in Judicial Elections," 12 *J. Am. Judicature Soc.* 178 (Apr. 1929).
62. Kermit Hall, *Popular Election of Judges,* 368.
63. 9 *Transactions of Commonwealth Club of California,* 311–12 (1914), in Lamar T. Beman, *Election versus Appointment of Judges,* 65 (1926).
64. William H. Taft, "The Selection and Tenure of Judges," 38 *A.B.A. Rep.* 418 (1913).
65. Id., 423.
66. Id., 422.
67. Judge Harvey Keeler, 25 *Green Bag* 147 (1913), cited in Lamar Beman, *Election vs. Appointment of Judges,* 49 (1926); Ohio State Bar Association, *Proceedings of the Thirty-Seventh Annual Session,* 188 (1916).
68. Berkson and Caufield, *Judicial Selection in the United States.* Iowa, Kansas, and Pennsylvania all tried nonpartisan judicial elections but reverted to partisan elections.
69. See Chris W. Bonneau and Melinda Gann Hall, *In Defense of Judicial Elections* (2009) for a summary of these studies.
70. Roscoe Pound, "The Causes of Popular Dissatisfaction with the Administration of Justice," 20 *J. Am. Judicature Society* 178, at 186.
71. John Parker Hall, "Methods of Selecting Judges," Address to the Ohio State Bar Association, Dec. 29, 1915, in Beman, *Election versus Appointment of Judges,* 66–67.
72. Michal Belknap, *To Improve the Administration of Justice: A History of the American Judicature Society* 1–20 (1992).
73. Glenn R. Winters, "The Merit Plan for Judicial Selection and Tenure: Its Historical Development," in *Judicial Selection and Tenure: Selected Readings,* 29, 33–36 (Glenn R. Winters ed., 1973).
74. Philip L. Dubois, *From Ballot to Bench: Judicial Elections and the Quest for Accountability,* 3 (1980).

75. Susan B. Carbon and Larry C. Berkson, *Judicial Retention Elections in the United States*, 4 (1980).
76. Id., 35. Edward Martin studied the bar's role in judicial selection in Chicago, but oddly preferred selection by the chief judge rather than a commission that included bar leaders. Edward Martin, *The Role of the Bar in Electing the Bench in Chicago* (1936).
77. Martin, *Role of the Bar*, 354–55.
78. F. L. Reinhold, "Philadelphia's Bar Primary," 24 *National Municipal Review* 205 (1934); Martin, *Role of the Bar*, 363.
79. Id., 354; Scott McReynolds, 9 *California State Bar Journal* 66 (1934).
80. Id.
81. Conference Committee on the Merit System, *The Merit System in Government: Report of the Conference Committee on the Merit System* (1926); Oliver Clark Short, *The Merit System: A Monograph* (1928); Charles W. Eliot, *The Merit System and the New Democratic Party*, National Civil Service Reform League (1913); Dean Lewis, *The Scope of the Merit System under the New Deal* (A.B. honors thesis, Harvard University, 1942); Hon. Frederick Gillett, *The Democratic Administration and the Merit System* (1913); Benjamin Fletcher Wright, "The Merit System in American States," *University of Texas Bulletin*, Feb. 1, 1923. The Pendleton Act of 1883 is credited with establishing a federal civil service system and a check against partisan patronage, sometimes described as a "merit system." Glenn C. Altschuler and Stuart M. Blumin, *Rude Republic: Americans and Their Politics in the Nineteenth Century*, 257 (2000).
82. Louise Rutherford, *The Influence of the American Bar Association on Public Opinion and Legislation*, 156 (1937).
83. Id., 157.
84. Richard Hofstadter, *The Age of Reform: From Bryan to FDR*, 131–48 (1955); Robert Wiebe, *The Search for Order, 1877–1920* (1967); Elizabeth Saunders, *The Roots of Reform* (1999); Shelton Stromquist, *Reinventing the People: The Progressive Movement, the Class Problem, and the Origins of Modern Liberalism* (2005).
85. For the interpretation of progressivism as liberal corporatism and anti-populism, see Gabriel Kolko, *The Triumph of Conservatism: A Reinterpretation of American History, 1900–1916* (1963); Samuel Hays, "The Politics of Reform in Municipal Government in the Progressive Era," 55 *Pacific Northwest Quarterly* 157 (1964); R. Jeffrey Lustig, *Corporate Liberalism: The Origins of Modern American Political Theory, 1890–1920* (1962); Nancy Cohen, *The Reconstruction of American Liberalism, 1865–1914* (2002); Stromquist, *Reinventing the People*.
86. Belknap, *To Improve the Administration of Justice*.

9. The Great Depression, Crime, and the Revival of Appointment

1. Earl Warren, "Organized Crime vs. Unorganized Law Enforcement," *California Journal of Development*, June 1934, p. 18.

2. Note how Warren's metaphor of judge-as-umpire has a negative connotation, less like Chief Justice Roberts's embrace of the umpire metaphor (and its revival during the Sotomayor hearings). For a more recent elaboration on this metaphor, see Bruce Weber, "Umpires vs. Judges," *N.Y. Times*, July 12, 2009 (http://www.nytimes.com/2009/07/12/weekinreview/12weber.html?_r=1).

3. Warren, "Organized Crime," 19.

4. Marsha Puro et al., "An Analysis of Judicial Diffusion: The Adoption of the Missouri Plan in the American States," 15 *Publius: The Journal of Federalism* 85 (1985). Puro et al. find that nonprofessional legislatures were correlated with the adoption of merit selection, but nonprofessional legislatures are highly correlated with rural states.

5. Puro's suggestion that *Baker v. Carr* in 1962 triggered a rural effort to entrench judges was refuted by Dubois, "The Politics of Innovation in State Courts." See Chapter 10 for a discussion of Dubois's theory of AJS leadership. Another theory was that bar association activity was strongly correlated with merit adoptions. Judith Haydel, "Explaining Adoption of Judicial Merit Selection in the States, 1950–1980: A Multivariate Test," 99 (unpublished Ph.D. diss., University of New Orleans, 1987). Bar activity was probably a factor, but Haydel's study measured "bar activity" only from surveys in the late 1970s and 1980s, long after the merit plans in her study were adopted. The main measure was the bar's involvement in judicial reform, which may have been more an effect than a cause. This chapter also addresses a theory of partisan risk aversion: merit plans succeeded in states with more parity between the parties, and thus the party in power increased judicial independence from the parties out of a greater fear of losing power. F. Andrew Hanssen, "Learning about Judicial Independence," 33 *J. Legal Stud.* 431 (2004). This theory applies in California in the 1930s, but not in the wave of the 1960s–1970s.

6. Id.

7. Philip Dubois, "The Politics of Innovation in State Courts: The Merit Plan of Judicial Selection," 20 *Publius: The Journal of Federalism* 23, 34 (1990).

8. Missouri's and Arizona's merit plans mandated merit selection only for those states' urban areas.

9. Ruth Milkman and Daisy Rooks, "California Union Membership: A Turn-of-the-Century Portrait," *The State of California Labor* 7 (2003).

10. Leo Troy, "Distribution of Union Membership among the States, 1939 and 1953," NBER, www.nber.org/books/troy57-1#navDiv=6.

11. Warren biographers do not discuss Warren's leadership of judicial selection reform. Ed Cray, *Chief Justice: A Biography of Earl Warren*, 73–75 (1997); G. Edward White, *Earl Warren: A Public Life*, 33–34 (1987); Jim Newton, *Justice for All: Earl Warren and the Nation He Made*, 81–85 (2006).

12. Malcolm Smith, "The California Method of Selecting Judges," 3 *Stan. L. Rev.* 571, 571–72 (1951).

13. William Nancarrow, "Vox Populi: Democracy and the Progressive Era Judiciary, 1890–1916" (Ph.D. diss., Boston College, 2004).

14. Smith, "California Method," 573 (citing 8 *Transactions of the Commonwealth Club of California* 5 [1913]).

15. Smith, "The California Method of Selecting Judges," 573. The Club's founders included Herbert Hoover and future governors James Gillette and Sunny Jim Rolph, and future U.S. Senator James Phelan, who campaigned to "Keep California White" in 1920.

16. "Selection of Judges," 9 *Transactions of Commonwealth Club of California,* 311–12 (1914).

17. *Cleveland News,* May 25, 1926, in Lamar T. Beman, *Election versus Appointment of Judges* 105 (1926).

18. "Selection of Judges," 9 *Transactions of the Commonwealth Club* 305 (1914).

19. Id., 313, 317.

20. Chairman Lynn White, "Report on the Section on Delinquency," 21 *Transactions of the Commonwealth Club* 395, 399 (1926). The issue was titled "The 'Crime Wave.'"

21. Smith, "California Method," 576.

22. Id., 574–75.

23. F. L. Reinhold, "Philadelphia's Bar Primary," 24 *National Municipal Review* 205 (1934); Edward M. Martin, *The Role of the Bar in Electing the Bench in Chicago* 363 (1936).

24. W. W. Robinson, *Lawyers of Los Angeles* (1959).

25. "California's Crusade for Selection Reform," 19 *Journal of the American Judicature Society* 51 (1936).

26. Smith, "California Method," 578 (citing *Cal. Assn. Journal* 3187 [1933]; Letter from John Perry Wood to Malcolm Smith, Oct. 11, 1950; 6 *Proc. Ca. St. Bar Ass'n* 89 [1933]).

27. U.S. Census Statistical Abstract, 1920, 1930.

28. U.S. Census data (1910, 1920, 1930).

29. Bryan Burrough, *Public Enemies: America's Greatest Crime Wave and the Birth of the FBI, 1933–34* (2005).

30. Paul and Patricia Brantingham, *Patterns in Crime* 190 (1984); David Rubinstein, "Don't Blame Crime on Joblessness," *Wall Street Journal,* Nov. 9, 1992, at A10; William Stuntz, *The Collapse of American Criminal Justice* (2011).

31. "Crime Can Be Curbed," California Committee on the Better Administration of Law, 1938, p. 7 (archived at Yale Law Library); Joseph Knowland, "California Girds for War on Crime," *California Journal of Development,* July 1934, p. 11.

32. Knowland, "California Girds for War on Crime."

33. Earl Warren, *The Memoirs of Earl Warren,* 110 (1977).

34. Id.

35. Smith, "California Method," 579, n. 59.

36. Id., 579–80.

37. See id., 580–85.

38. Louise Young, *In the Public Interest: The League of Women Voters, 1920–1970* (1989); Naomi Black, *Social Feminism* (1989); Kristi Andersen, *After Suffrage: Women in Partisan and Electoral Politics before the New Deal* (1996).

39. Young, *In the Public Interest,* 45–46, 113–14; Black, *Social Feminism,* 270–71, 283, 287, 295.

40. Earl Warren, "Conversations with Earl Warren on California Government," an oral history, 1972, Regional Oral History Office, The Bancroft Library, University of California, Berkeley, 1981; Cray, *Chief Justice*, 72.

41. Smith, "California Method," 581.

42. Id., 582 (citing Statewide Committee Minutes 1–24, 1–25 [Feb. 16, 1934]).

43. Smith, "California Method," (citing Statewide Committee Minutes 1–17, 1–24, 1–25 [Feb. 16, 1934]).

44. Id., at 584 (citing Statewide Committee Minutes 17, Mar. 20, 1934) (the Committee Minutes can no longer be found in the archives, so the citations come from Smith's 1951 article); "Commonwealth Club's Plan for Selection of Judges (Revised) Initiative Proposal," 29 *Transactions of the Commonwealth Club* 131–32 (1934).

45. Cray, *Chief Justice*, 72.

46. "Curb Crime Plan Pushed," *Los Angeles Times*, June 1, 1934, A1.

47. Id. at 584.

48. The label "merit selection" became common beginning in Nebraska in 1962.

49. "Conversations with Earl Warren on California Government," 11; "California's Crusade for Selection Reform," 52.

50. White, *Earl Warren*, 34.

51. Knowland, "California Girds for War on Crime," 11, 16; "Major Groups Endorse Amendments to Curb Crime," *California Journal of Development*, Sept. 1934, p. 20; "Help Prevent Crime," *California Journal of Development*, Oct. 1934, p. 25.

52. "California's Crusade for Selection Reform," 51; "Former Judge Wood Calls Cost of Justice in Los Angeles Out of All Proportion," *Los Angeles Times*, Feb. 4, 1934, B9.

53. "California's Crusade for Selection Reform," 51.

54. Smith, "California Method," 579. Hollis R. Thompson, "Arguments in Favor of the Club's Revised Plan for selection of Judges," 29 *Transactions of the Commonwealth Club* 135 140 (1934).

55. "Selection of Judges," *Los Angeles Times*, Oct. 31, 1934, A4.

56. "California's Crusade for Selection Reform," 51.

57. Smith "California Method," 585; see also Joseph Grodin, "Developing a Consensus of Constraint: A Judge's Perspective on Judicial Retention Elections," 61 *U.S.C. L. Rev.* 1969, 1972 (1988).

58. Edward D. Vandeleur, "Arguments Against Club's Plan for selection of Judges," 29 *Transactions of the Commonwealth Club* 136 (1934).

59. Id., 139.

60. "California's Crusade for Selection Reform," 52.

61. F. Andrew Hanssen, "Learning about Judicial Independence," 33 *J. Legal Studies* 431 (2004). See also Mark Ramseyer, "The Puzzling (In)Dependence of Courts: A Comparative Approach," 23 *J. Legal Studies* 721 (1994); Matthew C. Stephenson, "'When the Devil Turns . . .': The Political Foundations of Independent Judicial Review," 32 *J. Legal Studies* 59 (2003).

62. See chart in Appendix H.

63. See chart in Appendix H.

64. Id., 586.

65. "California's Crusade for Selection Reform," 51.

66. Hastings Law Library, California Ballot Propositions (1911–present), http://holmes.uchastings.edu/cgi-bin/starfinder/0?path=calprop.txt&id=webber&pass=webber&OK=OK. "Earl Warren's Campaigns Volume II," Oral History Office, The Bancroft Library, University of California, Berkeley.

67. Smith, "California Method," 582.

68. California Committee on the Better Administration of Law, "Crime Can Be Curbed" (1936).

69. Martin, *Role of the Bar,* 336 n.3.

70. Cray, *Chief Justice,* 74.

71. Id., 75.

72. Id.

73. Id.

74. White, *Earl Warren,* 34.

75. Id.

76. Id., 42.

77. Smith, "California Method," 593 (citing *San Francisco Chronicle,* Aug. 1, 1940, p. 14).

78. Id., 592.

79. 18 *Cal. St. Bar J.* 222 (1943).

80. Louise Rutherford, *The Influence of the American Bar Association on Public Opinion and Legislation,* 152 (1937).

81. Id., 156; Martin, *Role of the Bar.*

82. Rutherford, *Influence of the American Bar Association,* 159.

83. Hon. Robert N. Wilkin, "An Appointed Judiciary: Its Place in the Balance of Government," 23 *ABA J.* 57 (1937).

84. William J. Donovan, "An Independent Supreme Court and the Protection of Minority Rights," 23 *ABA J.* 254, 256 (1937). Incongruously, Donovan also included southern states' rights in this mix of minority rights, undercutting his moral stance on racial and religious minorities. He also argued that the Supreme Court had protected labor's rights. The article seems grabbing at any example in its hodgepodge defense of the Supreme Court, primarily in opposition to the New Deal, but nevertheless, it is grabbing at European fascism as another reason to defend judicial independence.

85. Hon. John Perry Wood, "Basic Propositions Relating to Judicial Selection— Failure of Direct Primary—Appointment through Dual Agency—Judge to 'Run on Record,'" 23 *ABA J.* 102, 103 (1937).

86. Id., 108.

87. "Lay Organization Demands Better Method for Selecting State Judges," 23 *ABA J.* 528 (1937); Elwood Hutcheson, "The Administration of Justice as Affected by the Insecurity of Tenure of Judicial and Administrative Officers," 23 *ABA J.* 930 (1937).

88. Barry Cushman, *Rethinking the New Deal Court: The Structure of a Constitutional Revolution,* 13, 21 (1998). There is evidence that Justice Roberts decided to switch in favor of New Deal legislation before Roosevelt announced the Court-packing plan.

89. Barry Friedman, *The Will of the People* 225 (2009).

90. George Brand, "Michigan State Bar's Work for Judicial Appointment," 22 *J. American Judicature Society* 197 (Feb. 1939).

91. H. L. Barkedull, "Analysis of Ohio Vote on Appointive Judiciary," 22 *J. American Judicature Society* 197 (Feb. 1939). The *Ohio State Bar Journal* in 1938 contains no references to merit selection as an anticrime measure.

92. Barkedull, "Analysis of Ohio Vote on Appointive Judiciary."

93. Troy, "Distribution of Union Membership."

94. "Padberg Again," *St. Louis Post Dispatch,* Sept. 24, 1940. The most notable example was Judge Padberg, who was trained as a lawyer but instead became a pharmacist. A party insider nominated him to be a trial judge, and despite the bar's low evaluation of Padberg, he won his primary.

95. Floyd Calvin Shoemaker, *Missouri and Missourians: Land of Contrasts and People of Achievements,* vol. 2, at 377 (1943).

96. Id., vol. 2, at 377–78.

97. Richard A. Watson and Rondal G. Downing, *The Politics of the Bench and the Bar: Judicial Selection Under the Missouri Nonpartisan Court Plan* 10 (1969); Charles B. Blackmar, "Missouri's Nonpartisan Court Plan from 1942 to 2005," 72 Mo. L. Rev. 199, 200–01 (2007); Shoemaker, *Missouri and Missourians,* vol. 2, at 380.

98. Bryan Burrough, *Public Enemies: America's Greatest Crime Wave and the Birth of the FBI, 1933–34,* at 58 (2005).

99. *Missouri Bar Journal,* Aug. 1937, p. 114.

100. George G. Suggs Jr., *Rush Hudson Limbaugh and His Times* (2003).

101. Id., 133.

102. Id., 153–59.

103. Id., 115–16.

104. *Missouri Bar Journal,* Sept. 1937, p. 142.

105. Leland Hazard, Kansas City Bar, "Agenda for the M.I.A.J.," *Missouri Bar Journal,* Dec. 1937.

106. "The President's Annual Address," *Missouri Bar J.,* Oct. 1937, p. 172.

107. *Missouri Bar J.,* Dec. 1937, p. 272.

108. Id., Dec. 1937, p. 272.

109. Id., Feb. 1939, p. 26.

110. Id., 26, 28.

111. Statistical Abstract, U.S. Census, http://www.census.gov/prod/www/abs/statab 1901-1950.htm.

112. "Report of Committee on Criminal Law," *Missouri Bar J.,* vol. 10, no. 7 (Sept. 1939), pp. 110–11. Letter from J. Lionberger Davis, President, M.I.A.J. to bar members, Dec. 1, 1938; Letter from Kenneth Teasdale, Counsel to M.I.A.J. to bar members, Mar. 13, 1939; Kenneth Teasdale, Memo, "Efforts of the M.I.A.J. Finally Bear Fruit," June 17, 1939, in the Frank Atwood Papers, Western Historical Manuscript Collection—Columbia, University of Missouri/ State Historical Society.

113. "Criminal Law Reform," *Missouri Bar J.,* vol. 11, no. 7 (p. 101).

114. Blackmar, "Missouri's Nonpartisan Court Plan"; Jack Peltason, *The Missouri Plan for the Selection of Judges* (1944); *Missouri Bar J.,* Dec. 1940, 212–13.

115. Blackmar, "Missouri's Nonpartisan Court Plan," 201.

116. *St. Louis Post-Dispatch,* Nov. 8, 1938, 2c.

117. Id., Feb. 24, 1940, 4a.

118. Id., Oct. 31, 1941, 2d.

119. Id., Feb. 24, 1940.

120. Troy, "Distribution of Union Membership."

121. Young, *In the Public Interest;* Black, *Social Feminism;* Andersen, *After Suffrage.*

122. Peltason, *Missouri Plan,* 64.

123. *St. Louis Post-Dispatch,* Aug. 25, 1942.

124. *The Bench and Bar,* vol. 7, no. 1 (Oct. 1942), pp. 8–9.

125. Id., Sept. 22, 1942, 2b.

126. *St. Louis Post-Dispatch,* Sept. 23, 1942, 2c.

127. Id., Oct. 2, 1942, 2d.

128. Id., June 4, 1940, 2c.

129. Blackmar, "Missouri's Nonpartisan Court Plan," 203.

130. Id., 204. Its first effort, opposing Allen C. Southern in 1942, failed by a vote of three-to-one.

131. Blackmar, "Missouri's Nonpartisan Court Plan from 1942 to 2005"; Peltason, *Missouri Plan;* Robert A. Schroeder and Harry A. Hall, "Twenty-Five Years of Experience with Merit Judicial Selection in Missouri," 44 *Tex. L. Rev.* 1088 (1966); Watson and Downing, *The Politics of the Bench and Bar.*

132. "Talk Change in Method of Picking Judges Here," *Milwaukee Journal,* Dec. 19, 1947, p. 25; Justice James Douglas, "Judicial Selection and Tenure: 'Missouri Plan' Works Well in Actual Results," 33 *ABA J.* 1172 (1947) (this should be taken with a grain of salt, because the author was the chief justice of Missouri at the time); Jacob M. Lashly, "The Missouri Plan for Selection and Tenure of Judges," 21 *Conn. Bar J.* 288, 294 (1947).

133. See Watson and Downing, *Politics of the Bench and Bar,* 44.

10. The Puzzling Rise of Merit

1. Richard Hofstadter, *Anti-Intellectualism in American Life,* 224–28 (1962); Arthur Schlesinger Jr., "The Highbrow in Politics," 20 *Partisan Review* 162 (1953).

2. Hofstadter, *Anti-Intellectualism,* 12.

3. Id.

4. Missouri's and Arizona's merit plans mandated merit selection only for those states' urban areas.

5. Philip Dubois, "The Politics of Innovation in State Courts: The Merit Plan of Judicial Selection," 20 *Publius: The Journal of Federalism* 40–41 (1990). Specifically, he notes that "of the twenty-two states adopting the Merit Plan during [a twenty-year period, AJS] 'Citizens Conferences' were held in at least seventeen" to organize and rally support. At the same time, Dubois is careful about his claim: "It would be unwise to attribute the diffusion of the Plan during the 1960s and 1970s entirely or even primarily to this mobilization

effort. Further research is needed on the political conditions under which such activities were influential in stimulating reform." Id., at 41.

6. F. Andrew Hanssen, "Learning about Judicial Independence," 33 *J. Legal Stud.* 431 (2004).

7. See Appendix H for party balance date and discussion. The following states adopted merit plans while one party consistently controlled the state legislature during the merit campaign: Missouri, Kansas, Iowa, Nebraska, Oklahoma, Idaho, Vermont, Maryland, Tennessee, Florida, Wyoming, Kentucky, Nevada, Kentucky, and Hawaii.

8. San Diego Unions v. Garmon, 359 U.S. 236 (1959); Int'l Assoc. of Machinists and Aero. Workers v. Wisconsin Employment Relations Commission, 427 U.S. 132 (1976).

9. Robert B. Hobson, "NACCA—As Viewed by Defense Counsel," 20 *Kentucky State Bar Journal* 170 (1956).

10. John Witt, *Patriots and Cosmopolitans: Hidden Histories of American Law*, 242–60 (2007); Samuel B. Horowitz, "NACCA and Its Objectives," *NACCA L. J.* 10:17 (1953) at 26–28; Hobson, "NACCA."

11. Witt, *Patriots and Cosmopolitans*, 242–63; Richard A. Watson, Rondal Downing, and Frederick Speigel, "Bar Politics, Judicial Selection, and the Representation of Social Interests," 61 *American Political Science Rev.* 54 (1967), at 66, 70–71; Horowitz, "NACCA and Its Objectives"; Robert W. Gordon, "The America Legal Profession, 1870–2000," in 3 *The Cambridge History of Law in America* (Michael Grossberg and Christopher Tomlins, eds., 2008).

12. See Deborah Goldberg, "Interest Group Spending in Judicial Elections," in *Running for Judge: The Rising Political, Financial, and Legal Stakes of Judicial Elections*, 79 (Matthew J. Streb ed., 2007); Lawrence Baum, "Judicial Election & Appointment at the State Level," 77 *Ky. L. J.* 645, 652–57 (1988); Marie Hojnacki and Lawrence Baum, "Choosing Judicial Candidates: How Voters Explain Their Decisions," in *Judicial Politics: Readings from Judicature* 44, 49 (Elliot E. Slotnick ed., 1999).

13. Richard Primus, *The American Language of Rights* (1999); Mary Dudziak, *Cold War Civil Rights* (2000).

14. Hon. Robert N. Wilkin, "An Appointed Judiciary—Its Place in the Balance of Government," 23 *ABA J.* 57 (1937); William J. Donovan, "An Independent Supreme Court and the Protection of Minority Rights," 23 *ABA J.* 254, 256 (1937).

15. Justice Stanley Reed, "The Bar's Part in the Maintenance of American Democratic Ideals," 24 *ABA J.* 622 (1938); Arthur T. Vanderbilt, "Our Main Order of Business: The Administration of Justice," 24 *ABA J.* 187 (1938).

16. Jacob M. Lashly, "The Organized Bar and National Defense," 27 *ABA J.* 647 (1941).

17. See also Arthur T. Vanderbilt, "Internal Aspects of National Defense: The Special Responsibility of Lawyers," 27 *ABA J.* 221 (1947).

18. Joseph Henderson, "Making Secure 'the Blessings of Liberty,'" 30 *ABA J.* 597 (1944); Tappan Gregory, "The Bar Faces the Future," 33 *ABA J.* 971 (1947). Frank E. Holman, "Forms of Government," 32 *ABA J.* 190, 194

(1946) (Lawyers' obligation is to defend against "autocracy of every kind . . . whether it be the autocracy of Fascism, Naziism or of the proletariat or the autocracy of executive fiat").

19. Justice Robert Jackson, "The Rule of Law among Nations," 31 *ABA J.* 290, 292 (1945).

20. Tom C. Clark, "Civil Rights: The Boundless Responsibility of Lawyers," 32 *ABA J.* 457 (Aug. 1946).

21. Dale M. Hellegers, *We, the Japanese People: World War II and the Origins of the Japanese Constitution,* 655 (2001).

22. Id., 500–01.

23. Shoichi Koseki, *The Birth of Japan's Postwar Constitution,* 80 (1997); Hellegers, *We, the Japanese People,* 646.

24. Hellegers, *We, the Japanese People,* 502, 516, 518, 520, 522, 525, 527, 540, 541–3, 553–4, 578, 616, 645–8, 669, 792; Koseki, *Birth of Japan's Postwar Constitution,* 81, 213; Theodore McNelly, *The Origins of Japan's Democratic Constitution,* 73–74, 81–83 (2000); *1880 United States Federal Census,* Year: 1880; Census Place: Dedham, Norfolk, Massachusetts; Family History Film: 1254548; Page 531A; Enumeration District: 514: *Who's Who in America: A Biographical Dictionary of Notable Living Men and Women,* vol. 27, 1952–1953, 2534 (1953); *Twentieth Century Authors: A Biographical Dictionary of Modern Literature,* 1476 (Stanley J. Kunitz and Howard Haycraft eds., 1942).

25. Alex Gibney, "Six Days to Reinvent Japan," 20 *Wilson Quarterly* 76 (1996); Hellegers, *We, the Japanese People,* 491, 495, 499, 513, 515–18, 520–23, 525, 527, 578, 580–82, 583, 645–48, 667, 669; Koseki, *Birth of Japan's Postwar Constitution,* 70–71, 73, 80, 82, 99, 119; McNelly, *Origins of Japan's Democratic Constitution,* 59–60, 75.

26. Courtney Whitney, "Memorandum for Chief of Staff. Subject: Comments on Constitutional Revision Proposed by Private Group," *GHQ/SCAP Records; Government Section; Box No. 2225: "The Japanese Constitution" <Sheet No. GS(B) 02090–02092>,* Jan. 11, 1946, from the National Diet Library website, List of Documents Section 3–6, p. 3, National Diet Library, http://www.ndl.go.jp/constitution/e/shiryo/03/060/060tx.html.

27. Hellegers, *We, the Japanese People,* 648.

28. Id., 650–51.

29. "Check Sheet, From: Govt Sect., Subject: Japanese Draft Constitution," National Diet Library website, http://www.ndl.go.jp/constitution/e/shiryo/03/002_28/002_28_007l.html (accessed Aug. 5, 2010).

30. Hellegers, *We, the Japanese People,* 650–53.

31. Id., p. 16., http://www.ndl.go.jp/constitution/e/shiryo/03/002_22/002_22_016l.html.

32. Hellegers, *We, the Japanese People,* 650 n.5 (citing Charles L. Kades, interview by Hellegers, Dec. 12, 1973; Ellerman Notebook C [Michigan: Hussey Papers]; Milo E. Rowell, interview by Hellegers, May 4–5, 1972).

33. The minutes of the discussion state that this measure was intended to bring the judiciary "closer to the people." Ellerman Notes on Minutes of Government Section, Public Administration Division Meetings and Steering

Committee Meetings between 5 February and 12 February inclusive, National Diet Library, Ellerman Notes, SCAP Files of Commander Alfred R. Hussey, Doc. No. 7, p. 16, http://www.ndl.go.jp/constitution/e/shiryo/03/002_22/002_22_016l.html (accessed Aug. 5, 2010).

34. Charles L. Kades, interview by Hellegers, Dec. 12, 1973; Ellerman Notebook C (Michigan: Hussey Papers), at Hellegers, *We, the Japanese People,* 650.

35. Hellegers, *We, the Japanese People,* 654, n.16.

36. David M. O'Brien and Yasuo Ohkoshi, "Stifling Judicial Independence from Within: The Japanese Judiciary," in *Judicial Independence in the Age of Democracy: Critical Perspectives from around the World,* 50 (Peter H. Russell and David M. O'Brien eds., 2001).

37. Alfred C. Oppler, *Legal Reform in Occupied Japan: A Participant Looks Back,* 75–76 (1976).

38. Oppler, *Legal Reform in Occupied Japan,* 90.

39. David S. Law, "The Anatomy of a Conservative Court: Judicial Review in Japan," 87 *Tex. L. Rev.* 1545, 1566 (2009).

40. See, for example, the National Municipal League: Committee on State Government, *Model State Constitution, with Explanatory Notes* (1948).

41. Senator Alexander Wiley, "A Free Judiciary: America's System Contrasted with the Soviets," 34 *ABA J.* 441 (1948). See also Carl B. Rix, "Lawyers and Courts: Other Lands Seek Patterns of Law and Justice," 33 *ABA J.* 332 (1947) (calling for judicial independence around the world for constitutional democracy to defeat totalitarianism).

42. Charles Rhyne, "The Original Creation and Future Impact of Law Day: Law Empowering People to Be Free from 1958 to the New Millennium" (Address, Law Library of Congress Law Day Celebration, Thomas Jefferson Building, Washington, D.C., May 1, 2000). Available online at http://www.abanet.org/publiced/lawday/2008/history/rhyne2000.shtml.

43. Rhyne, "Original Creation."

44. Hofstadter, *Anti-Intellectualism.*

45. Nicholas Lemann, *The Big Test: The Secret History of the American Meritocracy,* 116–17 (1999).

46. Michael Young, *The Rise of the Meritocracy, 1870–2033: An Essay on Education and Equality* (1958).

47. Lemann, *Big Test,* 119.

48. Paul L. Martin, "A Message from the President," 7 *Nebraska State Bar J.* 5–6 (Jan. 1958); see also Flavel A. Wright, "President's Page," 9 *Nebraska State Bar J.* 69–70 (July 1960).

49. Hale McCown, "President's Page," 10 *Nebraska State Bar J.* 41–42 (Apr. 1961); Hale McCown, "President's Page," 10 *Nebraska State Bar J.* 114 (Oct. 1961).

50. George E. Sims, *The Little Man's Big Friend: James E. Folsom in Alabama Politics, 1946–1958,* 5–8, 22, 25, 32 (1985).

51. Id., 27.

52. Id., 36–37, 39, 51.

53. 321 U.S. 649 (1944).

54. Sims, *Little Man's Big Friend,* 80–82, 89; see Charles Zelden, *The Battle for the Black Ballot* (2004).

55. William D. Barnard, *Dixiecrats and Democrats: Alabama Politics, 1942–1950,* 104 (1974).

56. *Speeches of James E. Folsom 1947–1950* (Wetumpka, Alabama, n.d.), quoted in Barnard, *Dixiecrats and Democrats,* 183–84.

57. Barnard, *Dixiecrats and Democrats,* 129.

58. Horace Wilkinson, *Alabama Lawyer,* 10 (1949).

59. "Report of the Editor," 9 *Alabama Lawyer,* 371–72 (Oct. 1948). Birmingham grew in the nineteenth century as a mining and steel town (named after England's powerful industrial city), and in the twentieth century, it became the state center for banking, insurance, and the bar.

60. William A. Nunnelley, *Bull Connor,* 36 (1991).

61. Charles E. Connerly, *The Most Segregated City in America: City Planning and Civil Rights in Birmingham, Alabama* (2005); Nunnelley, *Bull Connor,* 2–5.

62. Nunnelley, *Bull Connor,* 2–5.

63. Barnard, *Dixiecrats and Democrats,* 60.

64. Id., 135.

65. William Logan Martin, "Alabama Judges Under Elective System—40 Per Cent. Originally Appointed by Governor—Rise and Fall of Pay of Judges," 10 *Alabama Lawyer* (Jan. 1949).

66. "Alabama Judicial Selection, California Minor Court Reform, Approved by Voters in November Elections," 34 *Judicature* 120 (1950).

67. Id.

68. Ala. Const. of 1901, amend. 83.

69. *Birmingham Post-Herald,* Nov. 4, 1950.

70. "Alabama Judicial Selection, California Minor Court Reform, Approved by Voters in November Elections," 34 *Judicature* 120 (1950).

71. *Birmingham Post-Herald,* Nov. 8, 1950.

72. Sims, *Little Man's Big Friend,* 136–37.

73. Michael Klarman, *From Jim Crow to Civil Rights* (2004).

74. "Afraid Judges Won't Get a Fair Shake," *News Tribune,* June 14, 1976.

75. "200 Faces for the Future," *TIME,* July 5, 1974.

76. "Judge Election Repeal Has Support," *Naples Daily News,* May 24, 1976.

77. Carl A. Pierce, "The Tennessee Supreme Court and the Struggle for Independence, Accountability and Modernization, 1974–98," in *The Tennessee Supreme Court,* at 272.

78. Minion K. C. Morrison, *African Americans and Political Participation,* 219 (2003); Michael Barone, Grant Ujifusa, and Douglas Matthews, *Almanac of American Politics, 1976,* at 809–810 (1975); Bill Terry, "Nun, Mortician Vie in Tenn. Hill Race," *N.Y. Times,* Aug. 1, 1974.

79. Thomas B. Stewart, "A Model Judiciary for the 49th State," 42 *J. American Judicature Society* 56 (1958); Victor Fischer, *Alaska's Constitutional Convention,* 113 (1975).

80. Statehood Committee Press Release, quoted in Stewart, "A Model Judiciary," 56.

81. Minutes of the Alaska Constitutional Convention, Day 35, Dec. 12, 1955 (Yule Kilcher).
82. National Municipal League, *Model State Constitution*, 25 (1954).
83. Id., 10–11.
84. Alaska Constitution of 1956, art. IV, sec.§§ 5, 6, 8.
85. Alaska Constitution (1956), Art. IV, Section 8.
86. Id., Section 5.
87. Id., Section 6.
88. See Ralph Rivers's comments in Minutes of the Alaska Constitutional Convention, Day 32, Dec. 9, 1955.
89. Fischer, *Alaska's Constitutional Convention,* 114.
90. Id. (Warren Taylor).
91. Minutes of the Alaska Constitutional Convention, Day 35, Dec. 12, 1955 (Herb Hilscher).
92. Stewart, "Model Judiciary," 59. For the theory that an interest in commerce and investment can prompt leaders to prefer judicial independence, see Douglas C. North and Barry Weingast, "Constitutions and Commitments," 49 *J. Econ. History* 803 (1989).
93. Alaska's adoption of merit selection is often attributed to the date of its joining the Union in 1959, after Kansas's amendment, rather than its convention over three years earlier.
94. R. Alton Lee, "The Triple Switch: How the Missouri Plan Came to Kansas," 73 *Journal of the Kansas Bar Association* 32 (2004).
95. Id., 28.
96. Id., 33.
97. Id.
98. See Stacie J. Sanders, "Kissing Babies, Shaking Hands, and Campaign Contributions: Is This the Proper Role for the Kansas Judiciary?" 34 *Washburn L. J.* 579–81 (1995).
99. Lee, "Triple Switch," 33.
100. Sanders, "Kissing Babies," 35.
101. "Selection and Tenure of Judges," 23 *Journal of the Bar Association of the State of Kansas* 93 (1954).
102. See, for example, "Selection, Tenure, and Retirement of Judges," 24 *Journal of the Bar Association of the State of Kansas* 70 (Aug. 1955).
103. Howard Maddux, "Civil Rights—Racial Segregation," 24 *Journal of the Bar Association of the State of Kansas* 265 (Feb. 1956).
104. D. Clifford Allison, "The Right to Work," 23 *Journal of the Bar Association of the State of Kansas* 387 (May 1955).
105. Id., 395.
106. Id., 396.
107. Jon C. Teaford, *The Rise of the States: Evolution of American State Government,* 193 (2003).
108. *Salina Journal* [Kansas], Sept. 21, 1958, p. 4.
109. Lee, "Triple Switch," 28, 32–34.
110. Id., 35.

111. Id., 36.

112. See, for example, Paul L. Martin, "A Message from the President," 7 *Nebraska State Bar J.* 45–47 (Apr. 1958).

113. Virgil Haggart Jr., "The Case for the Nebraska Merit Plan," 41 *Nebraska L. Rev.* 726–72 (1962).

114. Alfred Heinecke, "The Colorado Amendment Story," *Judicature* 51 (1967): 17–19; Chief Justice James Duke Cameron, "Merit Selection in Arizona—The First Two Years," *Arizona State L. J.* (1976), 427; Note, "Merit Appointment versus Popular Election: A Reformer's Guide to Judicial Selection Methods in Florida," 43 *Florida L. Rev.* 538–40 (1991); Stephen E. Lee, "Judicial Selection and Tenure in Arizona," 51 *Law & Social Order* 58 (1973).

115. "Critics Rip into Judicial Plan of Two Bar Groups," *Chicago Daily Tribune,* May 24, 1952; "Judicial Amendment and the Democrats," *Chicago Daily Tribune,* June 22, 1953; "Big 19 Report Asks Tax on All Working in City," *Chicago Daily Tribune,* Sept. 24, 1952; Robert Howard, "Illinois Senate Passes Bill to Revamp Courts," *Chicago Daily Tribune,* June 4, 1953; "Lawyers and Judges," *Chicago Daily Tribune,* Feb. 28, 1953; Johnson Kanady, "Debate Court Plan Revival," *Chicago Daily Tribune,* June 25, 1953.

116. Kanady, "Debate Court Plan Revival"; Johnson Kanady, "Stratton Gives Backing to Bar Judicial Plan," *Chicago Daily Tribune,* May 13, 1953.

117. "New Judicial Reform Bills in Legislature," *Chicago Daily Tribune,* June 27, 1961; "Court Reform Passed by House," *Chicago Daily Tribune,* June 30, 1961; "O.K. Judicial Reform for Blue Ballot," *Chicago Daily Tribune,* July 2, 1961; Robert Howard, "Blue Ballot Adopted by 260,857," *Chicago Daily Tribune,* Nov. 30, 1962.

118. Richard L. Thornburgh, "Delegate Defends Judicial Proposal," Letter to the Editor, *Pittsburgh Post-Gazette,* Jan. 4, 1968.

119. "Local Judge Selection Left to Voter by ConCon," *Pittsburgh Post-Gazette,* Feb. 20, 1968.

120. "Judge Selection Plan Approved," *Pittsburgh Post-Gazette,* Feb. 27, 1968.

121. Louise Young, *In the Public Interest: The League of Women Voters, 1920–1970* (1989); Naomi Black, *Social Feminism* (1989); Kristi Andersen, *After Suffrage: Women in Partisan and Electoral Politics before the New Deal* (1996).

122. Young, *In the Public Interest,* 155–57.

123. Id., 161, 168–69.

124. Id., 172–74.

125. Id., 195.

126. Id., 254–63.

127. Frank M. Mathews, "Drive Supports State Judges' Merit Selection," *Pittsburgh Post-Gazette,* May 2, 1969; "Another Vote for Court Reform," *Pittsburgh Post-Gazette,* May 5, 1969.

128. "Negro Judge Backs State Jurists Plan," *Pittsburgh Post-Gazette,* May 7, 1969.

129. Herbert G. Sheinberg, "Judges' Merit Plan Given DeMerits," *Pittsburgh Post-Gazette,* May 8, 1969.

130. "Judge Pick Plan Loses Statewide," *Pittsburgh Post-Gazette*, May 22, 1969.

131. Francis Wheen, *Strange Days Indeed: The Golden Age of Paranoia* (2009).

132. See the Disaster Center in association with the Rothstein Catalog on Disaster Recovery, "United States Crime Rates, 1960 – 2008," http://www.disastercenter.com/crime/uscrime.htm (accessed Aug. 5, 2010).

133. From 1960 to 1970, crime doubled or tripled in Colorado, Idaho, Oklahoma, Utah, Indiana, Tennessee, Florida, Kentucky, Arizona, Maryland, Nevada, and New York.

134. See Appendix H, "Partisan Balance during Merit Campaigns: Judicial Independence as Partisan Strategy."

135. "Crime Survey Finds Gaps in U.S. Court Administration," *Christian Science Monitor*, Apr. 1, 1967, p. 10.

136. "Task Force Report: Experts Tell Ways to Cure Court Ills," *Chicago Tribune*, May 23, 1971, p. 1.

137. Richard Tucker, "'Non-Political Courts' Plan Stirs Debate," *Rocky Mountain News*, Oct. 7, 1966.

138. Michael Pounds, "Denver Crime Rate Grows 6.1 Percent," *Rocky Mountain News*, Oct. 9, 1966.

139. Marguerite Selinger, "Letters from the People: Views on Capital Punishment," *Rocky Mountain News*, Oct. 19, 1996.

140. "The Governor and Crime," Staff Editorial, *Rocky Mountain News*, Oct. 20, 1966.

141. "High Court Speedup Needed, Zall Claims," *Rocky Mountain News*, Oct. 26, 1966; "18 Candidates Seek District Judgeships," *Rocky Mountain News*, Oct. 24, 1966; Del W. Harding, "Court Decisions Defended by Judge," *Rocky Mountain News*, Oct. 11, 1966.

142. *The Deseret News*, Jan. 27, 1967.

143. Disaster Center in association with the Rothstein Catalog on Disaster Recovery, "Tennessee Law Enforcement Agency Uniform Crime Reports, 1960–2008," http://www.disastercenter.com/crime/tncrime.htm (accessed Aug. 5, 2010).

144. Id.

145. *Tampa Tribune*, Mar. 8, 1972.

146. *Kentucky Courier-Journal*, Oct. 23, 1973; Nov. 2, 1975.

147. Mary Breasted, "City Bar Unit, in Rare Act, Urges Fuchsberg's Defeat," *N.Y. Times*, Oct. 25, 1974.

148. Mary Breasted, "Bar Unit Alleges Judgeship Deals," *N.Y. Times*, Oct. 31, 1973; "Some Judges Are Bums," Editorial, *New York Daily News*, Oct. 3, 1977; Marcia Chambers, "Political Payments to Get Judgeships Alleged Nadjari; Nadjari Charges Judges Bought Posts," *N.Y. Times*, Oct. 11, 1975, at p. 65.

149. Francis X. Clines, "Carey, in Message Today, Will Ask Judicial Reform," *N.Y. Times*, Jan. 8, 1975 p. 1.

150. "The Opposition," *New York Daily News*, Nov. 5, 1977. See Daniel Becker and Malia Reddick, *Judicial Selection Reform: Examples from Six States*, 21–22 (2003).

151. William Nelson, *The Legalist Reformation: Law, Politics, and Ideology in New York, 1920-1980,* at 349–50 (2001).

152. Thomas Poster, "Judges Blast Ballot $ Drive," *New York Daily News,* Nov. 7, 1977, p 28.

153. Daniel Becker and Malia Reddick, *Judicial Selection Reform: Examples from Six States,* 22 (2003).

154. Id., 23.

155. Id.

156. Thomas Poster, "Labor Chiefs Back Court Reform," *New York Daily News,* Nov. 7, 1977, p. 20.

157. American Judicature Society, "Judicial Selection Reform: Examples from Six States," http://www.judicialselection.us/uploads/documents/jsreform _1185395742450.pdf.

158. "Excerpts from Debate by Four Major Candidates in Race for Mayor of New York," *N.Y. Times,* Nov. 2, 1977.

159. Glenn Fowler, "Koch Acts to Speed Judge Selection and Open It to Scrutiny by Public," *N.Y. Times,* Apr. 14, 1978.

160. Steven R. Weisman, "Carey Stumps State in Pre-Election Push," *N.Y. Times,* Dec. 11, 1977; "Text of Carey's 'State of the State' Address Proposing New Round of Cuts in Taxes," *N.Y. Times,* Jan. 5, 1978.

161. Dubois, "Politics of Innovation in State Courts," 20.

11. Judicial Plutocracy after 1980

1. Pozen, "Irony of Judicial Elections," 265; Brian Z. Tamanaha, *Law as a Means to an End: Threat to the Rule of Law* 185 (2006) ("Prior to the 1970s, judicial elections were sleepy events garnering little attention and involving relatively small sums of money"); Richard Briffault, "Public Funds and the Regulation of Judicial Campaigns," 35 *Ind. L. Rev.* 819, 819 (2002); Marie Hojnacki & Lawrence Baum, "'New-Style' Judicial Campaigns and the Voters: Economic Issues and Union Members in Ohio," 45 *W. Pol. Q.* 921, 921 (1992). However, there is new evidence that judicial elections were more competitive in the mid-twentieth century than modern commentators had thought in terms of contested elections and close elections, but not yet evidence of aggressive campaigning as individual candidates relative to the turn of the twenty-first century. Herbert Kritzer, "Competitiveness in State Supreme Court Elections, 1946–2009," 8 *J. Emp. Legal Stud.* 237 (2011).

2. Donald Wright wrote People v. Anderson, 493 P.2d 880 (1972); Rockwell v. Superior Court, 556 P.2d 1101 (1976).

3. Frank Richardson; see http://cschs.org/02_history/images_c/02_c_richardson .html.

4. John H. Culver and John T. Wold, "Judicial Reform in California," in *Judicial Reform in the States* 155 (Anthony Champagne and Judith Haydel eds., 1993).

5. Escola v. Coca Cola Bottling, 150 P.2d 436 (Cal. 1944); Ybarra v. Spangard, 154 P.2d 445 (Cal. 1944).

6. Summers v. Tice, 199 P.2d 1 (Cal. 1948).

7. Greenman v. Yuba Power Products, 377 P.2d 897 (Cal. 1963); Vandermark v. Ford Motor Co., 391 P.2d 168 (Cal. 1964); Elmore v. American Motors Corp., 451 P.2d 84 (Cal. 1969); Christian v. Rowland, 443 P.2d 561 (Cal. 1968); Tunkl v. Regents of University of California, 383 P.2d 441 (Cal. 1963); Muskopf v. Corning Hosp. Dist., 359 P.2d 457 (Cal. 1961) (limiting governmental immunity); Gibson v. Gibson, 479 P.2d 648 (Cal. 1971) (limiting family immunities); Dillon v. Legg, 441 P.2d 912 (Cal. 1968) (emotional distress liability expanded); Molien v. Kaiser Foundation Hospitals, 616 P.2d 813 (Cal. 1980) (same); Li v. Yellow Cab Co., 532 P.2d 1226 (Cal. 1975); Tarasoff v. Regents of University of California, 551 P.2d 813 (1976).

8. John Witt, *Patriots and Cosmopolitans: Hidden Histories of American Law* 242–60, 364 (2007); Samuel B. Horowitz, "NACCA and Its Objectives," 10 *NACCA L. J.* 17 (1953); Richard A. Watson, Rondal Downing, and Frederick Speigel, "Bar Politics, Judicial Selection, and the Representation of Social Interests," 61 *American Political Science Rev.* 54 (1967), at 66, 70–71; Robert W. Gordon, "The America Legal Profession, 1870–2000," in *The Cambridge History of Law in America* (2008).

9. Melvin Belli, *Ready for the Plaintiff!* 11 (1956); Witt, *Patriots and Cosmopolitans,* 242–60, 364; Horowitz, "NACCA and Its Objectives," at 26–28; Robert B. Hobson, "NACCA—As Viewed by Defense Counsel," 20 *Kentucky State Bar J.* 170 (1956).

10. See Deborah Goldberg, "Interest Group Spending in Judicial Elections," in *Running for Judge: The Rising Political, Financial, and Legal Stakes of Judicial Elections* 79 (Matthew J. Streb ed., 2007); Lawrence Baum, "Judicial Election & Appointment at the State Level," 77 *Ky. L. J.* 645, 652–57 (1988); Hojnacki & Baum, " 'New Style,' " at 925; "Choosing Judicial Candidates: How Voters Explain Their Decisions," *in Judicial Politics: Readings from Judicature* 44, 49 (Elliot E. Slotnick ed., 1999).

11. Witt, *Patriots and Cosmopolitans,* 242–63; Watson, Downing, and Speigel, "Bar Politics, Judicial Selection, and the Representation of Social Interests," 66, 70–71; Horowitz, "NACCA and Its Objectives"; Gordon, "The American Legal Profession, 1870–2000."

12. Patrick Brown, "The Rise and Fall of Rose Bird," 4 (California Supreme Court Historical Society, 2007), http://cschs.org/02_history/images/cschs_2007-brown.pdf.

13. Dick Meister, "The Courage of Rose Bird," *LaborNET,* http://www.labornet.org/viewpoints/meister/rosebird.htm.

14. Patrick Brown, "Rise and Fall," 5–6.

15. People v. Caudillo, 21 Cal. 3d 562 (1978).

16. People v. Tanner, 151 Cal. Rprt. 299 (1978). Tann & Aikman, "The California Supreme Court Investigation," 4 *State Court Journal* 3–8 (1980). When the case was revisited by the court, a justice changed his vote so the original law was upheld. Brown, "Rise and Fall," 7–8.

17. "Complete List of Recall Attempts," http://www.sos.ca.gov/elections/complete-list-of-recall-attempts.htm.

18. Sindell v. Abbott Laboratories, 607 P.2d 924 (Cal. 1980).

19. Joseph Grodin, *In Pursuit of Justice: Reflections of a State Supreme Court Justice* 168 (1989), http://en.wikipedia.org/wiki/Special:BookSources /9780520066540.

20. "Looking to November," *Post-Record* (San Jose), Mar. 13, 1985.

21. "Farm Groups Back Campaign against High-Court Members," *Los Angeles Daily Journal,* Dec. 10, 1985: p. 2.

22. Grodin, *In Pursuit of Justice,* 169.

23. Amador Valley v. State Bd. of Equalization, 22 Cal.3d 208 (1978).

24. "Polls Show Surge of Support for Death Penalty," *San Francisco Chronicle,* Mar. 5, 1986: 1 and 6.

25. Brown, "Rise and Fall," 1.

26. See pamphlets such as "Putting Justice Back in the System," Box 1658 folder 1.

27. See *Los Angeles Times,* Dec. 23, 1985, p. 22.

28. "Survey Says Bird Rulings 'Biased,'" *Oakland Tribune,* Apr. 13, 1985.

29. Speaker Manual, CVCR.

30. Paul Reidinger, "The Politics of Judging," *ABA Journal,* Apr. 1, 1987: 54; "Pro Life Council Opens Anti-Bird Campaign," *Oakland Tribune,* Dec. 29, 1985; "Rose Bird's Popularity Slips 10 Points in Three Months," *Bakersfield Californian,* May 26, 1985; Frank Clifford, "GOP Pinning Hopes to Bird's Coattails," *Los Angeles Times* Oct. 24, 1986: A3; "Bird-Deukmejian Battle Heats Up as Vote Nears," *Los Angeles Times,* Oct. 18, 1986: 5; "Death Penalty: A Political Killer?" *Sacramento Bee,* Mar. 2, 1986; Larry Peterson, "Bird Challenge Shaping Other Contests: GOP Hopefuls Urge Opponents to Take Stand on Confirmation," *Santa Ana Register,* Dec. 1, 1985.

31. "Governor Tells Businessmen to Help Oust Bird," *Los Angeles Times,* Feb. 8, 1985: 3.

32. "Deukmejian Able to Praise, Lament California Business," *Long Beach Press Telegram,* Mar. 4, 1985.

33. "Deukmejian Unveils Anti-Crime Package," *Thousand Oaks News Chronicle,* Feb. 10, 1985.

34. "NOW Has Bird in Mind," *Long Beach Press Telegram,* Aug. 17, 1985; "Campaigns of Bird Outspent Foes 2–1 in Early October," *Los Angeles Times,* Oct. 28, 1986.

35. Paul Reidinger, "The Politics of Judging," *ABA Journal,* Apr. 1, 1987: 54.

36. Id.

37. "Democrats Won't Fly to Bird's Aid," *The Register,* Jan. 26, 1985: A3.

38. Culver and Wold, "Judicial Reform in California," 155.

39. Maura Dolan and Don Irwin, "Anti-Bird Drive Inspires Moves in Other States," *Los Angeles Times,* Oct. 25, 1986: 1, 18; Robert S. Thompson, "Judicial Retention Elections and Judicial Method: A Retrospective on the California Retention Election of 1986," 61 *S. Cal. L. Rev.* 2007 (1988); Michael Dann & Randall M. Hansen, "Judicial Retention Elections," 34 *Loy. L.A. L. Rev.* 1429 (2001).

40. Daniel Becker and Malia Reddick, *Judicial Selection Reform: Examples from Six States* 3–4 (2003); Anthony Champagne, "Judicial Reform in Texas," in *Judicial Reform in the United States* 90 (1993).

41. Roy A. Schotland, "Financing Judicial Elections, 2000: Change and Challenge," 2001 *Mich. St. L. Rev.* 849, 856.
42. www.odessa.edu/dept/govt/dille/brian/courses/2306C/unit8.pdf; Champagne, "Judicial Reform in Texas," 94–100.
43. Anthony Champagne & Kyle Cheek, "The Cycle of Judicial Elections: Texas as a Case Study," *Fordham Urban L. J.* (2002).
44. Anthony Champagne, "Interest Groups and Judicial Elections," 34 *Loyola L.A. L. Rev.* 1391 (2001).
45. Champagne, "Judicial Reform in Texas," 101–05.
46. Lynn LoPucki and Walter Weyrauch, "A Theory of Legal Strategy," 49 *Duke L. J.* 1405 (2000).
47. In the end, Pennzoil's verdict was reduced to $8.5 billion.
48. Champagne, "Judicial Reform in Texas"; Becker and Reddick, *Judicial Selection Reform*, 3–4.
49. Becker and Reddick, *Judicial Selection Reform*, 3–4.
50. Id.
51. Robert H. Swansbrough, *Test by Fire* 42 (2008).
52. Id.
53. BMW v. Gore, 646 So. 2d 619 (1994).
54. BMW v. Gore, 517 U.S. 559 (1996).
55. Joshua Green, "Karl Rove in a Corner," *The Atlantic,* Nov. 2004.
56. Id., Nov. 2004.
57. Id.
58. Id.
59. John Fund, "Wisconsin's Judicial Revolution," *Wall St. Journal,* Apr. 5, 2008.
60. Justice at Stake, "2000–2008 Worst Judicial Campaign Ads," http://www.youtube.com/watch?v=4Du_WEHjMMw.
61. Patrick Marley, "Gableman Team Suggests Ethics Complaint Is Harassment," *Wisconsin Journal-Sentinel,* July 8, 2009; Ryan J. Foley, "Supreme Court Deadlocks in Gableman Ethics Case," *Wisconsin State Journal,* July 1, 2010.
62. Phillips v. Mirac, Inc., 685 N.W.2d 174 (2004).
63. "She Said," *Detroit Free Press,* Dec. 10, 2008: 2A.
64. See O'Neal v. St. John Hosp. & Med. Ctr., 487 Mich. 485 (July 31, 2010) (see Weaver, J., concurring, and Young, J., dissenting).
65. The state-by-state campaign finance reporting is collected from the American Judicature Society and from the National Institute of Money in State Politics. See American Judicature Society, Judicial Selection in the States, http://www.judicialselection.us (last visited Sept. 6, 2009); National Institute on Money in State Politics, Follow the Money, http://www.followthe-money.org (last visited Sept. 6, 2009).
66. In 1998, two California incumbents raised over $700,000 each to defend against potential pro-life challenges, but no challenges developed. As explained in this chapter, California's system gives the governor the power to nominate, not the merit commission, and that reversal creates extra incentives to challenge an incumbent when the opposition knows that the governor will serve their interests.

67. Melinda Gann Hall, "Competition as Accountability in State Supreme Court Elections," in *Running for Judge: The Rising Political, Financial and Legal Stakes of Judicial Elections* 165, 167 (Matthew J. Streb ed., 2007).

68. See, for example, Richard A. Watson and Rondal Downing, *The Politics of Bench and Bar: Judicial Selection under the Missouri Nonpartisan Court Plan* 79 (1969); Stephen J. Choi, G. Mitu Gulati, and Eric A. Posner, "Professionals or Politicians: The Uncertain Empirical Case for an Elected Rather Than Appointed Judiciary," 26 *J. L. Econ. & Org.* 290 (2010).

69. Traciel V. Reid, "The Politicization of Retention Elections: Lessons from the Defeat of Justices Lanphier and White," 83 *Judicature* 68, 68 (1999); Herbert Kritzer, "Law Is the Continuation of Politics by Other Means: American Judicial Selection in the Twenty-First Century," 56 *DePaul L. Rev.* 423 (2007). Justice Russell Nigro of Pennsylvania lost his 2005 retention election, but Pennsylvania is not a merit state. He was replaced in a partisan election. The 2005 election was an unusual off-year election in which Pennsylvania voters were angry about the state legislature giving itself a pay raise. The question was never litigated before the Pennsylvania Supreme Court, but because the legislators were not on the ballot in 2005, the voters punished the only incumbents on the ballot—the judges. Marc Levy, "Nigro: 'Misguided' Outrage Cost Him Supreme Court Seat," *Beaver County Times*, Nov. 11, 2005: A15.

70. G. Alan Tarr, "Do Retention Elections Work?" 74 *Missouri L. Rev.* 605 (2009).

71. Sandhya Somashekhar, "Opponents of Same-Sex Marriage Target Iowa Judges," *Wash. Post,* Aug. 26, 2010; Iowa Ethics and Campaign Disclosure Board, Campaign Disclosure Reports, at https://webapp.iecdb.iowa.gov/PublicView/?d=IndepExpend%2f2010; Linda Casey, "Independent Expenditure Campaigns in Iowa Topple Three High Court Justices" (National Institute on Money in State Politics, 2011), http://www.followthemoney.org/press/PrintReportView.phtml?r=440.

72. Watson and Downing, *The Politics of Bench and Bar*, 78–118.

73. Allan Ashman and James Alfini, *The Key to Judicial Merit Selection: The Nominating Process* (1974); Barbara Luck Graham, "Do Judicial Selection Systems Matter? A Study of Black Representation on State Courts," 18 *Am. Pol. Q.* 316 (1990); Henry Glick and Craig Emmert, "Selection Systems and Judicial Characteristics: The Recruitment of State Supreme Court Judges," 70 *Judicature* 228 (1987); Malia Reddick, "Merit Selection: A Review of the Social Scientific Literature," 106 *Dickinson L. Rev.* 729, 742 (2002)

74. "Judicial minstrel" at the Bar Association of the City of New York, sung by Judge James Garrett Wallace. Charles E. Clark, and David M. Trubek, "The Creative Role of the Judge: Restraint and Freedom in the Common Law Tradition," 71 *Yale L. J.* 272 (1961).

75. Mark Hurwitz and Drew Noble Lanier, "Women and Minorities on State and Federal Appellate Benches: A Cross-Time Comparison, 1985–1999," 85 *Judicature* 84 (2001); Nicholas Alozie, "Black Representation on State Judiciaries," 69 *Soc. Sci. Q.* 979 (1988); Nicholas Alozie, "Distribution of Women and Minority Judges: The Effect of Judicial Selection Methods," 71 *Soc. Sci. Q.* 315 (1990); Beth M. Henschen et al., "Judicial Nominating Commissioners:

A National Profile," 73 *Judicature* 328, 334 (1990); Reddick, "Merit Selection: A Review of the Social Scientific Literature"; Kevin M. Esterling and Seth S. Andersen, "Diversity and the Judicial Merit Selection Process: A Statistical Report," in *Research on Judicial Selection* (1999) (focusing on increasing diversity on merit nominating commissions); M. L. Henry, *Characteristics of Elected versus Merit-Selected New York City Judges, 1977–1992* (1992); M. L. Henry, *The Success of Women and Minorities in Achieving Judicial Office* (1985); Karen L. Tokarz, "Women Judges and Merit Selection under the Missouri Plan," 64 *Wash. U. L.Q.* 903 (1986).

76. Watson and Downing, *Politics of Bench and Bar.*
77. http://www.showmebettercourts.com.
78. http://www.sedaliademocrat.com/news/font-24666-pushing-span.html.
79. See, e.g, Chris W. Bonneau and Melinda Gann Hall, *In Defense of Judicial Elections* (2009).
80. Reddick, "Merit Selection: A Review of the Social Scientific Literature"; Hurwitz and Lanier, "Women and Minorities on State and Federal Appellate Benches: A Cross-Time Comparison, 1985–1999"; Alozie, "Black Representation on State Judiciaries"; Alozie, "Distribution of Women and Minority Judges: The Effect of Judicial Selection Methods"; Henschen, et al., "Judicial Nominating Commissioners: A National Profile," 334; Barbara Luck Graham, "Do Judicial Selection Systems Matter? A Study of Black Representation on State Courts," 18 *Am. Pol. Q.* 316 (1990).
81. Esterling and Andersen, "Diversity and the Judicial Merit Selection Process: A Statistical Report" (focusing on increasing diversity on merit nominating commissions).
82. See, e.g., Philip L. DuBois, *From Ballot to Bench: Judicial Elections and the Quest for Accountability* (1980).
83. http://www.showmebettercourts.com.
84. Anecdotally, merit commissions nominate candidates with more experience. But studies are mixed on quality, in part because quality is so hard to measure. Watson and Downing, *The Politics of the Bench and the Bar*; Choi, Gulati, and Posner, "Professionals or Politicians: The Uncertain Empirical Case for an Elected Rather Than Appointed Judiciary" (finding that appointed judges' opinions are cited more often by other courts and academics, but elected judges produce more opinions); Philip DuBois, *From Ballot to Bench*, 8–20, 94–95, 249–51.
85. On the problem of "*tragic cycling*," see Guido Calabresi and Philip Bobbitt, *Tragic Choices*, 195 (1978).
86. Legislative confirmation is more pro forma in the states than in the federal government.
87. New Mexico and Illinois, respectively.
88. Remarks by Chief Judge Joseph Lambert, "The Debate over Judicial Elections and State Court Judicial Selection," 21 *Geo. J. Legal Ethics* 1347, 1359 (Fall 2008) (panel transcript).
89. New York Court of Appeals (but not lower courts), Delaware, and Hawaii.
90. Recently, voters and legislators in four states have rejected merit proposals or expansions of existing merit plans. Voters in Florida and South Dakota

rejected expansions of their merit plans to lower courts in 2000 and 2005, respectively. The legislatures of Texas and North Carolina also rejected merit reforms since 1990. G. Alan Tarr, "Politicizing the Process: The New Politics of State Judicial Elections," in *Bench Press* (Keith Bybee ed., 2007).

91. Daryl Levinson and Richard Pildes, "Separation of Parties, Not Powers," 119 *Harv. L. Rev.* 2311 (2006).

92. Watson and Downing, *The Politics of the Bench and the Bar: Judicial Selection under the Missouri Nonpartisan Court Plan.*

93. See John O. McGinnis and Michael B. Rappaport, "Reconsidering the Federal Judicial Appointments Process: Supermajority Rules and the Judicial Confirmation Process," 26 *Cardozo L. Rev.* 543 (2005). Germany has a supermajority rule for its judicial appointments in both the nominating committee and the legislature. See id. at 571 n. 77.

94. U.S. Chamber Institute for Legal Reform, "Promoting 'Merit' in Merit Selection: A Best Practices Guide to Commission-Based Judicial Selection," Oct. 2009.

95. Paul Reidinger, "The Politics of Judging," *American Bar Association Journal* 73 (April 1987): 58.

96. Julian N. Eule, "Judicial Review of Direct Democracy," *Yale Law Journal* 99 (1990): 1503, 1583, n.361.

97. Model Code of Judicial Conduct, Canon I (1990).

98. Stephen P. Croley, "The Majoritarian Difficulty: Elective Judiciaries and the Rule of Law," 62 *University of Chicago L. Rev.* 689 (1995).

99. See, for example, Daniel R. Pinello, *The Impact of Judicial-Selection Method on State-Supreme-Court Policy* (1995) (concluding that elected judges are more likely to respond to political pressure than are appointed judges); Stephen B. Bright & Patrick J. Keenan, "Judges and the Politics of Death: Deciding between the Bill of Rights and the Next Election in Capital Cases," 75 *B.U. L. Rev.* 759 (1995) (finding that elected judges are influenced by public opinion and thus are more pro–death penalty); Mark A. Cohen, "The Motives of Judges: Empirical Evidence from Antitrust Sentencing," 12 *Int'l Rev. L. & Econ.* 13 (1992); Victor Eugene Flango & Craig R. Ducat, "What Difference Does Method of Judicial Selection Make? Selection Procedures in State Courts of Last Resort," 5 *Just. Sys. J.* 25 (1979) (finding some differences, but concluding that selection methods are less significant than some studies suggest); Sanford C. Gordon & Gregory A. Huber, "The Effect of Electoral Competitiveness on Incumbent Behavior," 2 *Q. J. Pol. Sci.* 107 (2007) (finding that in Kansas, judges chosen by partisan elections sentence more severely than nonpartisan judges); F. Andrew Hanssen, "The Effect of Judicial Institutions on Uncertainty and the Rate of Litigation: The Election versus Appointment of State Judges," 28 *J. Legal Stud.* 205 (1999) (finding that judicial independence and decision uncertainty are impacted by selection methods); Gregory A. Huber & Sanford C. Gordon, "Accountability or Coercion: Is Justice Blind When It Runs for Office?" 48 *Am. J. Pol. Sci.* 247 (2004); Stefanie A. Lindquist & Kevin Pybas, "State Supreme Court Decisions to Overrule Precedent, 1965–1996," 20 *Just. Sys. J.* 17, 34 (1998) (suggesting that New Jersey's Supreme

NOTES TO PAGES 262-267

Court justices, appointed to seven-year terms, overturn precedents more often and are more "activist" than elected judges because they "may feel more insulated from the political process"); Alexander Tabarrok & Eric Helland, "Court Politics: The Political Economy of Tort Awards," 42 *J. L. & Econ.* 157 (1999) (finding damage awards, particularly those against out-of-state businesses, higher in elected courts and highest in states with partisan elections, and concluding that judges, not juries, were the cause); Gerald F. Uelmen, "Elected Judiciary," in *Encyclopedia of the American Constitution* 170, 171 (Leonard W. Levy et al. eds., supp. I, 1992) (showing meaningful differences between judges selected by executive appointment and judges selected by other methods, such as elections).

100. Colorado, Indiana, Iowa, Kansas, Maryland, Missouri, Tennessee, and Wyoming feature this system of short-term initial appointment, long-term retention.

101. FEC v. Wis. Right to Life, Inc., 551 U.S. 449 (2007); Citizens United v. FEC, 130 S. Ct. 876 (2010).

102. Republican Party v. White, 536 U.S. 765 (2002).

103. Citizens United v. FEC, 130 S. Ct. 876, 968 (2010) (Stevens, J., dissenting).

104. Caperton v. A. T. Massey Coal Co., 129 S. Ct. 2252 (2009).

105. Jed Shugerman, "In Defense of Appearances: What *Caperton v. Massey* Should Have Said (Clifford Symposium)," *DePaul L. Rev.* (2010).

106. William Glaberson, "New York Takes Step in Money in Judicial Elections," *N.Y. Times*, Feb. 14, 2011: A1; Editorial, "Bold Step for Fair Courts in New York," *N.Y. Times*, Feb. 14, 2011.

107. "ABA Votes to Adopt New Rules for Judicial Disqualification," http://newsandinsight.thomsonreuters.com/Legal/News/2011/08_-_August/ABA_votes_to_adopt_new_rules_on_judicial_disqualification/.

108. John Ferejohn and Larry Kramer, "Independent Judges, Dependent Judiciary," 77 *N.Y.U. L. Rev.* 962 (2002).

109. See, e.g., Lebron v. Gottlieb Memorial Hospital 930 N.E.2d 895 (Ill. 2010).

Conclusion

1. Massachusetts, New Hampshire, and Rhode Island.

2. Partisan elections (12 states): Alabama, Illinois, Louisiana, Michigan, New Mexico (with retention elections), Ohio, Pennsylvania, Texas, and West Virginia, plus the lower courts of New York, Indiana, and Tennessee. Nonpartisan elections: Arkansas, Georgia, Idaho, Kentucky, Minnesota, Mississippi, Montana, Nevada, North Carolina, North Dakota, Oregon, Washington, and Wisconsin.

3. Connecticut; Delaware; Washington, D.C.; Hawaii; Maine; New Jersey; Virginia (legislative appointment); South Carolina (legislative appointment); and the New York Court of Appeals.

4. The sixteen states that have merit selection and retention elections (the AJS Plan or Missouri Plan) are Alaska, Arizona, Colorado, Florida, Indiana, Iowa, Kansas, Maryland, Missouri, Nebraska, Oklahoma, South Dakota, Tennessee, Utah, Wyoming, and arguably California. Nine others have merit

commissions for initial appointments: Connecticut; Delaware; Washington, D.C.; Hawaii; Massachusetts; New Hampshire; New York (Court of Appeals); Rhode Island; and Vermont.

5. Thomas Jefferson to Samuel Kercheval, July 12, 1816, in *The Writings of Thomas Jefferson* 15:34 (Andrew A. Lipscomb et al. eds., 1903).

6. James M. Love, "The Election of Judges by the People for Short Terms of Office," 3 *So. L. Rev.* 28, 31 (1877).

7. *Proceedings of the Constitutional Convention of the State of Georgia Held in Atlanta,* 1877, pp. 223–24.

8. Tom Ginsburg, *Judicial Review in New Democracies: Constitutional Courts in Asian Cases,* 18–23 (2003); Ran Hirschl, *Towards Juristocracy: The Origins and Consequences of the New Constitutionalism* (2004); Mark Ramseyer, "The Puzzling (In)Dependence of Courts: A Comparative Approach," 23 *J. Legal Studies* 721 (1994); Matthew C. Stephenson, "'When the Devil Turns . . .'": The Political Foundations of Independent Judicial Review," 32 *J. Legal Studies* 59 (2003). Hanssen, "Learning about Judicial Independence," 431.

9. See North and Weingast, "Constitutions and Commitments."

10. See Chapters 4 and 5.

11. Richard Primus, *The American Language of Rights,* 7, 44–45 (1999).

12. Albert Dicey, *Introduction to the Study of the Law of the Constitution,* 179–92 (1908); Richard A. Cosgrove, *The Rule of Law: Albert Venn Dicey, Victorian Jurist* (1980); Brian Tamanaha, *On the Rule of Law* (2004); John Rawls, *A Theory of Justice,* 235–43 (1971); Frederick Hayek, *The Political Ideal of the Rule of Law* (1955). One of the twentieth century's great historians wrote, during one crisis between law and politics, "the rule of law itself, the imposing of effective inhibitions upon power and the defence of the citizen from power's all-intrusive claims, seems to me to be an unqualified human good." E. P. Thompson, *Whigs and Hunters: The Origins of the Black Acts* 266 (1975). Pozen, "Irony of Judicial Elections," 265.

Appendix F

1. See Jed Handelsman Shugerman, "Note: The Floodgates of Strict Liability: Bursting Reservoirs and the Adoption of Fletcher v. Rylands in the Gilded Age," 110 *Yale L. J.* 333 (2000). See also Jed Handelsman Shugerman, "Twist of Long Terms," 98 *Geo. L. J.* 1349 (2010).

Appendix H

1. Alabama, Arkansas, Louisiana, Mississippi, New Mexico, Texas, and West Virginia. Massachusetts had appointments and adopted no merit commissions, either.

2. Michigan, Minnesota, Montana, North Dakota, Ohio, Oregon, Washington, and Wisconsin. Connecticut, Delaware, and Maine had appointments and adopted no merit commissions.

Acknowledgments

I have been blessed with excellent teachers, generous colleagues, wonderful students, and a loving, supportive family. I am especially appreciative of all of their encouragement for me to tackle a few centuries of legal history, and for supporting my decision to offer normative conclusions about reform in the twenty-first century. Glenda Gilmore, Bob Gordon, and Bruce Ackerman have been extraordinary mentors, and they were the teachers who inspired me to pursue a career in legal history when I started law school. Each read most of the manuscript with wonderful insight. Among the many readers of the manuscript, I owe the deepest gratitude to Dick Fallon, John Goldberg, Mike Klarman, Sandy Levinson, Bill Nelson, and John Witt, who read all or most of the entire manuscript and offered detailed suggestions and corrections. They improved this book immeasurably.

I thank Steve Bright for being an outstanding teacher and for being the first to bring this issue to my attention. Steve introduced me to Penny White, a former Tennessee Supreme Court justice, and she told her story about how she became a justice and then a former justice—because of a single death penalty decision. They motivated me to investigate this topic, and my perspective first was driven by moral outrage. Through years of historical research, I began to understand that judicial elections had their own logic in their own time and that judicial appointments were certainly no perfect alternative. To my surprise, I have ended up endorsing (more or less) merit selection, the method that had removed her from the bench. Nevertheless, I am inspired by Steve and Penny, and I credit them for shaping my views about the importance of judicial independence.

The best working group anyone could ask for is the Harvard juniors lunch: Adriaan Lanni, Matthew Stephenson, Gabby Blum, Rachel Brewster, Jim Greiner, Jeannie Suk, Glenn Cohen, Ben Roin, Ben Sachs, and Mark Wu. Thanks for reading so many rough drafts, and thanks for your friendship. Many other colleagues and friends also improved parts of this book immeasurably. Bill Alford, David Barron, Richard Bernstein, Mary Bilder, David Blight, Steve Burbank, Lizabeth

Cohen, Kris Collins, Nancy Cott, Chris Desan, Charlie Donahue, Dan Ernst, Noah Feldman, David Fontana, Willy Forbath, Barry Friedman, Risa Goluboff, Sally Gordon, Sandy Gordon, Mark Graber, Morty Horwitz, Dan Hulsebosch, Andy Kaufman, Greg Keating, Duncan Kennedy, John Langbein, Renee Lettow Lerner, Ken Mack, Ben Madley, Bruce Mann, John Manning, Serena Mayeri, Caleb Nelson, Nick Parrillo, James Pfander, Robert Post, Mark Ramseyer, David Seipp, Alan Tarr, Richard Tuck, Mark Tushnet, Ted White, and Owen Williams offered insightful comments and wise advice on substantial portions of the book. Elena Kagan and Martha Minow, both as deans and as astute readers, generously supported my work. Bill Stuntz was an especially gracious reader and mentor. I can't say enough about him and what he gave to this project.

The Executive Session for State Court Leaders in the 21st Century at Harvard's Kennedy School was a remarkable opportunity to talk to state judges regularly and get their feedback from the frontlines. I also benefited tremendously from presenting parts of the book to the American University Junior Faculty Workshop; the Boston College Legal History Roundtable; the Boston University Legal History Colloquium; the Columbia Colloquium on Courts and the Legal Process; the Conference on Empirical Legal Studies; the Harvard Law School summer workshops; the Harvard Center for History and Economics; the Harvard Project on Justice, Welfare and Economics; the NYU Legal History Colloquium; the Princeton Government Workshop; the Stanford Legal History Workshop; the University of Alberta summer workshops; the Yale-Stanford Junior Faculty Forum; and the Yale Legal History Forum. I received generous support from the Cromwell Foundation, the Golieb Fellowship at NYU., the Richard J. Franke Fellowship, and the John M. Olin summer fellowship at Yale.

I owe a huge debt of gratitude to the staffs of the Harvard libraries; the American Judicature Society's archives at Drake University; the Buffalo Public Library; the California Chamber of Commerce; the California State Library; the Cambria County Library in Johnstown, Pennsylvania; the Historical Society of Pennsylvania; the Hoover Institution Library and Archives; Philadelphia's Jenkins Law Library; the Library of Congress; the Maryland State Archives in Annapolis; the Mississippi Department of Archives and History; the New York Public Library and New York State Library in Albany; the New York University Library; the University of Chicago's libraries; the University of Missouri Library; the University of Pennsylvania libraries; the Library of Virginia in Richmond; and Yale's Beinecke, Sterling, and Law Libraries.

Most of Chapter 2 was published as "*Marbury* and Judicial Reference: The Shadow of *Whittington v. Polk* and the Maryland Judicial Battle," 5 *University of Pennsylvania Journal of Constitutional Law* 58 (2002). Parts of Chapters 4, 5, and 6 were published as "Economic Crisis and the Rise of Judicial Elections and Judicial Review," 123 *Harvard Law Review* 1061 (2010). Part of Chapter 7 was published in "The Twist of Long Terms: Judicial Elections, Role Fidelity, and American Tort Law," 98 *Georgetown Law Journal* 1349 (2010). Leigh Peters-Fransen provided extraordinary research assistance. I also thank Michael Admirand, Anthony Aminoff, Andrew Bernie, Danny Cluchey, Abby Coyle, Stephen Dee, Philip Foust, Emily Goldberg, Benjamin Hand, Lauren Kuley, Nooree Lee, Christoph Luschin, Ross McConnell, Jon Menitove, Andrea Miller, Leif Overvold,

Amanda Ray, Jennifer Reiss, Andres Restrepo, Danny Rubens, Amelia Schmidt, Jay Schweikert, Matthew Seccombe, Nicole Simon, Matthew Singer, Meggie Sudderth, Kim Rusthsatz Stephens, Mackenzie Tan, and Burden Walker for their invaluable help. Carol Igoe, Rose Dawes, and Joei Perry have been outstanding faculty assistants.

Finally, I want to thank the people who were there from the very beginning, and I cannot thank them enough. My parents, Clem Shugerman and Harriet Shugerman, taught me the importance of social justice and personal fairness. My father was my first history teacher and my first editor, and if you read very closely, you can see the traces of his red pen shortening my sentences. I am also lucky to have such supportive in-laws, Neil and Carol Handelsman. Leor, Zachary, and Noa have brought so much joy and meaning during so many years of archival research and writing. While my head spends a lot of time in the past, they filled my heart in the present and the future. Danya is my best friend who helps me live in the present, too. I have learned more from you, Danya, than from anyone else in the world. Without your support and encouragement, I never would have followed my dream to go into legal history. Your love and your patience sustained my focus to complete this project. *Gam zeh y'avor.* I am happy to emerge from the nineteenth and twentieth centuries, and to return even more fully to Danya, Leor, Zachary, and Noa.

Index

www.ingramcontent.com/pod-product-compliance
Lightning Source LLC
Chambersburg PA
CBHW051727260326
41914CB00031B/1777/J